Emotionalizing Organizations and Organizing Emotions

Emotionalizing Organizations and Organizing Emotions

Edited by

Barbara Sieben

and

Åsa Wettergren

First published 2010 by
PALGRAVE MACMILLAN

Palgrave Macmillan in the UK is an imprint of Macmillan Publishers Limited, registered in England, company number 785998, of Houndmills, Basingstoke, Hampshire RG21 6XS.

Palgrave Macmillan in the US is a division of St Martin's Press LLC, 175 Fifth Avenue, New York, NY 10010.

Palgrave Macmillan is the global academic imprint of the above companies and has companies and representatives throughout the world.

Palgrave® and Macmillan® are registered trademarks in the United States, the United Kingdom, Europe and other countries.

ISBN: 978–0–230–25015–4 hardback

This book is printed on paper suitable for recycling and made from fully managed and sustained forest sources. Logging, pulping and manufacturing processes are expected to conform to the environmental regulations of the country of origin.

A catalogue record for this book is available from the British Library.

Library of Congress Cataloging-in-Publication Data.

    Emotionalizing organizations and organizing emotions / edited by
Barbara Sieben, Åsa Wettergren.
      p. cm.
      ISBN 978–0–230–25015–4 (hardback)
      1. Organizational behavior – Social aspects. 2. Emotions – Social aspects.
    I. Sieben, Barbara, 1965– II. Wettergren, Åsa.

HD58.7.E4377 2010
302.3′5—dc22   2010023945

10 9 8 7 6 5 4 3 2 1
19 18 17 16 15 14 13 12 11 10

Printed and bound in Great Britain by
CPI Antony Rowe, Chippenham and Eastbourne

Contents

Part II Organizing Emotions

Illustrations

Tables

Figures

Notes on the Contributors

Carmen Baumeler has been Head of the Swiss Federal Institute for Vocational Education and Training's national Research and Development Division since 2009. She has been Senior Assistant at the University of Lucerne's Sociology Seminar and earned her PhD at the University of Zurich. Her research focuses on economic sociology, organizational sociology and educational sociology.

Charlotte Bloch is Associate Professor of Cultural Sociology at the Department of Sociology, University of Copenhagen. She has researched and published articles and books within the field of the Sociology of Emotions. Her main research focus is on the complex relationships between structures, cultures, emotions and social relations. Within this framework she has studied quality of life in terms of flow and stress in everyday life and emotions and emotional culture in Academia. At present she is exploring bullying in the workplace.

Nicole Bornheim, MA in sociology, is Lecturer and Research Assistant focusing on gender and diversity in organizations at the School of Business & Economics, Freie Universität Berlin. She is also completing her dissertation thesis on the field of emotions and subjectivity in the workplace at the Research Center for Sustainability Studies (artec), University of Bremen.

Andrea Cossu is Lecturer at the College of Arts and Sciences, University of New Haven, USA. He has done postdoctoral research at the University of Trento and Yale University. His main research interest is the study of political culture in Republican Italy, with a recent focus on the making of communist identity.

Stephen Fineman is Professor Emeritus at the School of Management, University of Bath, UK. He has had a long and abiding interest in emotion in organizations, especially socially constructive and critical approaches that place emotions firmly in their organizational, institutional and political contexts. Recently he has turned his attention to the way 'age' across the lifecourse is constructed and politicized, in and by organizations. This is an attempt to move our understanding of age beyond that of the more sterile 'independent' or 'control' variable.

Helena Flam, PhD, has been Professor of Sociology at the University of Leipzig since 1993. Her main research areas are the sociology of emotions, theory, market and organizations and social movements.

Yiannis Gabriel is Professor of Organizational Theory and Deputy Dean of the School of Management at Bath University, UK. He is well known for his work into organizational storytelling and narratives, leadership, management learning, the culture and politics of contemporary consumption and social applications of psychoanalytic theories. He has authored ten books and numerous other publications.

Jeff Hearn is Professor in Gender Studies (Critical Studies on Men), Linköping University, Sweden; Professor in Management and Organisation, Hanken School of Economics, Helsinki, Finland, and Professor of Sociology, University of Huddersfield, UK. He is a UK academician in the Social Sciences. His main research interests include gender, sexuality, violence, organizations, management, transnationalization and post-colonialism.

Christian Imdorf, PhD, is Research Assistant at the Institute of Sociology, University of Basel. He has been Visiting Fellow at the Institute of Labour Economics and Industrial Sociology LEST (Aix en Provence) and at the Adam Smith Research Foundation (Glasgow). His research interests include the Sociology of Vocational Education and Training and the Sociology of Discrimination.

Debra King is a sociologist and Senior Research Fellow at the National Institute of Labour Studies, Flinders University. She conducts research on the health and social care workforces, focusing on understanding the meaning and experience of work and particularly the emotional and relational dimensions of work and workplace change.

Vesa Leppänen is Associate Professor at the Department of Sociology at Lund University in Sweden. His research interests focus on work organization and social interaction between workers and clients, for instance primary care nurses and patients, telephone advice nurses and callers, municipal home carers and clients, sales workers and customers and domestic workers and customers.

Wendy Parkin is a retired Principal Lecturer in Sociology and Social Work at the University of Huddersfield, UK. Her research interests cover the relationship between gender, sexuality, emotions, violations and power in organizations. A particular research interest has been the exploration of these issues in residential care settings.

Poul Poder, PhD, is Associate Professor at the Department of Sociology, University of Copenhagen. His main research interests are work and organizational life, organizational change, the effects on social relationships of implementing evaluation and quality measures in organizations, theory of agency and power, the sociology of emotions, positive organizational scholarship and social theory.

Alberto Martín Pérez is Post-doctoral Research Fellow at the Institute for Public Goods and Policies of the Spanish National Research Council (CSIC). His current research focuses on the access of immigrants to public services and on the street-level practice of social policy.

Silvia Paierl is a member of the PhD Programme at the Faculty of Social and Economic Sciences, University of Graz, where she is currently working on her dissertation thesis about the reform of the Austrian public employment service. She is also Research Assistant at the 'Institut für Arbeitsmarktbetreuung und -forschung' (Graz), researching and evaluating labour market policies.

Barbara Sieben is Assistant Professor of Human Resource Management focused on Diversity at the Freie Universität Berlin (Germany). She earned her PhD with a dissertation on the topic of management and emotions. Further research interests include gender and diversity in organizations and the management of service work. Her research is based on multiparadigmatic approaches, informed by critical management perspectives.

Sylvia Terpe works as a Sociologist at the University of Halle, Germany, where she completed her PhD in 2008. Her dissertation explores the relationship between perceptions of injustice and (de)motivating emotions. One of her current interests concerns the phenomenon of 'conscience' and its emotional expressions in guilt, shame, remorse or regret.

Åsa Wettergren, PhD, is Assistant Professor at the department of Sociology, Gothenburg University. Her main research areas cover the role of emotions for collective identity and identity construction in organizations and social movements, and the emotions of migration, social integration and social interactions.

Emotionalizing Organizations and Organizing Emotions – Our Research Agenda

Barbara Sieben and Åsa Wettergren

1 Tackling the topic of emotion in organizations

Organizations and organizing constitute a field of research where sociologists and social scientists from business and management schools typically meet for a fruitful exchange (e.g. Clegg et al. 2006; Adler 2009). This observation may be echoed for the study of emotion in organizations, and has inspired the conception of this volume.

Formerly, emotions were not at the top of the agenda in either sociology or organization and management research. However, in the last two decades, from 1990 onwards, there has been a considerable rise in scholarly interest in the role, function and importance of emotions – for society in general (e.g. Kemper 1990a; Clark 1997; Scheff 1997; Barbalet 1998; Collins 2004; Turner/Stets 2005; Wettergren et al. 2008; Hopkins et al. 2009; Röttger-Rössler/Markowitch 2009; Scherke 2009), for politics and social movements (e.g. Goodwin et al. 2001; Ahmed 2004; Flam/King 2005) and for organizations (e.g. Fineman 1993a; Albrow 1997; Fineman 2000a; Flam 2000; Hochschild 2000; Ashkanasy et al. 2000; Schreyögg/Sydow 2001; Lord et al. 2002; Payne/Cooper 2004; Bolton 2005; Fineman 2006; 2007; Sieben 2007a; Lewis/Simpson 2007; Rastetter 2008). These latter publications also testify to the trans- and interdisciplinary interest in emotions in organizations, as do a whole range of special issues of journals on 'emotions at work' or 'emotions in organizations', e.g. *The Annals of the American Academy of Political and Social Sciences* (1999, 561(1)), *Work and Occupations* (2000, 27(1)), *Human Resource Management Review* (2002, 12(2)) and *Human Relations* (2007, 60(4)). Since 2005 there has also been a specialist journal on the subject; the *International Journal of Work Organization and Emotion.* Despite different research aims and foci, writers in this field agree on one point at least: they all refute the idea of the purely 'rational' bureaucratic organization in the classic Weberian sense (*'sine ira ac studio'*, Weber 1948: 215f.) and highlight the myriad ways in which organizations can be seen as 'emotional arenas' (Fineman 1993b; 2000b).

The studies by the US American sociologist Arlie Russell Hochschild have been described as path breaking for this upsurge of interest (e.g. Simpson/Smith 2005: 1). In 1979 Hochschild published the article 'Emotion work, feeling rules, and social structure' in *The American Journal of Sociology.* There she outlined an interactive account of emotions and an emotion management perspective. In brief, Hochschild argued that human beings continuously – consciously or 'latently' – subject their own and others' feelings to cognitive assessments and attempts to fashion and control them. They do so by performing emotion work in relation to feeling rules that apply to the frames of each situated interaction. Thus, emotions do not 'happen' to people as the conventional stress on the irrationality of emotions would have it, but are part and parcel of the social and cultural world we live in. Work in organizations belongs to this world. Its distinguishing feature is that in this realm an alienation from the private experience of emotions may occur, as the management of emotion is required and performed in return for a wage.

> When the manager gives the company his enthusiastic faith, when the airline stewardess gives her passengers her psyched-up but quasi-genuine reassuring warmth, what is sold as an aspect of labour power is deep acting. (Hochschild 1979: 569)

Consequently, as Hochschild argues, emotion work is becoming commoditized as part of middle-class wage labour. She developed this argument on emotional labour further in the book *The Managed Heart* (1983), which was to become a fundamental building block and an obligatory reference work for researchers interested in emotions in organizations, be they emotion sociologists (e.g. Wouters 1989; Flam 2000) or organization and management researchers (e.g. Morris/Feldman 1996; Grandey 2000; Bolton 2005; Rastetter 2008).

While the growing interest in emotions in the social sciences is of course ultimately intertwined with a general societal attention to the subject, there are a number of possible explanations with regard to the social sciences in particular, among which we suggest some here. First, the cultural turn in the social sciences beginning in the 1960s brought with it a massive critique against the scientific production of knowledge and its implicit assumptions about objectivity. The main arguments have been that there are neither clear boundaries between 'reality' and its description, between an external (objective) and an internal (subjective) world, between knowledge and opinion (e.g. Rorty 1989), nor between culture, politics and economy or between private and public (e.g. Best/ Kellner 1997; Seidman 1997; Jameson 1998); that power constitutes and saturates social relations through knowledge regimes and praxis (e.g. Foucault 1976; 1995; Laclau/Mouffe 1985) and that the binary thinking of western logics distorts and represses the body, the senses, the sociality and interdependency of individuals (e.g. Butler 1993; Williams 2001; McDonald 2006). Hence, the cultural turn, while not per se leading to an interest in emotion, certainly opened up an academic space for it – or, as Kleres (2009: 7) puts it regarding the sociological theorization of emotion, the 'so-called emotional turn (...) is arguably bolstered by the other turns in our own and cognate disciplines'.

Second, a growing amount of research and literature from both the natural (e.g. Damasio 1999; 2005) and social sciences (notably Barbalet 1998, Flam 2000 and Fineman 2006) deals with the critical and radical approaches to emotions by arguing that emotion is inherent to rationality and rational decision-making rather than – as the conventional approach holds – opposed to it. As Barbalet (1998) argues, the conventional approach is based on cultural representations that obscure the role of 'background emotions' by labelling them 'attitudes' instead of feelings (ibid.: 60). Instead, feelings serve as internal guides, and they help us communicate signals that can also guide others. Moreover, feelings are neither intangible nor elusive. As Damasio (2005) shows in his elucidation of *Descartes' Error*, emotions are inextricably intertwined with cognitions and rationality – an observation that is taken up by numerous management researchers as it promises to deliver a more holistic understanding of organizational life (Callahan/McCollum 2002; Fineman 2006).

Third, a theory of emotions promises to account for the link between social structure and individual actors. This may enhance our understanding of the ways in which social structures are not only maintained and reproduced, but also altered, in social interactions through the mechanisms of power and status (Collins 1990; Kemper 2006), as well as through mechanisms of group conformity (Goffman 1959), the emotional orientation in the complex social landscape and the construction and internalization of social roles, identities and self-perceptions.

This aspect renders the topic of emotions pertinent to management and organization research. For instance trust (Kramer/Tyler 1996; Kramer 1999) is a relevant topic with regard to the emergence of 'flat' organizations, to the blurring of boundaries between home and work life (Hochschild 2000; Pongratz/Voß 2003) and to the augmentation of globally distributed and virtual work (Fineman et al. 2007).

Patterns of the management and representation of emotions in organizations (or emotional regimes in the sense of Reddy 2001) have often been ascribed to structural changes, e.g. the exclusion and delegation of emotion to private life in the course of industrialization (e.g. Stearns 1988) or the upgrading of emotional labour due to the growing service sector (e.g. Gerhards 1988). Hence, authors describe the transformation of the 'passionless bureaucracy' into the 'emotional organisation' (Bolton 2005: 14), along with an increasing disciplining followed and accompanied by an informalization of emotions (Mastenbroek 2000; Wouters 2007), a progressive management of emotions (Rafaeli/Worline 2001) or an advanced routinization of control. Meštrović even (1997) argues that we are living in a post-emotional society where the continuous assessment and management of emotions (in relation to feeling and display rules) leads to the loss of 'authentic emotions'.

On the other hand, it can be argued that there have never been a-emotional organizations, any more than a-emotional societies. The Weberian ideal-type 'sine ira ac studio' is rather to be seen as an organizational emotional regime where emotions are viewed with suspicion (Stearns 1994). For management concepts and practices it may be shown that the valorization of emotions (as either negative/destructive or positive/constructive) has always been ambivalent and has undergone several changes (Sieben 2007a). Today this is changing into an emotional regime that renders explicit the display and embrace of 'positive' emotions – such as trust, love, enthusiasm, niceness, happiness, self-confidence, self-love and self-enhancement – while it requires the control and management of 'negative' ones (anger, jealousy, envy, resentment, disappointment, sadness, ironic or disengaged distance) (cf. Wettergren, forthcoming). The contemporary focus on emotions is not equal to 'letting emotions out', rather it recognizes their existence and value while simultaneously demanding their use in accordance with norms of an 'intelligent' management of emotions (cf. Goleman 1996; for critical analyses: Fineman 2000c; Sieben 2007a; Neckel 2009). This argument brings us to the point where the very existence of 'authentic emotions' must be brought into doubt, because if there is no such thing as an a-emotional society, there can also be no society where emotions are *not* controlled and managed. The extent and variety of societal emotional regimes have been pointed out by social anthropologists (c.f. Harré/Parrott 1996; Reddy 2001) and historically oriented scholars (Elias 1982; Reddy 2001; Stearns 1994; Wouters 2007), as well as by research into the historically changing emotional regimes of organizations (e.g. Mastenbroek 2000; Krell/Weiskopf 2006). It thus makes sense to speak of emotional regimes as internalized emotional dispositions, analogous to Bourdieu's (1999) notion of habitus (cf. Illouz 2007). The perception of authentic emotions thereby becomes tied to the notion of an 'authentic self' (Tracy 2005; Tracy/Trethewey 2005), which is also a pervasive cultural representation that tends to enhance the autonomous biographical self as essence on behalf of the fragmented and situated self as it is produced in social interaction (Mead 1976; Garfinkel 1984; Collins 1988).

2 Defining emotions

Following Hochschild (1990: 119; cf. also Thoits 1990: 191f.) an emotion comprises four elements: 'a) appraisals of the situation, b) changes in bodily sensations, c) the free or inhibited display of expressive gestures, and d) a cultural label to specific constellations of the first three elements.' This definition is generally consistent with the overall literature regarding the components of an emotion, but it may be interpreted and qualified in a number of ways, following the debated issue of which of the psychobiological or social components is most salient.

The 'organismic' (Hochschild 1990: 119f.) or psychobiological (Scherer 1999) model of emotions, for instance, focuses upon the biological function of emotion and the display of feeling. From this perspective it can be argued that there are universal basic emotions – e.g. anger, fear, sadness, disgust and enjoyment – manifested in cross-cultural facial expressions (Ekman 1999; Scherer 1999; Thrift 2004). However, presumably basic emotions are also hard to define and delimit; the extent and depth of the socio-cultural shaping of emotions and emotional expressions make it difficult to provide evidence for any 'universal' set of discrete emotions (cf. Harré/Parrott 1996; Barbalet 1998).

The 'interactional model' advanced by Hochschild, and generally embraced by the body of social scientific literature on the topic, concentrates on emotions as social constructs. Moreover, the model integrates psychobiological aspects as socially shaped 'ingredients' (Hochschild 1990: 120). Consequently, on the one hand, Hochschild claims, counter to the organismic model, that emotions are not just there to be triggered, but also *become* in social interaction (see also Reddy 2001). On the other hand, she invites psychobiological aspects when she speaks about 'the signal function' of emotions (Hochschild 1983; 1990: 119). Thus, if we return to her definition of emotion above, the four elements are experienced simultaneously, even if not necessarily consciously. Together with our other senses, emotion allows us to intuit the situations in which we find ourselves, guiding our selection of appropriate actions and expressions in the social terrain. Thus, for the purpose of the social science, what can be retrieved of the universal claims mentioned above is that the physical apparatus enabling human beings to experience emotions is universal (Reddy 2001; Damasio 2005). The prominent emotion sociologist Thomas Scheff (1990) further argues that shame is a universal social emotion, as it can be seen as a 'master emotion' that monitors compliance with culturally specific feeling rules. As a corollary to this, the quest for self-esteem through *recognition* – a sign of belonging and group inclusion – can also be assumed to be a universal human trait (cf. Honneth 2000).

A fruitful approach is to see emotions as processes rather than objects. Barbalet (1998) points out that as emotions inhere in social relations, they transform them and through experiencing emotions give rise to new ones, and so on. 'Emotion is always situated' and involves 'the whole person' instead of 'an isolatable aspect or attribute of a person's body or psychology' (ibid: 79). When we name and speak of emotions, Barbalet contends, they become objects, but as such, they are merely 'hypothetical constructs' (ibid.: 180, 186).

> The notion that emotion is a hypothetical construct follows from the fact that emotion cannot be reduced to its indicators. The various conceptualizations of emotion in life and in science derive from the frameworks in which the indicators of emotion are placed. These vary with the context and purpose of those involved. Thus the definitions of emotions are necessarily culturally diverse, both across societies and within them. (ibid.: 80)

A structuralist approach to emotions in social science focuses on the way emotion is embedded in social structures such as class (Barbalet 1996–97; 1998), the (stratified) structure of interaction rituals (Collins 1990; 2004), or generally the structural relationships of power and status (Gordon 1990; Burkitt 1997; Kemper 1990b; 2001). Collin's approach, particularly, warrants attention in relation to the contents of this volume. Combining Goffman, Garfinkel and Durkheim, Collins

(1990; 2004) states that social interaction involving two or more persons sharing the same focus of attention is a ritual, and that its outcome – collective effervescence – results in solidarity for the collective and emotional energy for the individual. The latter concept, emotional energy, refers to 'a feeling of confidence, courage to take action or boldness in taking initiative. It is a morally suffused energy; it makes the individual feel not only good, but exalted, with the sense of doing what is most important and most valuable' (Collins 2004: 39).

Emotional energy varies along a continuum. At the lower end, the individual experiences low self-feelings and low degree of inclusion and recognition, while the opposite is true at the other end of the spectrum. Further, emotional energy is unequally distributed. Power and status are the social mechanisms that determine the individual's experience of emotional energy.

In summary, we approach and understand emotion in this volume as multidimensional. In this view, emotions are more than just inner (psychological or biological) states or processes. Rather, emotions are experienced in and shaped by interactions with others; they are framed and reproduced through language and social practice. Furthermore, the ways in which emotions are experienced and displayed are 'coined' by understandings, valuations and social structures that are themselves historically and socio-culturally grounded. In this sense, emotions are tied to and shape relations of power and interdependence. In particular, the study of the emotion-laden complexities of organizations and organizing calls for such a comprehensive view (cf. also Sturdy 2003). In order to enhance the understanding of emotions in organizational settings and to discuss the possibilities and limits of their manageability, research on emotion in organizations should strive to capture all these dimensions. Not every piece of research may focus on all dimensions, but different contributions on these aspects should be combined and contrasted. The purpose of this volume is to fulfil part of this task, as shown below.

3 Studying emotions in organizations

This volume's aim is to further research on emotions in organizations by looking into specific processes and interactions in organizations that are not often highlighted in the main body of literature. For instance, by looking at 'ordinary' routines and everyday situations such as queuing for residence permits, medical advice calls, the selection of trainees, bullying and sexual harassment it expands insights into organizational arenas where emotions are produced and where structural settings become tied to individual motives and actions through emotion.

To illustrate the relationship of this volume to the body of research into emotions in organizations we present the latter in a two-fold theoretical framework that has in turn been used to structure the contents of this volume. The first, a 'compass' to assist orientation in the field of research on emotions in organizations (Figure I1), refers to the research perspective taken. The second, a conceptual model of appearances of emotions in organizations (Figure I2), refers to the current focus of study. We will explain each part of the framework, and the way that it clarifies the contents of this volume, in proper order.

First, Figure I1 represents a 'compass' that helps orientation in the field of research on emotions in organizations (Sieben 2007a; b).[1] This compass differentiates common social scientific research perspectives – called here functionalist, interpretive, poststructuralist and (ideology) critical – with the goal of doing research on emotion in organizations. The horizontal dimension refers to the way of doing research, i.e. it captures where and how research concepts and problems originate. At the

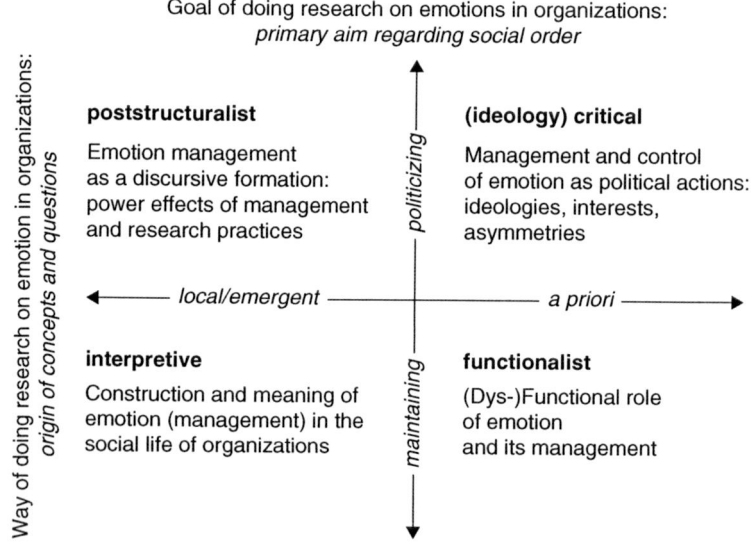

Figure I1   A compass to assist orientation in the field of research on emotions in organizations

Source: Adapted from Sieben (2007a: 138; Sieben 2007b: 567)

local/emergent end, studies are primarily explorative and/or hermeneutically oriented, emotion is regarded as emergent and studies seek to refine categories and to reformulate relationships found in situ. In contrast, at the a priori end we find the theory- and concept-driven research, e.g. based on categories like primary emotions, emotional labour and emotional intelligence, which often aims at testing hypotheses. The vertical dimension refers to the goal of doing research with regard to social order. On the one hand, the goal may be politicizing. In this case, studies draw on discourses and/or practices linked to emotion that are understood as powerful, conflicting and a source of domination; they seek to question self-evident assumptions and to indicate points of resistance. On the other hand, the goal regarding social order may be to maintain it. Such studies tend to draw on emotions as forces to be discovered, enhanced and managed: they search for insights on features, links and effects of emotions and try to understand or explain the ways in which they affect organizational life.

All the contributions to this volume may primarily be characterized as local/emergent with respect to the origin of concepts and questions and hence their way of studying emotions in organizations – a whole range of contributions based on case studies or on ethnographic or conversation-analytic approaches. These approaches allow us to describe emotional facets in rich detail and to elaborate emotion concepts in view of organizational context (e.g. Fineman, Bornheim, Bloch, King, Leppänen, Martín Pérez and Imdorf). Others draw on emotion (management) discourses emerging from emotion research, historical documents, management literature and the like (e.g. Gabriel, Poder, Flam/Hearn/Parkin, Cossu, Terpe/Paierl and Baumeler). Some of these contributions may instead be characterized as interpretive in that they concentrate on sense-making processes in organizations or on understanding how emotions are constructed through organizational processes and practices, e.g. Bornheim's analysis of the emergence of positive emotions, Imdorf's conceptualization of the role of emotion for hiring processes or Terpe's and Paierl's analysis of feeling rules emerging from bureaucratic prescriptions. Other contributions may be characterized as politicizing in that they engage critically with emotion management discourses and/or organizational structures and processes, e.g. Fineman's analysis of the side-effects of the 'emotionologies' in service organizations, Gabriel's psychoanalytically driven critique of emotion management in care work, Poder's critical elaboration of the empowerment concept, Flam, Hearn and Parkin's analysis of the discursive mechanisms and power effects of hushing up rape and sexual

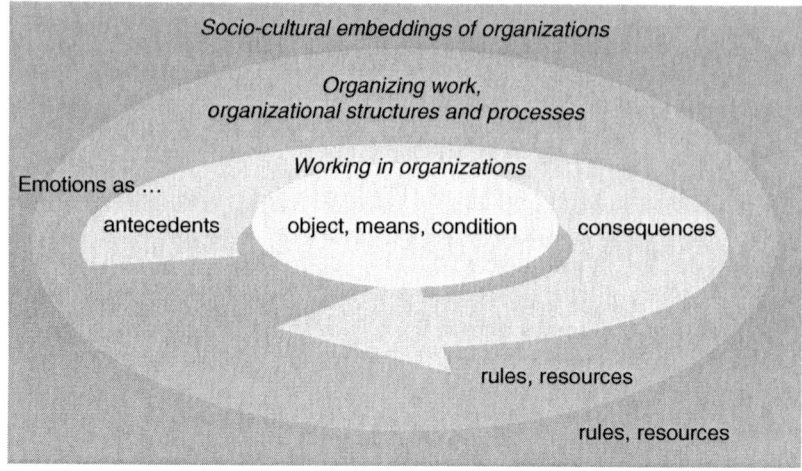

Figure 12   Appearances of emotions in organizations
Source: Adapted from Sieben (2005: 4)

harassment, Martín Pérez's analysis of how the emotions of queuing tend to (re)produce immigrants' social condition and Baumeler's analysis of emotional intelligence as an organizational regime of emotional conduct.

Second, the contributions can be characterized following their object of study, i.e. their thematic focus on emotions in organizations. Figure 12 represents a model of the appearances of emotions in organizations, i.e. a conceptualization of different forms in which emotion may be relevant to work in organizations. As such, this model is designed to outline the scope of the contents and will help to highlight the structure of the volume as well as the links between the contributions.

The model postulates differentiating analytically the levels of *working*, the *organizing* of work and the *socio-cultural embeddings* of organizations. If one focuses on these levels separately, emotion enters the picture in different manifestations. On the level of *working*, a job's activities may require a person to work on and with emotion, to perform emotion work in the sense of Hochschild (1983). Following the three-way division introduced by Dunkel (1988), emotion may represent:

- the *object* of work, if employees have to influence others' emotions, whether a service worker who lets clients feel well and attended or a team leader who seeks to establish an agreeable and cooperative atmosphere in the team;

- a *means* while working, if their own emotions and their expression are used to fulfil such tasks; and
- a *condition* of work, in the sense that one has to establish or redress a certain emotional state, to suppress or alter certain feelings – a vital task when dealing with others is at stake.

On the level of working, emotions may also appear as *antecedents* of work and as *consequences* resulting from work tasks. The antecedent-consequence array overlaps with the appearances of emotion as object, means and condition, but its range goes far beyond the work on and with emotion. Examples are joy with the work that motivate us, fear of a certain task or shame as result of a failure that hamper action and compassion or sympathetic feelings that cause a helping behaviour towards clients or colleagues. These examples clarify in addition, what the curved form symbolizes: antecedents and consequences are emotional processes that are not always easy to distinguish. At times, they may mutually cause each other or coincide: emotions that result from working will have consequences for further working behaviour.

On the level of *organizing*, numerous characteristics of the work setting influence, cause or modify the appearances of emotion. Emotion enters the picture on this level in the form of organization-specific *emotion rules and resources*. Rather than only shaping working behaviour, emotion rules and resources are produced and reproduced in this process. The same holds for the last level, *the socio-cultural embeddings* of work: social structures like gender, class or race may influence, cause or modify appearances of emotion. On this level, professional as well as broader socio-cultural emotion rules and resources enter the picture, again as appearances of emotion produced and reproduced in the process of social interaction at work.

With the appearance of emotion as *rules*, we understand the feeling rules (Hochschild 1979) and the display rules (cf. e.g. Rafaeli/Sutton 1989) embedded in the social norms that govern how emotion should be experienced and expressed. Such norms or emotional regimes may differ on the organizational, professional and societal level. On the organizational level, emotion rules may be explicitly stated, e.g. in mission statements or codes of conduct. But rules may also be implicitly demonstrated, experienced and reproduced, especially those emotion rules and emotional regimes tied to and arising from the broader socio-cultural embedding. With the appearance of emotion as a *resource*, we refer to Callahan's (2004: 1433) structuration-theorist notion of emotion resources as the 'source of control over the experience and expression of emotion'. Callahan differentiates between emotion as authoritative, if it is externally controlled by the organization, and as allocative, if it is controlled individually. With regard to emotion as an authoritative resource we may also add the 'emotions of control' as analysed by Fineman and Sturdy (1999), referring to the ways in which emotion is embedded and becomes manifest in power relationships and mechanisms of organizational control. By emotion as an allocative resource, Callahan (2004) understands the job-related application of emotion, which may bypass organizational policies for the worker's own social and economic needs. This notion of a deliberate emotion management beyond organizational control is also echoed by Bolton (2005) in her labour-process oriented analysis of emotional labour. These last two appearances of emotion, as *rules* and *resources*, thus complete the picture. Rather than representing additional components, they are present in the whole process of work. As structuring forces, they contribute to the emotional landscape of the organization.

The model of appearances of emotion in organizations depicts the range of emotional links to organizational work and serves as a blueprint for the structure of this volume. It also symbolizes the interplay of its two parts and of the individual contributions' thematic foci. The first part, *Emotionalizing Organizations,* highlights the role of emotions in organizational processes and structures, showing that feelings are instrumental to organizations and in many ways interwoven with work processes, e.g. as an antecedent and a consequence of work in organizations. The second part, *Organizing Emotions,* details how organizational structures and processes contribute to the learning and the control of emotions. It gives insights into specific emotional regimes and the application of emotion rules and resources. The question here is of how organizational structures and processes take effect on customers and employees, how organizational members are urged into various emotional regimes and how desired feelings are instigated.

In Part I, *Emotionalizing Organizations, Stephen Fineman* suggests that the turn towards the feelings of the customer and the shift within public social work organizations from caring for clients to servicing customer leaves the individual social worker without safety net when clients decide to push complaints ad absurdum. Based on an empirical case study he exemplifies how the emotionologies and emotional sub-cultures of organizations give rise to feelings in the employee that manifestly influence her/his self-worth and trust in others and that these feelings may even cause illness and necessitate sick leave. *Yiannis Gabriel* adds a psychoanalytical edge to the traditional focus on emotion management in care work. In a critical vein he argues that care work involves feelings and experiences from early childhood and is thus not as easily managed and scripted as has often been assumed. There is not just scripted emotion work in care work, but also sympathies and antipathies that are deep seated in each interactant and that shape the way the carers provide service to their clients and how the interactants perceive each other. Drawing on the example of professional elderly care, *Nicole Bornheim* analyses the emotional experiences of service providers. In terms of the model of appearances of emotions postulated here, she shows that positive emotions emerge on all levels – of working, of organizing and of the socio-cultural embeddings. As the most relevant triggers of positive emotions she identifies certain organizational conditions, namely working conditions and corporate philosophies. Based on a study of organizational procedures for personnel selection, *Christian Imdorf* examines affective decision-making in the hiring of trainees, showing the way that emotion and especially what is popularly called 'gut feeling' orientate the process of selecting appropriate candidates. They do so by coordinating and aligning the selection along criteria related to the different worlds of the firm and by reducing ambiguity in the face of insufficient information. *Poul Poder* elaborates an interactional approach to empowerment. As he argues, existing theories of empowerment focus either on the individual or the organization, treating empowerment either as a result of psychological aspects such as self-confidence or as an outcome of structural preconditions (e.g. in flat organizations), but they fail to take into account the importance of social interactions. Instead, he asserts that self-confidence and other positive emotions related to empowerment result primarily from interaction with colleagues and superiors, a process that not only grants recognition, but also the access to resources relevant to performing given tasks.

Combining Goffman's theory of face-threatening acts, Scheff's theory of emotions and social bonds and Clark's theory of emotions and social place, *Charlotte Bloch* elaborates a framework for the categorization of negative acts and bullying in organizations. The results of her qualitative analysis of negative acts by the type of face-threatening acts with a focus on emotions and interactional processes allow us to better understand the range of consequences for the victims. *Helena Flam, Jeff Hearn and Wendy Parkin* examine the issue of violations in organizations at the macro, meso and micro levels with a focus on organization violations, gender relations and emotions. The theoretical framework developed assesses the nature of violations and the severity of their consequences, and illuminates the way that nationalist and organizational discourses coincide in the effort to silence victims of rape and sexual harassment. The silence in turn reproduces the myths of the rational organization as well as the loving and secure family and nation. *Alberto Martín Pérez* presents an ethnographic study of the emotions in and around queuing for residence permits in Spain. As he shows, on the immigrants' side anxiety, humiliation, anger, resignation and happiness link into one another and are acted upon individually and in groups. The way these feelings are expressed is deeply connected to the immigrants' social status as they will suppress anger and reframe the situation in order not to endanger the permit they want to get. Emotions of anxiety and resignation are also identified on the civil servants' side, along with emotions of frustration and a patronizing attitude towards the clients. The findings thus reveal how nation state structures position both public servants and immigrants as powerless subjects of ritualistic bureaucratic processes of inclusion/exclusion and gatekeeping, giving rise to the permanent emotional turbulence of 'immigrant-hood', as well as emotional strain and a 'non-responsibility' attitude among public servants.

In Part II, *Organizing Emotions, Andrea Cossu* highlights the ambiguous role and use of emotion in the bureaucratic organization of the Italian Communist Party, focusing on the role of rituals. On the one hand, the party repressed emotion to promote a 'rationalist' image where positive emotions were a side-effect of politics, while negative ones were ascribed exclusively to the 'enemy'. On the other it provided detailed behavioural scripts that implied a thorough emotion management imposed on the communist in his and her daily individual life. *Sylvia Terpe and Silvia Paierl* draw on the reform of labour administration in Germany in order to examine the relationship between organizational processes, feeling rules and the ensuing emotions. They focus on the new processing rules for the 'modern service providers' – the case managers who attend to the unemployed. Based on a reinterpretation of the results of a qualitative study, they show in particular which feeling rules the case managers are subjected to and how they actively deal with them. The authors analyse the relationship of 'voluntary' emotion work and 'forced' emotional labour, and develop a typology that characterizes groups of employees by the feeling rules they feel obliged to obey and by their emotional reactions. In her qualitative analysis of the implementation of the 'Learning by Listening' concept, *Debra King* studies how techniques for the enhancement of the emotional intelligence of the staff and children in childcare institutions were developed and implemented. Focusing on the ensuing change in childcare routines and the way that the care staff worked with the emotions concerning and around these changes, she offers insights into the sometimes far-reaching personal and private consequences of the organizational emotional regime and its production of preferred organizational identities. *Vesa Leppänen* presents a conversation analytic study of interactions between telephone advice nurses and people seeking medical help. The fine-grained analysis of their verbal exchanges reveals nurses' microstrategies for controlling the callers' potential anxiety about disease and guiding them within the framework of emotional neutrality, which is the preferred emotional regime of the bureaucratic setting. The results not only show that the nurses steer the interaction and the emotional expressions of the caller, but also that the structural contexts of the conservations put the caller in a subordinate position vis-à-vis the nurse. Finally, *Carmen Baumeler* discusses the concept of emotional intelligence as an organizational regime of emotional conduct conducive to flexible capitalism. Basing her work on Elias, Foucault, Hochschild and Reddy, she shows that the development towards increased interdependency and functional relationships, as well as modern bureaucratization, do not do away with emotions but indeed bring them back onto the agenda in order to create self-disciplining idealized subjects.

In view of these multifaceted topics and approaches, we may proudly state that this volume delivers a strong contribution to the broadening field of research on emotions in organizations. With its trans-disciplinary and multiparadigmatic character it conveys deep insights into the multidimensional 'nature' of emotion and its appearance in organizational structures and processes.

Last but not least, we wish to recognize that the realization of this volume is indebted to the existence of the European Sociological Association's Research Network on the Sociology of Emotions (RN11). The network began in 2004 and is, in itself, a powerful sign of the growing interest in emotions in the social science. The network has quickly expanded since then, today encompassing both junior and senior researchers from Europe, Australia and the USA.[2] In the volume *Theorizing Emotions* (Hopkins et al. 2009), members of the network engage in the theoretical expansion of emotion sociology. The cornerstones of that volume, as well as those of the current one, on emotions in organizations were laid in sessions of the RN11 at the 8th Conference of the European Sociological Association in September 2007. Additionally, we are proud to have attracted further junior, as well as prominent senior, researchers from outside the network such as Stephen Fineman and Yiannis Gabriel.

With all these contributions we are able to offer original pieces of work from the research front, and a further demonstration of the fruitful cooperation of sociologists and organization and management researchers in tackling the topic of emotions in organizations. We thank all the contributors for the fantastic cooperation and for staying with us till the glorious end!

Notes

1. The development of this compass is based on Deetz' (1996) revision of the classic Burrell and Morgan (1979) framework of research perspectives in organizational research. The metaphor of a compass is to underscore the flexibility of different ways and goals of doing research, and the understanding of research perspectives as discursive orientations that are produced and reproduced in the very process of doing research. The framework's construction and its adaptation to research on emotion in organizations are outlined in more detail in Sieben (2007a).
2. For details on the foundation and development of the network, along with the history of the sociology of emotions in Europe, see Jochen Kleres' (2009) excellent preface to *Theorizing Emotions*.

References

Adler, P.S. (2009) *The Oxford Handbook of Sociology and Organization Studies: Classical Foundations*, Oxford: Oxford University Press.

Ahmed, S. (2004) *The Cultural Politics of Emotion*, Edinburgh: Edinburgh University Press.

Albrow, M. (1997) *Do Organizations Have Feelings?*, London: Routledge.

Ashkanasy, N.M., Härtel, C.E.J. and Zerbe, W.J. (eds) (2000) *Emotions in the Workplace. Research, Theory, and Practice*, Westport, Connecticut: Quorum.

Barbalet, J.M. (1996–97) 'Class action and class theory: Contra culture, pro emotion', *Science & Society*, 60(4), 478–85.

Barbalet, J.M. (1998) *Emotion, Social Theory, and Social Structure – A Macrosociological Approach*, Cambridge: Cambridge University Press.

Best, S. and Kellner, D. (1997) *The Postmodern Turn*, New York: Guilford.

Bolton, S.C. (2005) *Emotion Management in the Workplace*, Houndsmills: Palgrave MacMillan.

Bourdieu, P. (1999) *Distinction – A Social Critique of the Judgement of Taste*, London: Routledge.

Burkitt, I. (1997) 'Social relationships and emotions', *Sociology*, 31(1), 37–55.

Burrell, G. and Morgan, G. (1979) *Sociological Paradigms and Organisational Analysis. Elements of the Sociology of Corporate Life*, London: Heinemann.

Butler, Judith (1993) *Bodies That Matter: On the Discursive Limits of Sex*, New York: Routledge

Callahan, J.L. (2004) 'Reversing a conspicuous absence: Mindful inclusion of emotion in Structuration Theory', *Human Relations*, 57(11), 1427–48.

Callahan, J.L. and McCollum, E.E. (2002) 'Conceptualizations of emotion research in organizational contexts', *Advances in Developing Human Resources*, 4(1), 4–21.

Clark, C. (1997) *Misery and Company. Sympathy in Everyday Life*, Chicago: University of Chicago Press.

Clegg, S.R., Hardy, C., Lawrence, T.B. and Nord, W. (2006) *The Sage Handbook of Organization Studies*, 2nd edn, London: Sage.

Collins, R. (1988) 'Theoretical continuities in Goffman's work', in P. Drew and A. Wootton (eds) *Erving Goffman – Exploring the Interaction Order*, Cambridge: Polity Press, 41–63.

Collins, R. (1990) 'Stratification, emotional energy, and the transient emotions', in Kemper (1990a), 27–57.

Collins, R. (2004) *Interaction Ritual Chains*, Princeton: Princeton University Press.

Damasio, A.R. (1999) *The Feeling of What Happens: Body and Emotion in the Making of Consciousness*, New York: Harcourt Brace.

Damasio, A.R. (2005 [1994]) *Descartes' Error*, New York: Penguin Books.

Deetz, S. (1996) 'Describing differences in approaches to organization science: Rethinking Burrell and Morgan and their legacy', *Organization Science*, 7(2), 191–207.

Dunkel, W. (1988) 'Wenn Gefühle zum Arbeitsgegenstand werden. Gefühlsarbeit im Rahmen personenbezogener Dienstleistungstätigkeiten', *Soziale Welt*, 39(1), 66–85.

Ekman, P. (1999) 'Darwin, Charles Robert', in Levinson et al. (1999), 177–79.

Elias, N. (1982) *The Civilizing Process*, New York: Pantheon Books.

Fineman, S. (ed.) (1993a) *Emotion in Organizations*, London: Sage.

Fineman, S. (1993b) 'Organizations as emotional arenas', in Fineman (1993a), 9–35.

Fineman, S. (1996) 'Emotion and organizing', in S.R. Clegg, C. Hardy and W.R. Nord (eds) *Handbook of Organization Studies*, London: Sage, 543–64.

Fineman, S. (ed.) (2000a) *Emotion in Organizations*, 2nd edn, London: Sage.

Fineman, S. (2000b) 'Emotional arenas revisited', in Fineman (2000a), 1–24.

Fineman, S. (2000c) 'Commodifying the emotionally intelligent', in Fineman (2000a), 101–14.

Fineman, S. (2006) 'Emotion and organizing', in Clegg et al. (2006), 675–700.

Fineman, S. (ed.) (2007) *The Emotional Organization. Passions and Power*, Oxford: Blackwell.

Fineman, S. and Sturdy, A. (1999) 'The emotions of control – A qualitative exploration of environmental exploration, *Human Relations*, 52(5), 631–64.

Fineman, S., Maitlis, S. and Panteli, N. (2007) 'Virtuality and emotion', *Human Relations*, 60(4), 555–60.

Flam, H. (2000) *The Emotional 'Man' and the Problem of Collective Action*, Frankfurt a.M.: Lang.

Flam, H. and King, D. (eds) (2005) *Emotions and Social Movements*, London: Routledge.

Foucault, M. (1976) *La volonté de savoir*, Vol. 1, Paris: Gallimard.

Foucault, M. (1995) *Discipline and Punish: The Birth of the Prison*, New York: Random House.

Garfinkel, H. (1984) *Studies in Ethnomethodology*, Malden: Polity/Blackwell.
Gerhards, J. (1988) 'Emotionsarbeit. Zur Kommerzialisierung von Gefühlen', *Soziale Welt*, 39(1), 47–65.
Giddens, A. (1979) *Central Problems in Social Theory: Action, Structure and Contradiction in Social Analysis*, Los Angeles: University of California Press.
Goffman, I. (1959) *The Presentation of Self in Everyday Life*, New York: Doubleday.
Goleman, D. (1996) *Emotional Intelligence. Why Can it Matter More than IQ*, London: Bloomsbury.
Goodwin, J., Jasper, J.M. and Polletta, F. (eds) (2001) *Passionate Politics – Emotions and Social Movements*, Chicago: University of Chicago Press.
Gordon, S.L. (1990) 'Social structural effects on emotions', in Kemper (1990a), 145–79.
Grandey, A. (2000) 'Emotion regulation in the workplace: A new way to conceptualize emotional labor', *Journal of Occupational Health Psychology*, 5(1), 95–110.
Harré, R. and Parrott, W.G. (eds) (1996) *The Emotions: Social, Cultural and Biological Dimensions*, London: Sage.
Hochschild, A.R. (1979) 'Emotion work, feeling rules, and social structure', *American Journal of Sociology*, 85(3), 551–76.
Hochschild, A.R. (1983) *The Managed Heart – Commercialization of Human Feeling*, Los Angeles: University of California Press.
Hochschild, A.R. (1990) 'Ideology and emotion management: A perspective and path for future research', in Kemper (1990a), 117–44.
Hochschild, A.R. (2000) *The Time Bind. When Work Becomes Home and Home Becomes Work*, New York: Owl Books.
Honneth, A. (2000) *Das Andere der Gerechtigkeit*, Frankfurt a.M.: Suhrkamp.
Hopkins, D., Kleres, J., Flam, H. and Kuzmics, H. (eds) (2009) *Theorizing Emotions: Sociological Explorations and Applications*, New York: Campus.
Illouz, E. (2007) *Cold Intimacies*, Cambridge: Polity Press.
Jameson, F. (1998) *The Cultural Turn. Selected Writings on the Postmodern, 1983–1998*, London: Verso.
Kemper, T.D. (ed.) (1990a) *Research Agendas in the Sociology of Emotions*, Albany: State University of New York Press.
Kemper, T.D. (1990b) 'Social relations and emotions: A structural approach', in Kemper (1990a), 3–26.
Kemper, T.D. (2001) 'A structural approach to social movement emotions', in Goodwin et al. (2001), 58–73.
Kemper, T.D. (2006) 'Power and status and the power-status theory of emotions', in J.E. Stets and J.H. Turner (eds) *Handbook of the Sociology of Emotions*, New York: Springer, 87–113.
Kleres, J. (2009) 'Preface: Notes on the sociology of emotions in Europe', in Hopkins et al. (2009), 7–27.
Kramer, R.M. (1999) 'Trust and distrust in organizations: Emerging perspectives, enduring questions', *Annual Reviews of Psychology*, 50, 569–98.
Kramer, R.M. and Tyler, T.R. (eds) (1996) *Trust in Organizations – Frontiers of Theory and Research*, London: Sage.
Krell, G. and Weiskopf, R. (2006) *Die Anordnung der Leidenschaften*, Wien: Passagen.

Laclau, E. and Mouffe, C. (1985) *Hegemony and Socialist Strategy – Towards a Radical Democratic Politics*, Thetford: Thetford Press.

Levinson, D., Ponzetti, J.J. and Jorgensen, P.F. (eds) (1999) *Encyclopedia of Human Emotions*, Vol. 1, New York: MacMillan.

Lewis, P. and Simpson, R. (eds) (2007) *Gendering Emotions in Organizations*, Houndsmills: Palgrave Macmillan.

Lord, R.G., Klimoski, R.J. and Kanfer, R. (eds) (2002) *Emotions in the Workplace. Understanding the Structure and Role of Emotions in Organizational Behavior*, San Francisco: Jossey-Bass.

Mastenbroek, W. (2000) 'Organisational behavior as emotion management', in Ashkanasy et al. (2000), 19–35.

McDonald, K. (2006) *Global Movements. Action and Culture*, Oxford: Blackwell.

Mead, G.H. (1976) *Mind, Self and Society*, Chicago: University of Chicago Press.

Meštrović, S.G. (1997) *Postemotional Society*, London: Sage.

Morris, A.J. and Feldman, D.C. (1996) 'The dimensions, antecedents, and consequences of emotional labor', *Academy of Management Review*, 21(4), 996–1010.

Neckel, S. (2009) 'Emotion by design: Self-management of feelings as a cultural program', in Röttger-Rössler/Markowitch (2009), 181–98.

Payne, R.L. and Cooper, C.L. (eds) (2004) *Emotions at Work. Theory, Research and Applications for Management*, Chichester: Wiley.

Pongratz, H.J. and Voß, G.G. (2003) 'From employee to "entreployee". Towards a "self-entrepreneurial" work force?', *Concepts and Transformation*, 8(3), 239–54.

Rafaeli, A. and Sutton, R.I. (1989) 'The expression of emotion in organizational life', *Research in Organizational Behavior*, 11, 1–42.

Rafaeli, A. and Worline, M. (2001) 'Individual emotion in work organizations', *Social Science Information*, 40(1), 95–123.

Rastetter, D. (2008) *Zum Lächeln verpflichtet. Emotionsarbeit im Dienstleistungsbereich*, Frankfurt a.M.: Campus.

Reddy, W. (2001) *The Navigation of Feeling – A Framework for the History of Emotions*, Cambridge: Cambridge University Press.

Rorty, R.M. (1989) *Contingency, Irony, Solidarity*, Cambridge: Cambridge University Press.

Röttger-Rössler, B. and Markowitch, H.-J. (eds) (2009) *Emotions as Bio-cultural Processes*, New York: Springer.

Scheff, T. (1990) 'Socialization of emotions: Pride and shame as causal agents', in Kemper (1990a), 281–304.

Scheff, T. (1997) *Emotions, the Social Bond and Human Reality. Part/Whole Analysis*, Cambridge: Cambridge University Press.

Scherer, K.R. (1999) 'Cross-cultural patterns', in Levinson et al. (1999), 147–56.

Scherke, K. (2009) *Emotionen als Forschungsgegenstand in der deutschsprachigen Soziologie*, Wiesbaden: VS.

Schreyögg, G. and Sydow, J. (eds) (2001) *Emotionen und Management. Managementforschung 11*, Wiesbaden: Gabler.

Seidman, S. (ed.) (1997) *The Postmodern Turn – New Perspectives on Social Theory*, Cambridge: Cambridge University Press.

Sieben, B. (2005) *Interplay of Emotion and Virtual Work*, paper presented at the 21st EGOS Colloquium, Berlin.

Sieben, B. (2007a) *Management und Emotionen. Analyse einer ambivalenten Verknüpfung*, Frankfurt a.M.: Campus.

Sieben, B. (2007b) 'Doing research on emotion and virtual work: A compass to assist orientation', *Human Relations*, 60(4), 561–80.

Simpson, R. and Smith, S. (2005) 'Introduction', *International Journal of Work, Organization and Emotion*, 1(1), 1–3.

Stearns, P.N. (1988) 'Anger and American work: A twentieth-century turning point', in C.Z. Stearns and P.N. Stearns (eds) *Emotion and Social Change. Towards a New Psychohistory*, New York: Holms & Meier, 123–49.

Stearns, P.N. (1994) *American Cool – Constructing a Twentieth-Century Emotional Style*, Vol. 3, New York: New York University.

Sturdy, A. (2003) 'Knowing the unknowable? A discussion of methodological and theoretical issues in emotion research and organizational studies', *Organization*, 10(1), 81–105.

Thoits, P.A. (1990) 'Emotional deviance: Research agendas', in Kemper (1990a), 180–206.

Thrift, N. (2004) 'Intensities of feeling: Towards a spatial politics of affect', *Geografiska Annaler*, 86B(1), 57–78.

Tracy, S.J. (2005) 'Locking up emotion: Moving beyond dissonance for understanding emotion labor discomfort', *Communication Monographs*, 72(3), 261–83.

Tracy, S.J. and Trethewey, A. (2005) 'Fracturing the real-self ↔ fake-self dichotomy: Moving toward "crystallized" organizational discourses and identities', *Communication Theory*, 15(2), 168–95.

Turner, J.H. and Stets, J.E. (2005) *The Sociology of Emotions*, New York: Cambridge University Press.

Weber, M. (1948) 'Bureaucracy', in H.H. Gerth and C.W. Mills (eds) *From Max Weber: Essays in Sociology*, New York: Routledge, 196–244.

Wettergren, Å. (forthcoming) 'Managing unlawful feelings – the emotional regime of the Swedish migration board', appears in *International Journal of Work, Organization and Emotion*.

Wettergren, Å., Starrin, B. and Lindgren, G. (eds) (2008) *Det sociala livets emotionella grunder*, Malmö: Liber.

Williams, S. (2001) *Emotion and Social Theory*, London: Sage.

Wouters, C. (1989) 'The sociology of emotions and flight attendants: Hochschild's managed heart', *Theory, Culture and Society*, 6, 95–123.

Wouters, C. (2004) *Sex and Manners. Female Emancipation in the West, 1890–2000*, London: Sage.

Wouters, C. (2007) *Informalization*, London: Sage.

Part I
Emotionalizing Organizations

1
Emotion in Organizations – A Critical Turn

Stephen Fineman

1 Introduction

Over the last 15 years or so, the study of emotions in organizations has come a long way. For a subject that was in near obscurity in the early 1990s, we now witness a veritable explosion of interest. In addition to edited books, monographs and journal articles, specialist conferences and dedicated websites have sprung up, adding thrust to debate in the area.

A closer look at this work reveals a dominant perspective on emotion: something that occurs 'inside' the person, an experience or 'competency' that can individually or with others lead to 'better' or 'worse' leadership, change, decision making, creativity or some other organizationally related outcome.[1] Within this genre, emotional intelligence has gained a high profile – as a means of achieving all manner of 'goods' in organizational life, especially enhanced performance (Salovey et al. 2008). Similarly, 1950s 'positiveness' (Peale 1952/1996) has been reinvented and much augmented by positive psychologists and positive organizational behaviour scholars (Fineman 2006; Frederikson/Cohn 2008). Again, the productive benefits of being positive are extolled, alongside its value as an experiential or moral tonic.

Such psychologizing of emotion – looking inwards to individual, micro and process (personality, bio-somatic changes, cognitions, appraisals) – attests to a long and distinguished tradition of emotion theory going back to William James's monumental oeuvre, *Principles of Psychology*, in 1890. It is hardly surprising, then, that organizational psychologists should follow suit. We see this, for example, in recent reviews of research into emotions in organizations, such as in Elfenbein (2007). She pays considerable attention to the intrapersonal processes that follow the registration of a 'stimulus' or 'event', as in affective events theory (Weiss/Cropanzano 1996). The events, or the things that happen to people in organizations, are taken for granted in the model. They are themselves neither problematized nor deconstructed as part of a wider ethical, value or control system. Emotion is more an inside-out affair than outside-in. We witness a similar orientation in Ashkanasy and Coopers' (2008) edited *Research Companion to Emotion in Organizations*, marking 'the latest work from leading scholars in the field of emotion'. Wider societal issues are hinted at in the introduction, but the weighty volume is shaped substantively by chapters on 'within-person phenomena' and 'individual differences'. These are building blocks for subsequent chapters covering dyadic, group and (in just six of the total of 38 chapters) organizational levels of analysis.

What is missing, or much underworked, in these formulations is a sense of criticality. By this, I do not mean lively internal debates, which abound. I refer to the space defined by critical theory and critical management studies. Critical management studies (CMS), broadly speaking, asks us to think out of the box (and indeed to recognize that we are boxed) that frames our inquiries and to reflect on the implicit values embraced or reproduced, including our own as individual researchers. It draws attention to the way much current organizational theorizing often serves narrow, managerialist, goals, rather than wider community benefit or less oppressive practices.

CMS takes issue with the prevalence of instrumentality or performativity: enhanced output and profit as taken-for-granted end points for management research. The ethical and political consequences of these ends are rarely questioned, such as the way they reinforce class, gender or racial divisions; buttress dysfunctional bureaucracies; privilege the control of the many by an elite few or undermine the very sustainability of the planet. Importantly, CMS regards these issues as not simply 'fixable' by courses on ethics or anti-discrimination, or by initiatives from human resource departments. Indeed, it is the (re)construction of people as 'resources' that is regarded as part of the problem, sending a strong message about the way individuals are to be defined, used and, if necessary, discarded. It is to wider social and ideological structures that we must turn.

While most critical scholars would resonate with the above description, it would be wrong to characterize CMS as a unified corpus. There are divisions and tensions aplenty (e.g. Adler et al. 2007; Bridgman/ Stephens 2008). This is partly due to the different theoretical strands and allegiances that inform different critical scholars. The critical, cognate, fields are often sociological rather than psychological, and thus more attuned to organizational studies than to traditional psychology. For example, the reader trying to make sense of CMS will be confronted with a heady cocktail of Marxism, labour process theory, symbolic interactionism, feminism, postmodernism and poststructuralism (e.g. Alvesson/Willmott 1992; Deetz/Mumby 1990; Edwards 2006; Edwards 1979; Salaman 1981; Weedon 1997). Together, these draw attention, especially, to the way power circulates in and around organizations. Not only through structural (e.g. role) and ideological (e.g. managers/workers, men/women, old/young) divisions, but in the deployment of specific narratives and forms of language that produce and reproduce particular meanings and, consequently, colonize people's subjectivities – who or what they think they are.

These features may be more or less imposed, more or less oppressive, but they often insinuate themselves into shaping a social order, almost by default – and are therefore hard to desist or resist. Extreme structuralists (and some postmodernists) claim that individual resistance is pretty futile; there are bigger forces at play out there. Others, though, are more agentic in their theorizing: the cage we inhabit is more plastic than it appears and is responsive to individual and collective pressure, while structures are susceptible to a range of meanings and interpretations (Fitzghughj/Leckie 2001; Gubrium/Holstein 1995). This provides space for 'tempered radicals', those inside organizations who will push hard for major cultural changes (e.g. on race, sexual orientation or gender), but will also be prepared to serve the broad productive aims and objectives of the organization (Meyerson/Scully 1995).

A key strand of critical thought, inspired by Michel Foucault's writings (e.g.1970), concerns the role of knowledge in defining and propagating power. Knowledge and power are mutually constitutive. Knowledge in organizations – be it from managers, unionists, IT specialists, human resources staff, accountants or social scientists – is never neutral. It is both politicized and ethicized, and can be a positive or negative force. It enables certain outcomes or possibilities while excluding others. So, for example, the psychologizing – and quantification – of emotion is captured and validated by mainstream academic journals, many of them applied to a managerial outlook on organizations. Accordingly, it becomes axiomatic to researcher identity and their departmental prestige to exclude other, more critical or qualitative, voices. However, at the same time, the very act of being 'othered' nourishes resistance to the mainstream. Resistance is expressed in critiques of the managerialist assumptions that underpin some emotion theories and in favouring more qualitative and ethnographic inquiries (cf., e.g. Fineman 2004; Fineman 2005).

2　The critical emotion landscape

Through a critical lens, the emotional order of an organization is often fragile, and under strain. Wider economic/market pressures combined with entrenched divisions of power, resources and privilege embed the potential for tension and disputation. A cocktail of anxiety, insecurity and ambivalence across the organization can coalesce into resistance to executive prerogative or, in the extreme, a defensive, bullying, culture. Positive feelings, such as pleasure and ease are certainly not unattainable in this scenario, but are likely to be derived at the expense of others. Tension is exacerbated when the organization becomes preoccupied with its own survival. Some organizations respond to such circumstances by attempting to reinvent themselves, such as by installing new leaders, new images and a new rhetoric of control. The 'bad' past is camouflaged, silenced or even vilified, as organizational members are subject to 'revaluation', with some having to reapply for their old jobs. The restructuring rationale may have profound, unanticipated, emotional effects akin to a miasma, polluting the atmosphere with anxiety and fear (Fineman 2003: 87). Gabriel graphically portrays the miasma that attended one such 'renewal':

> An outstanding characteristic of the new organization was the constant undermining of individuals' self confidence by the very fetishization of the organization's new image. A very pernicious critical ethos installed itself in the organization, one that affected nearly every person I had an opportunity to talk to and many activities. Its core message was 'X is not good enough', where X could stand for a person, an activity, a department, groups of customers, suppliers etc. This criticism was rarely rationally driven – for example, unsuccessful projects had often evaded criticism and become 'no go areas' of discussion; yet, many routine and successful activities came to be criticized as flawed and ineffective. People too were criticized, by focusing on whatever aspect of their performance could be criticized, no matter how effective or successful they were in everything else they did. Many of them were said to be 'past their sell-by date'. (2008: 8)

The 'past their sell-by date' allusion draws attention to the way that certain narratives and labels are loaded emotionally within a culture or sub-culture, especially when imposed hierarchically. I have myself participated in an academic department where its executive board, in anxious response to a national programme to scrutinize and grade university research, labelled a proportion of its academic staff as 'at risk' because of their 'inadequate' or 'inappropriate' research. As these designations began to circulate, the demoralizing effect was palpable, stigmatizing (rather than 'motivating') their targets and contributing to a general sense of unease and cynicism.

3   Emotionologies and identities

Poststructural accounts of individual and social identity point to how identity formation requires a constant supply of identity work as self- and other-ascribed narratives are assembled, disassembled and temporarily resolved. Some of the narratives reflect *emotionologies*, society's 'take' on the way, and to whom, certain emotions are to be expressed, such as what we should feel towards asylum seekers, royalty, children, the police, doctors, single parents, gays, lesbians, the work shy or street beggars (Fineman 2008a; Parrott/Harre 2001; Stearns/Stearns 1985). Emotionologies are politico-ideological constructs part shaped by prevailing currents of nationalism, ethnocentrism, racism or homophobia, as well as by governmental, religious and party-political dogmas. They encapsulate emotions' stocks of knowledge, vocabularies, feeling and display rules (see Stets/Turner 2008). Articulated through parenting, teaching, newspapers, television, radio, films and the Internet, they provide a vocabulary, rationalization and 'place' to feel or express attitudinally 'appropriate' emotions, such as admiration, hate, love, pity, fear, anger or indignation towards particular sections of society.

Emotionologies colour the way specific occupational groups are valued. Through regular surveys we learn, for example, that Americans currently feel good about their firefighters, doctors, nurses and police officers, while their bankers, stockbrokers and estate agents are much scorned (HarrisInteractive 2007). Prison correctional officers in the USA face a societal discourse of low prestige that denigrates correctional institutions, and understanding this is important, argues Tracy (2008), in appreciating why many of them feel alienated, depressed and burned out with their work. Generational or economic shifts and upheavals – accelerated in postmodern times – are likely to trigger targeted emotionological reframings. For example, there has been the widely circulated discourse of 'greed and selfishness' associated with the 'bonus culture' enjoyed by top executives and financial traders during the world recession of the early twenty-first century (Partnoy 2004). It follows that such people can be openly derided or despised.

Emotionologies are important structural shapers of emotion. But systems of emotion and feeling are also nuanced within a particular culture or organizational sub-culture, often supporting a dynamic of competing or contradictory emotions. Elsewhere I have referred to such settings as emotional zones – symbolic or physical spaces in organizations where a local emotional order is tacitly negotiated and distinct from adjacent zones (Fineman 1993; 1996). In a similar vein Rosenwein (2002) speaks of 'emotional communities', such as families and neighbourhoods where, she suggests, that the researcher's focus should be on:

> what these communities (and the individuals within them) define and assess as valuable or harmful to them; the evaluations they make about others' emotions; the nature of the affective bonds between people that they recognize; and the modes of expression that they expect, encourage, tolerate, deplore. (ibid.: 842)

The interplay between regnant emotionologies and local competing or 'contra' emotionologies is currently under theorized – such as how much, and what sort of, difference or tension is sustainable. It is important for the practices of the earlier-mentioned tempered radicals, and central to what happens when people choose to deviate from strict secular, gender, religious or familial codes – such as on dress, education, sexual abstinence, diet, marrying 'out', child bearing or abortion. The 'deviant's' feelings about themselves and their actions, and others' feelings towards them, hinge upon how the tension between emotional orders – the omnipresent and the deviant – is addressed or resolved.

The grip of societal or community emotionologies can vary in strength. Some can be oppressive, effectively exploiting those who have little power to resist. For example, Afro-American integration into white mainstream culture suffered for many years from the white construction of their emotions as 'inferior' (Corrigan 2002).[2] Racist emotionologies can infuse the workplace. Mirchandani (2008), for instance, highlights the plight of transnational call-centre workers operating in India. In this competitive, high growth, market, indigenous operators are trained and monitored to 'please the customer', 'not to take the rude behavior of customers personally', and 'arguing back is a strict no no' (ibid.: 90). Mirchandani highlights workers' anguish and emotion work as they struggle to retain a sense of dignity in the face of racist slurs with colonial overtones. Many callers, especially from America, resent the operators' 'broken English' and, sheltering behind the anonymous technology and trained subservience of the operators, feel free to express racist views. As one operator recalled:

> I still remember a call from a very old guy, and after doing all the things possible to satisfy his needs he made a statement, 'You know V–, you did a great job, however I hate you because I hate all Indians. And my son is unemployed because of you, because the jobs are being outsourced to India'. (ibid.: 92)

And another reminisced:

> Then you get a lady.... she just called up to say that you people are so scripted and the I hate you people and I hate you Indians just because of that. (ibid.: 92)

These examples encapsulate a trend towards consumer capitalism (Miles 1988) or the 'sovereign consumer' (Fournier/Grey 2000). As the service economy has grown, power has shifted from the service provider or producer to the consumer or customer. Indeed, the very notion of 'customer' is imbued with symbolism, to suggest an overt or tacit commercial exchange where 'the sale', and repeat sales, are paramount. In terms of emotionologies, the once passive, silent or long-suffering client, passenger, patient, student or tax payer is now free, or freer, to express how they feel about the institution that has provided the service and, more poignantly, the person who has served them.

While some redress in the balance of power is to be welcomed, it is not without its dark side as far as the worker is concerned, as indicated above. Korczynski and Bishop (2008) amplify the point in their study of front-line staff in a job centre. Job centres in the UK are localized government organizations where the unemployed 'sign on' to receive their unemployment benefits and, as 'customers', are offered advice on job vacancies and applications. Staff are trained to be customer focused, to personalize their service (e.g. wearing a name badge) and to make the encounter an enjoyable one – for the customer. However, such appearances and 'skills' gloss over the coarse realities of dealing with aggrieved or disaffected clients, especially those who are insulting or violent. The training language sanitizes violence and abuse, and downplays its emotional effects. In the words of a front-liner, 'In training we have "challenging" customers... challenging situations – not violent customers; not drug addicts – people with "different lifestyle choices"!' Korczynski and Bishop speak of a 'legitimizing ideology for forms of violence and abuse' (2008: 75). Front-liners were taught to see themselves as culpable, personally responsible, for not containing or deflecting any anger or rage expressed towards them, which, on occasions, could be especially threatening, such as 'smashing windows up; smashing computers, jumping over the counter and hitting staff' (ibid.: 74). They were encouraged to frame such incidents as 'bad customer handling skills' reminiscent of Hochschild's (1983) flight attendants, 'recurrently trained' to take passenger insults with a smile.

The discourse of consumer sovereignty has now extended beyond 'the emotional proletariat' (Macdonald/Sirianni 1996) to the traditional professions, such as teachers, medical practitioners and social workers. In recasting the balance of power, customary emotionologies are challenged and reframed. The net effect can give the client greater voice and transparency. But this occurs, also, at a time when managerial discourses on accountability, risk minimization and standardization have begun to supplant professional missions of service, care or calling in the public services. In the name of efficiency, such 'new managerialism' can create a defensive, risk averse, culture where resource/budget caution, throughput, record keeping and time frugality become ends in themselves (Deem 1988; Grey 1996). It cultivates a 'tick box' approach that, in effect, can deskill the professional and undermine their discretion and confidence.

This scenario is well illustrated by social work – which I will explore here in some detail through a case study.

4 A case in point: The social worker

4.1 Emotionology of social work

In the UK – and elsewhere – the wider emotionological climate towards social work is at best cautious, at worse derisive. Public perceptions are fuelled by a stream of public inquiries and media exposés that purport to reveal social worker incompetence or neglect (LeCroy/Stinson 2004). Against this backcloth, social work practice has undergone radical transformation over the past decade, described by Dustin (2007) as a form of McDonaldization. The McDonaldization thesis, following Ritzer (1993), views the uncertainties, flux and fluidity of postmodernism as overstated; they exist alongside organizational structures that are decidedly modern – standardized and scripted in both work procedures and emotions. In UK social work, professional judgements are now heavily circumscribed and controlled by standardized methods and assessment forms, routinizing and flattening encounters with clients. The infusion of managerialism is symbolized by a shift away from casework to 'care management'. Care *management*, in many social workers' eyes, is deskilling, a dilution of their special expertise and unique professional contribution as a professional caseworker (Carey 2007). As care managers, it can seem that others – almost any others – can do what a social worker now has to do. Case management also appears far removed from the 'person-centred' philosophy of traditional casework training, and some argue that it fatally undermines it; it is a pale imitation of the 'real' client care that is driven by humanistic values and feminist ideals (Gray 1995; Innes et al. 2006; McAuley et al. 1999).

The social worker-cum-care manager now has to go to the commercial market to source services that were once state funded – such as nursing care and residential homes. The client's needs have to be balanced against the price of the services, where the cheaper the better is the norm for an organization that is budget led. The social worker as care manager, suggests Dustin, is sandwiched uncomfortably between 'two different sides, their responsibility to the organization to provide services at the right price and also their responsibility to see those clients' rights are guaranteed within the service' (Dustin 2007: 69). A final characteristic is a shift from 'client' to 'consumer' or 'customer'. In the marketized, managed, economy of social services, the service user is now publicly referred to a *customer* (Harris 2002),[3] valorized in terms indistinguishable from the customer of a supermarket or car dealership. As a customer, he or she has the right to 'excellent service' and 'full satisfaction' – rights that, in practice, are difficult or impossible to meet in a resource stretched, underfunded, service.

In sum, through a critical lens, the emotionalities of social work practice are located firmly in its structural and political context. The social worker's feelings are to be understood as far more than a matter of their 'stress resilience' or 'coping capacities' (e.g. Fineman 1985; Lloyd et al. 2002). They are produced from a combination of a disparaging public emotionology, role ambiguities, surveillance technologies, political double-binds and a culture of managerialism – summed up by one of Dustin's social workers: 'It's mad to feel bad about talking to a service user beyond the time allocated for a needs assessment' (2007: 70); and by another as '... "anti" everything you were trained to do' (69).

The finer details of these dynamics are exposed by the following case. It concerns Eve, a social worker in an elderly mental health team, part of a social services department in a UK metropolis. Eve had carefully documented her experiences and permitted me access to her notes and the organization's official correspondence. I met her regularly outside of work over a three-month period in 2009. She candidly revealed her feelings and dilemmas as events unfolded.

4.2   Eve's story: Social work and the tyranny of the customer

When we first met, Eve was into her second year of employment in a social services department in the UK. This was her first 'proper' job in social work. She was a member of a multi-disciplinary team with statutory responsibility for the needs of the elderly mentally ill in the local community – some at home, some in care centres, some in hospitals. For Eve, social work was an exciting, mid-life, career change. She had studied long and hard for it at graduate and postgraduate levels, with excellent academic results, as well post-qualification training. In training, the managerialist approach and assessment routines were discussed, but so too was the importance of maintaining a 'person-centred' approach for effective practice.

Eve said, wearily, that she found her work demanding. It was tiring, with much unexpected bureaucracy:

> Forms, ticking boxes for the sake of it, mixed or confusing messages from management and only sporadic supervision. A huge amount of paperwork. I was trained in person-centred social work but the *person* soon gets lost in the organization's administrative demands, report writing and bureaucracy – much of which I have to take home. Only today we received a new instruction to log every phone call we make – who, how long – all of which is collated by someone somewhere – for what?

Client assessments and care plans were dictated more by prescribed questions-and-answer categories than by her professional judgement. Regardless of the care plans that she wrote, the resources for her clients, 'service users', were strictly rationed; there was a constant conflict between what a client wanted or needed and what could actually be offered. Moreover, what, how and when available resources could be provided was 'often mysterious and mystifying', underpinned by the principle of 'the cheapest provider' or, less predictably, the 'whims of my manager'. This added to her feelings of impotence, as well as her doubts about the validity of her training.

Because of a 'culture of illness' in her department, 'some are off sick for ages', she often had to take on others' cases, adding considerably to her administrative load. But she prided herself on 'managing it' and 'not being one of the sickies'. Office politics – who would talk to whom, back biting and disaffection with management – consumed much emotional energy, as well as providing an occasional light release. Meanwhile, there was an ever-replenishing or repeating client load.

Throughout, however, direct client work is what attracted her and where she felt most comfortable:

> I haven't given up – yet. It does make it worthwhile when I can build real relationships and connections with clients and make a difference, even feel appreciated, even if it's just a bit.

To emphasize the point, Eve recounted her warm feelings for particular clients and her pleasure at hearing their personal life stories '... and sometimes I have to introduce myself from scratch every time I visit, because of their failing memory – but that's OK!' She exuded empathy. Her dedication, thoroughness and commitment, although shaken, were still intact, something noticed – and praised – by her colleagues and immediate manager (see Gabriel's discussion on 'authentic care' in this volume).

4.3 A turning point

In one of our meetings, Eve looked especially distressed and close to tears. She had just been informed by her manager that the daughter of one of her long-standing clients had written a formal complaint to the organization about the 'lack of assessment, planning and support' that her mother had recently received from Eve, and wanted a written apology from both the organization and from Eve. She also demanded reassurance that the organization would improve its service in future and that Eve would get suitably trained to put right her inadequacies. Eve was devastated – and angry.

4.4 The background to the complaint

Eve's principle client was an elderly woman with whom she had had regular contact for over two years, without problems. Things changed following the death of the client's husband; her daughter then wanted 24-hour care for her mother. In discussions with Eve, it was agreed that the daughter would seek out suitable care homes, but the daughter subsequently changed her mind and requested 24-hour care at the family home. Eve pointed out that this was not possible without a full assessment of her mother's needs, which would involve outside agencies and take some time to organize. Meanwhile, because the possibility of 24-hour care at home was unusual and expensive, Eve consulted her line manager about the best way of supporting her client and her family. The manager said firmly that the only option was to offer respite for the family while the assessment was being put into place. It would mean the client would need to go temporarily into a care home. Eve put this to the client's family, but the daughter was unhappy about the suggestion – so much so that she wrote a formal complaint to the agency, with a demand that Eve be replaced because they 'had lost confidence in her'.

Eve's immediate manager defended Eve's decision in a letter to the daughter, but at the same time agreed to assign a new social worker to the case. The new worker quickly provided most of the resources that the daughter had wanted. Eve was stunned. She felt, bewildered and undermined.

The story might have ended there, were it not that the daughter chose to press home her advantage. She demanded a formal apology from the organization for its 'poor service' and a personal apology from Eve, in which Eve would acknowledge her 'lack of listening, lack of experience and need for re-training'. She 'clearly wanted blood; it's personal now', said Eve shaking.

4.5   Navigating the complaints procedure

In our further meetings, Eve became progressively more agitated, swinging between righteous anger and deep despair. A formal complaint from a customer meant a formal process, itself laden with bureaucracy. The department's complaint procedure was enshrined in a 15-page document, tightly packed with prescriptions on what the 'investigating officer' should and should not say or do at the different 'levels' of the complaint process. It promised 'adequate support for everyone involved', but its fundamental slant was exposed in a culminating instruction:

> A letter is to be written to the complainant that contains a robust apology to satisfy the complainant that they no longer feel aggrieved, even if their complaint is not upheld; it should demonstrate a thorough response which presents a good image.

Pleasing the customer was paramount. Eve was warmly supported by her immediate colleagues ('this could be anyone of us Eve') but isolated by her management – and fast losing voice. No one, it appeared, wanted to hear her side of the story. Even the manager who had supported her action went silent (and then left the department). Meanwhile an investigating officer interviewed the complainant and, subsequently, summoned Eve to a meeting with her. In that meeting it was made clear that Eve's side of the story was 'not relevant' and that she would be 'well advised' to write a letter of apology to the complainant. The investigating officer then presented Eve with a pre-prepared letter to sign in which Eve admitted to her past shortcomings as well as her need for further training. Eve was aghast:

> I felt bullied – by both my organization and the daughter. I could, in effect, be openly slandered by the relative of a client and have no recourse. Rather than supporting and protecting me, hearing me out and dealing with the complaint for me, my organization was victimizing me. All they were interested in was getting the complaint out the way – at my cost. I did exactly as I had been advised by my manager and I was now getting crucified for it. No way was I going to sign that letter! And my training needs had absolutely nothing to do with the daughter; that's up to me and my manager.

The only active support that Eve could find was through her union, but this was more procedural than substantive. Meanwhile the emotional costs were mounting: sleepless nights, inability to concentrate and exhaustion. Her anger and indignation were mixed with feelings of helplessness, loss of confidence and depression as she felt she was now fighting the system, very much alone. There were soon signals from managers that it 'wouldn't help her career' if she decided to hold out, and the investigating officer accused her of 'paranoia' in her response to the situation.

Eventually, Eve felt worn down. Fearful of the vindictiveness of her own organization, she capitulated. She sent a letter, but in her own words, apologizing to the daughter. It was copied to, and 'approved', by the investigating officer. Simultaneously a 'grovelling' (Eve's words) letter of apology was sent by the investigating officer, assuring the complainant that new procedures in management and practice were already in place, described by Eve as 'patently untrue'. Eve felt scarred; however, the whole stressful business was now over.

But it was not. Some two months passed when the complainant wrote again to say that she was not convinced that Eve's apology was genuine, and unless she received a sincerer apology from her, she would escalate her complaint to a higher level, as permitted in the formal procedure.

> I felt as if I was falling off a cliff. I'd just about got my act together and it all kicked off again. But I did believe that the organization would take it on this time and tell her, firmly but politely, that the matter was now closed.

And indeed, she felt encouraged by her senior departmental manager, who said the letter she had already written was more than adequate and that she was right not to have signed the one originally penned for her by the investigating officer.

> At last, some real support, I thought. But not for long. E-mails began to whiz around the department and between departmental managers and senior managers in Social Services – and they all stopped talking to me. Then the very manager who had just supported me said that I should write another letter after all – '... as tough as it is Eve ... we all have to do something like this in our career.... you shouldn't feel bad about it Eve ... going to Level 2 could be very hard on you ... you don't have to take this personally'. I felt betrayed.

Eve's moral indignation was palpable. It appeared that managers were closing ranks and, to avoid embarrassment and exposure from a persistent and articulate complainant, they were prepared to sacrifice Eve. Eve finally buckled under the stress of it all and was signed off sick for a fortnight by her doctor – her first absence in two years.

> This has been a terrible period. Not only have I felt physically wrecked and drained of confidence, but the clock has been ticking on Level 2, which can only be stopped if I write another damn letter. For my managers this is simply an operational matter and one of convenience to them. For me it goes to the heart of moral conduct, my identity as a social worker, and trust in my employer.

After much agonizing, and advice from friends who were distressed to see how ill she was becoming, Eve, very reluctantly, wrote another letter of apology. She also wrote a letter to her manager, which she asked to be put on record. It included the following statements:

> As you are probably aware, I have complied with this latest request against my better judgement and in response to the pressure that I have felt placed on me by those handling this complaint. My initial letter to the complainant accurately reflected my true feelings after two years fieldwork with my client, most of which had been more than satisfactory.
>
> Throughout, the complaints procedure has been based exclusively on the complainant's account and views, including derogatory personal comments about me – which I perceive as inappropriate, not

least insulting. At no point have I been able to officially respond with my side of events. It leaves the firm impression that clients are free to say whatever they like about a social worker's practice and person and – crucially – she/he is left in limbo, no one interceding or moderating on his/her behalf.

In what appeared a rapid attempt at damage limitation, Eve's manager wrote to her, thanking her for 'going the extra mile', praising her 'excellent social work' and adding, 'It's fair to say that, with the benefit of hindsight, the complaint could have been dealt with differently'. Eve was unimpressed. She felt that her relationship with her department, and her practice, would never be the same again.

4.6 Understanding Eve's emotions

A psychological interpretation of Eve's emotions would point to her coping capacities and her vulnerabilities when under threat – indeed the very standpoint of some of her managers. A critical perspective alerts us to rather different considerations, especially how power and control is exercised in her organization. We see how the agency's public rhetoric of customer satisfaction, a quasi-emotionology, becomes a bureaucratic end in itself. It is to be protected in a climate where the activities, especially statutory ones, of nervous/wary social services departments are publicly scrutinized. Accordingly, the newly empowered consumer who shouts the loudest is very likely to be heard – and must be appeased. In Eve's case, this appears as a meta-discourse that preoccupies, even obsesses, management, over and above Eve's progressively precarious position and growing distress. Echoing Korczynski and Bishop's job centre staff, not only is Eve bullied by the complainant, but her organization's thinly veiled threats and complicity with the complainant's version of events, compound the bullying and effectively silences Eve.

Her silence, though, is superficial. In her resistance, she experiences a gamut of powerful emotions: humiliation, anger, fear, indignation, betrayal and depression. These feelings are to be understood as a product of an organization that is trapped in its own audit and surveillance procedures and that projects its anxieties onto its subordinate staff. It is keen to defend its external image, even if this means sacrificing the welfare of a rank-and-file member who is struggling to make sense of her role and responsibilities. However, the individual managers who contributed to Eve's malaise should not necessarily be construed as malicious in intent. A critical management perspective alerts us to the hierarchical cascade of anxiety that infuses an organization's culture when there is a mismatch, even gulf, between the organization's strategic aims and what it can realistically deliver. In social services, efficiency pressures from government, resource scarcity, legal culpability, image sensitivity in a stressful domain and generally poor remuneration make a potent mix that contributes to an edgy culture. This goes some way to explain why Eve was treated in the way she was. But it does not excuse it.

5 Conclusion

In this chapter, I have argued for a shift in our thinking about emotion in organizations from the individual-psychological to the politicized contexts in which emotions are socially constructed – territory informed by CMS. The levers to emotion lie substantially in the structures and flows of power that infuse an organization and its principal agents. The shaping of others' emotions is achieved though the direct and indirect impression of emotionologies, buttressed by mechanisms of hierarchical control and surveillance. This can be especially pernicious when policy-makers, managers or empowered consumers are able to dictate terms in ways that cannot be queried or challenged by those who are on the front line of the service. In sectors ill-attuned and ill-matched to an ethic of consumer sovereignty and marketization, the service worker can become more, rather than less, self-protective – as our examination of social work suggests. The seeds are sown for *contra* emotionologies – a local order of distrust and wariness of management as well as of certain clients or consumers.

A critical perspective on emotion also implies a recasting of traditional, psychologically driven models of organizational change and development. It is a move away from therapeutic-style interventions aimed at enhancing coping and leadership skills to ones that ask probing questions about the moral and emotional orders that an organization takes for granted and sustains, and about whom they best serve.

Notes

1. For example, see the topics covered in the *2008 International Conference on Emotions and Organizational Life.* http://www.uq.edu.au/emonet/emonet-2008/index.html
2. More generally, we see how 'odd' or 'inappropriate' emotional displays in public readily invite exclusion or pathologization. Emotionologies reach deep into prevailing norms of mental stability.
3. See www.dundeecity.gov.uk/socialwork/customers/

References

Adler, P.S., Forbes, L.C. and Willmott, H. (2007) 'Critical Management Studies', in Brief/Walsh (2007), 119–79.

Alvesson, M. and Willmott, H. (eds) (1992) *Critical Management Studies*, London: Sage.

Ashkanasy, N.M. and Cooper, C.L. (eds) (2008) *Research Companion to Emotion in Organizations*, Cheltenham: Edward Elgar.

Bridgman, T. and Stephens, M. (2008) 'Institutionalizing critique: A problem of critical management studies', *ephemera*, 8(3), 258–70.

Brief, A. and Walsh, J. (eds) (2007) *The Academy of Management Annals*, Vol. 1, Amsterdam: Elsevier.

Carey, M. (2007) 'White-collar proletariat? Braverman, the deskilling/upskilling of social work and the paradoxical life of the agency care manager', *Journal of Social Work*, 7(1), 93.

Corrigan, J. (2002) *Business of the Heart: Religion and Emotion in the Nineteenth Century*, Berkeley: University of California Press.

Deem, R. (1988) 'New managerialism and higher education: The management of performances and cultures in universities in the United Kingdom', *International Studies in Sociology of Education*, 8(1), 47–70.

Deetz, S. and Mumby, D. (1990) 'Power, discourse and the workplace: Reclaiming the critical tradition in communication studies in organizations', in Anderson, J. (ed.) *Communication Yearbook 13*, Newbury Park, CA: Sage, 18–47.

Dustin, D. (2007) *The McDonaldization of Social Work*, Aldershot: Ashgate.

Edwards, P. (2006) 'Power and ideology in the workplace: Going beyond even the second version of the three-dimensional view', *Work, Employment & Society*, 20(3), 571–81.

Edwards, R. (1979) *Contested Terrain*, New York: Basic Books.

Elfenbein, H.A. (2007) 'Emotion in organizations: A review and theoretical integration', in Brief/Walsh (2007), 315–86.

Fineman, S. (1985) *Social Work Stress and Intervention*, Aldershot: Gower.

Fineman, S. (1993) 'Organizations as emotional arenas', in S. Fineman (ed.) *Emotion in Organizations*, London: Sage, 9–35.

Fineman, S. (1996) 'Emotion and organizing', in S. Clegg, C. Hardy and W. Nord (eds) *Handbook of Organization Studies*, London: Sage, 543–64.

Fineman, S. (2003) *Understanding Emotion at Work*, London: Sage.

Fineman, S. (2004) 'Getting the measure of emotion – and the cautionary tale of emotional intelligence', *Human Relations*, 57(6), 719–40.

Fineman, S. (2005) 'Appreciating emotion at work: Paradigm tensions', *International Journal of Work, Organization and Emotion*, 1(1), 4–19.

Fineman, S. (2006) 'On being positive: Concerns and counterpoints', *Academy of Management Review*, 31(2), 270–91.

Fineman, S. (2008a) 'Introducing the emotional organization', in Fineman (2008b), 1–11.

Fineman, S. (ed.) (2008b) *The Emotional Organization: Passions and Power*, Oxford: Blackwell.

Fitzghughj, M.L. and Leckie, W.H. (2001) 'Agency, postmodernism, and the causes of change', *History and Theory* (40), 58–81.

Foucault, M. (1970) *The Order of Things*, London: Tavistock.

Fournier, V. and Grey, C. (2000) 'At the critical moment: Conditions and prospects for critical management studies', *Human Relations*, 53(1), 7–32.

Frederikson, B.L. and Cohn, M.A. (2008) 'Positive emotions', in Lewis et al. (2008), 777–96.

Gabriel, Y. (2008) 'Separation, abjection, loss and mourning: Reflections on the phenomenon of organizational miasma', *ESRC Seminar Series: Abjection and Alterity in the Workplace*, University of Leicester, 28th May.

Gray, M.E.L. (1995) 'The ethical implications of current theoretical developments in social work', *British Journal of Social Work*, 25(1), 55–70.

Grey, C. (1996) 'Towards a critique of managerialism: The contribution of Simone Weil', *Journal of Management Studies*, 33(5), 592–611.

Gubrium, F. and Holstein, J. (1995) 'Individual agency, the ordinary, and postmodern life', *The Sociological Quarterly*, 36(3), 555–70.

Harris, J. (2002) *The Social Work Business*, London: Routledge.

HarrisInteractive (2007) 'Firefighters, scientists and teachers top list as "Most Prestigious Occupations," according to latest Harris Poll', www.harrisinteractive.com/harris_poll/index.asp?PID=793 (accessed 15 August 2009).

Hochschild, A. (1983) *The Managed Heart*, Berkeley: University of California.

Innes, A., Macpherson, S. and McCabe, L. (2006) *Promoting Person-centred Care at the Front Line*, York: Rowntree Foundation.

James, W. (1890) *The Principles of Psychology*, New York: Holt.

Korczynski, M. and Bishop, V. (2008) 'The job centre. Abuse, violence, and fear on the front line: Implications of the rise of the enchanting myth of customer sovereignty', in Fineman (2008b), 74–87.

LeCroy, C.W. and Stinson, E.L. (2004) 'The public's perception of social work: Is it what we think it is?', *Social Work*, 49(2), 164–74.

Lewis, M., Haviland-Jones, J.M. and Barrett, L. (eds) (2008) *Handbook of Emotions*, 3rd edn, New York: Guildford Press.

Lloyd, C., King, R. and Chenoweth, L. (2002) 'Social work, stress and burnout: A review', *Journal of Mental Health*, 11(3), 255–65.

Macdonald, C.L. and Sirianni, C. (eds) (1996) *Working in the Service Economy*, Philadelphia: Temple University Press.

McAuley, W.J., Teaster, P.B. and Safewright, M.P. (1999) 'Incorporating feminist ethics into case management programs', *Journal of Applied Gerontology*, 18(1), 3–24.

Meyerson, D. and Scully, M. (1995) 'Tempered radicalism and the politics of ambivalence and change', *Organizational Science*, 6(5), 585–600.

Miles, S. (1988) *Consumerism*, London: Sage.

Mirchandani, K. (2008) 'The call centre: Enactments of class and nationality in transnational call centres', in Fineman (2008b), 88–101.

Parrott, G.W. and Harre, R. (2001) 'Princess Diana and the emotionology of contemporary Britain', *International Journal of Group Tensions*, 30(1), 29–38.

Partnoy, F. (2004) *Infectious Greed: How Deceit and Risk Corrupted the Financial Markets*, New York: Holt.

Peale, N.V. (1952/1996) *The Power of Positive Thinking*, New York: Ballantine.

Ritzer, G. (1993) *The McDonaldization of Society*, Thousand Oaks, Calif.: Pine Forge Press.

Rosenwein, B. (2002) 'Worrying about emotions in history', *The American Historical Review*, 107(3), 821–45.

Salaman, G. (1981) *Class and Corporation*, London: Fontana.

Salovey, P., Detweiler-Bedell, J.B. and Mayer, J.D. (2008) 'Emotional Intelligence', in Lewis et al. (2008), 533–47.

Stearns, P.N. and Stearns, C.Z. (1985) 'Emotionology: Clarifying the history of emotions', *American Historical Review*, XC, 813–36.

Stets, J.E. and Turner, J.H. (2008) 'The sociology of emotions', in Lewis et al. (2008), 32–46.

Tracy, S.J. (2008) 'The prison. Power, paradox, social support and prestige: A critical approach at addressing correctional officer burnout', in Fineman (2008b), 27–43.

Weedon, C. (1997) *Feminist Practice and Poststructualist Theory*, 2nd edn, Oxford: Blackwell.

Weiss, H.M. and Cropanzano, R. (1996) 'Affective events theory: A theoretical discussion of the structure, causes and consequences of affective experiences at work', *Research in Organizational Behaviour* (18), 1–74.

2

Beyond Scripts and Rules: Emotion, Fantasy and Care in Contemporary Service Work

Yiannis Gabriel

> What if emotions were honoured? That is, if people regularly *attended to* and *engaged* others' feelings? ... What if this type of interaction – where human beings engage a fuller and deeper range of their own and others' feelings – was the norm rather than the exception?
>
> (Meyerson 2000: 168)

> If we think of emotions as having a life of their own, which might be in contradiction to, or expressed fully or partially through our cognition to different degrees in different times, we can think through all sorts of situations with which most people must be familiar: experiencing feelings we cannot express to our satisfaction; having feelings that we can express but that others find difficult to understand; and most important perhaps, the regular experience of contradictions between our thoughts and our feelings
>
> (Craib 1998: 110)

1 Introduction

The rise of contemporary consumerism has forced a radical revaluation of a wide range of organizational phenomena. In the field of organizational studies there has been a broad recognition of the emergence of a triangle (Leidner 1991) involving the worker, the manager and the customer, whose endlessly mutating dynamics form the basis of a wide range of organizational processes. Politics, identity, structure, culture and so forth can no longer be viewed from a perspective of the old-fashioned tug-of-war between workers and bosses. Instead they must be viewed through a 'lens' that acknowledges the triadic nature of contemporary work and organization. Triads, as Simmel (1950) recognized, are more unstable than dyads, involving shifting alliances and conflicts in which the third party can be the stakes or the beneficiary. The entry of the consumer as an important figure into the world of organizations has therefore radically reshaped the nature of contemporary work, the more so as different parties of the triad are frequently found to swap masks and adopt each other's positions. Just like the worker, the manager is an employee of the organization. The manager becomes a worker in her dealings with her superiors and she becomes a customer in her relations with different departments within the same organization. The customer often re-enters an organization as manager or worker.

One of the consequences of the rise of contemporary consumerism has been a preoccupation with the cathedrals of consumption, like shopping malls, tourist destinations, theme parks and so forth, and the nature of the service interaction between employee and consumer. This, in turn, has resulted in numerous insights into the nature of emotions in today's workplaces that radically depart from classic formulations. Formerly, organizations had been looked at, as Fineman nicely put it, as 'emotionally anorexic' (1993b: 3). In the last 15 years or so, much scholarship has been reoriented to view emotion as an integral part of the service interaction and the ethos of 'customer care' (du Gay/Salaman 1992; Fineman 1993a; 2000a; 2003; Sturdy 1998). As such, emotion has been found to be liable to similar rationalizing tendencies as affect all work in capitalist societies – in short, it can be planned, standardized, deployed and controlled in the interest of profit and sales.

Scholarship in this area has been dominated by the twin perspectives of labour process and emotional labour. The dynamics of control, resistance and identity delineated for the industrial worker have been reconfigured for service work, through the realization that emotion is a vital feature of such work. Emotional labour involves the performance of different emotional scripts, dictated by or designed for different circumstances, specific to different jobs and the requirements of different employers. Thus the battle for control of emotional scripts and performances, the resistance to exploitative emotional demands and other such phenomena have been sharply delineated (see, e.g. several contributions in Grugulis/Willmott 2001; Sturdy et al. 2001; Korczynski/Macdonald 2008).

In spite of the insights generated by this approach, it presents, in my opinion, a partial view, one that tends to deny emotions any autonomy, ultimately subordinating them to cognition and the logic of capitalist controls. Emotions, from this perspective, are socially constructed to suit the logic of management and profit generation. If emotions are socially constructed, then, along with every other social construction, they follow the logic of power and privilege; they become capital ('emotional capital') to be deployed as a legitimate basis for accumulation of privilege, power and profit. In this paper, I will question some of the assumptions of this view, offering an analysis of the emotional dynamics involved in service work and the service relationship, and in particular the relationship between carer and cared for, a relationship that is capable of generating very powerful emotions in both parties, turning them into objects of positive and negative fantasies for each other. Customer care, I will argue, cannot be conceptualized merely as a discursive formation aimed at dominating the worker and seducing the customer. Using current ideas from both the ethics of care literature and psychoanalytic literature, I show that caring emotions have their origins in early life experiences and cannot be reinvented at the whim of management. Caring cannot be domesticated within routinized interactions, but invariably triggers off powerful positive and negative emotional relations, which, in many cases, are unmanaged and, even, unmanageable.

2   Emotional labour and some unanswered questions

The concept of emotional labour was first proposed by Arlie Hochschild (1983) following her earlier use of 'emotion work' (Hochschild 1979), and opened radical new possibilities for the sociological study of emotion. First, emotions were detached from instinctual expressions and were shown to be capable of being learned, performed and scripted, in short, to a substantial degree to be *socially constructed*. Language plays a large part in this process of construction, enabling us to identify different emotional states in ourselves and others and make fine distinctions of nuance and intensity. Second, consistent with current thinking in neurology and physiology (see, e.g. Damasio 1994; Sacks 1995), emotions are not opposed to rationality but often support or qualify it. Third, emotions – far from being automatically cast as disruptive forces to order, stability and organization – were viewed as capable of supporting organizational activities. In this way, emotions emerged as vital resources that could be marshalled and controlled, in a manner not dissimilar to other resources such as money, information or materials. Putnam and Mumby noted that 'through recruitment, selection, socialization and performance evaluations, organizations develop a social reality in which feelings become a commodity for achieving instrumental goals' (1993: 27). In this way, bureaucratic rationality can expand to colonize affectivity and emotions. Mature bureaucracy, in opposition to its Weberian ideal counterpart, need no longer be afraid of emotions – rather it may commandeer them, control them and deploy them as it does other resources, like knowledge, money or technology. Writers like Ferguson (1984), Mumby and Putnam (1992) and Ashforth and Tomiuk (2000), as well as Hochschild (1983) herself, criticized the resulting self-estrangement, inauthenticity and burn-out suffered by employees who, under pressure from management, adopt the emotions and even the feelings required by their roles.

I do not wish to deny the systematic commodification of emotions, aptly captured in the title and subtitle of Hochschild's (1983) groundbreaking book, *The managed heart: Commercialization of human feeling*. However, the emphasis on commercialization of emotion (and the attendant surge of excitement about emotional intelligence) has resulted in a new kind of blindness. If Weber and his successors were blind to emotions in organizations and at the workplace, it seems to me that Hochschild and many of her successors have become blind to feelings unless scripted and controlled. This is something that certain scholars are beginning to realize. Some recent contributions to the emotional labour debate have noted that people at work often engage with others emotionally in ways that are not directly tied into the formal job requirements (most obviously, developing warm and supportive relationships with either co-workers or customers in the workplace out of personal choice; see, e.g. Bolton 2005). Korczynski (2003), for his part, has referred to groups of employees forming warm and supportive emotional relationships as 'communities of coping'. Maybe most interestingly, Fineman (1996; 2003) has for the past ten years been arguing for a distinction between feeling and emotion, which unfortunately, however, has not been taken up by others.

What I would like to challenge goes beyond the view that emotions can be domesticated into a predictable resource that can be deployed in line with the dictates of capital. More fundamentally, I would like to argue that emotional work cannot be reduced to the management of emotional appearances and performances, the smile, the smirk and the shrug, and the costs they exact. Instead, I will propose that emotional work involves both internal and external work; the 'internal' work of coping with contradiction, conflict and confusion and the 'external' work of reconciling fantasy and desire with the demands of different social situations. I have long tried to argue (see, e.g. Gabriel 1995; 1997; 1998) that fantasy, a concept that scarcely features in the work of Hochschild and her successors, is of vital importance for an understanding of emotion. This is especially relevant to service interactions, which may depart from rationalizing and controlling scripts – such interactions may entail flirtation (Hall 1993; Guerrier/Adib 2000), harassment (Folgero/Fjeldstad 1995), emotional blackmail (Rosenthal et al. 2001) or toxic exchanges (Stein 2007). The emotional dynamics at the interface of the service worker and the customer can be unpredictable and uncontainable. Emotional performances are often disrupted by powerful feelings, positive and negative, unleashed at the interface between service worker and customer.

Let me start with a simple question. Does the service worker *care* for her customers? Does the teacher care for her pupil, the social worker for the homeless person, the call-centre employee for the caller, the cabin crew member for the passenger or the nurse for the patient? A Weberian answer would clearly be negative. A Marxist answer would be negative, except in as much as the worker is liable to false consciousness and alienation at work. Extending this, a labour process theorist would add that a service worker may exact benefits by caring for her customers, and may even exact concessions from her managers and employers in order to offer a high quality of care. The question still remains. Does the service worker *really* care for her customers? Avoiding the obvious pitfalls of generalization, we need to acknowledge that some workers, some of the time, *do* really care for their customers. Let us push the question: why? Following Hochschild (1979: 39ff.; see also Ashforth/Tomiuk 2000), emotional labour theorists might argue that workers really care in as much as they *deep act* emotional performances that have them caring for their customers. Deep acting involves experiencing the emotions dictated by the parts actors are playing rather than merely 'simulating' the emotional displays, which is referred to as 'surface acting'.

But, the question remains: what decides whether employees deep act or surface act, whether they genuinely feel the emotions of caring or merely display them? And what causes the disruption in acting that changes conformity to an emotional rule into its violation? Using one of Hochschild's own illustrations, what *emotional forces* are at play in the following incident?

A young businessman said to a flight attendant, 'Why aren't you smiling?' She put her tray back on the food cart, looked him in the eye, and said, 'I'll tell you what. You smile first, then I smile.' The businessman smiled at her. 'Good,' she replied. 'Now freeze, and hold that for fifteen hours.' Then she walked away. (1983: 127)

Hochschild views this as a 'smile-fighter's victory' (ibid.) in the smile war. In this way, the incident is seen as a deliberate act of resistance, through which one set of emotional rules is violated because it is seen as unjust and unreasonable (the set that dictates that flight attendants should smile all the time) and is replaced by another (that states flight attendants earn status and the respect of their peers if they can be rude to offensive customers and get away with it). But is this displacement of one set of rules by another unrelated to any emotions that exist beyond performances (Fineman 1996; Fineman/Sturdy 1999; Sturdy/Fineman 2001)? Could it be that the slippage from one performance to a different one was brought about by something in the 'young businessman's' appearance, smirk or hair style that reminded her of her ex-boyfriend or her general irritation at having to fly to Seattle when she expected to go to New York where she could spend a few hours with her current boyfriend? While emotional labour captures well the quality of work that the employee performs in *controlling* her own emotions and *evoking* emotions 'appropriate' to a situation, the judgement of what is 'appropriate' may itself the product of emotional forces and may require emotional work of a different type. It is a judgement that adopts the customer as a deserving and needy fellow human, or conversely as a spoilt and irksome parasite. On what basis is this judgement made?

Hochschild (1979) links different regimes of emotional control to different styles of upbringing. In particular, she argues (on rather meagre evidence) that working-class children are raised through control of their behaviour whereas middle-class children are raised with greater emphasis on presenting appropriate emotions. On this basis, she concludes that middle-class people are more emotionally prepared for occupations in which emotion work is a large part. What Hochschild did not examine is the rather more profound influence that a child's prolonged state of infantile dependency has on his/her emotional development – how does being cared for over a long period of time affect subsequent attitudes and experiences of caring and being cared for?

3　Ethics of care discourse

Roughly at the same time that Hochschild developed her theory, Carol Gilligan (1982) published her influential book, *In a Different Voice*, in which she put forward the view that girls follow a different path of moral development from boys, one that does not revolve around rights, rules and abstract principles of justice, but centres on compassion, care and the ability to sustain intimate relationships. This provided the basis for a rich debate on the nature of caring relations and their relevance to ethics. While this debate has had a profound influence on numerous disciplines ranging from moral philosophy to psychology and international relations, it has not had much of an impact on the sociology of emotions or organizational theory. This is interesting, given the huge amount of research devoted to the service relationship. It is also interesting in the light of the rapidly ageing population in rich societies and the constant calls for increased levels of care work. People in developed and developing countries live longer and are prepared to go to ever greater lengths to prolong their agonies of death. This translates into constantly increasing demands for caring for the elderly and infirm, a demand that may be met by relatives, the state, freelance workers (especially immigrants) or various voluntary and other organizations. It seems to me that some of the insights generated by ethics of care theorists can be of great value to discussions of emotion in service occupations.

Since the publication of Gilligan's (1982) influential and controversial book, caring for others has been increasingly recognized as a vital dimension of most human interactions and as the foundation of a particular type of morality (e.g. Noddings 1986; Ruddick 1989; Tronto 1993; Kittay/Feder 2002; Held 2006). In contrast to the 'ethics of justice' that have long dominated the thinking of moral philosophers, ethics of care theorists argue for a different system of morality, one that does not rely on dubious claims of universality, absolute judgements of right and wrong and perfect virtues. Instead, they advocate a morality that grows out of a recognition that all people are embedded in different webs of social relations, being dependent on others for their survival and well-being and capable of supporting others in their moments of need and helplessness. A large part of this debate concerns the gendered nature of care, whether, in other words, women are more disposed by nature, culture or other factors for caring than men and how this affects power relations between the genders. What does it mean to care for other people? Caring is attending to the needs of others to whom we feel close and for whom we are prepared to take responsibility. Caring is not a scripted emotional performance and cannot be reduced to emotional labour. Caring involves some of the qualities that are currently and fashionably grouped under the title of emotional intelligence (e.g. by Salovey/Mayer 1990; Goleman 1998; but see also Fineman 2004). Yet, unlike emotional intelligence, caring entails no suggestion of emotional manipulation or deception. Instead, caring involves sensitivity to the emotional needs of the other person and an ability to guide and control these emotions through wide range of actions, utterances and expressions. It requires a constant state of watchfulness and an ability to anticipate the needs and vulnerabilities of the person cared for. It also requires the ability to filter out all that is irrelevant or secondary. But above all, Noddings points out the following:

> To act as one-caring [...] is to act with *special regard for the particular person in a concrete situation*. We act not to achieve for ourselves a commendation but to protect or enhance the welfare of the cared-for. [...] The one-caring displays a characteristic *variability in her actions – she acts in a nonrule-bound fashion* in behalf of the cared-for. (2003: 24 f., emphasis added)

Ethics of care has been evolving as a discourse in moral and political philosophy, psychology, gender studies and areas ever further afield, such as international relations (for overviews, see Noddings 1986; Sevenhuijsen 1998; Kymlicka 1991; Kittay/Feder 2002; Held 2006). While numerous debates are still unfolding on the different dimensions of caring, there is a fair degree of agreement on the following:

1. Every child spends a prolonged period of *dependence* in the care of others – this leaves deep residues for later life. Caring for others and being cared for are experiences that are liable to awaken powerful fantasies and emotions from a person's earliest past, and to evoke reminiscences of infantile dependency and powerlessness (e.g. Ruddick 1989).
2. Caring is *relational*, and there are limits to the extent to which it can be depersonalized or mechanized; machines and systems may facilitate care work but cannot replace the work of the carer (e.g. Sevenhuijsen 1998).

3. Caring for another person is an *individualized* form of work – it relies on face-to-face interaction. In this sense, it resists bureaucratization and formalization (e.g. Bubeck 1995).
4. Caring evokes *complex emotions and fantasies* in both the carer and the cared for; these include positive emotions such as love, gratitude and trust, but also negative ones such as envy, fear and anxiety. Most caring relations, therefore, are liable to entail some *ambivalence* (e.g. Ruddick 1989).
5. In spite of their importance, caring activities are *systematically devalued*, underpaid and disproportionately occupied by the relatively powerless in society (e.g. Tronto 1993).
6. Caring and being cared for are vitally important, if problematic, aspects of individuals' *identities* (e.g. Meyers 2002).

While philosophers and psychologists have been developing these themes, a considerable body of literature has grown on the 'caring professions'. Yet, the two discourses have scarcely taken notice of each other. Care clearly defines the predominant character of many occupations (such as nursing, teaching, therapy, counselling and so forth), including many of those working with the elderly, the sick and the young. As I argue presently, caring also represents one of the major features and failures of leadership. Care work is a feature of all service work; it is heavily gendered both as domestic labour and across virtually all the caring professions, which are characterized by low status and low pay. In spite of the considerable aptitudes and talents it demands, care work is widely viewed as low skill and low cost. It therefore neatly conforms to the outsourcing and off-shoring logics of our times. Outsourcing and off-shoring are strategies not only of multinational corporations, but also of individuals and families as they seek to transfer responsibility of caring for older relatives, younger children or needy dependents onto others (Parreñas 2008).

In a culture that lionizes the sovereign consumer who spends her money as she pleases, the individual dependent on the care of others cuts a distinctly dejected figure. Being cared for – whether by relatives, by the state or by other organizations cannot shake off its associations with dependency, decay and failure. As Fraser and Gordon (1994) have demonstrated, the concept of dependence has not only gradually narrowed down to represent a fault or failure of individuals, but it has been feminized and racialized to set it up as the 'other' of independence, particularly as represented by the Anglo male wage-earner. Interestingly, the carer *as well as* the cared for is tarnished by this association with dependence. In a prototypical way, the caring mother as much as the cared-for child is seen as enmeshed in dependency relations decidedly inferior to the myth of independent men going about their businesses as they please (Meyers 2002). The mother's caring relationship to her child renders her dependent on a purportedly independent man who assumes a privileged position in this relationship. The caring man, in turn, becomes dependent on his employer. Caring for others creates a secondary or derivative dependency (Fineman 1995; Kittay 1999); it becomes a fetter, holding back careers, identities and achievements and, above all else, restricting freedom.

In spite of these associations, a caring orientation remains a valued quality, even in our highly narcissistic and individualistic culture. The expression 'Nobody cares' instantly evokes a reprehensible state of affairs where people are driven only by self-interest. A 'caring person' may not be the commonest self-description seen in today's inflated resumés, but it remains the description of a valued and valuable person. We may note this in the common usage of the term 'care': frequently we hear people say about a person – often a 'leader' – that 'He does not care', habitually accompanied by 'He only cares about himself'. The affinity between servant and leader has been explored by Greenleaf (1978). Caring is one of the most powerful fantasies that followers project onto their leaders (Gabriel 1997). Leaders who care are those who are willing to give generously of their time, advice, recognition and support; who are genuinely concerned for the realization of a mission or a project and who are prepared to treat others with consideration and respect, rather than as pawns on a chessboard. By contrast, leaders who do not care are those who treat others as means to their own aggrandizement, and those who lack generosity and sensitivity.

Although caring is often seen as a sign of altruistic orientation, caring leaders are by no means averse to conflict, hardness and resolution. On the contrary, the real test for caring leaders, as for all people who genuinely care for someone else, comes when they have to fight in order to defend those for whom they care, rather than opt for easy compromises. Far from being a soft and universally mild attitude, caring means taking responsibilities for others and being prepared to take personal risks in discharging these. The same can be said about the caring attitude of service workers, whether they work in overtly caring roles, such as nurses and social workers, or as employees in call centres or retail outlets. An employee who cares for the customer is one who is prepared to 'go the extra mile' in order to offer a proper service, and, by the same token, a company that cares for its customers is one that is prepared to faces its responsibilities even if this has an adverse impact on bottom lines.

Another significant element of care that is frequently commented upon by ethics of care theorists is the *personalized* bond that binds the carer with the cared for (see, e.g. Held 2006). Care seems to eschew the principle of equality in the most blatant manner. A mother will discriminate in favour of her child with little concern for the implications of this for other mothers and other children. She will barge to the head of every queue in the interest of her child. She will bend every moral principle if the interest of the child demands it, since she views categorical imperatives and absolute norms as secondary to the pressing needs of her child. As Held argued:

> Those who conscientiously care for others are not seeking primarily to further their own individual interests; their interests are intertwined with the persons they care for. Neither are they acting for the sake of all others or humanity in general; they seek instead to preserve or promote an actual human relation between themselves and particular others. (2006: 12)

I had ample opportunity to observe both of these aspects of care (i.e. 'going the extra mile' and disregard for the principle of equality) during a recent round of interviews and focus groups with clinical staff in a London hospital aimed at identifying different ways in which 'patient care' is socially constructed.[1] A large number of stories exemplifying good patient care were collected and nearly all of them identified 'care' with personalized attention given to specific patients, often at the expense of other patients. This is evident in the following comment by a junior doctor in a gynecology department.

> A pregnant woman came in through A&E [Accident and Emergency]. She was having problems with her pregnancy. I asked the registrar what to do. They decided that the best thing to do was get the woman scanned to find the problem. However, being a night shift there were no porters to be seen and the scanning units were closed. I felt that the anxious woman could not stay in A&E surrounded by drunks and druggies as it was inappropriate. Instead of calling for porters, which would have taken time, I and the registrar moved the

pregnant lady to the maternity ward ourselves where we opened up a scanning unit to find out what was wrong with the lady's pregnancy. I was proud of the leadership that I had received from my registrar; not every registrar would have done this but he solved the problem and delivered good patient care in the process. The problems were resolved within an hour with only skeletal night staff.

Here we notice a striking contrast between the individualized care reserved for the deserving patient and the virtual indifference towards the plight of the anonymous 'drunks and druggies'. Their treatment was negatively affected by the preferential treatment offered to the pregnant woman. An ethics of care perspective in this instance seems to neutralize the clinician's professional ethics that would require all patients to be treated equally.

Another interesting feature brought out by an ethics of care perspective is the notion that the carer may know the needs of the cared-for person better than the latter does him- or herself. This is evident in the case of children when a carer is said to act 'in loco parentis', that is in place of the parent who is assumed to know *better* than the child what is good for the child. But health care throws up numerous similar situations, especially if a patient suffers from a condition that impairs their judgement, such as senility or a personality disorder.

An ethics of care perspective is highly visible in the relations between clinician and patient, but it is also a dimension of many other service relations, not least between teacher and pupil, social worker and client, but even between call-centre employee and customer. Caring for others means treating them in a personalized way, going beyond the call of duty and, sometimes, acting in ways that suggest that the carer understand the needs of the cared for better than the latter does. Yet, this relation between carer and cared for should not be thought of as a blissful idyll, free of tensions and conflicts, far from it. At times, the emotional dynamics of such relations can reach extremes, but virtually every such relationship is bound to generate some ambivalence in both parties, where positive images compete with negative ones and tender emotions compete with hostile ones. Korczynski (2001; 2003) has observed this ambivalence between feelings of closeness to the needy and deserving customer and feelings of resentment towards the others in many service employees. The customer now generates affectionate feelings of care and consideration, now resentful feelings of vengefulness and envy. This ambivalence is linked to a split between two images of the customer in the mind of the caring person. On the one hand, there is the deserving customer, the customer with a human face who is often a 'regular'; this customer is invariably an individual with individualized tastes and needs, who evokes affection and sympathy. On the other hand, there is the hard 'sovereign' customer, who is often seen as privileged, regal, pampered and parasitical, and who provokes resentment and envy. At times the two images may merge into one, generating simultaneous affection and antipathy.

Sahlin (1996) notes a similar split in images of the poor and other 'client groups' of local housing authorities, which tend to oscillate between two extreme poles: they resemble either pitiable 'wretches' or shameless 'villains'. According to Sahlin, these are stereotypes associated with two divergent attitudes towards authority: submission or challenge. As such, they are not based on the generalization of *real* clients but constructed through the moral justification and legitimation of particular actions towards specific individuals. Stereotypes of the other, such as the parasite, the helpless victim, the deserving sufferer and the aggressive sponger all draw their emotional power by triggering *fantasies* fantasies that draw much of their power from our experiences in early life.

4 From social construction to fantasy – A psychoanalytic contribution

Powerful images of the other may be viewed as social constructions – they recur in numerous contexts. The term 'social construction', however, fails to acknowledge their symbolic power, their ability to stir up powerful emotions, some of which are in conflict with each other. Psychoanalysts argue that many of these images are linked to fantasies that grow out of early childhood experiences of helplessness and dependency. In later life, certain experiences of dependency or caring are liable to trigger off some of these fantasies (e.g. 'I will be abandoned'; 'I am the most important person in the world', 'My mother is here to serve me' or 'My father wants to punish me') releasing the same powerful emotions as before. The underlying process is called *transference*, a key psychoanalytic concept regarding emotion. Unlike the emotional labour approach that views emotions ahistorically, psychoanalysis insists that our feelings and emotions have histories that parallel our own histories as individual subjects. They are liable to return whenever we find ourselves in a situation that evokes an earlier one that left a powerful emotional mark on us. Transference is a process whereby feelings (e.g. admiration, fear, resentment) and images (e.g. omnipotence, mystery, beauty) once attached to parental figures become transferred onto figures who come to occupy similar unconscious locations in later life (Freud 1912; Gabriel 1998, 1999; Stein 1999). Freud (1926) first noted that, compared to all other primates, the human child appears to be born prematurely: infants spend a prolonged period in a state of total dependency; they can undertake no actions of their own and must rely on others for the satisfaction of every one of their needs. This has a favourable effect on the bonding process between the child and the parents, who appear omnipotent, but it creates, in the child, acute feelings of anxiety lest its needs should not be met. Even short periods of separation from the carer can lead to acute rage on the part of the child. Subsequently, situations of extreme helplessness are liable to evoke feelings of anxiety and powerful fantasies similar to those experienced in the earliest period of life. Seeing another person in a position of dependency is also liable to generate powerful emotions that can range from unbearable pity to abject contempt.

Freud's theory of the consequences of infantile dependence was further developed by psychoanalyst Melanie Klein (1987) who identified the nature of the fantasies evoked by these situations. She argued that the key feature of these fantasies is a psychological *splitting* between good and bad. Splitting was viewed by Klein as the most primitive defence against anxiety, and in particular the anxiety created by ambivalence, that is, the simultaneous experience of something as bad and good. Splitting first becomes manifested when a child desires the maternal breast and fails to find it. The breast is then imagined as two separate objects, a 'good breast' that is always available and nourishing and a 'bad breast' that is absent or withheld. Subsequently, the child projects the split onto the mother herself, who at times is experienced as a 'good mother', caring and available, and at times as 'bad mother', cold and indifferent. The splitting of objects into good and bad 'part objects' is later adopted as a way of coping with the anxiety provoked by objects that are both good and bad. Klein extended her theory to include other defence mechanisms, but continued to view 'splitting' as a fundamental process that is regularly deployed in later life whenever we experience such anxieties. Thus, we find it impossible to view a person as both unfortunate and toxic – a 'wretch' and a 'villain' in Sahlin's (1996) conceptualization – or both good and bad, as this would create intolerable anxieties and conflicts.

It is now possible to argue that the caring dimension of the service relationship can reawaken in both care worker and cared-for customer some of the fantasies they first experienced in early life. Each becomes for the other an *object of fantasy and desire*, charged with extreme positive or negative qualities, rather than ordinary people caught up in a contractual relationship. The customer may then experience the service worker as generous, helpful and considerate or, conversely, as withholding, unhelpful and deliberately impudent. Equally, the service worker may experience the customer as a deserving and needy subject or, conversely, as spoilt and undeserving. In each case, powerful emotions are generated, infusing the worker-customer relationship with some of the potentially explosive emotional qualities we associate with family relationships. Many emotions are thus ambivalent, involving both positive and negative aspects, love and hate and respect and fear. Ambivalent emotions, although very common, can be very confusing and disorienting – we like to organize our loves and our hates and our likes and dislikes in a consistent manner. For this reason, we often repress those emotions that we experience as dangerous or unacceptable.

That the relationship between service worker and customer can become so charged with fantasy and emotion should not surprise us. The 'servant' has long been a familiar character in myths, stories, parables, drama and literature. The character of Figaro, who gives his name to a prominent French newspaper, represents the servant who, without directly confronting his master, learns how to manage him, not least by reading and exploiting his master's emotions, reminding us that the control of others' emotions is not the sole prerogative of those in power. The master-servant relationship, with its ambiguities and subtleties, is explored in numerous works of art. Moxnes (1999) has argued that the servant represents an archetype, a highly charged symbolic image in the sense of Jung (1968), one that springs from the collective symbolic heritage of humanity flowing through each and every human being. Moxnes proposes that the servant exists in both positive and negative variants – as loyal, dedicated, caring and giving or, conversely, as malevolent, treacherous, devious and mendacious.

Whether the servant should be included in the great archetypes of humanity may be disputed, but it seems to me that something of the multifaceted quality of the relationship between master and servant is present in most service relationships, including those that are mediated by consumerist and capitalist structures. Servant and master are not fixed on a simple Marxist axis of exploitation and oppression. They are caught in a relationship that involves trust and mistrust, loyalty and resentment, identification and distancing and emotional manipulation and emotional neutralization, as captured in Genet's play *The Maids* and numerous other works of art. Master and servant know many of each other's secrets and therefore have a disproportionate ability to inflict damage on one another. It is a relationship that constantly has the potential of veering towards fantasy, and like all profound forms of human bonding invariably harbours unpredictable and potentially unmanageable possibilities. This, of course, makes the master-servant relationship such a rich seam for sexual fantasy, one constantly mined by erotic literature and pornography alike.

5 Conclusions

Throughout this essay, I have examined the relationship between service worker and customer through the prism of fantasy rather than through the dominant theory of emotional labour. What are the implications of this view? First, the ambivalence of emotions immediately becomes transparent, along with their disproportionate intensities and their ability to mutate into different and unpredictable ones. More importantly, however, once we acknowledge that the emotional lives of people in a service relationship cannot be scripted in line with the expediencies of efficiency, control and profit, we are forced to recognize that the interface between service worker and customer entails unmanaged and unmanageable elements, including flirtation, tenderness, antipathy, jousting, repartee, deception, dissimulation and so forth. Sometimes, this interface may blossom into passion and full-scale romance (e.g. Mano/Gabriel 2006), and in not a few cases it can lead to violence (e.g. Diamond 1997).

Let us recapitulate. The arrival of consumerism and the service economy has prompted social scientists to reflect on emotions as an essential dimension of work. Emotions are no longer seen as either irrelevant or detrimental to organizational functioning; on the contrary – in Fineman's (1993b; 2000b) apt term – organizations are viewed as 'emotional arenas', as places where the expression and control of emotions are contested. Emotions are both the forces driving the contest and the contest's stakes. Emotional labour, like manual or intellectual labour, is liable to regulation through rules and scripts (emotional rules and emotional scripts), which, in turn, are subject to contest and resistance. In this way, emotions become a vital dimension in the labour process. While accepting the value of this conceptualization, I have argued that it presents a too narrow and regimented account of emotions, one that denies them a life of their own and subordinates them to cognition and to the logic of organizational controls. By focusing on care as an important domain of service work, I have argued that emotions can be unmanaged and unmanageable. Like other intense human experiences, such as falling in love, mourning or rising up to an insult, caring opens up many unpredictable possibilities, where our emotions seem at odds with our thoughts, our actions and with each other. Caring emotions cannot easily be domesticated and channelled to appropriate organizational ends. Therefore, care work cannot be reduced to a simple enactment of different emotional scripts or resistance to them.

Along with ethics of care theorists, I proposed that care can neither be mechanized nor bureaucratized the way that many other forms of work can. Instead, care work generates certain emotional dynamics that stem from early life experiences originating in the human state of infantile dependency that forces us to rely on others for our survival and well-being. This prompts a deep ambivalence for both workers and customers, one that has been widely recognized by many of the scholars who have examined the service interaction in detail. Following the argument of Melanie Klein, I proposed that a splitting emerges as one of the crucial defence mechanisms through which people seek to cope with such ambivalence. Splitting exacerbates positive and negative images and fantasies by keeping them apart. Fantasy comes to play a far greater role in the experiences of service workers than it does for manufacturing workers, leading to a degree of unpredictability and even unmanageability at the service interface.

Consequently I suggested that carers and cared for easily become fantasy objects for each other, evoking corresponding emotions. These are most evident when the product being delivered is integral to the interaction between service worker and recipient, for example, clinical staff and patients or teachers and students, as well as sex workers and other professionals and their clients. It is not accidental that these types of interaction feature regularly in every kind of contemporary narrative such as films or novels. Such interactions regularly unleash early life fantasies and desires of power, dependency, submission, vulnerability and many others. Although these fantasies may be less decisive for service interactions of the more separable sort, they are not absent from the work experiences of, for instance, waiters, retail workers and call-centre employees. Such employees may sometimes imagine themselves as the champions of the customer frustrated by the exigencies of efficiency, as being under siege from unreasonable, parasitical or 'irate' customers or as being asked to prostitute themselves for the sake of the customer. Fantasies may be directed at customers, at managers or at fellow workers, about whom strong positive and negative images are constructed.

If we take the fantasy aspect of service work seriously, we will begin to understand why emotions in such jobs frequently and unexpectedly depart from the scripted set pieces, why they can be in contradiction or conflict with each other and why they can lead to unexpected and unpredictable turns of events that lend such endless fascination. We will then begin to discern some of the unmanaged and unmanageable aspects of service organizations that at the moment we are rather too eager to disregard or to domesticate. As social scientists, we may then claim that we do not only take notice of emotions in social life but also start to honour them.

Note

1. The project described, *Leadership and Better Patient Care: From Idea to Practice* (Principal Investigator Paula Nicolson), enabled by an SDO Grant, was carried out in September 2006. Thanks are due to researchers Paula Lökman and Emma Rowland who conducted most of the interviews.

References

Ashforth, B.E. and Tomiuk, M.A. (2000) 'Emotional labour and authenticity', in Fineman (2000c), 184–203.

Bolton, S.C. (2005) *Emotion Management in the Workplace*, Houndsmills, Basingstoke: Palgrave Macmillan.

Bubeck, D.E. (1995) *Care, Gender, and Justice*, Oxford: Oxford University Press.

Craib, I. (1998) *Experiencing Identity*, London: Sage.

Damasio, A.R. (1994) *Descartes' Error. Emotion, Reason, and the Human Brain*, New York: Putnam.

Diamond, M.A. (1997) 'Administrative assault: A contemporary psychoanalytic view of violence and aggression in the workplace', *American Review of Public Administration*, 27(3), 228–47.

du Gay, P. and Salaman, G. (1992) 'The cult(ure) of the customer', *Journal of Management Studies*, 29(5), 615–33.

Ferguson, K. (1984) *The Feminist Case Against Bureaucracy*, Philadelphia: Temple University Press.

Fineman, M. (1995) *The Neutered Mother, the Sexual Family, and Other Twentieth Century Tragedies*, New York: Routledge.

Fineman, S. (ed.) (1993a) *Emotion in Organizations*, London: Sage.

Fineman, S. (1993b) 'Organizations as emotional arenas', in Fineman (1993a), 9–35.

Fineman, S. (1996) 'Emotion and organizing', in S. Clegg, C. Hardy and W.R. Nord (eds), *Handbook of Organization Studies*, London: Sage, 543–64.

Fineman, S. (2000a) 'Commodifying the emotionally intelligent', in Fineman (2000c), 101–15.

Fineman, S. (2000b) 'Emotional arenas revisited', in Fineman (2000c), 1–24.

Fineman, S. (ed.) (2000c) *Emotion in Organizations*, 2nd edn, London: Sage.

Fineman, S. (2003) *Understanding emotion at work*, London: Sage.

Fineman, S. (2004) 'Getting the measure of emotion – and the cautionary tale of emotional intelligence', *Human Relations*, 57(6), 719–40.

Fineman, S. and Sturdy, A. (1999) 'The emotions of control: A qualitative exploration of environmental regulation', *Human Relations*, 52(5), 631–63.

Folgero, I.S. and Fjeldstad, I.H. (1995) 'On duty – off guard: Cultural norms and sexual harassment in service organizations', *Organization Studies*, 16(2), 299–313.

Fraser, N. and Gordon, L. (1994) 'A genealogy of dependency: Tracing a keyword of the U.S. welfare state', *Signs*, 19(2), 309–36.

Freud, S. (1912) *The Dynamics of Transference*, London: Hogarth Press.

Freud, S. (1926) *Inhibitions, Symptoms and Anxiety*, London: Hogarth Press.

Gabriel, Y. (1995) 'The unmanaged organization: Stories, fantasies and subjectivity', *Organization Studies*, 16(3), 477–501.

Gabriel, Y. (1997) 'Meeting God: When organizational members come face to face with the supreme leader', *Human Relations*, 50(4), 315–42.

Gabriel, Y. (1998) 'Psychoanalytic contributions to the study of the emotional life of organizations', *Administration and Society*, 30(3), 291–314.

Gilligan, C. (1982) *In a Different Voice: Psychological Theory and Women's Development*, Cambridge, Mass.: Harvard University Press.

Goleman, D. (1998) *Working With Emotional Intelligence*, London: Bloomsbury.

Greenleaf, R.K. (1978) *Servant, Leader & Follower*, New York: Paulist Press.

Guerrier, Y. and Adib, A.S. (2000) ' "No, we don't provide that service": The harassment of hotel employees by customers', *Work Employment and Society*, 14(4), 689–705.

Hall, E.J. (1993) 'Smiling, deferring, and flirting: Doing gender by giving good service', *Work and Occupations*, 20(4), 452–71.

Held, V. (2006) *The Ethics of Care: Personal, Political, and Global*, Oxford: Oxford University Press.

Hochschild, A.R. (1979) 'Emotion work, feeling rules, and social structure', *American Journal of Sociology*, 85(3), 551–75.

Hochschild, A.R. (1983) *The Managed Heart. Commercialization of Human Feeling*, Berkeley: University of California Press.

Jung, C.G. (1968) *The Archetypes and the Collective Unconscious*, London: Routledge.

Kittay, E.F. (ed.) (1999) *Love's Labor. Essays on Women, Equality, and Dependency*, New York: Routledge.

Kittay, E.F. and Feder, E.K. (eds) (2002) *The Subject of Care: Feminist Perspectives on Dependency*, Lanham, Md.: Rowman & Littlefield Publishers.

Klein, M. (1987) *The Selected Melanie Klein*, ed. by J. Mitchell, New York: Free Press.

Korczynski, M. (2001) 'The contradictions of service work: Call centre as cus-
tomer-oriented bureaucracy', in Sturdy et al. (2001), 79–101.
Korczynski, M. (2003) 'Communities of coping: Collective emotional labour in
service work', *Organization*, 10(1), 55–79.
Korczynski, M. and Macdonald, C. (eds) (2008) *Service Work: Critical Perspectives*,
New York: Routledge.
Kymlicka, W. (1991) *Contemporary Political Philosophy. An Introduction*, Oxford:
Oxford University Press.
Leidner, R. (1991) 'Serving hamburgers and selling insurance: Gender, work and
identity in interactive service jobs', *Gender and Society*, 5(2), 154–77.
Mano, R. and Gabriel, Y. (2006) 'Workplace romances in cold and hot organizational
climates: The experience of Israel and Taiwan', *Human Relations*, 59(1), 7–37.
Meyers, D.T. (2002) *Gender in the Mirror: Cultural Imagery and Women's Agency*,
Oxford: Oxford University Press.
Meyerson, D.E. (2000) 'If emotions were honoured: A cultural analysis', in
Fineman (2000c), 167–83.
Moxnes, P. (1999) 'Deep roles: Twelve primordial roles of mind and organiza-
tion', *Human Relations*, 52(11), 1427–44.
Mumby, D.K. and Putnam, L.L. (1992) 'The politics of emotion', *Academy of
Management Review*, 17, 465–86.
Noddings, N. (1986) *Caring: a feminine Approach to Ethics & Moral Education*,
Berkeley, Calif.: University of California Press.
Noddings, N. (2003) *Caring: A Feminine Approach to Ethics & Moral Education*, 2nd
edn, Berkeley, Calif.: University of California Press.
Parreñas, R.S. (2008) 'The globalization of care work', in Korczynski/MacDonald
(2008), 154–71.
Putnam, L:L. and Mumby, D.K. (1993) 'Organizations, emotion and the myth of
rationality', in Fineman (1993a), 36–57.
Rosenthal, P., Peccei, R. and Hill, S. (2001) 'Academic discourse of the customer:
"Sovereign beings", "management accomplices" of "people like us"', in Sturdy
et al. (2001), Basingstoke: Palgrave Macmillan, 18–37.
Ruddick, S. (1989) *Maternal Thinking. Toward a Politics of Peace*, Boston: Beacon
Press.
Sacks, O. (1995) *An Anthropologist on Mars*, Oxford: Blackwell.
Sahlin, I. (1996) 'From deficient planning to "incapable tenants". Changing
discourses on housing problems in Sweden', *Scandinavian Housing & Planning
Research*, 13(4), 167–81.
Salovey, P. and Mayer, J.D. (1990) 'Emotional intelligence', *Imagination, Cognition
and Personality*, 9, 185–211.
Sevenhuijsen, S. (1998) *Citizenship and the Ethics of Care: Feminist Considerations
on Justice, Morality, and Politics*, London: Routledge.
Simmel, G. (1950) 'The triad', in W. Kurt (ed.) *The Sociology of Georg Simmel*,
Glencoe, Ill.: Free Press, 145–69.
Stein, H.F. (1999) 'Countertransference and understanding workplace cataclysm:
Intersubjective knowledge and interdisciplinary applied anthropology', *High
Plains Applied Anthropologist*, 19(1), 10–20.
Stein, M. (2007) 'Toxicity and the unconscious experience of the body at the
employee-customer interface', *Organization Studies*, 28(8), 1223–41.

Sturdy, A. (1998) 'Customer care in a consumer society: Smiling and sometimes meaning it?', *Organization*, 5(1), 27–53.

Sturdy, A. and Fineman, S. (2001) 'Struggles for the control of affect: Resistance as politics *and* emotion', in Sturdy et al. (2001), 135–57.

Sturdy, A., Grugulis, I. and Willmott, H. (eds) (2001) *Customer Service: Empowerment and Entrapment*, Basingstoke: Palgrave Macmillan.

Tronto, J.C. (1993) *Moral Boundaries: A Political Argument for an Ethic of Care*, New York: Routledge.

3
Organizational Conditions for Positive Emotions in the Workplace – The Example of Professional Elderly Care

Nicole Bornheim

1 Introduction

This article deals with the emotional experiences of employees providing person-related services. Unlike a considerable body of research on service that which concentrates on the strains tied to emotional labour, my focus lies on positive emotions, which are assumed to contribute to employees' health and well-being. My question is how and why positive emotions emerge in the workplace. Rather than treating emotion as an individual given and positive emotions as the outcome of individual traits, I show that organizational factors play a decisive role in the emergence of positive emotions.

Professional elderly care is one of the prominent examples that rebut the traditional picture of the neutral organization. Here, organizational structures and processes are deeply infused with emotion. My findings as to the triggers of positive emotions stem from case studies carried out in three nursing homes. As a result of my interviews and observations, it turned out that caregivers experience the entire spectrum of emotions at work. That is, all elderly care nurses reported on upsetting and shattering emotional experiences at work as well as on 'really beautiful' moments and work situations. As a comparative analysis of the case studies shows, the latter type of experiences, which are linked to positive emotions, may be traced back to certain organizational conditions, namely working conditions and corporate philosophies.

Based on rich accounts of emotional experiences in service work, the chapter aims to deliver a differentiated picture of the role of organizational conditions for positive emotions. This is an important basis for the design of humane working conditions able to promote employees' health and well-being.

2 Background: The focus on positive emotions in the workplace

2.1 Features and implications of positive emotions at work

Emotions are the subject of different scientific disciplines with different topics and interests of research. Correspondingly, there exist different definitions of and several points of view about the nature of emotions and their significance for human actions. Nevertheless there is broad consent that there exist specific emotions that are distinguishable from each other because people do not just feel, but they feel in a specific way (they are happy, sad, angry, etc.). Differential emotion research suggests that, depending on the quality of the emotions experienced and their effects, specific emotions can be divided into positive and negative ones (cf. Izard 1994: 68). Referring to this, I use the term 'positive emotions' for feelings that are characterized by a positive experience component (e.g. joy, pride, love, etc.).[1]

According to psychological research, positive experiences act as a stress compensation factor and promote the health and well-being of the individual. Thus, in many work and organizational approaches positive emotions are considered to interact strongly with job satisfaction, work motivation and individual productivity (cf. Wegge/van Dick 2006: 34). In contrast, negative emotions are considered to interact with frustration, decline in motivation and burnout as potential individual risks for employees, leading to undesirable fluctuation, decline in output and recruitment problems at an organizational level (cf. Rastetter 2001: 114).

2.2 The interest in positive emotions at work

Emotion has – at least in US research – 'become something of a fashionable topic within work and organizational psychology but also in management research, sociology, and organizational behaviour' (Briner 1999: 328) since the middle of the 1990s (cf. also Sieben 2007). Nevertheless, very little attention has been paid to positive emotions. A large body of research concentrates on negative emotions with the objective of identifying their negative consequences – like stress, burnout or depression – and on eliminating their causes (e.g. Rastetter 2001).

However, there are exceptions: positive emotions are getting more and more attention in the current management discourse (cf. Fineman 2006), for instance through concepts like emotional intelligence (e.g. Goleman 1998) or organizational energy (e.g. Bruch/Goshal 2003). Based on the results of emotion psychology, such writers pick up on the supposed activating and performance-enhancing potential of positive emotions. Thus, they regard positive emotions as an important individual resource for employability and work motivation, which promote the individual workableness and lead to reduced absenteeism. Moreover, positive emotions are considered a resource that should be activated to enhance work processes and product quality, and a key factor for organizational success (e.g. Becke et al. 2003). As Poder (in this volume) shows, they may also be regarded as important factors for the generation of empowerment.

Thus, as Schreyögg and Sydow (2001: VII) conclude, in novel management concepts the feelings of the employees almost become of value in themselves, emotional intelligence being a prominent example (for critical analyses cf. e.g. Fineman 2004; Sieben 2007). Following Neckel (2005: 422), in this way emotional self-control and external control become a novel blueprint for the solution of various problems of modern management efficiency. According to his critique in the accompanying counselling literature emotional self-fulfilling postulates, strategic emotional lore and the promise of subjective satisfaction are linked in such a way that emotions are displayed not for their own sake, but because of their usefulness for organizational purposes. Thus, from a critical perspective, the suspicion is that the renewed interest in subjectivity and emotionality in the workplace would only make the heteronomy of workers more closed in and extensive.

In contrast to this perspective, I follow authors like Becke et al. (2003: 2) in assuming that the consideration of subjectivity and emotionality at work may help to identify key features of humane working conditions. These are essential starting points for developing recommendations as to the operational job design. Moreover, to counter the overwhelming pathogenetic focus of emotion research (cf. e.g. Caza/Cameron 2009: 101), I take up a research perspective that is deduced from the concept of salutogenesis (Antonovsky 1989) in medical sociology. While traditional pathogenetic approaches ask about the causes of disease and how disease can be prevented, the crucial question in salutogenetic approaches is: what are the causes of health and how can health be strengthened? Transferred to my research approach this means: assuming that positive emotional experiences in the workplace play an important role for health, well-being, and (job) satisfaction, looking from a salutogenetic research perspective for those organizational conditions that mainly contribute to the emergence of positive emotions.

The underlying assumption is that the experience of positive emotions at work may have a double dividend effect for employees and the organizations: the preservation of employees' health and well-being represents for the organization an essential prerequisite for their performance and motivation, which in turn will pay off in organizational outcomes (reduced absenteeism, increased group and organizational performance, etc.).

2.3   Positive emotions and job satisfaction

As seen, positive emotions are considered to be linked to (an increase in) job satisfaction. In a great body of research (as well as in management practice) the construct of job satisfaction itself is still considered an appropriate indicator for the degree of positive and negative experiences at the workplace (cf. Rafferty/Griffin 2009: 196). In psychological research, job satisfaction has become widely accepted as the measure of various individual comparisons between the employee's needs, objectives or motives on the one hand and the job characteristics on the other (cf. Temme/Tränkle 1996: 277).

However, as critical analyses show, this approach cannot provide satisfactory results in terms of the employees' emotional experience of work because it largely discounts specific qualities of emotions and it does not allow explicit conclusions about the actual experience of emotions at work (ibid.: 275ff.). Accordingly, Briner (1999: 325) criticizes the construct of job satisfaction as a too non-specific approach and illustrates this by an analogy from medicine: 'If we were medical professionals, interested in understanding and treating people's physical well-being, we would certainly not describe people just "well" or "ill" but rather look for much more specific types of intervention.' In addition, Temme and Tränkle (1996: 276ff.) criticize the survey of job-satisfaction levels because they are mostly confined to cognitive-motivational aspects. But as they point out, the concept of job satisfaction as a cognitive-evaluative attitude varying with the working situation also implies emotional aspects, which had been 'completely ignored' in job satisfaction research before then. Therefore, they strongly advocate an extension of the research perspective into emotional aspects. This requirement is also underlined by Wegge and van Dick (2006: 25f.). From an analysis of recent research findings related to the Affective Events Theory (Weiss/Cropanzano 1996), they come to the conclusion that a more precise analysis of specific emotions, in fact, provides additional insights that are overlooked when using classical indicators of job satisfaction.

In line with these approaches, job satisfaction may be regarded as a longer-term subjective valuation of the work situation, which is essentially based on the experience of specific emotions at work. Specific emotions on their part are assumed to be triggered by specific situations and events in the workplace (cf. Wegge/van Dick 2006: 18ff.). That is why in my approach I touch upon the job satisfaction of care givers; however, I focus mainly on the experience of specific positive emotions and the concrete work situations and contexts, in which they appear.

While psychological researchers seek the individual aspects of emotion, sociologically oriented approaches focus on the socio-cultural background of emotions (e.g. Gerhards 1988; Flam 2002). In order to meet the requirements of the complexity and multidimensionality of emotions, both aspects should be considered because on the one hand emotion conditions are individually experienced and on the other they are always embedded in and shaped by a socio-cultural context (cf. Fineman 2003).

Therefore, I do not only look for the structural conditions that conduce the experience of positive emotions in organizations, but also concentrate on the socio-cultural factors under which emotions are constructed in the context of organizations – which at the same time is also a politicized context (cf. Fineman in this volume).

3 Empirical approach

3.1 The example of professional elderly care

While organizational structures and conditions of professional care have been studied in a large body of research, emotional aspects (in the experience) of professional nursing activities were for a long time largely ignored. As Glaser and Höge (2005: 6ff.) point out, most research on healthcare refers exclusively to medical aspects. Furthermore, most studies are based on a pathogenetic research perspective, because they focus exclusively on strain factors, which may hinder efficient and effective action in professional care. According to such studies, elderly care nurses are considerably disadvantaged as regards their psycho-physical health compared to many other professionals (cf. Büssing/Glaser 2003: 103). Therefore, Büssing and Glaser ironically speak of a 'nursing emergency' in Germany – characterized by low job satisfaction and rapid staff turnover in professional care, as well as a high rate of job exit.

Regardless of the research perspective, almost all studies referring to German-speaking regions show that the workload of nurses has clearly increased in recent years (cf. Glaser/Höge 2005: 6). The reason for this is mainly seen in the health care reform legislation that became effective in Germany in 1994 and has led to a fundamental strengthening of the socio-economic conditions in the field of health and nursing. In particular, the modified conditions are characterized by increased financial pressure and rigid performance standards. The economization of care is particularly expressed in the expansion of requirements for documentation and the standardization of individual care services. As a consequence, only medical nursing services can be taken into account, so that nurses have only a little time for giving emotional care and holding conversations with the residents (cf. Kumbruck/Senghaas-Knobloch 2006: 30f.). Thus, in many residential care facilities the changes have led to increased medical and organizational requirements for the nurses, and a decline in their social relationship with the care receivers (cf. Dahme et al. 2005). Against this background, the identification of organizational conditions in professional elderly care that allow or encourage positive emotions at work becomes even more pressing as these feelings can support the nurses in coping with workload and organizational change processes.

3.2   Method

A whole range of scales has been developed to measure overall job satisfaction as well as (positive) emotions at work. Hence, a considerable body of research on the topic is based on surveys using standardized questionnaires, which allow one to examine the type of specific emotions and to measure the frequency of their appearance (e.g. van Katwyk et al. 2000). However, with such quantitative approaches real-life experiences of emotions at work cannot be examined, nor may one dig deeper into the backgrounds of their formation (cf. Fineman 2006). Only a qualitative approach can deliver rich accounts of how and why positive emotions emerge at work. As I am interested in such questions of 'how' and 'why' I opted for a case study design, as proposed by Yin (2003). This allows me to examine the factors that trigger or influence positive emotions at work.

The study was carried out from October 2006 to June 2007 in three nursing homes situated in northern Germany, which are presented below. In each nursing home I got access to facility-specific documents, conducted extensive interviews with the general managers and the nursing managers and had the opportunity to visit the residential care facilities and observe the nurses' work activities, following which I conducted detailed narrative interviews with them.[2]

3.3 The cases: Three nursing homes

The case study includes three nursing homes, one home led by the Diaconie (named The Bells) and two public homes (named The Residence and The Sunshine).

The Bells is a long-term care facility for the elderly, and is sponsored by the church. Originally solely intended for deaconesses, nowadays the house is a modern nursing home for the elderly. With the decline in number of deaconesses in recent decades, their organizational cultural influence was also decreased. Therefore, today The Bells is confronted with the task of preserving the Christian-spiritual profile of the home in a modernized form (even without the uncontemporary model of deaconesses). The consequences of these cultural changes were intensified by the introduction of health care reform with its billing structures and its documentation requirements.

The Residence and The Sunshine both belong to the same non-profit foundation, that seemingly forms the overarching umbrella of the two nursing facilities. On the one hand, the individual institutions are largely autonomous in their governance structure and how they organize care. On the other, both nursing homes fall under a common management, which dictates the financial framework and the corporate political and cultural orientation. Since the introduction of long-term care insurance, the foundation has also been affected by changed economic conditions and a rise in competitive pressure. According to the general manager, the foundation is in the midst of a cultural change with the aim of establishing a new conception of professional care. Despite the common guidelines, the two nursing homes differ from each other with regard to the everyday organization of care.

In The Residence the care is provided in a small and traditionally organized department where the mostly wealthy residents are served and cared for extensively. According to the guidelines of the general manager, The Residence has to implement new forms of care, which are characterized by expanding ambulatory forms of care.

The required restructuring is already relatively well implemented in The Sunshine. The entire inpatient care area is divided into so-called home communities, each centred on an eat-in kitchen. Responding to the economic pressures, the management of The Sunshine has modified its employment practice. To replace staff as cheaply as possible, new employees receive only part-time contracts (with reduced benefits). In addition, the management draws more and more on nurses from temporary agencies.

4   Findings: The experience of positive emotions in the workplace

In this section, I present the findings I have drawn from the interviews with the nurses. First of all, it should be noted that the nursing staff of all three institutions declare a high level of job satisfaction and a strong attachment for their respective nursing homes. All the nurses experience (in some cases very strong) positive emotions in the context of their work. This is also the reason why they 'definitely would choose again' if they had to decide on a job again (Nurse, The Sunshine).

For the analysis and structuring of the emotions triggering situations and circumstances I refer to the characteristics of service work laid out by Krell (2001) and to the model of appearances of emotions in organizations (Sieben/Wettergren in this volume). Both postulate an analytical distinction of the different levels on which emotions figure for work in organizations. Accordingly, I differentiate three levels for the experience and occurrence of emotions in elderly care: the level of working, the level of the organizational environment in which the work takes place and the level of the socio-cultural embeddings of the organization.

4.1   The level of working: Elderly care as interaction work

According to Krell (2001: 14), the interactions between service givers and recipients give distinction to person-related service work and give rise to emotional consequences. Correspondingly, at the working level elderly care can be characterized as interaction work between the nurses and the residents with physical (e.g. lifting the residents), mental (e.g. knowing which resident needs which kind of care) and emotional components (e.g. consoling the residents), all of which lead to the appearance of emotions.

To begin with, all the nurses interviewed are very happy in practising their profession – even if professional elderly care is physically and mentally very demanding work that is often accompanied by emotional strains. Indeed, the nurses often feel emotionally stressed by job-related events: patients' illness, dying and death. Without doubt, they realize that their workplace is 'ultimately a terminus' for the residents; however, they often feel sad when someone 'has to go'. Despite such recurrent and emotionally (very) oppressive work situations, all of the nurses described their profession as a 'really beautiful job', which goes along with the experience of many (strong) positive emotions such as love, enthusiasm and pride.

According to the nurses' statements the most important and frequent source for positive emotions is due to the *personal interaction* with the residents of the nursing homes. The caregivers narratives show that the direct interaction with the cared for people often leads to strong positive emotions. 'What makes me happy? Honestly, the contact with the residents (...) I love it, to interact directly with the people' (Nurse, The Sunshine). Caregivers working in fields with highly emotional requirements in particular (e.g. caring for dementia patients or working in terminal care), astonishingly, often spoke about the occurrence of strong positive emotions at work. They adduce that the reason is because they get back 'so much in return' from the residents – for example a smile or a hug, a spontaneous expression of feelings ('Oh, how nice that you are here') or a happy face. All the nurses describe this kind of feedback from the residents as giving them a very uplifting feeling, by which they get 'motivated to continue again and again'. Hence, the nurses' statements suggest that the interaction with the residents is not only a core task of professional elderly care (cf. Glaser/Höge 2005: 8f.) but also a central source of positive emotions.

4.2 The level of the organizational environment

4.2.1 Interactions with colleagues and executives

As Krell (2001: 14) points out, in an organizational context elderly care is associated with further interactions (e.g. with colleagues, executives and relatives). These can act as work stressors on the one hand or, on the other, as resources that are helpful in coping with strains – and may be accompanied by positive emotional experiences.

A *good relationship with colleagues* is highlighted by all the nurses as particularly significant for the experience of positive emotions at work. In particular, the nurses emphasize the importance of a good working atmosphere and a trusting relationship with their teammates. They regard an 'adequate' team composition as a prerequisite for this: team members should share common views about 'good care' and how it should be executed.

The caregivers frequently mention the mutual assistance of the team-mates as another important source of positive emotions. This refers specifically to psychological and emotional support from colleagues. According to the nurses, the team represents an important platform for coping with difficult and stressful work situations, as is also shown in other studies (e.g. Rastetter 2001). Informal discussions between the teammates are described as a particularly important emotional resource for quickly reducing emotional burdens at work.

A good relationship with the executives, particularly to the charge nurse and to the nursing manager, was also mentioned as an important influence for the experience of positive emotions in the working routine of the care givers. In particular, leadership behaviour that is characterized by benevolence, acknowledgment and respect, and a relationship to the (direct) executives that is characterized by mutual trust, are named as central sources for positive emotions. The nurses describe 'ideal' superiors as trustworthy persons who give them a feeling of security and of being backed. They mention periodical performance appraisals and constructive feedback given by the executives as being important in this context.

4.2.2   The organizing of work

As Krell (2001: 15ff.) points out, interactions are embedded in the formal and social hierarchy of any organization. Thereby an organization sets the framework for the execution of service work, e.g. through target times and the associated staffing level, through the provision of operating resources in sufficient quantity and quality, through the form of work organization (e.g. individual or group work) or through mission statements. All these aspects may trigger emotions as the case of elderly care shows.

A first important factor is the *personnel and employment policy*, especially a policy that guarantees personnel continuity. This is the case in The Bells, where the staffing level and the conditions of employment are mentioned as sources of positive emotions. The employment policy of this institution has until now been characterized by tenure and personnel continuity. The nurses ascribe the experience of positive emotions to this personnel policy as it initially enables good care.

By contrast, in the two homes of run by the foundation it looks very different. The nurses of The Residence regard the policy of cost-cutting on personnel of their home as a definite barrier to positive emotions at work, because they have experienced how this leads to uncertainties among the employees and to reduction in the quality of care. This is also the case at The Sunshine. Moreover, there, the nurses lament the meanwhile quite regular use of agency workers. The nurses agree that the execution of 'good care' is only possible 'if one is somehow connected to the nursing home. If you know the residents and the staff with whom you work. If you know exactly what to do. And if you get yourself involved with it' (Nurse, The Sunshine). The nurses of The Sunshine assess the increased use of agency workers as 'negative for all concerned participants', as it has led to a significant decline in the working atmosphere and to uncertainties among the established employees. Hence, this employment policy is regarded as a further barrier to the experience of positive emotions in the workplace.

Involvement in organizational (decision-making) processes is mentioned as another important source for the experience of positive emotions. The nurses in The Bells, in particular, have been actively involved in important decision-making processes and participated in the development of the organization-specific mission statement. Accordingly, they consider the organizational change processes as positive or neutral. In contrast, in the other two institutions the organizational change processes are (almost) exclusively regarded as a barrier to positive emotional experiences at work: because the nurses are not involved in decision-making processes they feel helpless in the face of further savings on staff and the decline of direct interaction with the residents that result from the restructuring processes. As mentioned, direct interaction with clients had been one of the most important sources for positive emotions.

Further factors are the *spirit of the institution and quality standards.* Whereas the nurses of The Sunshine mention no emotional triggers related to its organizational culture, the caregivers in The Bells and The Residence highlight the specific spirit of the home as being very significant for the experience of positive emotions. The nurses of The Bells characterize this specific spirit primarily by the existence of a very respectful tone within interpersonal relationships with the residents and their relatives, as well as to the employees. The nurses of The Residence ascribe the specific spirit of the home to 'a very friendly working atmosphere' that (according to the nurses) is also perceived very positively by the residents and their families. In conjunction with a high-quality standard of work, which means that the people 'are really well cared for', the spirit of the institution notably contributes to the good reputation of their homes. This conjunction represents a further key point for the nurses' experience of positive emotions at work.

4.3 The level of the socio-cultural embeddings of the organization: Perceptions of 'good care' and the legislation on long-term care insurance

As Krell (2001: 17) points out, organizations are themselves in turn embedded in the power structures and the socio-economic conditions of the surrounding society. Thus, service organizations represent institutional patterns of society and reflect social changes, as well as their related social discourses. Again, this organization level is connected to the appearance of emotions. In the case of elderly care, the socially constructed image of the 'caring angel' (Rieder 1999), and connected normative assumptions as to 'good care', may be taken as one of these embeddings – connected with the arousal of positive emotions. Instead, another important embedding represents an impediment to positive emotions: health care reform, a socio-economic condition, which is coupled with social discourse about good care and its financing.

As for *perceptions of good care*, my findings show that the nurses' experience of positive emotions at work is significantly tied to these. Their subjective perceptions of good nursing correspond in turn to the achievement of a high-quality standard of care. In the opinion of the care givers interviewed, good care is basically characterized by the fact that 'the resident gets a good medical care and does not sustain any consequential damage through the nurses' activities'. Ideally, good care leads to a better state of health for the residents, so that they 'obtain a bit more quality of life'. The nurses stressed that the medical aspect is not the primary objective. It is much more important 'to hold the person's hand and to keep the hand a bit and to say something nice to him. To have a keen sense of the people, that's essential.' However, this perception of good care is contrary to the main public discourse about the conditions that are necessary for the provision of a high-quality standard of care.

In particular, *the legislation on long-term care insurance* has been found to have a negative impact. With regard to the statutory provisions of the health care reform legislation, the nursing staffs of all three institutions agree that these significantly affect emotions at work. In contrast to other factors, the statutory provisions are exclusively described as a negative factor, which acts as a barrier to the experience of positive emotions. As the practical experiences of the caregivers show, the legal requirements are calculated in such a way that the same work as before has to be done in a shorter time and with fewer qualified nursing staff. Consequently, there is not enough time or personnel available for the individual care of the residents. Accordingly, the nurses associate the resulting time pressures and loss of quality with the experience of negative emotions at work.

5 Comparative analysis: The most relevant influencing factors

Summing up the previous step of analysis, all three levels influence the appearance of positive emotions in elderly care. Thereby, at the levels of both working and the socio-cultural embeddings, the frequency and quality of positive emotions is very similar in all three nursing homes. However, with regard to the level of the organizational environment the analysis reveals significant differences between the three institutions. This raises the question of how and why the organization-specific differences in the emotional experiences at work arise in detail.

To be able to analyse the respective differences between the studied nursing homes, first of all, the similarities in their organizational framework conditions have to be acknowledged.

5.1 Similarities in organizational framework conditions

To begin with, factors in the organizational structure such as the size of the nursing homes, the number of beds, hierarchical structures, etc. are largely comparable for all three facilities. What all three homes have in common, in particular, is that they are under (financial) pressure to make organizational changes. On the one hand, this pressure results from the statutory provisions of the health care reform legislation, which are associated in particular with an increasing financial pressure, tighter competition from private providers and the elimination of state subsidies (cf. Dahme et al. 2005). On the other hand, the pressure for change stems from a cultural shift, which is affiliated with the general professionalization of nursing. In The Bells the cultural change primarily becomes visible in the elimination of the deaconesses, who acted as cultural carriers and as labour resources that were always available. In the institutions of the foundation, the cultural change is visible in the new job-related requirements. These are characterized by an increase in medical care and organizational tasks, and a decline in the social relationship with the care receivers.

These conditions are comparable in all three institutions, therefore they cannot explain the different emotional experiences of the nurses. Hence, the question is: which factors distinguish the three nursing homes? What is different? My findings suggest that the differences are significantly associated with different corporate philosophies and leadership, and that these in turn are considerably mediated by managerial perceptions within the individual institutions.

Since The Residence and The Sunshine are under the corporate guidelines of the same foundation, I will initially consider the differences between these institutions, on the one hand, and the The Bells, on the other. The causes for the differences between the two institutions of the foundation are considered in the second step. For these steps of analysis, I will draw on findings stemming from interviews with the managers of the three institutions.

5.2   Different managerial perceptions of 'good care'

A major difference lies in the executives' perception of the opportunities and risks connected to the changes in the health care system. While the management of the foundation sees the health care reform as an opportunity for building up new forms of autonomy-targeted caring principles, the general manager of The Bells regards the reform basically as a threat to the longer-term provision of good care. Accordingly, the (political and operational) approaches to problem-solving are very different in the studied institutions. Although both general managers try to save on personnel costs by providing more part-time employment contracts and by reducing non-tariff benefits, the practical implementation of measures and approaches is very different.

The management of The Bells still adheres to the principle of permanent employment and vehemently rejects the use of temporary workers. The general and the nursing managers both regard the continuity of staff and a high standard of qualifications among the caregivers as essential for achieving a high quality of care. Consequently, in The Bells we find a relatively high proportion of qualified nurses.

In the foundation, the general manager considers that good care is characterized by reasonable assistance from the existing social networks of the residents rather than by the provision of a 'wraparound-care' which in his opinion is often performed by an over-qualified and, by implication, over-expensive nursing staff. Accordingly, here savings on staff are associated with a structural transformation of the individual nursing homes, through which many caring activities are no longer carried out by nurses, but by cost-efficient housekeeping staff on the one hand and through the participation of relatives and volunteers on the other. That is to say, staff savings and the reduction of working hours lead to a tranformation of the personnel structure; here we find a comparatively high proportion of nursing assistants, housekeeping staff and temporary workers.

5.3 Different perceptions of 'good leading'

A further difference lies in the leadership styles of the two general managers.

Leadership philosophies and resultant leadership styles are based on the subjective perceptions of good leading. These are closely linked with the concept of humankind (cf. Schein 1995), which can be deduced from the respective managers' ideas of appropriate ways of dealing with personnel (cf. Krell 2001: 17).

In The Bells the general manager's subjective perceptions of dealing with the nurses is based mainly on Christian principles focused on human dignity. Corresponding to this, he shows a keen interest in 'his' personnel. He tries to include the personnel's needs in the company's policy decisions and to integrate their interests with the financial and structural conditions. For him it is important that all the members of the institution 'act in concert'. Therefore, he attaches great importance to transparency and openness in communication of necessary organizational measures concerning personnel policy. In addition, he believes that good work can take place only in a good psycho-social working atmosphere. Accordingly, he considers the creation of an atmosphere of esteem and trustful interaction between executives and employees, as well as a sense of security for the nursing staff, as important requirements for leadership. The general manager stressed that he wants to bring together a staff within which 'humanness still counts, and not just nursing'. Thus, the management philosophy in The Bells is centred on the needs of the employees and on the aspect of social relations in the workplace.

In contrast, in the foundation, the general manager's concept of humankind is based mainly on the fundamental idea of a high level of personal responsibility for self-fulfilment and personality development. According to this, the general manager considers the most important demand for good leadership to be the creation of individual development opportunities with the aim of enabling the employees to make 'experiences of self-efficacy, autonomy and creativity in their own action'.

Comparing the management philosophies (and the resultant organization-specific requirements) with the emotional experiences of the nurses, the intertwining of the two factors is clearly recognizable. For positive emotions to occur at work, it seems to be particularly important that the caregivers' subjective perceptions of good caring fit with those of the management.

The interviews and observations have shown that in The Bells the management and the nurses pull together and work hand in hand.

They share common perceptions about the characteristics of good care, and about necessary organizational conditions. According to their own statements, the nurses feel themselves to be 'in good hands', because of the high level of emotional support they receive from the management of their organization.

In contrast, in the foundation, opinions as to what organizational conditions are necessary for the provision of good care partially differ. This is particularly evident in the managerial perceptions of the consequences of health care reform. The foundation's general manager considers these reforms as an opportunity to build up new caring arrangements that are more oriented on the care receiver's autonomy, and which go hand in hand with a 'huge win for all involved, whether residents or employees'. As mentioned above, this view collides with the nurses' subjective perceptions of good care, on the one hand, and with their experienced reality in the everyday work life, on the other.

At this point, the question arises of how to explain the differences between the emotional experiences of the nurses in 'The Residence' and 'The Sunshine', even though they are under the same general management.

5.4   Differences between the foundation's nursing homes

Although the nursing homes of the foundation have the same underlying financial, political and cultural guidelines, the nursing homes are largely autonomous with regard to the individual facility's management structures and the implementation of the foundations' guidelines into the daily care routine. As my findings show, the perceptions of the foundation's general manager have only indirect effects and are mediated by the managers of the individual nursing homes. In particular, the nursing managers who are responsible for the inpatient care area and stay in direct contact with the caregivers play a key role in this. Comparing the nursing managers of The Residence and The Sunshine, it is striking that they have very different perceptions of good care and good leadership.

The nursing manager of The Residence herself worked as a nurse for a long time and she (therefore) feels responsible for 'her' nurses in a special way. She is very interested in the caregivers' well-being and tries to motivate them even though the conditions under which they have to operate are getting more difficult. Since she still shares the same ideas on good care as the nurses, she attempts to adapt the execution of the foundation's guidelines to the demands of the nurses.

The nursing manager of 'The Sunshine' also emphasizes the importance of having good relations with the nursing staff. In particular, he tries to establish this relationship by visiting all nursing areas daily and by talking with the nurses. However, he feels detached from the nursing staff and stresses that he is a member of the upper management. He considers his relative lack of relationship to the nurses as rather positive, because as an executive he sometimes 'must take decisions that do not quite correspond to the opinions of employees.' Concurring with the foundation's general management, the nursing manager of The Sunshine regards the structural changes induced by the health care reform as an opportunity for the improvement of care, since it enables the nurses to concentrate entirely on the care activities while all other tasks will be done by housekeeping staff and aides. However, from the nurses' perspective this looks very different, as noted above. They mainly regard the restructuring as a loss of quality. As a nurse at The Sunshine puts it: 'now we only do daily care, medical care, documentation. And then we must do it pretty fast in order to accomplish the whole thing.' In summing up these differences, the nursing manager of The Sunshine all – but represents the extended arm of the foundation's general management, whereas the nursing manager of The Residence acts as a (sort of) moderating variable, or a 'buffer', between the foundation's general management and the nursing staff on the spot.

6 Conclusion

The aim of this analysis of positive emotions connected to professional elderly care was to detect their main triggers, especially to identify the role of organizational conditions. This is an important basis for the design of humane working conditions that are able to promote employees' health and well-being.

As the analysis shows, a concentration on emotional experiences at work may deliver more differentiated insights than the examination of overall job satisfaction: in all three facilities that I studied, the nurses reported a high level of job satisfaction. However, by digging deeper into their emotional experiences at work, by distilling those connected to positive emotions and analysing their triggers, a more differentiated picture appeared. With traditional, i.e. cognitive-evaluative, approaches and measurements of job satisfaction the variety of influencing factors presented here would not have been distinguishable. Whether this is based on the construct of job satisfaction as too non-specific an approach (cf. Briner 1999), or on the common quantitative empirical approach, has to be left undecided here. In any case, my study reflects further evidence that job satisfaction is related to individual experiences of emotions at work (cf. Wegge/van Dick 2006: 21) and that a more detailed analysis of emotional experiences may provide additional insights.

My special focus lies on the triggers of positive emotions at elderly care homes. In contrast, most studies on the care sector concentrate particularly on identifying the workload factors that negatively affect nurses' mental and physical health and which subsequently lead to negative implications for the employing organization (e.g. staff turnover, increased sick leave or lower product quality). Time pressure, responsibility for too many residents and too little time for the psychosocial care of residents are identified in particular as the main burdens in professional elderly care (e.g. Zimber et al. 1999). This is also confirmed by my findings. Moreover, coping with disease, dying and death, frequent work breaks and, sometimes, dealing with difficult relatives are regarded as further central stress factors in professional elderly care (cf. Glaser/Höge 2005: 14f.). In my findings these statements can only be confirmed in a modified form. As the study has shown, the nurses experience strong positive emotions especially in working situations that are supposed to be emotional stressful (e.g. dementia or terminal care). As long as appropriate organizational framework conditions are provided, direct interaction with the care recipients is a great (re)source for the emergence of positive emotions and helps the nurses to compensate for many encumbering influences.

Moreover, my study on professional elderly care shows that the experience of positive emotions significantly depends on the structural *working conditions* within the employing organization. These conditions, which were derived from the nurses' descriptions of good care, can also be found in the concept of 'enabling organizations' (Haipeter/Voss-Dahm 2002: 215). Enabling organizations imply the creation of lasting employment and the provision of adequate human and material resources by the organization's management, and furthermore comprehensive human resources development, holistic job designs and the provision of sufficient scopes and rights of participation for the employees while protecting them from excessive demands.

The empirical findings clearly reveal that as regards organizational resources and measures it is not only the 'what' that is crucial for the experience of positive emotions at work, but also the 'how' – the way they are implemented. The nurses' statements show that *the leadership style* and *the corporate philosophy* play an especially crucial role, as they influence the working atmosphere of the entire organization. As the caregivers point out, an atmosphere of respect, esteem and cooperative working has a major influence on their experience of positive emotions.

Thereby, the caregivers positively underlined the 'inner attitudes' of the executives as long as they were not based only on economic indicators, but also on the well-being of employees as an important resource for delivering a high quality of care. As shown, the managerial perceptions of good care differed in the studied organizations, gave rise to different leadership styles and moderated the implementation of the corporate philosophy. Thus, in addition to the structural working conditions that are usually emphasized in occupational science (e.g. Latniak 2006), these factors also turn out to be vitally important for the experience of positive emotions at work.

To summarize, the experience of positive emotions in the field of professional elderly care is influenced by three factors: first, the subjective perceptions of good care, second, the structural working conditions within the nursing facilities and, third, the dominant organizational culture that is reflected, inter alia, in the routines of dealing with each other and the leadership style of the executives within the institutions (cf. also Neubauer 2003: 30). The last point, especially, seems to play a crucial part in determining whether positive emotions in the workplace occur or not. To what extent the results are transferable to other (person-related) service work has to be explored in further studies.

Notes

1. As Izard (1994: 68) notes, the division into 'positive' and 'negative' may serve only as a classification that cannot be rigidly applied to each emotional experience. Moreover, the qualification as positive or negative refers only to the experience of an emotion and not to its (e.g. behavioural) effects. Thus, positive emotions can produce both positive and negative outcomes (cf. e.g. Caza/Cameron 2009: 110).
2. In my methodology I apply the mixed-method approach laid out by Becke and Senghaas-Knobloch (2004: 15ff.).

References

Antonovsky, A. (1989) 'Die salutogenetische Perspektive. Zu einer neuen Sicht von Gesundheit und Krankheit', *MEDUCS*, 2, 51–7.
Becke, G. and Senghaas-Knobloch, E. (2004) *Forschung in Aktion – Betriebliche Veränderungen im Dialog*, artec-paper Nr. 121, Universität Bremen.
Becke, G., Nagler, B., Punke, W., Senghaas-Knobloch, E. and Wegner, G. (2003) *Balanceakt Begeisterung – mit Leib und Seele in der Arbeitswelt. Konzeption eines gemeinsamen Entwicklungsvorhabens für 'gute Arbeit'*, artec-paper Nr. 105, Universität Bremen.

Briner, R.B. (1999) 'The neglect and importance of emotion at work', *European Journal of Work and Organizational Psychology*, 8(3), 323–46.

Bruch, H. and Ghoshal, S. (2003) 'Unleashing organizational energy', *MIT Sloan Management Review*, 45(1), 45–51.

Büssing, A. and Glaser, J. (2003) 'Arbeitsbelastungen, Burnout und Interaktionsstress im Zuge der Reorganisation des Pflegesystems', in A. Büssing and J. Glaser (eds) *Dienstleistungsqualität und Qualität des Arbeitslebens im Krankenhaus*, Göttingen: Hogrefe, 101–29.

Caza, A. and Cameron, K.S. (2009) 'Positive Organizational Scholarship: What does it achieve?', in S.R. Clegg and C.L. Cooper (eds) *The SAGE Book of Organizational Behaviour*, (2) *Macro Approaches*, Los Angeles: Sage, 99–116.

Dahme, H.-J., Kühnlein, G. and Wohlfahrt, N. (2005) *Zwischen Wettbewerb und Subsidiarität. Wohlfahrtsverbände unterwegs in die Sozialwirtschaft*, Berlin: Edition Sigma.

Fineman, S. (2003) *Understanding Emotion at Work*, London: Sage.

Fineman, S. (2004) 'Getting the measure of emotion – and the cautionary tale of emotional intelligence', *Human Relations*, 57(6), 719–40.

Fineman, S. (2006) 'On being positive: concerns and counterpoints', *Academy of Management Review*, 31(2), 270–91.

Flam, H. (2002) *Soziologie der Emotionen: eine Einführung*, Konstanz: UVK.

Gerhards, J. (1988) *Soziologie der Emotionen. Fragestellungen, Systematik, Perspektiven*, Weinheim: Juventa.

Glaser, J. and Höge, T. (2005) *Probleme und Lösungen in der Pflege aus Sicht der Arbeits- und Gesundheitswissenschaften*, ed. by Bundesanstalt für Arbeitsschutz und Arbeitsmedizin, Dortmund.

Goleman, D. (1998) *Working with Emotional Intelligence*, New York: Bantam.

Haipeter, T. and Voss-Dahm, D. (2002) 'Nachhaltige Dienstleistungsarbeit? "Front-Line-Work" in der IT-Branche und in Banken', in G. Bosch, P. Hennicke, J. Hilbert, K. Kristof and G. Scherhorn (eds) *Die Zukunft von Dienstleistungen. Ihre Auswirkungen auf Arbeit, Umwelt und Lebensqualität*, Frankfurt a.M: Campus, 214–34.

Izard, C.E. (1994) *Die Emotionen des Menschen. Eine Einführung in die Grundlagen der Emotionspsychologie*, 3rd edn, Weinheim: BeltzPVU.

Krell, G. (2001) 'Zur Analyse und Bewertung von Dienstleistungsarbeit. Ein Diskussionsbeitrag', *Industrielle Beziehungen*, 8(1), 9–37.

Kumbruck, C. and Senghaas-Knobloch, E. (2006) *Das Ethos fürsorglicher Praxis im Wandel – Befunde einer empirischen Studie*, artec-paper No. 137, Universität Bremen.

Latniak, E. (2006) 'Auf der Suche nach Verteilungs- und Gestaltungsspielräumen. Eine Bilanz der Organisationsveränderungen seit den 90er Jahren', in S. Lehndorff (ed.) *Das Politische in der Arbeitspolitik*, Berlin: Edition Sigma, 33–70.

Neckel, S. (2005) 'Emotion by Design. Das Selbstmanagement der Gefühle als kulturelles Programm', *Berliner Journal für Soziologie*, 15(3), 419–30.

Neubauer, W. (2003): *Organisationskultur*, Stuttgart: Kohlhammer.

Rafferty, A.E. and Griffin, M.A. (2009) 'Job Satisfaction in Organizational Research', in D.A. Buchanan and A. Bryman (eds) *The SAGE Book of Organizational Research Methods*, Los Angeles: Sage, 196–212.

Rastetter, D. (2001) 'Emotionsarbeit – Betriebliche Steuerung und individuelles Erleben', in Schreyögg/Sydow (2001), 111–34.

Rieder, Kerstin (1999) *Zwischen Lohnarbeit und Liebesdienst. Belastungen in der Krankenpflege*, Weinheim: Juventa.

Schein, E.H. (1995) *Unternehmenskultur: ein Handbuch für Führungskräfte*, Frankfurt a.M.: Campus.

Schreyögg, G. and Sydow, J. (eds) (2001) *Emotionen und Management. Managementforschung 11*, Wiesbaden: Gabler.

Sieben, B. (2007) *Management und Emotionen. Analyse einer ambivalenten Verknüpfung*, Frankfurt a.M.: Campus.

Temme, G. and Tränkle, U. (1996) 'Arbeitsemotionen. Ein vernachlässigter Aspekt in der Arbeitszufriedenheitsforschung', *Arbeit. Zeitschrift für Arbeitsforschung, Arbeitsgestaltung und Arbeitspolitik*, 3, 275–97.

van Katwyk, P.T., Fox, S., Spector, P.E. and Kelloway, E.K. (2000) 'Using the job-related affective well-being scale (JAWS) to investigate affective responses to work stressors', *Journal of Occupational Health Psychology*, 5, 219–30.

Wegge, J. and van Dick, R. (2006) 'Arbeitszufriedenheit, Emotionen bei der Arbeit und organisationale Identifikation', in L. Fischer (ed.) *Arbeitszufriedenheit. Konzepte und empirische Befunde*, 2nd edn, Göttingen: Hogrefe, 11–36.

Weiss, H.M. and Cropanzano, R. (1996) 'Affective events theory: A theoretical discussion of the structure, causes and consequences of affective experiences at work', in B.M. Staw and L.L. Cummings (eds) *Research in Organizational Behavior*, 18, Greenwich: JAI, 1–74.

Yin, R.K. (2003) *Case Study Research: Design and Methods*, 3rd edn, Thousand Oaks: Sage.

Zimber, A., Albrecht, A. and Weyerer, S. (1999) 'Arbeitsbedingungen und Arbeitsbelastungen in der stationären Altenpflege', in A. Zimber and S. Weyerer (eds) *Arbeitsbelastung in der Altenpflege*, Göttingen: Hogrefe, 185–99.

4
Emotions in the Hiring Procedure: How 'Gut Feelings' Rationalize Personnel Selection Decisions

Christian Imdorf

1 Introduction

Sociological research on personnel selection has repeatedly shown the significance of emotions and feelings when managers or other organizational gatekeepers make decisions about whom to hire. Even though managers think of themselves as rational, they often make their hiring decisions based on feelings rather than on facts (Miller/Rosenbaum 1997: 512). Emotions seem to guide even the most professionalized personnel specialists when they match vacant job positions to one out of numerous job candidates (Voswinkel 2008). Usually, 'gut reaction' in hiring refers to face-to-face job interviews, when personnel specialists judge candidates' characteristics such as interests, motivation, positive attitude, work ethic or self-presentation (Lee/Wrench 1983: 26; Neckerman/Kirschenman 1991: 441). 'Gut feelings' were repeatedly mentioned when Moss and Tilly (2001: 230) asked employers about how they judge job candidates' self-presentation. Jenkins (1986: 61f.) goes beyond this restriction to job interviews and assumes that emotion-based judgements are crucial for decision-making in all contexts of the hiring process. Likewise, Eymard-Duvernay and Marchal (1997: 145ff.), in their talks with recruitment specialists, have observed the frequent occurrence of expressions of intuition and feelings from the very beginning of the recruitment processes when applications are initially screened.

However, the relevance of emotion-based decision-making in hiring as an empirically evident fact causes problems from a theoretical perspective and is often overlooked by sociological theories of organizations, even though 'bounded rationality' (Simon 1957: 200) is taken into account. In the research on personnel selection mentioned so far, emotional decision-making has been theorized to different degrees. In earlier works the commonsense distinction between objective and subjective selection factors (Lee/Wrench 1983: 26) was commonly mentioned. As 'subjective' is often referred to as informal, emotional and irrational, its counterpart 'objective' appears to be associated with a more formalized, cognitive and rational selection process. Hence, Moss and Tilly (2001: 209) believe that more formal techniques reduce the degree of subjectivity and subsequent emotion-based space for prejudice in judgements about whom to hire. In their view, formalizing selection procedures promises to reduce the influence of emotions in the selection process – a claim I will challenge further below.

More straightforward than the analysed distinction between 'objective' and 'subjective' in understanding the relevance of emotions in organizational decision-making – which becomes normative in the sense that professional personnel selection is supposed to be objective rather than subjective – are those accounts that claim that feelings help to cope with insecurity in the selection process. Miller and Rosenbaum (1997: 512f.) have argued that a major problem for employers is obtaining trustworthy information about candidates. Their mistrust of information other than their own feelings leaves them without an acceptable alternative, even though they are aware that emotion-based methods can lead to bad hiring decisions. According to Eymard-Duvernay and Marchal (1997: 146), uncertainty in recruitment is due to a lack of consensus on the required competences, and intuition then serves as a resource for holistic judgements. Consequently emotion-based choices are a matter of both past experience and associations between a current candidate and memorized 'friends' (ibid.: 158). Other authors also support the link between emotions in hiring and previous experiences (Lee/Wrench 1983: 26). Jenkins (1986: 62) and Voswinkel (2008: 5004) go further when they argue that experience-based emotional judgements can be legitimately defended if they are justified as being rooted in a recruiter's professional socialization, or if a claim of subjectively saturated reality based on experience is more convincing than illusionary scientific rationality. Thus, emotion-based decision-making in hiring can be presented as a professional way to select new employees rather than an illegitimate strategy admitted by one employer interviewed by Moss and Tilly (2001: 209) who stated: 'I hate to say this, but a lot of it is gut feeling.'

How do feelings affect personnel selection in work organizations? Why are they indispensable in ensuring that even bureaucratic procedures such as the screening of applications work properly? Referring to the moral sociology of Boltanski and Thévenot (2006), the sociology of emotions and my own empirical data drawn from interviews with employers in 81 mostly small Swiss companies, I will discuss in this paper the organizational relevance of affective decision-making in hiring with regard to two important dimensions: (1) emotions as moral claims for legitimate job requirements and (2) emotional assessment of the competences, 'quality' or 'value' of job candidates. I will therefore first draft a sociological model of personnel selection, which combines insights of organizational studies with a theory of justification (section 2). I will then incorporate emotion into this framework and outline two essential functions for feelings in personnel selection (section 3), which I will lastly illustrate with my own data (section 4).

The subsequent theoretical modelling of hiring processes has been developed in the course of an empirical investigation into apprentice selection in small Swiss companies,[1] during which the expert interview-based approach revealed the relevance of emotion-based agency in decision-making. In this qualitative survey, based on semi-structured face-to-face interviews, employers were asked to outline and justify their procedures and criteria for apprentice selection.[2] Although my discussion refers to the selection of apprentices in small companies, the model may enable us to understand personnel selection in the context of any work organization.

2 A sociological model of personnel selection[3]

The starting points for my conceptual considerations are the needs and constraints of training companies, forced to survive in the market of their industrial sector. Sooner or later, the training of apprentices must result in a profit and contribute to the preservation of the company. The main challenge for a company when appointing new apprentices is to match its well-known, experience-based requirements (such as the occupational and social fit) with mostly unknown candidates. Due to numerous structural problems (such as multidimensional, partly conflicting requirements constituting the internal job profile), a candidate who 'fits best' cannot be found. Profit maximization doesn't work and companies cease their efforts to search for adequate candidates once they have found one who sufficiently satisfies their needs (according to the idea of *satisficing*, see March/ Simon 1958: 169). Such pragmatic matching therefore needs to fulfil an essential precondition: the result of the selection needs to be credible both inside and outside of a company's walls. The potential protest from the company's own workforce and external customers must be minimized.

2.1 Personnel selection in the different worlds of the company

To handle complexity and ambiguity when personnel decisions need to be made, companies depend on forms and orders of justification (as proposed by Boltanski/Thévenot 2006), which enable them to legitimize the resultant choices.[4] Personnel decisions can be justified, if they refer to selection rules that are considered just and fair by both the employer and internal and external stakeholders, that is by the workforce and customers who constitute the public of small companies. Selection criteria are usually accepted in public if they serve a common good (Eymard-Duvernay 2004: 98), for instance with regard to the social cohesion of a rural community or to the solidarity of a superordinate polity (e.g. the welfare state).[5]

An important assumption is that the provision of a public good through workplace action necessitates a specific form of *coordination* of humans with each other (but also among humans and objects, such as tools, machines and equipment) to adjust their behaviour mutually (ibid.: 66). Work organizations thereby require different forms of coordination from their members during a typical workday, such as working alone or together at the workbench (or at the assembly line in larger companies), having a friendly chat with colleagues during the break to relax from stress at work, dealing with customers in the front office, and so on. Accordingly, gatekeepers[6] have diverse but limited norms of coordination at their disposal in order to assign *worth* to applicants in the selection process and justify their resultant decisions. Job candidates possess worth if they reflect the potential to coordinate in a specific situation (Boltanski/Thévenot 1999: 363). Boltanski and Thévenot (2006) now distinguish between different *cités* and 'worlds', each characterized by its own form of coordination and worth. I outline three of these worlds: the industrial world, the domestic world and the market world, as they seem especially helpful for understanding the selection of apprentices in small companies.

In the *industrial world* of the firm, the fabrication of consumer goods or the provision of services requires an efficient production process, which benefits by not being disturbed by a new apprentice. In this world, coordination within the workforce, as well as between workers (and eventually objects), depends on regular actions, which in turn are based on plans, schedules and impersonal rationales (Boltanski/ Thévenot 1999: 362). Persons are considered worthy when they are efficient, productive and operational. Relationships can therefore 'be said to be harmonious when organized, measurable, functional, standardized' (ibid.: 373). The bureaucratic organization generally confines itself to the coordination principles of the industrial world.

However, the integration of a new member into the firm not only requires the rearrangement of the technical interrelationship, but also affects existing social relations. Such an integration impacts on the group climate, bringing about or changing emotions in the staff (Laske/Weiskopf 1996: 312). Thus, the needs and requirements of a firm's *domestic world* are inherent in co-deciding whom to hire. This world comprehends interpersonal relations and expectations within the staff, in line with the model of traditional family relations. Hence, social bonds and coordination between people are based upon a generalization of kinship and respect for tradition and lineage (Boltanski/ Thévenot 1999: 370). 'It's a neighbouring space, polarized by the opposition between what is far or close, what is here or there, who are associates or strangers' (Thévenot 2001: 414). This world is characterized by trust, respect and dependency, as well as by traditional gender roles and gender relations. Firm members often refer to the 'spirit of the house' and candidates are assessed on how well they might 'fit in' and integrate into the same 'house'.

Last but not least, apprentices adopt an additional value once they have direct contact with the firm's customers. Through his or her appearance, manners, language and ascribed social identity (e.g. gender or ethnicity as outlined by Jenkins 1996: 141f.), an apprentice may appeal more or less to customers and hence influence a firm's customer retention in the *market world*.[7] Employers represent their own clientele when they select new personnel and evaluate a future employee from the clients' point of view.[8] Hence, resources of coordination, such as 'soft skills' in the exchange with clients, are part of the productive resources of the firm (Eymard-Duvernay 1994: 326).

Together the three outlined worlds account for multiple social orders in work organizations. Apprentices and new employees in general pose both a potential risk and a chance for the continuance of these worlds. To appoint a new apprentice means to assess and avert the risk that he or she could disrupt any of the outlined worlds. To allow the firm's further existence, each world tends to reproduce itself by relying on its own hiring principles of personnel valuation and justice. All promising candidates have to prove their industrial, domestic and market suitability, as well as compliance, for success in the selection process.

2.2 Reality tests: Assessing the worth of job candidates

How can people be qualified and their worth in a situation of (future) workplace coordination be assessed when firms appoint new employees? To categorize persons according to their worth, Boltanski and Thévenot (2006) introduce the concept of *reality test* or 'test of worth'. A reality test is based on an agreed principle of worth (and of coordination), hence enabling the judgement process to reach a justifiable agreement. By qualifying people with reference to principles of worth, reality tests serve to minimize inaccuracy and ambiguity when new employees are being hired.

The modalities of how people are valued in the selection process depend on the agreed 'order of worth' that is considered to coordinate staff members adequately in an organization (Eymard-Duvernay 2004: 92). *Industrial* worth can, among other things, be measured and tested on a scale of professional capabilities based on technical performance. New apprentices are chosen on grounds of school qualifications, 'hard skills' and work virtues like punctuality, orderliness and dependability. In contrast, to test worth in the *domestic* world, firms apply what Thévenot (2001: 415) calls a 'test of confidence'. For example, worth is reflected in human warmth (*chaleur humain*, Thévenot 1995: 152). It also depends on a hierarchy of trust based on a chain of personal dependencies (Boltanski/Thévenot 1999: 370). Persons are judged as valuable if they can show that they accept domestic control structures, that is, by showing respect for long-serving employees and senior members of staff, and by recognizing older co-workers' authority as well as the gender-specific division of labour (Thévenot 1995: 161).

The assignment of worth in the selection process therefore requires decisions based on two important aspects of assessment: *justice* and *accuracy* (Eymard-Duvernay: 2008). On the one hand, the legitimate world of coordination is at stake and, together with its principle of equivalence, needs to be clarified. On the other, an acceptable process of evaluation and assessment of a person's worth in such a clarified world is necessary. First, the *principle of equivalence* is based on people's consenting to the form of coordination in place in order to reach and sustain a common good. Identification of the adequate coordination principle necessitates a qualitative evaluation of what is *just* (ibid.: 57f.), and is a normative or moral decision. The principle of equivalence (such as efficiency or seniority), which allows for assessing the valence of humans in a given situation, can therefore be considered as a *moral principle* of coordination, referring to the agreed principle of justice and equivalence in any given situation. Second, this agreed principle enables personnel specialists to establish a *measurement order*, which allows accurate classification of candidates. Given diverse forms of information and observation – such as application forms or letters, short placements, job interviews or telephone conversations – two or more candidates can now be assessed, compared and ranked in a legitimate way (Eymard-Duvernay 2004: 73f.). I will show below that emotions are essential for both aspects of assessment in personnel selection, that is, the identification of the just principle of coordination and the measurement of a candidate's worth in a specific world of the work organization.

3   Integrating emotions into the personnel selection model

How do emotions impact on our model of work organization and personnel selection provided so far? On the one hand, emotions are indispensable to guarantee the coordination of people in different worlds of work organizations. On the other, they are integral components of reality tests used to judge the worth of job candidates. Before I discuss these issues, I want first to outline a coherent concept of emotion relevant for our model of personnel selection.

3.1   Organizational emotions

3.1.1   Social emotions in organizations

To account for emotions in personnel selection, I have chosen the strategy of incorporating a coherent notion of emotion into the hitherto emotion-free organizational framework, as proposed by Sturdy (2003: 97). In doing so, I refer to *social emotions*, which, in contrast to subjective sentiments, clearly have a social basis (Barbalet 2001: 94). In this view, emotions have meaning only in the context of social relations, as they situate social actors and conduct the evaluation of their behaviour in their relations with each other (ibid.: 133). Translating an argument by Keltner (1999: 468) into organizational contexts, I assume that social emotions serve *social functions* by prioritizing and organizing ongoing behaviours in ways that optimize the adjustment of organizational members to organizational demands. This functional account claims that social emotions adapt to the problems of organizational continuity and survival. As will be outlined below, they are 'means of coordinating social interactions and relationships' (Keltner/Haidt 1999: 508) in different organizational worlds. Hence, I go beyond social emotions and refer to *organizational emotions*, when the former helps individuals to review and rearrange organizational priorities and cause their attention to be directed to the reproduction of different organizational worlds (Howard 1993: 616). As far as organizational reproduction is concerned, feelings are not individual, but rather result from the successful usage of the staff by the company. In participating in the company's daily routines, a manager gets a feeling about who will fit into the company and who will not. Thus, as incorporated organizational resources of decision-making, emotions reduce ambiguity.[9] Scenarios of threat, which can negatively affect the firm's survival in the market, if only in a firm's projected nightmare, are perceived and avoided by refusing certain job candidates at an early stage.

3.1.2 Affective-cognitive cultures of coordination

Ciompi (2003; 2004) offers a promising comprehensive meta-theory of interaction between emotion and cognition. Based on both evolutionary biology and, more importantly, systems theory, it is compatible with my functional model of personnel selection. Whereas Ciompi's notion of affect implies emotional phenomena in general, he refers to cognition 'as the capacity of perceiving and further processing sensory differences' (2003: 183). Such distinctions are continuously associated with affects, such as harmless/dangerous, interesting/uninteresting or pleasant/unpleasant, and are linked to corresponding tendencies for action (2004: 30). Furthermore, affects have so called operator-effects on cognitive calculations, as they deeply influence what is perceived and experienced. Such affects focus attention on specific cognitive contents, which are seen to be vital in a specific context, especially by excluding others (2003: 185). Thus, feeling and thinking are inseparably intertwined. The most important social function of affects (sympathy and antipathy or liking and disliking among others) is to act as a motor behind mental and social processes and to reduce complexity (2004: 42).

Cognitive elements that are systematically linked with similar affective connotations into a greater cognitive entity then generate an affect-dominated type of thinking. Referring to Ciompi's model of affect-logic, affects store and mobilize cognitive elements with similar emotional 'colour' into greater cognitive entities, which lead to global affect-dependent judgements such as 'a friendly country' or 'a nice man' (2003: 185). I assume that such frames of references build on cognitive distinctions with specific emotional valences that constitute cultures of coordination in organizations. Work organizations, or rather the different worlds they consist of, depend on their own affective-cognitive subcultures to assure reproduction and continuance. Such cultures shape everyday thinking (including prejudices and stereotypes) and guide the behaviour of organizational members in general and of decision-makers, in particular, when they have to match job positions with job applicants. Thus, if I use notions such as (gut) feelings, sentiments or affects, I refer to social emotions, which are part of affective-cognitive cultures[10] in the different worlds of the firm.

3.2   Emotions as a prerequisite for organizational coordination

Social emotions have an indisputable place in the dynamics of workplace coordination (Thévenot 1995: 154). According to Fineman (1996: 546) feelings and emotions are basic processes, which underlay social order and social functioning. Emotions and emotional expressions help coordinate routine operations and social interactions, so as to meet the superordinate goals of the work group (Keltner/Haidt 1999: 511). They are central rather than deviant or even 'irrational' to the everyday operations of organizational processes (Barbalet 2001: 3). 'Background emotions' (ibid.: 60) are required for the instrumental rationality of different (industrial, domestic, market) worlds.

Traditional theories of bureaucracy have usually stressed the function of a work organization's *industrial world*, which was considered as passionless due to its being based on efficiency (Fineman 1994: 75). However, emotions such as a distaste for waste of resources and time underlie the coordination of this world, as well as relying heavily on satisfaction in one's work (Barbalet 2001: 60). Furthermore, trust, such as confidence in technologies and plans, is essential in the industrial world.

Moving 'from an employee as a malleable instrument of production, to a more complex soul with [...] peer and family loyalties' (Fineman 1994: 76) points to the relevance of the *domestic world* of the firm. Workers have feelings such as trust, attachment and belonging for a work group and feel committed to the group task and spirit (Fineman 1996: 544). Within groups, experience and display of emotions help individuals define and negotiate their group-related roles and status (Keltner/Haidt

1999: 512). Working in groups as a source of identity can raise feelings of embarrassment or fear, similar to the tensions and dramas of family life (Fineman 1996: 549). Thévenot (2001: 414) places the feeling of trust first and foremost in the domestic world. On a temporal gradient, trust refers to precedent, which endures through ingrained customs and bridges between generations. On a spatial gradient, enduring relations of local proximity matter. On a hierarchical gradient, trust between employees and a superior depends on the domestic authority of the patron (Eymard-Duvernay 2004: 78f.).

Finally, Adam Smith (2006/1790) stated that forms of social coordination based on a *market order* cannot be sustained without 'moral sentiments'. The instrumental rationality of market competition can only get by because emotions act as an important background to the impersonal pursuit of commodities (Barbalet 2001: 59). Furthermore, emotions have turned out to be important resources to tie customers into 'personality markets'. In the context of customer services, where clients have to be met with warmth and smiles, the commodification of emotions helps to improve customer satisfaction and resultant sales (Fineman 1996: 554).

To summarize, the way social orders are maintained in multiple organizational worlds reverts to different emotion rules in terms of specific emotional commitments between organized actors (Fineman 1994: 82). Therefore some feelings such as trust, or 'the confidence that another's actions will correspond with one's expectations' (Barbalet 1996: 78), are essential for cooperation and organizational functioning in multiple worlds. Barbalet (1996: 80) proposes that loyalty is the feeling of confidence that the organization will perform its tasks and provide the required output because trust between workers can be maintained in the long run.

3.3 Critical and radical approaches to emotions in personnel selection

The main issue of this paper, however, is not the 'emotionality' of working and enhancement of productive performance through adequate emotions. Rather, I focus on emotions within the fabric of organizational *decision-making* (Fineman 1994: 79) when firms appoint new members. Thus, the interweaving of emotion and judgements in processes of organizational evaluation comes to the fore. What role do feelings play when managers assess the worth of job candidates in the different worlds of the firm? In the next section, I will elaborate, in the context of personnel selection, on the proposition of Thévenot

(1995: 170) that emotions are embedded in debates between different orders of worth, as well as within one single social order when worth is assessed.

To distinguish these two issues, it seems helpful to clarify further the relationship of feeling and rationality in my concept of organizational emotions. Fineman (1996) and Barbalet (2001) both outlined three different ways through which emotions and rationality can relate to each other as concepts. In the *conventional approach* (ibid.: 33ff.) of traditional organizational theory, emotions are in opposition to and interfere with rationality (Fineman 1996: 547ff.). In a more *critical approach* (Barbalet 2001: 38ff.), emotions can be seen as a solution to problems when reason alone cannot solve the problem. In such a case, emotional processes serve rationality (Fineman 1996: 550). Finally, a *radical approach* (Barbalet 2001: 45ff.) assumes that instrumental action is founded upon particular emotions. According to Fineman (1996: 550f.), emotions and cognitions are inextricably entwined and (cognition-based) rationality is a myth. My concept of emotions in organizational decision-making accounts for both the critical and radical approaches.

3.3.1   Emotional reduction of ambiguity in reality tests

I refer to the *critical approach* when I analyse how organizational gate-keepers make use of anticipatory emotions, in the sense of Kemper (1978: 74f.), to assess the future worth of job candidates in different organizational worlds. Reality tests can indeed be localized on a con-tinuum of quantitative measures of accuracy and rightness (assessing worth by 'hard facts') and qualitative forms of assessment, by express-ing feeling regarding the appropriateness of a person's status (Eymard-Duvernay 2008: 57). In Jenkins' study, an interviewee referred to gut feelings as being 'some measure of confidence the person has given during the interview [and as] difficult to quantify' (Jenkins 1986: 62). Ambiguity and uncertainty are usually reduced through the accumulation and retrieval of meaningful information (March 1994: 207f.). However, once 'hard facts' are not available, decision-makers use emotional signals such as hunches and gut feelings to anticipate an ambiguous future and unlock the problem of decision-making (Fineman 1996: 550). According to Luhmann (1968), emotions like trust or mistrust, are very effective tools for reducing the complexity of an unknown and unknowable future world and resolve ambiguities in decision-making. These emotions bring the future, which by def-inition cannot be known or rationally 'calculated', into the present by providing a sense of certainty (Barbalet 1996: 81f.; 2001: 101). Hence, confidence, trust and loyalty allow social agents to act with regard to an unknown and unknowable future, as only an emotional apprehension of circumstances can do this, while thought and reason cannot (Barbalet 1996: 82).

3.3.2 Emotions claiming a just moral order

In the *radical approach*, emotions are not just a substitute for reason in situations where the hands of the latter are tied because adequate information is lacking. Following David Hume, passion directs will. Thus emotions motivate actions, which are executed by the means selected and applied through reason (Barbalet 2001: 31; Howard 1993: 613). Hence, emotions obtain a role in decision-making complementary to that of reason. I refer to the radical approach to emotions to understand how managers decide about the order of worth they consider to be just in a situation of personnel selection. These decisions are 'moral' because they refer to a decisive form of coordination, which *should* be considered in order to judge a job candidate, based on shared norms about how members ought to behave (Turner 2007: 115). Thus each organizational world implies a moral community whose morality ties individuals to each other (Haidt 2007: 1000). From this point of view, emotions are primary expressions for defining and negotiating social relations in a moral order (Lutz/White 1986: 417). Positive (e.g. affection) and negative emotions (e.g. anger) express either promises or threats to moral communities (Fineman 1996: 550; Howard 1993: 620f.). As 'moral sentiments', they are the sense of approbation and disapprobation and the sense of *justice* (Barbalet 2001: 57). Following Solomon (1995: 32), justice first allows a way of participating in the world, a way of being with other people and 'a set of feelings of affection and affiliations that link us [...] with other people', rather than a set of principles or policies. Thereby, Solomon claims that the feeling of anger provides an assessment of broken fairness. This view is supported by Barbalet (2001: 144) and Keltner (1999: 474), who argue that moral anger enables the restoration of just relations when changes in the principles and rules of social relationships occur.

Next I will investigate empirically the two modes of emotional judgements in personnel selection. I will first discuss some options for, and limitations of, the detection of emotions in our interview data. I will then show how emotional expressions reflect moral statements about the appropriate order of worth for comparing job candidates, and how anticipatory emotions enable the assessment of their worth in different worlds.

4   Empirical evidence for emotions in personnel selection

4.1   Detecting social emotions in expert interview data

Jenkins (1986: 61) has noted that 'gut feeling' is tricky to pin down in a research interview, as it is difficult to expand upon verbally. Nevertheless, I was able to track down emotion-related statements throughout my analysis. They were indeed omnipresent in the statements of gatekeepers under investigation. With Kövecses (2003: 2ff.), I can distinguish between descriptive and expressive emotion words or expressions. A statement such as 'it's gut feeling' *describes* an emotional experience and therefore qualifies as a descriptive phrase. Such a statement verifies that feelings have played a role and their valence needs to be reconstructed out of the context. The extent to which people use descriptive emotional language may depend on the language. My data are based on conversations in Swiss German, which proved to be a rather rich language for making very basic emotional statements. Respondents often used words such as *to feel* (*fühlen*), *feeling* (*Gefühl*), *flair* (*Gespür*) or *emotionally* (*gefühlsmässig*).[11]

In Kövecses' study, examples of *expressive* emotion words include *shit!* when angry, *wow!* when enthusiastic or *yuk!* when disgusted (2003: 2). I expand these forms and also include non-verbal expressions such as laughter, loud breathing, raised voices, knocking on the table, and so on in the range of expressive statements. Thereby, the reconstruction of feelings reflected by expressive statements is very much a question of adequate observation and documentation during the interview. My phenomenological approach to expressive emotions is somewhat restricted, as the analysis of emotions was not an original intention of the research. The observations are, among others, limited to audible parts of expressive emotions during the interviews, as no visual observations such as facial expressions or posture were taken into account.

4.2   How moral emotions provide a compass for legitimate job requirements

Referring to some examples of interviews with gatekeepers in private dental surgeries, who offer an apprenticeship for dental assistants, the following cases show how the emotional expressions of dentists reflect moral judgements about the appropriate world of coordination[12] when comparing job applicants. In the first quote, a dentist underlines the relevance of the domestic world (teamwork) and of the market world (communicating to clients) in the selection process:

> You do not only expect from a person to dully assist, or just to siphon off saliva, do you? The aim is rather teamwork, and this involves three persons, namely [knocks on the table with each naming] the patient, the dental assistant, and the dentist. This requires rather much from the assistant, because she is standing very close to the patient, and sometimes she communicates much more with the patient than does the dentist (dentist A, private dental surgery)

The quote shows how the interviewee highlights certain worlds and simultaneously devalues the requirements of the industrial world by knocking emotionally on the table. Industrial skills do not meet all the job requirements; rather evidence of domestic and market worth is required.

Another dentist was asked how he deals with male applicants, as statistically, dental assistant apprentices are exclusively female. The answer of the dentist was short and emotional: 'No, I don't need this [laughter], I want to be the only male in the surgery, no, I don't [laughter]' (dentist B, private dental surgery). While this dentist made his claim based on expressive emotions, a third one, dentist C, confronted with the same question during the interview, expressed his emotions in a more descriptive manner. He underlined that he couldn't imagine a man in the position of a dental assistant, 'because there would still remain a certain role play'. He went on arguing, that 'this might be unfamiliar for patients, if two males work over them'. Moreover, he stated that his arguments were 'weird, just unusual, and basically absurd'. However, he further justified his response. 'But from an emotional point of view, emotionally, I would say no. To be honest, if a man is introducing himself, I would tell him that I rather look for a woman' (dentist C, private dental surgery). Dentists B and C both refer to the coordination principles of the domestic world – that of patriarchy and gender roles respectively. Their feelings clearly highlight the relevance of this world as a dominant and gendered order of coordination in private dental surgeries. In the case of dentist C, the tolerance of clients towards male dental assistants in the market world of the dental surgery is additionally put into question.

Hence, emotions call employers' attention to important worlds and distract their perception from other forms of coordination, such as the industrial world. This is particularly the case when it comes to male applicants, who in my interviews with dentists are never considered seriously as suitable medical or dental assistants, though males don't lack the necessary skills to do the job. However, (male) dentists put the suitability of male assistants in the domestic world emotionally into question on moral grounds. Thus, emotions speak for or against the compatibility of an applicant with regard to relevant principles of coordination. They express a moral contest and their affective narratives enable a methodological access to the everyday morals (Neckel 2006: 133f.) of dentists in their surgeries.

There remains, however, a serious methodological problem when I attempt retrospectively to analyse moral emotions (particularly expressive ones) from data gained through interviews. It remains unclear to what extent the emotions shown by my interviewees correspond to the decisive moral emotions they showed during the selection process. Hence, participant observation would be a more appropriate way to investigate the relevance of expressive moral emotions in personnel selection. In addition, the last two examples show that it is sometimes difficult to separate the moral and the anticipatory dimension of emotions in the data. If dentists militate against male assistants, they do not only highlight the morality of the domestic world, they simultaneously deny (and thus, assess) the domestic worth of male candidates.

4.3   Affective assessment of job candidates' worth

Once the legitimate order of coordination is sorted out, anticipatory emotions discriminate between applicants through reality tests. The analysed empirical data contain numerous stories regarding how employers make judgments about job candidates grounded on gut feelings. In the *domestic world*, emotions help individuals define group boundaries and identify potential group members (Keltner/Haidt 1999: 512). This is illustrated by the words of a medical assistant in a private surgery whose justification for refusing a young 'foreign' female was based on emotions aroused during initial contact through a short placement:

> Well, in my case, it was just sympathy; I didn't want her from the beginning. – *Yes* [voice getting louder] but I know, it is difficult to say. – Yes, it was gut feeling, so one can hardly put it into words. She probably was somehow alien to me with her whole way.

Further, gatekeepers judge if somebody will fit in with the team by gut feeling. In the words of one dentist: 'The apprentice should somehow fit in. If I don't have a good feeling, it won't turn out great.' Another dentist insisted that intuition plays a central role in judging if a (female) job candidate will fit in the team or not.

Feelings are also omnipresent when gatekeepers estimate the worth of applicants in the *market world* of the training firm. For example, a garage owner unorthodoxly voted for female car mechanics: 'We are a "women's garage", and I have the feeling, a woman in our garage attracts additional customers.' One of the dentists, in contrast, feared losing 'good patients', if he hired particular apprentices – ones with foreign-sounding surnames:

> It gives a bad impression, lets say for *Swiss*. They are used that people here are called [gives some Swiss surnames] 'Hugentobler', or 'Steinauer' or so, thus a name, which sounds normal and Swiss. As soon as there is a foreign...– I have the feeling [...] this results in attracting other patients at the end [...]. I simply have the feeling that good, long standing Swiss patients could jump off because of such names.

Last but not least, emotions also help to assess requirements in the *industrial world*. A garage owner relies on his feelings to interpret school credentials:

> These damn school reports always look different, excuse me. Over there that way, here this way [...]. Thus I view them very subjectively, as I feel it down in my gut, and I say, ok, this is a good report [...]. Well, this is not very scientific.

One manager said that she assigns limited opportunities for short place-ments of potential apprentices (which are used to test worth in real terms) according to her emotional evaluation of the written applications: 'How is the wording of the job application? Does it appeal to me or not? Well, this is somewhat difficult to measure; it's all about how it affects me.' In a similar vein, a garage owner admits to judging through emotions if the verifiable manual skills of applicants are within the normal range:

> Of course, there is a report of the mechanic about his working skills, and the test piece he [the apprentice] had to manufacture on his own, plus the school grades, and those calculations, the essay [...] and so on. This sets the framework that one could say, yes, we have the feeling that he is our guy.

Emotions thereby help to process the appointment of new employees from the beginning until the very end of the recruitment and selection process. At the outset of the selection process, gatekeepers use feelings to screen written applications. For instance, the director of an automotive paint shop screens the photos that make up part of the application forms[13] based on his intuition ('inner instinct'). In this way, he detects if somebody will be suitable and sympathetic to the firm's needs. A clerk in a trade association referred – besides other criteria such as grades and tidiness of the application – to his gut feeling when he selects candidates for job interviews. One auto body painter 'can say yes or no' from the first impression based on a gut level when somebody steps into the company's premises for the first time. In contrast, other gatekeepers have highlighted the fact that they take an emotion-based final decision about whom to hire at the very end of the selection process. The words of a doctor and clinic director testify to this: 'At the end, gut feelings play a role. One has to decide amongst two, three [candidates; C.I.] who are in the running, and you may have no hard facts to say, this one is better than the other.'

To sum up, feelings are crucial throughout the selection process when gatekeepers are taking decisions about whom to hire. On the one hand, feelings enable the preselection of candidates under conditions of time pressure and uncertainty through emotion-based screening. On the other, they accelerate decision-making and facilitate the termination of the selection process at its end. Thus, no process of personnel selection takes place without the utilization of feelings, at least in small companies.

5   Conclusion

In this study I have observed affective decision-making in hiring all along the evaluation process, from the initial screening of applications until the end, when organizational decision-makers have to select one of several 'equivalent' candidates. Thereby, the colloquial 'gut feeling' can be considered as a metaphor for experience-based as well as belief-based and biased organizational forms of judgement, incorporated and naturalized in organizational gatekeepers. My analysis shows that reference to one's own feelings does not necessarily harm the justification of a decision outcome (Voswinkel 2008), as emotions allow for rationalization in the evaluation of applicants. On the one hand, employers' gut feelings express a moral contest for legitimate criteria of coordination and selection in the multiple worlds of the firm. On the other, they help in coping with ambiguities if little or no trustworthy information is available for assessing the worth of job candidates. These two modes of emotion-based decision-making can overlap when managers refer to their feelings. In the particular case that a manager's 'gut feeling' serves to reduce ambiguities in measuring the worth of a job candidate, and as much as this feeling represents a *biased* form of judgement linked to a social characteristic of the candidate (e.g. gender or ethnicity), emotion-based hiring results in discrimination.[14] For instance, when some candidates are considered as not fitting to the existing team due to their stigma of being 'foreigners', then their worth in the domestic world is based on wrongful emotional grounds. Rather than being measured 'industrially', their domestic worth is systematically *felt* by the gatekeeper (Imdorf 2010b), based on stereotypes and on existing power relations in the company.

Finally, an important organizational function of emotions is their value in accelerating and, ultimately, terminating the selection process. As such, they allow for organizational efficiency, particularly, when time and information are scarce. In small companies, they furthermore enable the substitution of more formal procedures, which generally allow for legitimate decision-making. However, my research shows that even formalized routines do not work without feelings as long as humans are involved.

Notes

This chapter was developed during two research visits at the Laboratoire d'Économie et de Sociologie du Travail (Aix-en-Provence) and at the Adam Smith Research Foundation (University of Glasgow), subsidized by a research fellowship of the Swiss National Science Foundation. I thank Verena Marshall, Bridget Fowler, Hélène Buisson-Fenet, Barbara Sieben and Åsa Wettergren for helpful comments.

1. The original research project 'The selection of trainees in small and medium-sized enterprises: Integration and exclusion at the transitional stage between school and vocational training' was subsidized by the Swiss National Science Foundation within the National Research Programme 'Social Integration and Social Exclusion' (contract no. 405140–69088; see http://www.nfp51.ch).
2. The sample I refer to in this paper consists of 81 small and medium-sized enterprises (SMEs) in German-speaking Switzerland, which were investigated in 2005. The companies at hand were chosen according to the provision of selected apprenticeships in different industries: automobile painters (trained in paint shops), mechanics (in garages), carpenters (in joiner's workshops), dental and medical assistants (in dental and medical surgeries)

and clerks (in SMEs' offices, multiple branches). Companies were chosen by following unsuccessful applications, which resulted in a non-representative sample, despite its size. Most of the SMEs contacted turned out to be very small (25 companies with one to nine employees including apprentices) or small companies (31 with 10–49 employees). Thus, the data mainly enable a comprehensive reconstruction of apprentice selection processes in small companies.

3. This section summarizes two papers (Imdorf 2010a and 2010b), which outline my sociological model of personnel selection in more detail.

4. Professionalized organizations usually justify their personnel choice by legitimate procedures of recruitment and selection (Meyer/Rowan 1977). However, managing people in SMEs is often pragmatic and led by experience and improvisation, as well as by instinct (*Fingerspitzengefühl*), not by formalized procedures and policies (Pichler et al. 2000: 51). Hence, as long as no reliable and legitimate selection procedures are available, other resources for justification are required.

5. If the social cohesion of a local community is considered to be the most important common good, than the selection of a local apprentice (for example an employee's family member) rather than somebody unknown who lives outside the community would be considered legitimate by the (local) public of a small firm. However if social peace, based on a social contract, is regarded as the relevant public good, then a selection criterion that favours the inclusion of a disadvantaged person rather than their proximity would count as legitimate. Efficiency in turn can be justified as a selection criterion if it enables not only the prosperity of the company, but the wealth of the municipality through company taxation (see Boltanski/Thévenot 2006: 63ff. for a discussion of different political philosophies of the common good).

6. I call both professionalized and non-professionalized personnel relations specialists 'gatekeepers', as they represent specific institutional and organizational contexts and because they structure the life courses of the applicants (Struck 2001).

7. Admittedly, the term 'market world' is an imprecise one to account for the main principles of coordination when employees come into direct contact with the company's clientele and, hence, influence customer retention. Rather, the advancement of customer ties goes beyond one single coordination principle. The worth of an employee in exchanges with customers is based on a compromise of different principles, such as those of the domestic, projective and market worlds (see Imdorf 2010a for a more detailed account). For simplification, I use the term 'market world' in this text to refer to the worth of new employees in appealing to previous and new customers, as perceived by managers.

8. See also the question of Ortlieb and Sieben (2008) on why people with a migration background are employed or not employed in organizations. They answer the question through the resource dependencies of the organization. How organizational decision-makers assess clients' expectations plays a decisive role for the resulting typology of diversity strategies.

9. The prejudices and stereotypes of co-workers are resources for reducing organizational complexity and ambiguity, which are primarily of

organizational relevance. A personnel manager trusts an organizational member with risks of the company, and, to a lesser extent with his or her own personal risk (Luhmann 1968: 58 and 124).

10. In this text, I focus only on subcultures based on organizational emotions as outlined above. Of course, companies also shelter further peer group subcultures, which needn't be in line with the organizational goals of the company, and which are ignored by our theoretical approach to personnel selection.

11. Whereas Kövecses (2003: 3) refers to basic descriptive emotion words such as anger, sadness, fear, joy or love, I am concerned only with utterances that show that emotions have played a role in the course of action and assessment.

12. Swiss employers are mainly free to apply any selection criteria when they hire apprentices. There is no anti-discrimination law and hardly any formal rules exist to govern the hiring process as long as the employer respects the labour law. One of the few formal rules requires that the apprentice is at least 16 years old once the apprenticeship contract is concluded.

13. Standards of job application forms differ considerably between Anglophone countries (UK, USA, Australia, etc.) and German-speaking countries (Germany, Austria, Switzerland) (for a comparison see Huesmann 2008, 120ff.). Whereas in the former asking for photos is considered inappropriate and illegal, in the latter they are often required explicitly, especially as far as applications for apprenticeship positions are concerned.

14. See Imdorf (2010b) for an extensive discussion on how discrimination relates to my model of personnel selection. Emotion-based reality tests can provide an organizational opportunity structure for discrimination (Peterson/ Saporta 2004) once gatekeepers depend on the collectivistic exploitation of social characteristics to assess the worth of job candidates in multiple worlds.

References

Barbalet, J. (1996) 'Social emotions: confidence, trust and loyalty', *International Journal of Sociology and Social Policy*, 16(9), 75–96.

Barbalet, J. (2001) *Emotion, Social Theory, and Social Structure. A Macrosociological Approach*, Cambridge: Cambridge University Press.

Boltanski, L. and Thévenot, L. (1999) 'The sociology of critical capacity', *European Journal of Social Theory*, 2, 359–77.

Boltanski, L. and Thévenot, L. (2006) *On Justification: Economies of Worth*, Princeton: Princeton University Press.

Ciompi, L. (2003) 'Reflections on the role of emotions in consciousness and subjectivity, from the perspective of affect-logic', *Consciousness and Emotions*, 4, 181–96.

Ciompi, L. (2004) 'Ein blinder Fleck bei Niklas Luhmann? Soziale Wirkungen von Emotionen aus Sicht der fraktalen Affektlogik', *Soziale Systeme*, 10, 21–49.

Eymard-Duvernay, F. (1994) 'Coordination des échanges par l'entreprise et qualité des biens', in A. Orléan (ed.) *Analyse économique des conventions*, Paris: PUF, 307–34.

Eymard-Duvernay, F. (2004) *Économie politique de l'entreprise*, Paris: Éditions La Découvert.

Eymard-Duvernay, F. (2008) 'Justesse et justice dans les recrutements', *Formation Emploi*, 101, 55–69.

Eymard-Duvernay, F. and Marchal, E. (1997) *Façons de recruter. Le jugement des compétences sur le marché du travail*, Paris: Éditions Métailié.

Fineman, S. (1994) 'Organizing and emotion: towards a social construction', in J. Hassard and M. Parker (eds) *Towards a New Theory of Organizations*, London: Routledge, 75–86.

Fineman, S. (1996) 'Emotion and organizing', in S.R. Clegg, C. Hardy and W.R. Nord (eds) *The Handbook of Organization Studies*, London: Sage, 543–64.

Haidt, J. (2007) 'The new synthesis in moral psychology', *Science*, 316, 998–1002.

Howard, N. (1993) 'The role of emotions in multi-organizational decision-making', *Journal of the Operational Research Society*, 44, 613–23.

Huesmann, M. (2008) *Arbeitszeugnisse aus personalpolitischer Perspektive. Einsatz, Gestaltung und Wahrnehmungen*, Wiesbaden: Gabler.

Imdorf, C. (2010a) 'Wie Ausbildungsbetriebe soziale Ungleichheit reproduzieren: Der Ausschluss von Migrantenjugendlichen bei der Lehrlingsselektion', in H.-H. Krüger, U. Rabe-Kleberg, R.-T. Kramer and J. Budde (eds) *Bildungsungleichheit revisited. Bildung und soziale Ungleichheit vom Kindergarten bis zur Hochschule*, Wiesbaden: VS, 263–78.

Imdorf, C. (2010b) 'Die Diskriminierung "ausländischer" Jugendlicher bei der Lehrlingsauswahl', in U. Hormel and A. Scherr (eds) *Diskriminierung. Grundlagen und Forschungsergebnisse*, Wiesbaden: VS, 197–219.

Jenkins, R. (1986) *Racism and Recruitment. Managers, Organisations and Equal Opportunity in the Labour Market*, Cambridge: Cambridge University Press.

Jenkins, R. (1996) *Social Identity*, London: Routledge.

Keltner, D. (1999) 'Functional accounts of emotions', *Cognition and Emotion*, 13, 467–80.

Keltner, D. and Haidt, J. (1999) 'Social functions of emotions at four levels of analysis', *Cognition and Emotion*, 13, 505–21.

Kemper, T.D. (1978) *A Social Interactional Theory of Emotions*, New York: Wiley.

Kövecses, Z. (2003) *Metaphor and Emotion. Language, Culture, and Body in Human Feeling*, Cambridge: Cambridge University Press.

Laske, S. and Weiskopf, R. (1996) 'Personalauswahl – Was wird denn das gespielt? Ein Plädoyer für einen Perspektivenwechsel', *Zeitschrift für Personalforschung*, 10, 295–330.

Lee, G. and Wrench, J. (1983) *Skill Seekers – Black Youth, Apprenticeships and Disadvantage*, Leicester: National Youth Bureau.

Luhmann, N. (1968, 4th edn 2000) *Vertrauen*, Stuttgart: Lucius & Lucius; trans. N. Luhmann (1979) *Trust and Power*, Chichester: Wiley.

Lutz, C. and White, G. (1986) 'The anthropology of emotions', *Annual Review of Anthropology*, 15, 405–36.

March, J.G. (1994) *A Primer on Decision-making. How Decisions Happen*, New York: Free Press.

March, J.G. and Simon, H.A. (1958) *Organizations*, New York: Wiley.

Meyer, J.W. and Rowan, B. (1977) 'Institutionalized organizations: formal structure as myth and ceremony', *American Journal of Sociology*, 83, 340–63.

Miller, S.R. and Rosenbaum, J. (1997) 'Hiring in a Hobbesian world. Social infrastructure and employers' use of information', *Work and Occupations*, 24, 498–523.

Moss, P. and Tilly, C. (2001) *Stories Employers Tell. Race, Skill, and Hiring in America*, New York: Russell Sage.

Neckel, S. (2006) 'Kultursoziologie der Gefühle. Einheit und Differenz – Rückschau und Perspektiven', in R. Schützeichel (ed.) *Emotionen und Sozialtheorie. Disziplinäre Ansätze*, Frankfurt a.M.: Campus, 124–39.

Neckerman, K.M. and Kirschenman, J. (1991) 'Hiring strategies, racial bias, and inner-city workers', *Social Problems*, 38, 433–47.

Ortlieb, R. and Sieben, B. (2008) 'Exclusion, hazard, adding value, or learning? Diversity strategies focused on employees with a migration background', in G.T. Solomon (ed.) *Best papers proceedings of the sixty-seventh annual meeting of the Academy of Management* (CD), ISSN 1543–8643.

Peterson, T. and Saporta, I. (2004) 'The opportunity structure for discrimination', *American Journal of Sociology*, 109, 852–901.

Pichler, J.H., Pleitner, H.J. and Schmidt, K.-H. (2000) *Management in KMU. Die Führung von Klein- und Mittelunternehmen*, Bern: Haupt.

Simon, H.A. (1957) *Models of Man. Mathematical Essays on Rational Human Behavior in a Social Setting*, New York: Wiley.

Smith, A. (2006/1790) *The Theory of Moral Sentiments*, 6th edn, Mineola: Dover.

Solomon, R.C. (1995) *A Passion for Justice. Emotions and the Origins of the Social Contract*, Lanham: Rowman & Littlefield.

Struck, O. (2001) 'Gatekeeping zwischen Individuum, Organisation und Institution. Zur Bedeutung und Analyse von Gatekeeping am Beispiel von Übergängen im Lebensverlauf', in L. Leisering, R. Müller and K.F. Schumann (eds) *Institutionen und Lebensläufe im Wandel. Institutionelle Regulierungen von Lebensläufen*, Weinheim, München: Juventa, 29–54.

Sturdy, A. (2003) 'Knowing the unknowable? A discussion of methodological and theoretical issues in emotion research and organizational studies', *Organization*, 10, 81–105.

Thévenot, L. (1995) 'Émotions et évaluations dans les coordinations publiques', in P. Paperman and R. Ogien (eds) *La couleur des pensées*, Paris: Éditions de l'École des Hautes Études en Sciences Sociales, 145–74.

Thévenot, L. (2001) 'Organized complexity: conventions of coordination and the composition of economic arrangements', *European Journal of Social Theory*, 4, 405–25.

Turner, J.H. (2007) *Human Emotions. A Sociological Theory*, London: Routledge.

Voswinkel, S. (2008) 'Der Support des Bauches: Entscheidungsorganisation bei der Personaleinstellung', in K.-S. Rehberg (ed.) *Die Natur der Gesellschaft. Verhandlungsband des 33. Kongresses der Deutschen Gesellschaft für Soziologie*, Frankfurt a.M.: Campus, 4997–5007 (CD-ROM).

5
Empowerment as Interactions that Generate Self-Confidence – An Emotion-Sociological Analysis of Organizational Empowerment

Poul Poder

1 Introduction

Empowerment, understood as the delegation of authority, the flattening of organizational hierarchy and the effort to encourage employees to work independently and creatively, is a strong and widespread ideal. Many employees in contemporary work organizations are involved in empowerment programmes (Dahl 1999: 51; Jacobsen/Thorsvik 2007: 188). However, such programmes are often unsuccessful (Wilson 2004; Edwards/Wajcman 2005), and the processes that lead to effective empowerment have not yet been sufficiently understood (Conger/ Kanungo 1988; Eylon 1998: 17). This chapter aims to address this gap in understanding by theorizing how confidence and other positive emotions contribute to personal agency, which is an essential aspect of the empowerment process.

It is generally understood that confidence – meaning faith in oneself as opposed to conceit or arrogance – is essential to empowerment. For example, DuBrien advises managers to: 'Look for evidence of self-confidence in handling past assignments. It takes self-confidence to handle decisions on your own. (Of course, you could argue that being empowered builds self-confidence). Look for at least some past displays of self-confidence' (DuBrien 2000: 228f.). That one should look for *past* signs of self-confidence indicates that self-confidence in present efforts cannot be taken for granted. Moreover, the suggestion that being formally and structurally empowered builds self-confidence is not self-evident, since employees do not necessarily feel confident just because authority has been formally delegated to them (Brooks 2003). Furthermore, the fact that employees in hierarchical organization can act in empowered ways, while employees in formally empowered organizations may feel disempowered (Spreitzer 2008), proves that structural empowerment alone does not necessarily generate confidence. Like other empowerment researchers, however, DuBrien does not theorize the generation of confidence (e.g. Blanchard et al. 1999). The present chapter thus shows how confidence is not properly theorized by either the socio-structural or the psychological approaches, which are the two main ones within empowerment theory. Both are limited, one by taking confidence for granted and the other by understanding it exclusively in psychological terms. In order to advance our understanding of confidence, the present chapter suggests how it is generated by particular social interactions that promote recognition *and* access to relevant resources for action. Drawing on emotion-focused sociological theory about agency and emotional energy, and Fredrickson's 'build and broaden' theory of positive emotions, I argue that the focus on consciousness and intentionality as the defining features of human agency has led us to downplay the fact that agency is primarily an emotional phenomenon. As such, it is also dynamic and situational, since it is highly dependent on interactions that engender emotional energy and positive emotions that fuel and widen agency. As an example of such positive emotions, I focus in particular on confidence, a crucial factor in empowerment, since employees who are required to work independently and creatively must have confidence in themselves. On the basis of this interactional understanding of how agency is generated by particular interactions, the chapter will explain the unresolved paradox mentioned above.

In pursuit of this central aim I begin, first, by criticizing the existing theories of empowerment for failing to explain how confidence is generated, then I outline an interactional framework that supplements the mainstream structural or psychological approaches to empowerment theory. Second, I illustrate this alternative theory by presenting a few examples from a case analysis of organizational empowerment within a large international company (Poder 2004). Third, I discuss the implications of this theoretical contribution to our understanding of empowerment. By theorizing confidence as an emotion generated through interaction, I show that empowerment cannot be defined solely in structural terms (i.e. in terms of the amount of authority delegated) or in psychological terms (i.e. in terms of the extent to which employees perceive themselves as being in control of things). Rather, empowerment should be understood as the ongoing interactional generation of confidence as a necessary factor in enabling employees to act independently and creatively. Moreover, in presenting the generation of confidence as a fundamental social process, to be found in both hierarchical and non-hierarchical relationships, I show that empowerment is not essentially defined by the absence of hierarchical relationships. Finally, the conclusion emphasizes that confidence cannot be taken for granted, which is why it is crucial to investigate the extent to which interactional efforts to create empowerment succeed (or otherwise) in engendering confidence. The chapter can thus be seen as a theoretical contribution to a relational understanding of empowerment, one which draws on the sociology of emotions to highlight the essentially emotional dimensions of agency.

2   Psychological and structural approaches to empowerment

Empowerment has hitherto been considered primarily from a psychological or structural perspective (Scott/Jaffe 1991; Mark 1997; Pepitone 1998; Potterfield 1999). While both these perspectives capture essential dimensions of the phenomenon, they fail to grasp sufficiently the way in which self-confidence – an essential factor in empowerment – is generated through particular forms of interactions.

2.1   The socio-structural approach

The socio-structural approach theorizes how certain organizational structures are conducive to empowerment. The key idea is that empowerment takes place through the transfer of power from higher ranks of employees to lower ranks, and that employees can be empowered by the sharing of authority, command, information, knowledge and rewards (Potterfield 1999: 34). This approach is significant in understanding how empowerment is defined by specific managerial practices, such as delegating authority, sharing resources and making the organizational format less hierarchical (Blanchard et al. 1999). The idea of empowerment as an emancipation from hierarchical organization is expressed, for example, in the influential book *The 3 Keys to Empowerment – Release the Power Within People for Astonishing Results*, whose authors contend that the real core of empowerment consists in the emancipation of the knowledge, experience and motivational power already residing in employees (Blanchard et al. 1999). However, the empowerment literature has described on the one hand situations in which employees continue to feel disempowered even when all the structural tools of empowerment – the sharing of power, knowledge, information and rewards – have been deployed, and, on the other, situations in which employees have felt empowered and acted accordingly, despite the fact that the structural features of empowerment were absent from their workplace (Spreitzer 2008: 56). Thus empowerment has an experiential dimension that is not fully accounted for by the socio-structural approach. This level has been addressed by the psychological approach within empowerment theory, to which we now turn.

2.2 The psychological approach

The psychological approach concentrates on the experiential level of empowerment by addressing employees' perceptions of their working relationships and seeking to identify the key factors that characterize the experience of empowerment. Widespread support has been given within the interdisciplinary literature on empowerment to Spreitzer's (2008) theory of four key psychological states and cognitions that employees experience when they are genuinely empowered:

1. They perceive their work and organizational position as meaningful because their work role and beliefs, values and behaviours match one another.
2. They think of themselves as competent, i.e. as being able to carry out their tasks with skill and self-efficacy, which refers to the conviction that one can act in required ways in order to create particular outcomes (Bandura 1989).
3. They see themselves as self-determining, in the sense of having choice in initiating and regulating their actions. They consider themselves free to make their own decisions about their methods and pace of work and the amount of effort they devote to it.
4. They feel that they can make an impact on others and influence strategic, administrative or operating outcomes at work (Spreitzer 2008: 57).

Together, these cognitions reflect an active attitude towards one's work. The experience of empowerment is manifest in all four dimensions – if one dimension is missing, then the experience of empowerment will be limited (Spreitzer/Doneson 2008). For example, if a person has the discretion to make decisions (i.e. self-determination) but does not care about the kinds of decisions they make (i.e. they lack a sense of meaning), he or she will not feel empowered. Similarly, if people think they can make a difference but are not sure they have the skills and abilities to do their job well (i.e. they lack a sense of competence), they will not feel empowered.

Researchers writing from a psychological perspective focus on interpretative acts such as attribution, evaluation and envisioning (Conger/ Kanungo 1988; Thomas/Velthouse 1990). They emphasize how individuals interpret events in ways that make them feel in control of things. Changes in external working environments may promote empowerment but the emphasis is on how employees' interpretations of events enhance or detract from their feelings of competence and control (Potterfield 1999: 50). The psychological approach thus concentrates on empowerment as 'a subjective state of mind whereby an employee perceives that he or she is exercising efficacious control over meaningful work' (ibid.: 51).

The psychological perspective is valuable, since individuals' interpretations of themselves and social events frame or influence the way they act. Believing that one can accomplish a certain task makes it more likely that one will succeed (Bandura 1989). However, the psychological approach is centred on the individual (Spreitzer 2008: 57), concentrating on the intra-psychic perceptions/cognitions of individual employees. It emphasizes the fact that the experience of being empowered is dependent on the way in which employees interpret what is happening to them. If one perceives oneself as being more in control due to particular measures and efforts to increase empowerment, this will naturally influence one's *experience* of being empowered. The psychological approach thus captures an important experiential dimension of empowerment that is not addressed by the socio-structural approach. But as we shall see, the experience of employees is not defined by self-perceptions alone.

2.3   Limitations of the socio-structural and psychological approaches

Both the socio-structural and the psychological approaches offer limited understandings of how self-confidence is generated. With respect to the psychological approach, I would argue that confidence is not solely generated by interpretations that construct one as being in control. Belief in oneself is not identical with self-confidence. How people cognitively perceive themselves is not necessarily reflected in how they feel. In other words, individuals may *think* that they feel in control of their work without actually feeling that they are. Such self-efficacy, understood as the conviction that one can successfully execute the behaviour required to produce particular outcomes, is a cognitive evaluation (Quinn 2007: 75). My argument is therefore that the perception of one's own efficacy is not identical with self-confidence. The identification of confidence with a person's self-efficacy fails to grasp the way in which confidence is also constituted by other individuals' engendering of positive emotions in their interactions with the person concerned.

While the socio-structural theory provides an organization-centric perspective on empowerment, it nevertheless fails to address how confidence is generated by specific forms of interaction. Rather, it assumes that confidence pre-exists: 'People are empowered when they are able to more freely exercise whatever power they possess, such as using their own expertise' (DuBrien 2000: 231). The issue of how confidence is *generated* is not recognized as significant, because it is believed that flattening the organizational hierarchy will in itself liberate employees' potential. This approach overlooks the generation of confidence as a phenomenon requiring explanation, because it assumes that human initiative (confidence) will flourish as soon as allegedly stifling hierarchical structures are abolished. The sharing of resources and information is part of empowerment, but such sharing, or the fact that employees *think* of themselves as empowered, is not sufficient. They must also *feel* confident, in a way that enables them to act confidently. In sum, both mainstream approaches pay too little attention to the significance of the interactional level in generating confidence.

The next section therefore explores the relationship between social interaction and confidence in order to elaborate a framework that fully encompasses how confidence is socially (re)generated. By concentrating on interactions that are significant for agency, and that occur in both hierarchical and non-hierarchical organizations, an interactional theory may help to explain the paradox that employees may feel empowered, and act accordingly, in hierarchical organizations, and that conversely they may feel *dis*empowered in organizations where formal structures have been set up to empower them.

3 An interactional approach to empowerment

In order to develop a properly sociological or interactional approach to confidence it is necessary to address the issue of agency in a more fundamental sense. Through critiquing a common notion of agency, I pave the way for understanding it as an essentially emotional and dynamic phenomenon in which positive emotions such as confidence play a crucial role. Organizational empowerment involves the generation of personal agency: its aim is to enable employees to work more independently and creatively. It is therefore important to understand *how* such agency is generated. As I explain below, self-confidence is essential to the process of promoting agency. In order to demonstrate the significance of agency as an emotional phenomenon, I also consider other positive emotions that contribute to it. In brief, this section deals with the ways that positive emotions contribute to the generation of agency.

My starting-point is that individuals should not be seen as agents per se, as they are when we define agency in terms of consciousness and intentionality (Poder 2008). The prevailing view is that humans act on the basis of conscious intentions, whereas animals merely *re*act (Fuchs 2007). However, consciousness and intentionality are not sufficient to define agency, since they describe decision-making rather than agency as such. Making a decision is not the same as having the energy or will-power to act upon it (Campbell 1999). Thus rather than thinking of agency as a generic and given capacity, we would do better to understand it as variable and socially produced (Layder 2004). Consciousness and intentionality are generic features of human beings. But the energy to act on plans and intentions is dependent on the generation of emotional energy (Collins 2004) and especially on self-confidence, which is essential to any action aimed at going beyond mere routine actions.

Agency is thus predicated on emotional energy, which differs from the perception of self-efficacy in being an affective rather than a cognitive experience, since energy also involves 'an appraisal of a situation (usually unconscious), changes in body language, and affective arousal' (Quinn 2007: 75). Emotional energy arises out of ritual and bodily interaction, and is not merely the product of an individual's self-interpretation (Collins 2007), as elucidated by Collins' theory of interaction rituals (Collins 2004). In order to develop a more specific sociological appreciation of how confidence is generated in social interaction, I draw on Barbalet's theory of confidence, trust and loyalty as basic social emotions that are constitutive of agency on a personal, social and institutional level (Barbalet 1996). Here, I focus in particular on Barbalet's reflections concerning confidence, which are especially helpful in understanding how empowerment involves making employees going beyond routine acting and taking on new challenges.

Barbalet's theory posits confidence as an emotion that is fundamental to action: 'All action is ultimately founded on the actor's feeling of confidence in their capacities and the effectiveness of those capacities. The actor's confidence is a necessary source of action; without it, action simply would not occur' (ibid.: 90). Confidence is best understood as an emotion of *self-projection* that encourages one to go one's own way with the *assured expectation* of success (ibid.: 77). Both self-projection and assured expectation are essential to human agency, which is possible only in so far as the individual is able to project his or her capacities into the future. Confidence creates a sense of security vis-à-vis the unknowable future by bringing the possible future into the present. It implies non-conformism in so far as it involves a willingness to follow one's own path. Confidence can be described as the opposite of passive emotional states such as anxiety, sorrow, despair, shame, shyness or modesty, all of which operate as potential limitations to action (ibid.: 76).

Like other emotions, confidence has an occasion and an object, essentially relating to the future. Moreover, confidence involves three features that are associated with emotion in general: (1) a subjectively experiential aspect: one knows when one feels confident; (2) a physiological or behavioural aspect: others can see if a person appears confident and (3) an impulsive, motoric aspect indicated by the fact that people who feel confident often report pleasurable sensations or bodily reactions such as good muscular control or deep or relaxed breathing. But even though confidence, understood as self-assured projection, can be treated as a purely individual psychological state, the phenomenon does not arise only in the consciousness of the individual. From a sociological point of view, confidence arises out of social relations in which the person concerned is met with appreciation and granted access to relevant resources for future action (Barbalet 1998: 86). These resources are important not because they are necessarily needed immediately, but because access to them ensures that they are available for the future (Barbalet 1996: 87). Confidence does not feed on recognition or acknowledgement alone. Without admission to relevant resources, the individual cannot sustain the feeling of being able to act on his or her own in relation to the unknowable future. This points to the fundamental temporal aspect of confidence as based on secured *future access* to, or the right to use, resources. To feel confident about realizing a projection of oneself – confident, for example, that one will succeed in becoming a manager – one needs to know that one has entrée to resources of instrumental significance in this career development. Thus self-confidence is a genuinely social emotion, since the way we experience it, and whether we experience it, depends on the social context of relevant resources in which the person concerned is inevitably enmeshed. Access to resources for future action involves material social dependency on other actors. As a social phenomenon, confidence is thus more than a psychological matter of cognitions about, or interpretations of, the self.[1] It is generated through interactions in which individuals show one another recognition and accord one another the right to use relevant resources for action. This interactional and generative understanding of agency is supported by Fredrickson's (2001) innovative theory of how particular positive emotions *broaden* individuals' outlook on the world and their opportunities to act within it, and *build* resources that they can draw on in future action. Whereas negative emotions such as fear and disgust narrow our possibilities, positive emotions broaden the scope of attention, cognition, and action, widening the array of precepts, thoughts and actions that are presently in mind (Fredrickson/Branigan 2005: 315). Thus, as Fredrickson (2003) argues, *joy* creates an urge to play, to be creative and to push existing limits. *Interest* creates the urge to explore the world, take in new information and experience and expand the self in the process. *Pride* engenders an urge to share the news of one's achievements with others and to envision even greater achievements in the future. And *contentment* urges the individual to take time to savour current life circumstances, and to integrate these circumstances into new views of self and the world. These effects of positive emotions demonstrate in more detail the emotional nature of agency, for they transform the individual in ways that render him/her more capable of acting in the world. These emotions not only contribute to agency in the immediate sense of opening out a wider view of one's possible courses of action, but also broaden habitual modes of thinking, and in doing so make people more flexible, empathic and creative (ibid.: 174). In making individuals more empathic, positive emotions help to generate their agency vis-à-vis others, enabling them more easily to connect and interact. Fredrickson's theory thus describes how positive emotions contribute to agency in an *immediate* sense by broadening individuals' cognitive outlook on the world and on possible courses of action. In short, positive emotions render the individual more able to make considered and informed choices (Fredrickson/Branigan 2005). Fredrickson's theory thus explains how positive emotions other than confidence contribute to agency, and thereby offers us a fuller understanding of the emotional nature of agency in general.

Barbalet demonstrates that confidence is a *social* emotion by stressing how the experience of confidence is not merely a matter of individual perception but is dependent on social context – on the individual's being granted not only social recognition but also access to relevant resources for action. He thus provides a thoroughly sociological account to supplement the approaches discussed above. However, the fact that confidence as an emotion is essential to agency at the personal level does not mean that agency is necessarily episodic. The stability or otherwise of emotion-based agency depends on the extent to which the social interactions in which the individual is involved serve reliably to generate confidence.

The positive emotions described by Fredrickson often arise from social interactions (Watson et al. 1992) rather than from individual self-cognitions. They are also 'contagious' and can thus be transmitted through the members of an organization (Hatfield et al. 1994). This effect of emotional contagion is especially strong and effective if the parties in a given interaction share a mutual focus of attention (Collins 2004: 76). In organizational contexts leaders' positive emotions may be especially contagious, since a lot of attention is normally devoted to them (Quinn 2000) and their emotions have been shown to predict the performance of the groups of employees answerable to them (George 1995). Drawing on Fredrickson's theory, researchers in the emerging field of Positive Organizational Scholarship (Cameron et al. 2003a) analyse how particular positive interactions increase individuals' capacities for action (Dutton/Heaphy 2003; Dutton/Baker 2007; Dutton/Ragins 2007; Spreitzer/Doneson 2008). In his study of generative forms of interaction, Quinn explains how emotional energy arises: (a) when individuals *exchange resources* they value and need, for example in conversations where mutually useful information is communicated; (b) when the relationship between parties *constructs identities* that provide meaning and a sense of self-worth, as for example when husband and wife communicate together in ways that confirm that they are the kind of parents they want to be; (c) when individuals act together on the basis of feelings of connectedness and respect, which stimulates a sense of being capable of doing more than usual because one has the sympathy of others, and (d) when a relationship offers opportunities to learn in a way that makes the parties involved feel better able to master particular situations and tasks (Quinn 2007). Thus Quinn shows how various kinds of interaction are instrumental in generating energy as an essential dimension of agency.

In sum, the issue of agency is best understood in relation to particular emotionally generative interactions. I would emphasize that the challenging issue here is to understand precisely what determines the extent to which an individual is empowered to act. Rather than merely assuming that agency will flourish either as a result of cognitive perceptions of self-efficacy or of being set free from bureaucratic and hierarchical organizational structures, we need to understand what kinds of interaction promote (or discourage) agency. Moreover, it follows from this understanding of agency that it can be generated in both horizontal and vertical relationships, since individuals in both types of relationship can in principle express recognition and provide access to relevant resources for action. Theoretically, this framework does not privilege any actor in advance and thereby avoids overstating the significance of managers for organizations (Parker 2002). On a practical level, however, it shows that employees are deeply dependent on managers precisely because the latter have most say in the distribution of access to relevant work resources. Managers influence employees not only by according (or failing to accord) them recognition, but also in the extent to which they grant them access to relevant resources. Dependency on others, and on managers in particular, goes very deep since it influences the very generation of confidence in the individual employee.

The next section illustrates this emotion-oriented interactional theory by relating it to a particular case of organizational empowerment.

4   Illustrating the interactional theory

The interactional theory presented here, which concerns the way in which particular positive emotions constitute agency, suggests that it would be useful to investigate interactions empirically with respect to whether they express recognition of others or provide access to resources that are relevant to them. To illustrate this theory of confidence I will briefly present a particular case of organizational empowerment showing that self-confidence is an essential dimension of empowerment[2] and that it is engendered through generative and resource-oriented interactions, both between managers and employees and between colleagues. The organization in question saw empowerment not merely in terms of encouraging employees to identify normatively with corporate values, or of liberating them from bureaucratic structures, but as a generative endeavour. This was made clear by a corporate list of actions that managers were asked to engage in, in order to promote empowering of the employees.

The senior management considered empowerment a 'cornerstone value' and had defined it as 'pushing accountability and decision-making power as far out into the organization as possible'. All departmental managers were told to take active responsibility for creating an empowered organization: 'It's up to you as managers to make sure that the incredible potential of each individual is set free in a way that will contribute to our future goals' (cf. document issued by senior manager, see Poder 2004). This corporate empowerment *philosophy* was concretized

Table 5.1 Empowerment

The manager	The employee
Provides information	Contributes ideas
Focuses on performance	Takes on problems and solves them
Is available	Builds on colleagues' efforts
Creates a team environment	Challenges tradition
Helps and coaches	Helps to implement
Invites challenge	Seeks out information
Encourages ideas and listens	Works well in a team
Asks probing questions	Takes initiatives
Defends employees' decisions	Encourages discussion
Learns from mistakes	Provides feedback
Develops useful networks	Works cross-functionally
Gives others credit	Takes responsibility for results
Provides personal feedback	Qualifies him/herself for the demands of the future

Note: Entries as defined by managerial document (see Poder 2004).

into specific normative expectations concerning both managers and employees, which were displayed on the noticeboard in the employee lounge and in the employees' own offices (see table 5.1 above).

In order to meet such normative expectations the employee needs to feel self-confident. 'Taking on problems and solving them' or 'taking the initiative' requires confidence because taking on problems as opposed to carrying out routine tasks demands extraordinary effort and creativity. A person who lacks self-confidence is less likely to take on challenges and volunteer solutions. Similarly, 'contributing ideas' and 'encouraging discussion' both require self-confidence, i.e. the belief that one's thoughts, ideas or hunches may be worthy of consideration and discussion. Similarly, it requires a great deal of confidence to 'challenge tradition', since traditions are often highly valued and the subject of strong feeling. Customs and habits provide ontological security amid the constant changes and reflexivity of modern life (Giddens 1991). Moreover, traditions may serve to support and legitimize existing power structures (Weber 1991: 79). In this sense, challenging tradition may also mean challenging actors who benefit from the way things have been customarily arranged. Speaking out against these interests certainly requires self-confidence – the belief that one is not bound merely to follow the status quo but can set oneself apart by challenging it.

From this list of actions expected of an 'empowered employee' we can easily see how essential confidence is to empowerment.

Confidence is the more or less implicit precondition for being able to act as the ideal 'empowered employee'. By contrast, the list of normative expectations relating to the 'empowering manager', to which we will now turn, illustrates that the generation of confidence is an interactional matter. The list in question suggests how managers should contribute to employees' self-confidence by way of certain forms of interaction.[3] 'Providing information' relevant to the employee's tasks can be understood as giving access to information as a resource for the employee in meeting new and demanding assignments. Similarly, the manager should engage in 'helping and coaching' the employee, i.e. in providing adequate support and assistance as the employee faces new and difficult challenges. 'Encouraging ideas and listening' implies managerial recognition and acknowledgement of the employee's initiative and creativity. Recognition is fundamental to the employee's development of a feeling of empowerment. Such recognition is of course also involved in 'giving employees credit' for results achieved, a point likewise emphasized by the psychological approach to empowerment. Similarly, 'providing personal feedback' involves the expression of specific recognition or appreciation of the employee concerned.

However, empowering an employee involves more than giving recognition, as the following example shows. In this particular case, a manager delegated a task to an administrative employee, who initially felt insecure as to whether she could manage it: the task was new to her, it was more complex and demanding than her usual tasks and the manager had previously taken care of it. The manager expressed recognition of the employee's competencies by stressing how she had successfully taken on similar tasks in the past. He also told her that his door was always open if she needed any kind of assistance in solving the task. In other words, the manager could provide her with additional knowledge, information or advice if this proved necessary. This example shows that empowering employees is not merely a matter of expressing recognition; nor is structural change, such as the delegation of authority, a sufficient condition of empowerment. The key to developing empowerment is instead the resource-based creation of confidence when meeting new challenges. Barbalet's theory grasps this generative, dynamic nature of empowerment by understanding how self-confidence is not merely constituted by others' communicative recognition but is materially dependent on others providing access to relevant resources for action. In my analysis, the recognition given to the administrative employee was not by itself sufficient to give her confidence to take on the more demanding assignment; she needed to know she had access to support and information as well (Poder 2004).

This interactional perspective on agency thus suggests that becoming empowered is an ongoing process rather than an end state, as implied in the socio-structural focus on non-hierarchical organization. It also emphasizes the social interdependency of human beings. Individuals will always be dependent on others for the recognition and resources on which to build confidence, and each new task creates a new need for confidence. Organizational empowerment is sometimes understood as normative regulation exercised through organizationally endorsed values, beliefs and modes of sense-making (Ashforth/Mael 1998: 113). However, the interactional approach to empowerment indicates that it is not primarily to be understood as identification with particular corporate values, but as the continuous formation of agency in response to new challenges. The idealized list of actions that managers are urged to take vis-à-vis their employees illustrates how the development of confidence depends on specific forms of interaction.

This interactional framework thus identifies a significant function for managers in contributing to employees' confidence. But equally importantly, it resists exaggerating the manager's significance by emphasizing that employees can also energize one another by expressing recognition and granting others access to relevant resources for action, e.g. by sharing knowledge, information or work techniques. According to this framework everybody can add to others' self-confidence by expressing recognition or providing entry to relevant resources. In a previous study I showed that examples of such symmetrical generation of agency could be found in the different ways colleagues assisted and acknowledged each other during organizational restructuring (Poder 2004).

5   Discussion: Contributions and implications

In this section I will recapitulate the contribution made by this chapter and discuss two significant implications of my analysis of organizational empowerment from an interactional, emotion-oriented perspective. This interactional framework can be said to build further on the relational approach to empowerment (Spreitzer 2008: 58) by exploring confidence in particular as a significant social emotion that has hitherto been left unexamined in relational theory (e.g. Walsh et al. 1998; Fletcher 1998; 1999) and empowerment theory in general, as shown in this chapter.

In addition, two theoretical implications of the interactional framework deserve special attention. First, comprehending self-confidence sociologically also implies thinking about it in terms of power *over* resources. Embarking from Barbalet's emotionalized understanding of agency I argue that confidence, as a necessary constituent of agency, is in itself a power resource. Individuals who possess conventional power resources, such as knowledge, authority and money, are ineffective unless they also possess confidence. Emotionally generated agency is therefore a very fundamental power resource (Poder 2006). In terms of the notion of 'power games' over certain resources, the literature on empowerment often suggests that in empowering employees, and thus redistributing self-confidence as a power resource, both management and employees gain power: employees perform better, and the manager of the department thereby achieves better results and more time and energy to concentrate on other tasks. This assumption of a win-win situation suggests that empowerment takes us beyond the traditional zero-sum power game in which certain actors gain power at the expense of others. I agree that there is indeed a win-win component in so far as boosting the confidence of others is also likely to contribute to one's own self-confidence. Empowerment thus involves mutual influence and growth (Eylon 1998). In my view the generation of agency through positive emotions, such as confidence, that are so crucial to empowerment, is part of a generative game of renewable resources. However, I see this as a variable-sum rather than an infinite plus-sum game. This is because (a) personal sympathies and antipathies make it unlikely that a given individual is able to acknowledge all employees/colleagues equally and thus provide everyone with equal entry to action resources, and (b) the managers in charge of the distribution of various forms of corporate resources are crucial to the development of employees' confidence. It is up to them to decide which employees to encourage and trust and, on this basis, whom to invest in and devote most attention to.

A second important implication concerns the non-determining relationship between empowerment and non-hierarchical organization. The interactional framework explains the paradox that confidence/empowerment is not necessarily generated by delegating authority or reducing organizational hierarchy, since it is predicated on interactions that provide both recognition and access to relevant resources for action. In this sense confidence may be generated in both non-hierarchical *and* hierarchical organizations. The absence of hierarchy is *not* therefore an essential defining feature of empowerment. It is true that when an organization decentralizes and shares information to a higher degree than previously, employees get the chance to act more independently by gaining access to information that they can use in making decisions. But sharing information, e.g. by letting every member of a department participate in weekly departmental meetings, does not by itself ensure that employees will feel confident of acting independently. In other words, it is not certain that access to more information equals access to *relevant* information with respect to the tasks that the employee in question is meant to solve. More importantly, even in 'flat' organizations with a high degree of information-sharing, employees depend on others recognizing them *and* giving them access to resources in order to feel sufficient confidence to take on challenging tasks. This does not of course preclude the possibility that employees may be *more* dependent on others' help in a hierarchical organization with little sharing of information and knowledge. However, in hierarchical organizations employees and managers also have a choice as to whether or not to give one another acknowledgement (Abrahamson 2007). As far as confidence is concerned, the difference between hierarchical and non-hierarchical organization is therefore a matter of degree rather than of principle. Whether or not confidence is generated depends on whether or not the organizational interactions concerned provide recognition and access to relevant resources.

6 Conclusion

The theory developed in this chapter concerning the interactional and emotionally generative nature of self-confidence as an essential constituent of empowerment shows how particular interactions matter in making employees actually *feel* empowered, i.e. in helping give them the energy to act independently. The theory explains why empowerment is a continuous process by showing that confidence is an emotion that needs continuously to be produced and reproduced in empowerment contexts. From the interactional emotion-based perspective, the generation of self-confidence is seen as being inextricably bound up with power over the distribution of crucial resources for future action. It is only through this generative perspective that one can properly account for the success or otherwise of formal, structural empowerment initiatives in building self-confidence. Thus the interactional framework offers a solution to the paradox left unexplained by the socio-structural and psychological approaches. It articulates what is needed in social and emotional terms to generate the self-confident agency required to turn idealized empowerment programmes into real action. And it explains why and how it is possible to become energized by self-confidence without structural empowerment, but also why effective empowerment is impossible without employees being energized by the emotion of self-confidence.

I have critically assessed the limitations of the psychological perspective, which focuses on the individual's perception of him/herself in terms of self-efficacy: the active attitude towards one's work that makes one more predisposed to becoming an empowered employee. But adopting such an attitude is not the same as experiencing sufficient energy to be able to act more independently and creatively. I have also criticized the structural approach by showing that empowerment is not essentially defined by the adoption of a flat, non-hierarchical organizational format, and that even within formally empowered organizations the generation of confidence may be a matter of stratification. However, this is not to say that structural empowerment is futile. On the contrary, the more employees are given structural opportunities to share information/knowledge and participate in decision-making, the more likely they will be to have access to relevant resources which may help to generate self-confidence. But there is no guarantee that such positive emotions *will* be generated. That depends on how employees and managers act on such opportunities and interact together.

In sum, the chapter shows how particular kinds of social interaction produce positive emotions that generate agency, and why this is so crucial in understanding empowerment processes. The chapter thereby enhances our understanding of empowerment by elucidating how the generation of agency as an essential dimension of empowerment is dependent on particular forms of interaction. Any serious attempt to understand the processes of effective or non-effective empowerment thus requires an emotion-focused interactional approach to agency, in which the latter is seen as being much more dependent on social interactions than is the case in the predominant cognitive approach. In order to act on one's conscious deliberations and intentions one needs emotional energy, and such energy arises predominantly through interaction with others.

Notes

I am very thankful to both editors, Åsa Wettergren and Barbara Sieben, for their helpful comments in the process of working on this chapter.

1. It can be argued that if one *believes* one has access to relevant resources then one can feel confident. But if one only assumes rather than knows that one has access to resources relevant for realizing self-projections, one is more likely to experience a weaker degree of confidence.

2. See Poder (2004) for a more detailed analysis of the generation and managing of emotions during organizational restructuring in a big international company.

3. 'The empowering manager' was ideally expected to build self-confidence in the employees by providing information, help and coaching; encouraging ideas; listening and giving others credit. However, certain formulations of the managerial empowerment philosophy also assumed confidence as something latent, to be set free by changing hierarchical (authoritarian) structures and habits. Managers were told that if they trusted the employees more the 'incredible potential' of the latter would be set free. Consequently, the case data contain two (partially) contradictory ideas of empowerment: on the one hand, confidence is seen as an already pre-existing quality that simply needs to be liberated in some way, and on the other there is the idea that confidence has to be generated through interactions between manager and employee. As we have seen, the understanding of empowerment as a form of liberation process is commonly found in the empowerment literature in which a socio-structural approach is taken. However, according to the present emotion-oriented interactional theory this understanding is unproductive, since confidence is seen here as continuously produced and reproduced in a series of social interactions, rather than understood as a pre-existing, static quality that simply awaits liberation.

References

Abrahamson, B. (2007) *Hierarki – om ordning, makt och kristallisering*, Malmö: Liber.

Ashforth, B. and Mael, F. (1998) 'The power of resistance: sustaining valued identities', in R. Kramer and M. Neale (eds) *Power and Influence in Organizations*, London: Sage, 89–119.

Bandura, A. (1989) 'Human agency in social cognitive theory', *American Psychologist*, 44(9), 1175–84.

Barbalet, J. (1996) 'Social emotions: Confidence, trust and loyalty', *International Journal of Sociology and Social Policy*, 16(9/10), 75–96.

Barbalet, J. (1998) *Emotion, Social Theory, and Social Structure – A Macrosociological Approach*, Cambridge: Cambridge University Press.

Blanchard, K., Carlos, J. and Randolph, A. (1999) *The 3 Keys to Empowerment – Release the Power Within People for Astonishing Results*, San Francisco, CA: Berrett-Koehler.

Brooks, I. (2003) 'Systemic exchange: Responsibility of angst', *Organizational Studies*, 24(1), 125–41.

Campbell, C. (1999) 'Action as will-power', *The Sociological Review*, 47(1), 48–61.

Cameron, K., Dutton, J. and Quinn, R. (2003a) 'Foundations of positive organizational scholarship', in Cameron et al. (2003b), 3–13.

Cameron, K., Dutton, J. and Quinn, R. (eds) (2003b) *Positive Organizational Scholarship: Foundations of a New Discipline*, San Francisco: Berrett-Koehler.

Collins, R. (2004) *Interaction Ritual Chains*, Princeton University Press.

Collins, R. (2007) 'Reply to Erickson and Schwalbe', *Contemporary Sociology*, 36(3), 215–18.

Conger, J. and Kanungo, R. (1988) 'The empowerment process: Integrating theory and practice', *The Academy of Management Review*, 13(3), 471–82.

Dahl, P.N. (1999) 'Medarbejderinvolvering i ord og gerning – en kritisk diskursanalyse', *Dansk Sociologi*, 10(3), 47–67.

DuBrien, A. (2000) *Complete Idiot's Guide to Leadership*, Indianapolis: Alpha Books.

Dutton, J. and Baker, W. (2007) 'Enabling positive social capital in organizations', in Dutton/Ragins (2007), 325–45.

Dutton, J. and Heaphy, E. (2003) 'The power of high-quality connections', in Cameron et al. (2003b), 263–78.

Dutton, J. and Ragins, B. (eds) (2007) *Exploring Positive Relationships at Work – Building a Theoretical and Research Foundation*, New York: Lawrence Erlbaum Associates.

Edwards, P. and Wajcman, J. (2005) *The Politics of Working Life*, Oxford: Oxford University Press.

Eylon, D. (1998) 'Understanding empowerment and resolving its paradox – lessons from Mary Parker Follett', *Journal of Management History*, 4(1), 16–28.

Fletcher, J.K. (1998) 'Relational practice: A feminist reconstruction of work', *Journal of Management Inquiry*, 7, 163–86.

Fletcher, J.K. (1999) *Disappearing Acts – Gender, Power, and Relational Practice at Work*, Cambridge, MA: The MIT Press.

Fredrickson, B. (2001) 'The role of positive emotions in positive psychology: The broaden-and-build theory of positive emotions', *American Psychologist*, 56, 218–26.

Fredrickson, B. (2003) 'Positive emotions and upward spirals in organizational settings', in Cameron et al. (2003b), 163–75.

Fredrickson, B. and Branigan, C. (2005) 'Positive emotions broaden the scope of attention and thought-action repertoires', *Cognition and Emotion*, 19, 313–32.

Fuchs, S. (2007) 'Agency (and Intention)', in G. Ritzer (ed.) *Blackwell Encyclopedia of Sociology*, www.blackwellreference.com/public/tocnode?id=g9781405124331_chunk_g97814051243317_ss1–24 (accessed 7 December 2009).

George, J.M. (1995) 'Leader positive mood and group performance: the case of customer service', *Journal of Applied Social Psychology*, 25, 778–94.

Giddens, A. (1991) *Modernity and Self-Identity – Self and Society in the Late Modern Age*, Oxford: Polity Press.

Hatfield, E., Cacioppo, J. and Rapson, R. (1994) *Emotional Contagion*, Cambridge: Cambridge University Press.

Jacobsen, D. and Thorsvik, J. (2007) *Hvordan Organisationer Fungerer – Indføring i Organisation og Ledelse*, Copenhagen: Reitzels.

Layder, D. (2004) *Emotion in Social Life – The Lost Heart of Society*, London: Sage.

Mark, T. (1997) *Mastering People Management: Build a Successful Team: Motivate, Empower and Lead People*, London: Thorogood.

Parker, M. (2002) *Against Management*, Oxford: Polity Press.

Pepitone, J. (1998) *Motivating Employees*, Blacklick, OH: McGraw-Hill.

Poder, P. (2004) *Feelings of Power and the Power of Feelings: Handling Emotion in Organizational Change*, Ph.D. dissertation, Copenhagen University.

Poder, P. (2006) 'Ingen frihed uden magt, ingen magt uden emotionel energi', in M. Jacobsen and P. Poder (eds), *Om Bauman – kritiske essays*, København: Reitzels, 177–208.

Poder, P. (2008) 'The Sociology of Emotions – Managing, Exchanging and Generating Emotions in Everyday Life', in M. Jacobsen (ed.) *Sociologies of the Unnoticed*, London: Palgrave Macmillan, 299–352.

Potterfield, T. (1999) *Business of Employee Empowerment: Democracy and Ideology in the Workplace*, Westport, CT: Greenwood.

Quinn, R. (2000) *Change the World: How Ordinary People Can Achieve Extraordinary Results*, San Francisco: Jossey-Bass.

Quinn, R. (2007) 'Energizing others in work connections', in Dutton/Ragins (2007), 73–90.

Scott, C. and Jaffe, D. (1991) *Empowerment – Building a Committed Workforce*, Menlo Park, CA: Crisp Pubs.

Spreitzer, G.M. (2008) 'Taking Stock: A review of more than twenty years of research on empowerment at work', in C. Cooper and J. Barling (eds) *The Sage Handbook of Organizational Behavior – Volume 1 Micro Approaches*, London: Sage, 54–72.

Spreitzer, G. and Doneson, D. (2008) 'Musings on the past and future of employee empowerment', in T. Cummings (ed.) *Handbook of Organizational Development*, Thousand Oaks: Sage, 311–24.

Thomas, K. and Velthouse, B. (1990) 'Cognitive elements of empowerment´, *Academy of Management Review*, 15(4), 666–81.

Walsh, K., Bartunek, J. and Lacey, C. (1998) 'A relational approach to empowerment', in C. Cooper and D. Rousseau (eds) *Trends in Organizational Behavior*, New York: Wiley, 103–26.

Watson, D., Clark, L., McIntyre, C.W., and Hamaker, S. (1992) 'Affect, personality, and social activity', *Journal of Personality and Social Psychology*, 63, 1011–25.

Weber, M. (1991) 'Politics as Vocation', in H. Gerth and C.W. Mills (eds) *From Max Weber: Essays in Sociology*, London: Routledge, 77–128.

Wilson, F. (2004) *Organizational Behaviour and Work: A Critical Introduction*, 2nd edn, Oxford: Oxford University Press.

6
Negative Acts and Bullying: Face-Threatening Acts, Social Bonds and Social Place

Charlotte Bloch

1 Introduction

Modern working life is characterized by growing individualization and by increasing demands for flexibility. These trends nourish ambiguity about where we stand in relation to others and encourage individualized jockeying for position. In the last decades increased attention has been given to the question of bullying at the workplace (Adams 1992; Keashly 1998; Rainer 1998). So-called 'negative acts' constitute a central concept in this research. In the literature negative acts are defined as 'acts that are unwanted by the target that may be carried out deliberately or unconsciously, but clearly cause humiliation, offence and distress' (Einarsen 2003: 6). Such acts include common sense categories of social behaviour such as being laughed at, screamed at, ignored, threatened with sacking, maliciously teased, repeatedly criticized for one's work, subjected to excessive surveillance, etc. Individual negative acts as such do not necessarily constitute bullying. However, in quantitative approaches bullying is defined in terms of frequency and duration of exposure to negative acts.[1]

Research on bullying at the workplace has been dominated by quantitative approaches (Vartia 2001; Einarsen et al. 2003; Høgh 2005). Several scholars, however, emphasize the need for qualitative approaches to bullying as a dynamic relational phenomenon (Leymann 1996; Erikson 2001; Salin 2003; Thelin/Williamson 2004). Some studies also emphasize the importance of emotions in bullying as a process (Fors 1993; Gabriel 1998; Ahmed et al. 2001; Lindberg 2007).

The purpose of the present chapter is to explore why negative acts are so painful and why they may escalate into bullying. For that purpose I have conducted a qualitative analysis of negative acts with a focus on emotions and interactional processes. Negative acts at the workplace occur both on the horizontal level among equals and on the vertical level among superiors and subordinates. The present study is limited to negative acts among colleagues.

2   Materials and methods

The empirical study was based on a subgroup selected from a larger group of 40 employees who had reported experiences of bullying either as bystander, as victim or as perpetrator.[2] All 40 employees were asked to reconstruct episodes that they construed as bullying. They were asked about their emotional experiences, emotion management and experience of relationships in terms of power, status and popularity. The interviews were conducted according to phenomenological principles of interviewing and were all transcribed. Within this group of 40 employees a subgroup was selected according to the following criteria: (1) that the interviewee defined her/himself as a victim of bullying and (2) that the interview contained concrete and detailed descriptions of their experiences. Nine interviews were selected on this basis. Eight of them referred to bullying among colleagues, while only one concerned the bullying of a subordinate by a superior. In view of this imbalance I decided to focus exclusively on bullying among equals, i.e. colleagues. The selected subgroup comprised five women and three men aged between 30 and 50, all of whom were occupied partly in routine work and partly in vocational trained work. A screening of the eight selected interviews yielded 85 descriptions of episodes that the interviewees interpreted as negative acts. These were then subjected to a phenomenological analysis. The first step was to condense the interviewees' descriptions of individual negative episodes. Next I sought to explicate the experience and meanings embedded in these descriptions. Finally I tried to interpret the explicated descriptions from the perspective of theories about interaction and emotions, specifically Goffman's theory of face-threatening acts, Scheff's theory of emotions and social bonds and Clark's theory of emotions and social place.

The results of the analysis are presented in two parts. First, I present my interpretation and categorization of negative acts as face-threatening acts. This analysis draws in particular on Goffman's concepts. Second, I present my interpretation of emotional and social processes embedded in the different types of face-threatening acts. This analysis draws in particular on Scheff's and Clark's theories. In my presentation of the results I introduce each part of the analysis with a brief account of the theoretical concepts applied, then proceed to present the empirical results. We will begin by looking at negative acts in terms of face-threatening behaviour.

3 Negative acts as face-threatening interactions

According to Goffman (1967) we always interact within a social order, showing our respect for that order by following shared rules of conduct. In this interaction we also present our social self, or as Goffman puts it 'our face'. Our face refers to the valued image of self that we want to present to others. By presenting it, we expect certain responses from others and hope to have our interpretation and evaluation of self confirmed. Thus, according to Goffman, social interaction always involves the communication either of deference to and respect for, or of disrespect for the face of the other person. The individual's face is a sacred object to which she/he is profoundly attached, and as such it is a prime target for others. Others may seek not only to wound the individual's face unofficially, but even officially to destroy his/her face completely. Face-threatening acts arouse embarrassment not only in the victim but also among other participants. Such acts disrupt the smooth flow of interaction and the current social order and call for face-saving practices.

Elaborating on Goffman's theory of face-threatening acts, Brown and Levinson (1987) distinguish between threats towards aspects of the other's face and threats towards the other's face as such. They also distinguish between face-threatening acts 'on the record' and 'off the record'. 'On the record' acts are those in which the actor's intention is clear and unambiguous. Face-threatening acts 'off the record' are acts in which the actor's intention is ambiguous or hidden, as may happen for instance in gossiping or joking. In addition, some face-threatening acts are accompanied by redressive measures intended to counteract potential face damage through different strategies of politeness such as offering a little smile, providing a legitimizing explanation, etc. Other acts exclude this possibility of maintaining or restoring face.

The interviewees described a variety of acts that may be interpreted as face-threatening in the light of Goffman's theory . Inspired by Goffman's theory and by Brown's and Levinson's elaborations I have interpreted and categorized these acts according to (1) the ways in which the person's face is contested and (2) whether or not the act

Table 6.1 Main categories of face-threatening acts

Face-threatening acts	Examples in interviews	Number in the empirical material
Strong on-the-record rejection of the other's face without redressive acts.	Uncontrolled scolding, shouting and yelling; slamming the door in the other's face; strong and highly insulting accusations such as 'you are a liar', 'you are a thief', etc.	6
On-the-record denial of the other's face	Ignoring the other, not seeing the other, not replying to the other, not greeting the other, etc.	23
Contesting aspects of the other's face.	Discreet, subtle acts designed to induce insecurity in the other through correction, criticism, questioning, emphasizing obligations, etc.	44
Off-the-record derogatory construction of the other's face.	Negative gossip, slander and rumour.	11
On-the-record ambiguous construction of the other's face.	Humour, teasing, nick-names	1

leaves any opportunity for face-saving practices. On the basis of these criteria the 85 descriptions of negative acts have been reduced to five main categories. I present these categories in Table 6.1 above and now elaborate briefly on each.

Strong, on-the-record rejection of the other's face refers to the unrestrained expression of strong emotions, or highly offensive accusations, that show that the perpetrator does not care at all about the other's face. In the column 'Examples from interviews' various examples are presented. The extreme nature of this threat may make it difficult or impossible to mobilize face-saving responses. However, loss of emotional control is a norm-transgressing form of behaviour, and as such may also constitute a threat to the face of the perpetrator him/herself.

On-the-record denial of the other's face refers to acts such as overlooking, ignoring, not responding to or not greeting the other. As fundamentally socially responsive creatures, human beings follow shared codes of ritual conduct in social interactions, such as smiling, looking at people, maintaining an appropriate distance and greeting one another, by which we express mutual recognition and respect. When we deny another's face we suspend these rules of conduct, i.e. the social self of the other person is erased. This kind of face-threatening act differs from the strong rejection of the other in the sense that, in the case of denial, the interactional relationship is completely suspended. The denial is not accompanied by any redressive act, and no face-saving responses are available to the victim in relation to the offender. Denial of the other's face therefore represents a serious breach of the rules of social conduct.

Contesting aspects of the other's face refers to subtle ways of downgrading another person by contesting *aspects* of face such as specific behaviour, performance, expressed feelings, etc. By questioning or correcting a person, or by emphasizing obligations, we may induce feelings of inferiority and uncertainty in him or her. These feelings also indicate a sense of subtle downgrading within the micro social hierarchies of everyday life. Through such acts an offender may in subtle ways try to enhance his/her face at the expense of those of others. As seen in Table 6.1, the majority of the episodes described were instances of this type of face-threatening behaviour.

Off-the-record degrading and derogatory construction of the other's face refers to negative gossip, slander and rumour. Gossip is here defined as informal evaluative talk about someone who is not present (Eder/ Enke 1991). The literature emphasizes the positive as well as the negative aspects of gossip (Ben Ze'ev 2000). However, it is important to note that gossip may concern information that the target considers private and intimate, that in gossip the target is not present and able to defend her/himself and that through gossip the target may become subject to a process of 'othering'.[3] The accounts of gossip in this study all referred to acts that the target interpreted as negative or degrading constructions of his/her face. As gossip takes place behind the back of the target, she/ he may sense the gossip but is neither able to prove it nor to confront it. Thus she/he is denied the possibility of face-saving responses. Several of the interviewees talked about gossip at their workplaces. Some of them described how they had become accidentally aware of existing gossip about themselves. Other interviewees talked about gossip and slander as a prevailing feature of the culture of the workplace.[4]

On-the-record ambiguous construction of the other's face refers to acts such as irony, humour, teasing, nick-naming, etc. that by being ambiguous offer the target some opportunity for face-saving interpretation (Brown/ Levinson 1987: 69). Humour and teasing run along a continuum that extends from bonding to 'nipping' and 'biting' (Boxer/Cortes-Conde 1997: 279). However, what the audience may interpret as a joke the target may interpret as an attack or insult (Alexander 1986; Keltner et al. 1998; Agewall 2007). In my study the interviewees did not mention any episodes in which they saw themselves as the targets of humour or teasing.[5] However, there was one description of an episode that, from my perspective as a researcher, might be interpreted as an instance of humour but which the interviewee defined exclusively as a negative act. Interviewees also mentioned episodes in which they witnessed forms of teasing such as mocking imitations of the target's gestures or giving him/her a derogatory nick-name.

Goffman's theory explains why negative acts, understood in terms of face-threatening behaviour, may be so disturbing. Face-threatening acts not only contest our faces as sacred objects and arouse embarrassment and pain but may also contest the social order. As we saw above, the challenge to another person's face may either be directed at his/her entire social self, or it may be less radical, targeting only aspects of that person's face. Furthermore the different categories leave varying degrees of space for face-saving practices. In the case of 'on-the-record denial of the other's face', for example, the scope for restoring face is very limited because the very rules of social interaction as such are suspended. Similarly, in the case of 'off-the-record negative construction of the other's face', such as gossip or slander, there is limited scope for acts of restoration because the victim is excluded from the community of gossipers. Thus with the use of Goffman's theory and Brown and Levinson's distinctions we may conclude that certain types of face-threatening acts may be more damaging and disturbing to the victim than others. But Goffman focuses only on situated behaviour, on role expectations and the interaction order. He does not explore the actual experiences of the participants or look at what face-threatening acts mean to the ongoing interaction and social relationships. In order to explore these processes I will now draw on Scheff's theory of social bonds and Clark's theory of social place.

4 Face-threatening acts in terms of social bonds and social place

Scheff and Clark both emphasize the interplay between emotions and social interaction. Whereas Goffman focuses on embarrassment in connection with face-threatening acts, Scheff and Clark expand the emotional perspective to include shame, pride, anger and grief as well. Moreover, whereas Goffman concentrates solely on a person's behaviour at a given moment, Scheff emphasizes actors as individuals with personal biographies. Following this perspective we can say that the interactions and emotions of the moment are connected to and influenced by the individual's past experiences and in turn shape his/her future interactions.

The emotion of shame has a crucial place in Scheff's theory (1990; 1994; 2007). Shame refers to feelings of being rejected and includes a broad family of related emotions such as embarrassment, humiliation, guilt and uncertainty. Shame is a 'master emotion' that regulates social behaviour by warning us when our social bonds are under threat.[6] Thus shame may be used in a constructive way as a signal that a given relationship is problematic. However, as shame is not only painful but is also a stigmatized feeling in our culture, we try to suppress or ignore it. This unacknowledged shame generates recursive spirals of feeling, such as shame-shame spirals and shame-anger spirals, in which shame is suppressed and replaced by anger. These unacknowledged spirals of feeling may run as compulsive and recursive processes within an individual and between individuals, laying the ground for perpetually damaged social bonds.

Scheff distinguishes between secure social bonds, in which the individuals experience 'attunement', and damaged social bonds, in which they experience 'engulfment' and 'isolation'. In *attunement* the actors attend both to their own self and voice and to the other's self and voice, i.e. there is a balance between nearness and distance to self and the other. In *engulfment* the actor merges with the other, conforming to the other's view and emotions at the expense of his/her own self, i.e. there is too little distance to the other. In *isolation* the actor suppresses the other's self, ignoring the other's emotions and viewpoint in favour of his/her own voice. Not listening to the other, the actor hears only her/his own voice, i.e. there is too great a distance to the other. Compulsive and recurrent spirals of feelings are the unacknowledged fuel for damaged social bonds and for protracted conflicts in which the participants are mutually alienated from each other's views and emotions. Thus face-threatening acts of the moment may arouse social-emotional processes with far-reaching consequences for future interaction between the actors.

Emotions fuel our social bonds but also work as indicators of our social place within informal social structures. Clark (1990; 2004) uses the term 'social place' to refer to our position within the informal micro-hierarchies of everyday life. Social place is to the level of everyday life what formal position is to the organizational level or social status is to the societal level. However, whereas social position/social status refers to socially recognized and stable rights at the macro-structural level, social place is much more fluid, situated and subject to ongoing negoti-ation. Our social place becomes available to us through self- and other targeted feelings, such as humiliation, uncertainty, awe, pride, etc. These feelings form part of our situated selves, i.e. our feeling of the moment and our momentary consciousness of who we are and how we can act in the present. Because our social place becomes available through feelings we may impinge on others' emotions in order to gain social place. By showing exaggerated patience, for example, we may arouse feelings of humiliation in the targeted person and thereby a sense on his/her part that she/he has lost social place within the micro-hierarchy of every-day life. Thus, according to Clark, emotions convey information about where we stand in the informal social ranking system. But what does social place give access to within the micro-hierarchies of everyday life? According to Clark, it confers interactional rights, such as the right to interrupt others, arrive too late and be listened to; in other words social place confers discursive power and/or the right to define social reality.

Scheff's and Clark's theories offer theoretical tools to explore what face-threatening acts do to social relationships and why these may escalate into bullying.

In the analysis, the 85 descriptions of negative acts have been inter-preted from the perspective of these theories. The interpretation of emotions is based on a coding system developed by Retzinger (1990) and Scheff (1990; 1994) for verbal and non-verbal markers of emotions in discourse.[7] Furthermore, I was inspired by Kövecses' (2000) analysis of metaphors of emotions. The interpretation of social bonds and social place is based on an interpretation of the emotions, meanings and experiences expressed in the interviews. The interpretation of recurrent spirals of feelings requires a temporal perspective. Since this was absent from the present study, my interpretation of these spirals is based on the presence of the shame-anger-resentment compound.

A full presentation of the analysis of the 85 descriptions requires much more space than this chapter permits. However, to illustrate the analysis I have selected one example from each of the five main categor-ies of face-threatening act. These examples are presented below.

I will introduce each example with an excerpt from the interview in question, then proceed to the analysis. The emotional colouring of the interviewee's voice at various points is indicated by square brackets and followed by a closer description in parentheses. Capital letters represent particularly strong emphasis. 'I' in the excerpts re-presents the interviewer while the interviewee is represented by the abbreviation 'IP'.

4.1 Scolding

Here we will look at an example of 'strong on-the-record rejection without redressive acts'.

The following episode occurred in the context of recurrent conflicts between a senior and a junior laboratory technician. The particular conflict reported here concerned procedures relating to the removal of chemical substances from the storeroom, some of which had been ordered for use in student exercises. The interviewee reported the following:

IP: But she could go completely mad if I went in and took a chemical which was to be used for the exercises. And then I tried to explain to her that 'I'm taking this now, because I need it now, but I have ordered a new consignment that will be put on the shelf for chemicals used for the exercises and it will come', but no, [she raised the roof] (condensed talk) and I got a tremendous telling-off.

I: What did this telling-off consist of?

IP: ['YOU are not allowed to take this and it is ME who decides ... who do you think you are? That's paid by a different account and you MUST not touch this.] (loud and sneering voice). I was standing there, 'but, but, but it's just – I have ordered a new one and it's coming', but ['You MUST NOT touch it] (shouting) and ['you have to wait until you get your own chemicals'] (screaming voice) and it was my professor who had told me to go and take it. And I tried to explain this to her, but it's the professor who said ... ['NO, but you MUST NOT'] (shouting). It was really over the top.
And I was standing there; I was on the verge of tears. It happened many times. It really did. In various situations ...

I: Did you get frightened?

IP: Yes I did, frightened and insecure. Very frightened and very insecure – what should I do.

The excerpt indicates that the interviewee experienced her colleague as being emotionally out of control. As far as her own feelings are concerned, the term 'frightened' may be a general term for fear but it may also refer to a feeling of alarm/surprise at her colleague's violent reaction. From Scheff's perspective, the terms 'insecure' and 'on the verge of tears' could be interpreted as verbal markers of unacknowledged shame. The interviewee does not mention feelings of anger and resentment. Her use of a derogatory metaphor for the behaviour of the colleague and her sneering and shouting when imitating the way she talked may be interpreted as anger or resentment toward the colleague. In terms of the social bond, the excerpt shows how the interviewee and the colleague were alienated from one another in the sense that neither of them listens to, hears or considers the other's argument. The interviewee needs to borrow chemicals from among those reserved for student exercises and she proposes ordering a new consignment to replace them. The colleague, however, focuses on the fact that the chemicals are bought, stored and registered for student purposes so that removing them for a different purpose may lead to confusion. The combination of shame, anger and resentment, together with the participants' apparent alienation from each other's voices, may indicate the type of damaged social bond that Scheff refers to as 'isolation', which involves recurring cycles of shame and anger. This fits with other parts of the interview where the interviewee describes recurrent conflicts with the same colleague concerning various procedures. In these conflicts it was not only the colleague who got emotionally out of hand; the interviewee also described her own fury and loss of control.

Since the act of scolding shows no care for the other's face or social place, the interviewee may have experienced the episode as a humiliation and as a challenge to her social place. But fierce scolding is also a serious violation of social norms of behaviour. Thus the scolding in this case may also be interpreted as an episode in which the perpetrator herself loses face. No redressive acts accompany such fierce rejection of the other's face. The interviewee instead chose to withdraw from the situation and engage in emotional work such as categorizing the colleague as crazy and seeking support for this interpretation among other colleagues. By these means she sought to protect both her face and her social place. Other interviewees who had experienced this type of face-threatening act similarly responded either by withdrawing or by engaging in direct confrontation.

4.2   Ignoring

Ignoring is about 'denial of the other's face'. In this example, the interviewee had been employed for a couple of months. Suddenly she started feeling that certain colleagues refused to respond to her:

> IP: Suddenly one of the newcomers was against me, and I had no idea why, and the newcomer and X wouldn't look me in the eye, and when I asked X about something when we were working together just the two of us, or when there were only a couple

of people around, then suddenly she wouldn't answer me, even though I called her by name when I asked her about something. I mean, there's perhaps five metres between us. Why is she suddenly not answering? Is it bad hearing or is there something wrong with me, you know.

I: How did you feel about that?

IP: It was unpleasant, but then I asked her directly, I addressed her directly and I said: 'X, are you angry with me, or do you have something against me?' or whatever. ['No, no, why?'] (sweet, making a face – laughter) – then she's just like – oh – behaving like she's totally innocent, and for sure she's not. So then I said: 'I just find it odd that you don't answer me when I talk to you, and I've approached you directly three times today by name, and you don't respond.' But that behaviour took place from October until just before Christmas.

I: Where she ... ?

IP: Turned the cold shoulder on me.

The excerpt shows how the interviewee becomes confused about what is happening and why her colleague is ignoring her. She uses the term 'unpleasant' to describe her feelings – a verbal marker of unacknowledged shame. Later in the interview she also says that she had a feeling of being 'surrounded by cold air'. The metaphor of 'cold air' refers to feelings of rejection. She denies feeling angry at the perpetrator, but the sneering voice when imitating her and the statement that the perpetrator is 'for sure' not 'totally innocent' indicates resentment. In terms of the social bond between the two, the excerpt points to isolation. The interviewee shows her willingness to understand by asking the colleague for an explanation, but the latter insists that there is nothing to be explained. This answer contradicts the interviewee's own experiences and alienates her from the perpetrator's feelings or point of view. Shame may be turned inwards as grief and sadness or it may be turned outwards as anger and hate. In this case, the interviewee reported feeling sadness and lost motivation during the period in which these negative events took place. Other interviewees subjected to denial of their faces instead emphasized feelings of anger, hate and resentment towards the perpetrator. Several also described feelings of distrust, particularly towards the perpetrators.

The denial of the other's face in terms of non-greeting or ignoring the other may occur accidentally, but if it is intentional and continuous it may be experienced as a very offensive attack on the victim's social self.

It implies that the social bond has been voluntarily cut: in other words, the victim has been symbolically excluded from the community. As a consequence she/he is deprived of the interactional right to be heard and thereby also to defend her/himself. 'Denial of face' is therefore more severe than simply downgrading the other in the micro-hierarchy of everyday life. It is an act that transcends the realm of face-saving and may give rise to strong negative feelings towards the perpetrator. In this particular case the interviewee was subjected to denial of her social self for a relatively limited period (a few months). However, among all the interviewees who reported being subjected to denial, the experience was associated with long-term feelings of resentment and distrust.

4.3   Challenging professional identity and feelings of pride

The type of face-threatening that I call 'contesting aspects of the other's face' was the one most commonly reported. In this case a recently employed laboratory technician was being instructed by a senior colleague. She reported:

> When we were doing exercises with the students, if I took a pipette then my colleague would say 'when you are going to do... [THEN YOU HAVE TO DO IT IN THIS WAY' and 'Now I will show you how to make a 1 to 4 solution, right?'] (loud and sneering voice) I'm an educated laboratory technician and I've worked as a technician for three years. It's part of the education to know and to have a constant overview of what you're doing with your solutions and what you're writing down. So I thought to myself: she's not an educated technician herself.

This excerpt clearly indicates that the interviewee found the very detailed instruction professionally humiliating. According to Scheff, feelings of humiliation are part of the shame family. The interviewee does not mention anger, but the loud sneering voice when imitating the colleague and the presentation of her as an abusive order-giver '*YOU HAVE TO*...' signals anger. The statement about the colleague's lack of education may also be interpreted as a hostile attempt to bring her down a notch. Thus there is a mixture of shame and anger. In terms of the social bond it is difficult to judge whether the colleague intended to humiliate the interviewee or whether the interviewee misinterpreted her attempt to offer optimal, detailed instructions to a new employee. Nevertheless the participants were mutually alienated from each other's voices, i.e. the social bond was one of mutual isolation. At the workplace, professional authority and success are valued aspects of face through which the employee may gain social place. In the example the interviewee experienced a downgrading of her professional qualifications, leading to a loss of social place. Face-threatening acts within the category of 'contesting aspects of the other's face' are often subtle and part of the everyday negotiation of social place; sometimes the victim is hardly conscious of what is going on. In the example the interviewee defends her social place by cognitive emotional work, expressed in her statement about the perpetrator 'she is not an educated technician herself'.

4.4 Negative gossip

Negative gossip is an example of 'off-the-record derogatory construction of the other's face'.

In the following excerpt an interviewee describes two instances of disclosure of gossip about intimate aspects of her life:

> *IP*: They make personal remarks, but always indirectly. [I always find out about it indirectly] (tearful voice). They don't say it directly to me. [But there was a situation where somebody suddenly says to me ... for some time I suffered from intestinal wind because I had stomach trouble. Then suddenly somebody came and told me that I shouldn't be unhappy about that, because it's a side effect when you have that kind of thing] (low voice, inaudible, sigh) [And this person shouldn't normally know anything about it, you see. That kind of thing. All the time ...] (Loud intense voice)
>
> *I*: When you had the feeling that they had been talking about you ...
>
> *IP*: Yes, talking, right. [For some time] (soft voice) I like mackerel, so I brought mackerel for my lunch. And one morning we were sitting at the lunch table and suddenly someone started talking about food, and someone said: ['Now let's keep quiet about this] (loud voice). We have to agree that we don't criticize other people's food.' Somebody said: ['Yes, there is some mackerel that always stinks'.] (loud distorted voice) – ALL THE TIME. It wasn't even something that was addressed to me directly, because then you could say that NOW you're going too far. But I don't get the chance to do that. It has been really bad. And it has been much worse than now. Now I have the impression that the 'VIPs' [researchers] have started to do something about the problem, not saying anything directly, but doing something indirectly.

In both episodes reported in this excerpt the topic of the gossip is smell, in one case the interviewee's bodily smell and in the other the smell of her food. Smells belong to the realm of intimate life and according to Pelzer (2005) violation of the boundaries of smell may arouse disgust towards the person who smells.

Regarding the first episode the interviewee describes how she became aware of the gossip because a colleague suddenly showed concern about her stomach problem. The interviewee focuses not on the colleague's concern but rather on the fact that she/he revealed knowledge about her intimate life. No emotions are mentioned, but her first tearful then almost inaudible voice and the sighs when she describes her gas problem may indicate feelings of shame and sadness. Her loud excited voice in the last sentence may be interpreted as a marker of anger or resentment. In the second episode the interviewee became aware of gossip about the smelly mackerel she eats. The colleagues do not explicitly address her eating of mackerel, but one of them makes a general statement that mackerel stinks. This passage also illustrates cultural norms concerning legitimate topics of gossip, for instance: 'we have to agree that we don't criticize other people's food.' In response the interviewee expresses feelings of helplessness and powerlessness; she is deprived of any possibility to defend herself because the gossip takes place behind her back. Her loud, shouting and distorted voice when quoting the gossipers may be interpreted as a marker of anger and resentment.

Gossip ranges from small talk to severe accusations, ridicule and 'othering' of the absent target. Negative gossip is a face-threatening derogatory construction of the target's face, and one of its distinctive features is that the construction of negative face lies outside the reach of the victim. In line with this, all the interviewees who reported being subjected to gossip expressed feelings towards their colleagues not only of shame and anger but of distrust, suspicion, uncertainty and apprehension of betrayal. As the interviewees were unable to control the gossip they tried instead to censor, hide and control access to any kind of information that revealed aspects of their private and intimate selves. As another interviewee put it: 'everything can be used against you'.

Gossip may contribute to group formation at the expense of othering an absent third person. In so far as gossip transgresses shared moral rules, it may arouse feelings of shame and guilt in the gossipers.[8] These emotions may be managed through 'engulfment' in the group and 'isolation' towards the target of the gossip. The victim, however, is ostracized from the gossiping community. In Clark's terms the targeted person has no place within the group; she/he is structurally excluded, which means that the person in question is deprived of interactional rights to define social reality. Disclosure of negative gossip arouses very strong feelings of betrayal. One of the interviewees said: 'I can try to forgive, but I will never forget.'

4.5 Humour

The category 'ambiguous construction of the other's face' may be expressed in humour.

In my data the interviewees made no mention of episodes in which they saw themselves as targets of humour. They did, however, mention episodes that from my perspective as a researcher could be interpreted as instances of humour, but which the interviewees defined exclusively as face-threatening acts.

The following is an example of humour that the interviewee/target interprets as a violation. The interviewee is employed in the airport business and at the time of interview she had recently been transferred from one department to another, i.e. she had just started work in a new department. She works with her colleagues in an open-plan office with a counter for customers. She reports:

And then I was sitting and typing in the data on a plane and at the same time one of my former colleagues from the transit department was sitting opposite me at a table and typing something, and then he asks me about something new that we had just introduced before I changed departments, and he asks me about how we do this. And then I go and help him, and I say, then you just have to do this and this, and then someone from my new department says: ['Don't you think we'll soon have to charge warehouse rent for that Thai plane you're dealing with?'] (distorted loud voice), because [she thought that I spent too much time on it] (inaudible/condensed). And we shouldn't be nice and help each other. And I just can't accept that kind of stuff.

Immediately I felt that I was being watched, which I didn't expect and it wasn't at all what I'd come from, you see, where we were a full department helping each other a lot. So at first I felt that I was kept under surveillance, and I thought: What is this about? And then I felt that [it was patronizing] (low voice), I mean, like I didn't do my work, and I did. I mean, I think it was humiliating that she had to say it <u>out loud</u> in the department, too. First, there are eight-ten of us sitting there, and she shouldn't have started shouting at me, <u>not at all</u>, I mean, [she said it very loud] (rapid speech) anyhow. And there are customers at the counter and stuff, so I [just think it was improper] (inaudible/condensed).

The crucial sentence in this excerpt is 'Don't you think we'll soon have to charge warehouse rent for that Thai plane you're dealing with?'. This may be interpreted as humour that bites a little. However, the interviewee interprets the message solely as an attack on her work performance. She describes how she felt that she was being watched, and how she felt patronized and humiliated. The almost inaudible voice may be interpreted as a marker of shame whereas the distorted voice when she quotes the perpetrator may be interpreted as an indicator of resentment. The perpetrator communicates a cultural norm about 'attending to your [own] work' in a sarcastic way while the interviewee interprets the message as a violation of her autonomy and an attack on the moral norm of helpfulness. Thus emotionally and cognitively the bond is characterized by mutual 'isolation'. The interviewee in this example remains silent, not being familiar with the speech style of her present workplace. Thus the perpetrator gains social place in so far as she has been able to 'bite' the victim within the normal flow of conversational moves (Collins 2004: 21). The victim feels publicly humiliated, which implies a loss of social place.

4.6   What do face-threatening acts do to social bonds and social place?

Above I have illustrated through concrete examples what different types of face-threatening acts may do to the social bonds and social place of the people subjected to them.

The results of the analysis of the 85 descriptions of negative acts are summarized in Table 6.2 below.

Table 6.2 shows that a mixture of shame and anger, as well as damaged social bonds leading to a sense of isolation, are associated with all types of face-threatening acts. Following Scheff, this shame-anger compound may indicate recurrent shame-anger spirals, which, coupled with isolation, indicate a mechanism through which negative acts may escalate. The analysis of emotions further shows that some face-threatening acts have a stronger potential for exclusion than others. 'Denial of the other's face' and 'derogatory constructions of the other's face' not only give rise to unacknowledged shame and anger but also to a fundamental loss of trust, which equates to loss of the emotional basis for cooperation. By losing trust the person loses faith in both him/herself and others. Feelings of lost trust were connected to face-threatening

Table 6.2 The effect of face-threatening acts on social bonds and social place

Face-threatening act	Emotions	Social bonds	Social place
Strong on-the record rejection of face without redressive acts (e.g. scolding)	Fear, insecurity, helplessness, anger, resentment	'Isolation'	(Fierce, uncontrolled acts are norm-transgressing, which is why the perpetrator, according to the interviewees, most often loses social place.)
On-the-record denial of face (e.g. ostracism)	Unpleasantness, grief, sadness, insecurity, resentment, coolness, distrust	'Isolation'	Social exclusion of social self
Contesting aspects of face	Humiliation, resentment, revenge, shame, being attacked	'Isolation'	Downgrading of situated self
Off-the-record derogatory construction of face (e.g. slander, gossip)	Powerlessness, defencelessness, grief, anger, rage, distrust	'Isolation'	Social exclusion of social self
On-the-record ambiguous construction of face (e.g. humour, nick-naming, teasing)	Humiliation, anger, resentment	'Isolation'	Downgrading of situated self

acts that not only downgraded the person within the micro-hierarchies of the workplace, but in fact expelled him/her from the community and deprived him/her of interactional rights, including the discursive power to define social reality. Thus Clark's theory of social place also highlights the micro-political struggles that may contribute to the escalation of conflict and exclusion.

5 Summary

The questions that the present study seeks to answer are: why are negative acts so painful, and why and how do negative acts escalate into bullying? In the present chapter I have presented an exploratory study of negative acts among colleagues in the workplace. First, drawing on Goffman's theory, I have interpreted negative acts as various types of face-threatening act. Goffman's theory explains why negative acts create such disturbance. However, the analysis also showed how the various face-threatening acts work through posing differing kinds of threats to the face, and leaving different degrees of scope for face-restoring practices. In the analysis, the negative acts were reduced to five main categories. It was also suggested that two of the five types of face-threatening acts identified in my data, namely 'on-the-record denial of the other's face' and 'off-the-record derogatory construction of the other's face', can be seen as particularly damaging and difficult to redress. Goffman understands face-threatening acts as disturbances to the social order. Thus Goffman's theory also explains why negative acts not only hurt and traumatize the victim but also affect and stress other members of the workplace.

Second, in order to explore how negative acts affect social bonds and social place, I drew on Scheff's and Clark's theories to analyse the five types of face-threatening act. The analysis revealed a mixture of shame, anger and resentment; damaged social bonds in terms of 'isolation'; contested or lost social place and sometimes lost interactional rights. All these processes may contribute to the escalation of conflict into bullying. The analysis also showed that, as well as contributing to the shame-anger compound, the types of negative acts mentioned above – namely 'on-the-record denial of the other's face' and 'off-the-record derogatory construction of the other's face' – also led to loss of trust, which is a basic condition for cooperation. These negative acts were also connected to social processes of exclusion from the community. Thus this second part of the analysis qualifies and elaborates on what was indicated in the first part.

The present study has its shortcomings. It is based on limited empirical material. The focus is more on the structure of experiences than on their development. Thus a temporal perspective is needed in order to provide full empirical evidence for recurrent spirals of feeling. As far as future perspectives are concerned, further systematic research is needed into the emotional and interactional dynamic of negative acts among colleagues, and among superiors and subordinates. From an interactional perspective bullying is to be interpreted as a process in which not only the victim but also bystanders and perpetrators are participants. Future research should include studies of how the other participants, including bystanders and perpetrators, contribute to the escalation of negative acts into bullying.

Notes

I am indebted to the Danish Working Environment Research Fund for their support of the present study. I am also indebted to Thomas Scheff and to my colleagues from NFA for comments on the first draft of this chapter.

1. In quantitative research, bullying is measured by an inventory consisting of negative acts. The most widely used inventory was constructed by Einarsen (2003).
2. The study was conducted as part of a larger investigation of bullying in Danish workplaces (Høgh et al. 2009), which included a quantitative study of the psychosocial work environment and bullying in 20 organizations. On the basis of employees' responses to questions concerning daily, weekly or monthly experiences of bullying, 40 employees at four different workplaces were selected and invited to participate in a qualitative interview.
3. 'Othering' refers to gossip in which the identity of the gossipee is rendered uncertain and ambiguous in relation to social categories (Jaworsky/Coupland 2005: 670).
4. Rumour and slander are related concepts to gossip. However, gossip may be unsubstantiated because very often it takes place behind the scenes. In rumour, however, spreading the unsubstantiated is an intentional goal-directed activity (Ben-Ze'ev 2000). Tallbut (1983: 164) defines slander as false and intentionally published or communicated claims/assertions.
5. For a presentation of the more subtle differences between teasing, humour, and nick-naming, see Boxer/Cortes-Conde (1997), Keltner et al. (1998) and Agewall (2007).
6. As a master emotion, shame interferes with our experience and handling of other emotions as well such as anger, grief, fear and even shame itself (Scheff 1994: 54).
7. See the coding system in Scheff (1994: 151ff.), as well as Bloch (1996).
8. Derogatory gossip is a norm-transgressing activity, which is why it may also threaten the face of the gossipers (Jakowsky/Coupland 2005: 689).

References

Adams, A. (1992) *Bullying at Work. How to Confront and Overcome It*, London: Virago.
Agewall, O. (2007) 'Mobbning, interaction och meningsproduktion. Lokale kulturer, individuella trakasserier och kategoriell uteslutning', in Carleheden et al. (2007), 164–89.
Ahmed, E., Harris, N., Braithwaite, J. and Braithwaite, V. (2001) *Shame Management Through Reintegration*, Cambridge: Cambridge University Press.
Alexander, R.D. (1986) 'Ostracism and indirect reciprocity: The reproductive significance of humour', *Ethnology and Sociobiology*, 7, 253–70.
Ben-Ze'ev, A. (2000) *The Subtlety of Emotions*, Cambridge, MA: MIT.
Bloch, C. (1996) 'Emotions and Discourse', *Text*, 16(3), 323–43.
Boxer, D. and Cortes-Conde, F. (1997) 'From bonding to biting: Conversational joking and identity display', *Journal of Pragmatics*, 27, 275–94.

Brown, P. and Levinson, S.C. (1987) *Politeness. Some Universals in Language Usage*, Cambridge: Cambridge University Press.

Carleheden, M., Lindskog, R. and Roman, C. (eds) (2007) *Social interaction: förutsättninger och former*, Stockholm: Liber.

Clark, C. (1990) 'Emotions and micropolitics in everyday life: Some patterns and paradoxes of "place"', in T.D. Kemper (ed.) (1990) *Research Agendas in the Sociology of Emotions*, Albany: State University of New York Press, 305–33.

Clark, C. (2004) 'Emotional gifts and "you first" micropolitics: Niceness in the socioemotional economy', in A.S.R. Manstead, N. Frijda and A. Fischer (eds) *Feelings and Emotions*, Cambridge: Cambridge University Press, 402–21.

Eder, E. and Enke, J.L. (1991) 'The structure of gossip: Opportunities and constraints on collective expression among adolescents, *American Sociological Review*, 56, 494–508.

Einarsen, S. (2003) 'The concept of bullying at work: the European tradition', in Einarsen et al. (2003), 3–31.

Einarsen, S., Hoel, H., Zapf, D. and Cooper, C.L. (eds) (2003) *Bullying and Emotional Abuse in the Workplace. International perspectives in research and practice*, London: Taylor & Francis.

Erikson, B. (2001) 'Mobbning: en sociologisk diskussion', *Sociologisk Forskning*, 2, 8–44.

Fors, Z. (1993) *Obalans i magt. Fallstudier av barnmobbning*, Ph.D. Thesis, Göteborg.

Gabriel, Y. (1998) 'An introduction to the social psychology of insults in organizations', *Human Relations*, 51(11), 1329–54.

Goffman, E. (1967) *Interaction Ritual. Essays on Face-to-Face Behaviour*, London: Penguin Books.

Høgh, A. (2005) *Aggression at work*, Copenhagen: NFA.

Høgh, A., Hansen, Å.M., Bloch, C., Mikkelsen, E.G., Maier, C.M., Persson, R., Pedersen, J., Giver, H. and Olsen, O. (2009) *Mobning og negativ adfærd på arbejdspladsen*, Copenhagen: NFA.

Jaworsky, A. and Coupland, J. (2005) 'Othering in gossip: "you go out you have a laugh and you can pull yeah okay but like..."', *Language in Society*, 34, 667–94.

Keashly, L. (1998) 'Emotional abuse in the workplace. Conceptual and empirical issues', *Journal of emotional abuse*, 1, 85–117.

Keltner, D., Young, R. and Oeming, C. (1998) 'Teasing in hierarchical and intimate relations', *Journal of Personality and Social Psychology*, 75(5), 1231–47.

Kövescses, Z. (2000) *Metaphor and Emotion*, Cambridge: Cambridge University Press.

Leymann, H. (1996) 'The content and development of mobbing at work', *European Journal of Work and Organizational Psychology*, 5, 165–84.

Lindberg, O. (2007) 'Mobbningsoffrens erfarenhet av skam och skamrelaterade känslor. En teoretisk fördjupning', in Carleheden et al. (2007), 189–207.

Pelzer, P. (2005) 'The hostility triad: The contribution of negative emotions to organizational (un-)wellness', *Culture and Organizations*, 11(2), 111–23.

Rainer, C. (1998) 'Workplace bullying: Do something!, The journal of Occupational Health and Safety – Australia and New Zealand, 14(6), 581–85.

Retzinger, S. (1990) *Violent Emotions*, London: Sage.

Salin, D. (2003) 'Ways of explaining workplace bullying: A review of enabling, motivating and precipitating structures and processes in the work environment', *Human Relations*, 56(3), 1213–32.

Scheff, T. (1990) *Microsociology*, Chicago: University of Chicago Press.

Scheff, T. (1994) *Bloody Revenge*, Oxford: Westview Press.

Scheff, T. (2007) *Goffman Unbound! A New Paradigm for Social Science*, London: Paradigm Publishers.

Thelin, A. and Williamson, H. (eds) (2004) *Dokumentation av en forskerkonferens om mobning 24–25 september 2003 i Stockholm*, APN, Nordiska Ministerråd, Köpenhavn.

Vartia, M. (2001) 'Consequences of workplace bullying with respect to the wellbeing of its targets', *Scandinavian Journal of Work, Environment and Health*, 27(1), 63–9.

7
Organizations, Violations and their Silencing

Helena Flam, Jeff Hearn and Wendy Parkin

1 Introduction

Organizations have long been portrayed as rational, unemotional and neutral entities. However, recent research has shown the significance of violence, emotions and gender in and around organizations. For instance, Hearn and Parkin (1995) demonstrated the power and paradox of 'organization sexuality' – the interconnection between gender, power and sexuality and its pervasive influence in supposedly agendered, asexual rational worlds. Organizations, however, are not only sexualized and gendered. Emotions, though often not formally acknowledged, are ever-present in organizations (Flam 1990; 1993; 2000; Fineman 1993; 2000; 2007; Gabriel 1993; 1995). Academic, policy and workplace resistance literature has pointed to a frequent structural co-occurrence of violence, gender relations and emotions in and around organizations (Kondo 1990; Jermier et al. 1994; O'Toole/Schiffman 1997; Hearn 1998; 2003; Heise et al. 2002; WHO 2002; Ferguson et al. 2004).

In this text we first propose a research framework that addresses these organizational issues (Hearn/Parkin 2001; 2007). We argue for working with the concept of violations, rather than just violence, on the grounds that this broadens our perspective, bringing many hitherto unrelated issues together. Then we outline a framework for analysing organization violations, gender relations and emotions – ranging from macro structures resulting in plural forms of oppression and violation to meso domains, with their often allegedly 'neutral' organizational principles veiling various forms of violation, and to the micro level, with its mundane taken-for-granted violations, like racist jokes, but also physical violence involved in extreme forms of bullying and sexual harassment. Although there is a dearth of research in this area, in the second part of this chapter we shift focus to gendered, sexualized violence as well as to the strategies and discourses – both organizational and national – that help to silence it (based on Flam 2008). We show that responses to sexual violence and rape are in fact gendered and involve strong emotions. However, organizations rely not only on the 'silencing emotions', but also on several different strategies to silence their victims. Organizational and national discourses frame these strategies, helping to sustain the illusion that organizations constitute agendered, emotionless and pacified or civilized units.

2   Violence and violations in organizations

2.1   Violence

Violence has not been a central concern of mainstream organization theory. Although a contested term, it usually implies recognition that somebody's conduct is seen as problematic, unacceptable or threatening. Conflicts over its definitions are intense and involve various moral referents. These have been central to the social construction, social experience and social reproduction of violence.

Debates and dilemmas around the definition of violence – particularly what it includes and excludes – make an issue of whether or not there is (i) intention to harm; (ii) actual physical contact; (iii) harmful effects and damage; (iv) perceived/acknowledged/visible violence from the point of view of the violator, violated and onlookers and (v) interpersonal and structural violence.

Violence is often equated with physical violence (Hearn 1998). In criminal law it is equated with the 'unjustified' use of physical force. In organizational contexts, 'violence' may be seen to extend to cover harassment and bullying – two issues usually kept separate. It then includes repeated shaming and contemptuous behaviour intended to diminish and/or hurt the victims. Violence in this sense can also be seen as 'persistent attempts by one person to torment, wear down, frustrate or get a reaction from another' (Bast-Petterson 1995: 50). A third definition stresses that experience of violence can result from generalized intimidation, interrogation, surveillance, persecution, subjugation, discrimination and exclusion, what Judith Bessant (1998) calls 'opaque violence': inequality easily turns into violence where power disparities are long-term, as is the case in workplaces and other institutions.

We will now turn to the concept of organization violations. This is a broader concept than violence and includes structured oppression and discrimination; harassment, bullying and violence and mundane, everyday violations within and around organizational worlds.

2.2 Organization violations

Violations range across verbal, emotional, representational and visual attacks, threats and degradation; enactment of psychological harm; physical assaults; use of weapons and other objects; destruction of property; rape and murder.

Violation can be dramatic or subtle, occasional or continuous, chronic and endemic (as in slave workplaces), generally invisible and 'unnecessary' (as inequalities are so entrenched), normalized and naturalized (as in the acceptance of sexual harassment as part of some jobs), an indication of changing power relations or a reassertion of power by dominant groups (as in men's responses to women's power).

Focusing on various types of violence *as violation* brings together debates on different forms of violence that have usually been kept separate. Here, we approach these forms of violence on the structural (macro), organizational (meso) and individual (micro) levels of analysis.

By macro structures behind violations we understand structural power differences, including patriarchal social relations, systems of capitalist and imperialist exploitation and national exclusions, structural racism and xenophobia. Structural oppression usually takes a plural form, entailing exploitation, marginalization, powerlessness, cultural imperialism and violence (Young 1990). Oppressive social divisions, such as age, ethnicity, disability, gender, sexuality and class, have each been among the macro structural causes of violations, and as such of political mobilization. These oppressive social divisions are reproduced, even though in a modified form, in and by organizations. Structural inequalities in power may violate without direct resort to physical violence when they link with the organizational level, as when hiring committees opt mostly for white males to the exclusion of white women and women and men of colour, or with the micro 'mundane' level, as when widespread racism is present in one-to-one racist language and patriarchal power relations demonstrated in sexist 'joking'.

The meso level of analysis refers to the organizational domains in terms of both the extent of their social power and their internal organizational structures, hierarchies and power relations. These can contribute to violations in their own right, for example, in the construction of different decision-making principles or categories of people, but are also a vehicle for the reproduction of macro-structural violations. Supposedly neutral (in terms of power or gender, age or 'race' relations) 'management practices', 'organizational dynamics' or 'decision-making' (Martin 2001), but also organizational cultures and authority structures, are focal at this level. As decision-makers, managers in gatekeeping positions can reproduce their own organizational profile by shaping rules, procedures, hiring and decision-making practices with this aim in mind.

A more specific set of meso domain questions concerns organizational orientations to violations, specifically their place in relation to the aims and tasks of the organization. One way of conceptualizing violations in and by organizations is to recognize that organizations can have an explicit or an implicit relation or orientation to violation, and more specifically to violence: the police and the army exemplify one extreme, with the other extreme being an organization of dedicated pacifists.

Violations also occur within routine micro intra-organizational processes, perpetuated by specific managerial discourses and work cultures, in ordinary enactments of authority and in the very existence and ordinary functioning of organizations, whereby certain people are given preferential treatment. In such ways those lacking power and authority can be liable to be demeaned and violated.

Violations in and around organizations can be ways of reinforcing and refining relations of domination and subordination, and of scapegoating, but also – less frequently – of developing and affirming resistance (Gabriel 1998). Hence, at the micro – interpersonal or individual – level of analysis there are day-to-day organizational processes and cultures of power and authority through which people are exploited and violated and through which macro and meso logics of exploitation and violation are acted out.

As for the emotions involved, violations and the enactment of violence may involve both positive (pleasure in winning, sadism, conquest) and negative (anger, self-disgust, guilt, depression) emotions, as well as the numbing of emotions. Increasing pressure on employees to work longer hours, organizational crisis, work stress, strong internal competition and time pressures may all be associated with, for example, bullying (Einarsen et al. 1994; Vartia 1996). Teamworking can generate conflict between co-workers whereby intense pressure to meet deadlines may lead to aggression towards those who have difficulty complying with required production levels.

Johnson (1986) argues that in industrial workplaces similar processes to those in military, prison and police organizations – where violence is more openly legitimated – can operate to dehumanize workers. Where great work and production pressures exist, managers and supervisors may push workers to work in ways that are dangerous, exhausting or a threat to health or even life. Managers may contribute to organizational cultures that increase tension and/or vulnerabilities, which may facilitate intentionally harmful behaviours in the workplace. Johnson sees such violence as underwritten by authorization – through bureaucratic organizing, procedures and rules and isolation of the organization from mainstream moral values and regular external review (cf. ibid.: 188ff.). Workplace cultures are important in constraining or facilitating the emergence of violations. Possible 'motivating factors' (Salin 2003) include the nature of the reward system and expected benefits, the presence of very high- or very low-performing colleagues or subordinates and changes in the workgroup that lead to dominant subgroups engaging in resistance to those changes. Violation may also be an outcome of perceived injustice (for either subordinate or dominant groups) within or by organizations (Folgerø/Baron 1996). It is also more likely to occur where gendered workplace cultures are characterized by heavy drinking and/or intense competition between employees within or in different organizations (Bennett/Lehman 1996).

2.3   Working with violations

A number of work sectors appear to present particular risks of physical violence from clients or customers. These include those handling valuable goods; lone workers; providers of care, advice, education and services and those working with potentially violent people (Cardy 1992; Woods/ Whitehead 1993; Bishop et al. 2005). In and around some organizations direct violence and violation are compounded by the threat of violence and violation, themselves often unpredictable, and the consequent fear, insecurity and anxiety. This is perhaps clearest in situations of war, paramilitary violence, organized crime and state terror (Sluka 2000), but the more general implications of threat and fear apply also in more mundane situations (Bourne 2004). Military, paramilitary and similar organizations find it difficult to maintain the potential for physical violence meant for 'enemy' while minimizing internal violence (Dixon 1976). Paradoxically even in organizations created to reduce or abolish violence, 'violence' becomes an element in routine work practices. This is most clearly seen in psychiatric institutions, criminal justice agencies and some anti-violence and peace organizations. Also of interest is that agencies that deal with violent men are staffed mostly by men who may mirror or take over the excuses and justifications of their clients. They may collude in avoiding the topic of violence or in treating it as a decontextualized activity, divorcing the issue of male violence from the general question of male power and control. This exemplifies just one of many discursive strategies that help to reproduce violence and violations in and around organizations.

2.4 Gendering organization violations

At present most recognized forms of violations in organizations are sexual and racializing forms of harassment. Sexual harassment is often not perceived as so 'severe' or 'serious' as other forms of physical violence, downplaying its importance as a violent act per se. While not all bullying is gendered, most sexual harassment is a form of bullying and violence to the individual. The similarities in terms of physical and psychological harm, intimidation, persistence or undesirability need to be recognized. Hushing up their occurrence, as well as treating them as separate phenomena, contributes to their very persistence.

Scapegoating, bullying and harassment have for long been treated as distinct from work satisfaction, interpersonal workplace conflicts, industrial relations disputes, exploitation and class and gender conflicts. This representation of violence as separate from social inequalities is part of what aids their very reproduction. The broad violations embedded in patriarchy, capitalism and nationalism are rarely considered in literature on bullying and physical sexualized violence, as if the latter occur in a world free from gender, class and racializing distinctions that all constitute and produce violence.

Dominant forms of violation and violence in organizations are by men to women, children or other men. Closely linked is the dominant male presence throughout organizations and their hierarchies in business, governments, the police, the judiciary, the church and the armed forces. Patriarchal organization violations follow from the unequal power relations between men and women in organizations (Gwartney-Gibbs/Lach 1994). Micro-level violations often entail particular groups of men routinely producing violations, such as harassment, through the perpetuation of practices that reproduce men's dominant organizational cultures (Collinson/Hearn 1996). Just because an organization is not obviously male-dominated it does not mean that men's power is not being exercised. The hierarchies of occupations, professions and indeed entire organizations are clearly gendered, as both facilitators and constraints these are relevant to the contextualization and practice of harassment, bullying and physical violence. Masculinization of workplaces sets the norms by which women who seek to join must behave, as well as norms and rules regulating the acceptable expression of emotions.

Management with an emphasis on 'strong', aggressive masculinist ways of acting is still widely seen as the desirable type (Collinson 1988; Einarsen/Raknes 1997). Such a management culture may be imposed on personnel regardless of their gender, with women having to comply in order to advance and men having to comply to avoid being seen as 'soft' or 'feminine'. Typical organizational discourses violate women as capable, committed workers when they – portrayed as sexual beings or those solely responsible for the emotional and caring work – are contrasted with 'rational organizational men' (Gutek 1989; see also Rastetter 1994). For men, violations stem rather from pervasive patriarchal cultures in organizations and in society when these discourage demonstrations of fear, softness or 'femininity' on their part (see Howell/Willis 1990). In this discursive context the reluctance of men to complain about bullying can be interpreted as their unwillingness to deviate from the masculinist image. Some men accept the 'all's fair in business' maxim so much that they suppress their emotional reactions and refuse to label negative experiences as bullying or violation (Wright/Smye 1997). Being perceived as emotional and not being able emotionally to handle negative experiences may be experienced as a sign of weakness, even if men are as emotional as women (Hearn 1993).

Organization violations involve both the damaging event(s) and the emotional responses to damage that are embodied, material and discursive. The organizational relationship between the violator and the violated is crucial in understanding how violence and violation relate to organizational dynamics. Such relationships might include violence between workers and managers, between organizational peers or between clients and professionals. Being violated involves emotions such as hurt, shame and humiliation (see Bloch, this volume). It may also lead to a cutting off from emotions, especially where violation is very sudden, traumatic, severe and long-term (Hodgkinson/Stewart 1991; Scott 2001). Violation denied by the violated can still be discomforting and emotionally disturbing.

While trying to understand sexual harassment of women in organizations, one discovers that this constitutes part of a larger phenomenon of the deployment of (sexual) violence against women. Sexual violence directed against women spans across domestic, organizational and national life, flaring up during war and postwar mass rapes. Moreover the 'silencing emotions' and the very silence about sexual violence directed against women links home, workplace and wars – whether civil or international. The remainder of this chapter focuses on sexual harassment and rape, and the multifaceted dynamics involved in denial of them at the individual, organizational and national levels.

3   Rape, silence and emotion

3.1   Rape and sexual harrassment

Rape is about not only sex and sexuality, but also assertion of power and control that relies on sexual violence. Likewise, battery, harassment and bullying are an assertion of power and control that may, but not necessarily, rely on violence, sex and/or rape. Sexual harassment can take place in everyday situations, but it is often more narrowly seen as a form of assertion of an already pre-existing positional power of men against women in work organizations. In the US, the Working Women United Institute provided one of its first definitions of sexual harassment in 1978 (Gruber/Björn 1982: 273) as:

> any repeated and unwarranted verbal or physical sexual advances, sexually explicit derogatory statements or sexually discriminatory remarks made by someone in the workplace which is offensive and objectionable to the recipient or which causes the recipient discomfort or humiliation or which interferes with recipient's job performance.

The U.S. Equal Employment Opportunity Commission links this concept much more tightly to job opportunities:

> Unwelcome sexual advances, requests for sexual favors, and other verbal or physical conduct of a sexual nature constitute sexual harassment when this conduct explicitly or implicitly affects an individual's employment, unreasonably interferes with an individual's work performance, or creates an intimidating, hostile, or offensive work environment (EEOC 2009).

Here the focus is on sexual harassment by co-workers rather than by or indeed of customers (for exceptions see Folgerø/Fjeldstad 1995; Guerrier/Adib 2000). Those especially exposed to severe forms of sexual harassment are (young) women entering male occupations or job sectors in visible numbers to occupy low-status positions, particularly when they are of colour or have minority/migrant status (Gruber/Bjorn 1982: 274f., 291; Clair 1998: 76; Hearn/Parkin 2001: 53ff.), or, alternatively, more powerful women, with higher education and tenure levels, working in male-dominated settings with many employees or much customer contact (de Coster et al. 1999: 42). In general, worker power and the proportion of female employees seem to decrease the risk for sexual harassment, although the actual risk depends on the nature of that power and the form of harassment. While supervisor harmony and co-worker solidarity offer protection against 'patronizing' sexual harassment, they do not necessarily help against its more severe 'taunting' and 'predatory' forms. The most threatening forms of sexual harassment are most likely when workers face employment insecurity, have physically demanding jobs in gender-mixed groups with masculine, sexualized work cultures or in large, anonymous organizations without built-in protection against the most extreme forms of sexual abuse (de Coster et al. 1999: 41f.; Chamberlain et al. 2008: 286ff.). On the other hand, employer policies adopted to stabilize the labour force and increase job satisfaction, not only lessen stress while increasing workers' intention to stay with the organization, but also – often inadvertently – decrease sexual harassment (Mueller et al. 2001: 434ff.).

3.2 Emotions of rape

A typical interpretative text[1] on rape starts by citing statistics on sexual violence against women but then asserts that this is just a tip of an iceberg. Indeed most crimes of this sort remain vastly unreported. Scant literature on rape implies that what we can call *silencing emotions* cause the silence about rape:

1. *Shame*: it is most often argued that women are too ashamed to report sexual harassment and/or rape. This shame is often treated as a major cause of silence (Hoerning 1985: 333; Yuval-Davis 1997: 110; Clair 1998: 74f., 91, 94; Hearn/Parkin 2001: 51; Sharlach 2002: 118; Schäfer 2005: 144; Moe 2007: 685).
2. *Fear*: this second silencing emotion is less frequently mentioned. While women raped outside the workplace fear violence, for their (and their children's) physical security and/or rejection by their own families and communities (Schäfer 2005: 144), at work, they fear intimidation and for their careers (Clair 1998: 74f.; Hearn/Parkin 2001: 54, 71, 78). Clair (1998: 74f.) points out that sexually harassed women fear challenging the status quo with their testimony.
3. *Indifference, lack of empathy/compassion, hostility*: even when raped women report what happened to them, they often face indifference and/or lack of empathy and compassion. The usual reaction is that of disbelief, hostility, suspicion and of trivialization or dismissal of the report (Schaefer 2005: 144f., 147; Moe 2007: 677, 681, 684, 692, 694). These negative reactions are typical of male-dominated families, communities or institutions to which the victims turn for help.

4. *Men's solidarity and guilt*: as far as institutions are concerned, there seems to be much less difference than is often assumed between so-called 'modern' and 'traditional' societies. The institutions to which raped women turn, such as the courts, police or military, enterprises and public institutions, are often staffed by men who consciously or unconsciously uphold patriarchical-fraternal structures and male cultures. These men feel solidarity towards each other and bond or ally with each other (even sometimes across deep social divisions) to ignore, excuse, dismiss, disbelieve and trivialize women's reports. They may themselves be guilty of what women wish to report and by their negligence they encourage even more transgressions (Hoerning 1985: 331; Yuval-Davis 1997: 142; Clair 1998: 74f., 87; Hearn/Parkin 2001: 52f.; 97; Schaefer 2005: 147f.; Moe 2007: 681, 694).

This brief literature review shows that it is crucial to consider such emotions as embarrassment, humiliation and guilt as the *silencing emotions* imposed on the victims by the feeling rules of the patriarchal society and its institutions, such as family, courts, police, hospitals or care centres. Even if the victims do not feel ashamed at the outset, they are likely to end up feeling embarrassed, humiliated, ashamed and guilty after being let down, ignored, dismissed or blamed by the institutions entrusted with the task of helping them (Gruber/Bjorn 1982: 294f. ; Clair 1998: 91; Moe 2007: 692). All these emotions produce isolation and result in silence. Clair (1998: 94) argues that when victims respond with embarrassment, shame, guilt and humiliation, their very emotions reinforce dominant discourses and structures. The victims are thereby triply punished: by the demeaning assault itself, by their initial shame and sense of degradation and, finally, when disbelieved and dismissed, by the emerging sense of embarrassment and guilt. The term 'secondary victimization' has been coined to highlight that the rape denials, emotional dismissals and questioning of women's culpability or sexual history practised by the family, friends, police, courts and other parties are extremely hurtful and discouraging to the victim. Martin (2005) analyses some NGOs that constitute a rare exception to this rule.

There are voices which praise 'modern' societies for having made the notions of shame and honour that bring about violence no longer relevant to their members as compared to the members of 'traditional' societies. Research on sexual violence defies such a view. It shows that the 'west' is not that different from 'the rest'; men are still expected to dominate females and to engage in male bonding while treating women, their sexuality and their reproductive capacities, as men's property – a property that once damaged should be condemned, shamed and cast away.

3.3 Organizational silencing practices

Even though the same basic structure of the argument – the victim's shame causes silence – is found in texts on domestic or international violence as in those on formal organizations, some exceptions can be found in a few texts on work organizations that go beyond this structure and provide insights into the *silencing practices in and by these organizations*. For example, when sexually harassed women speak out, they are individualized and pathologized by their work organizations (Clair 1998: 83). Sexual harassment – as also other forms of violence – remains un- or only partly acknowledged. Most often sexual harassment becomes dismissed by being framed as a single act of an isolated harasser on an isolated and individualized victim (Hearn/Parkin 2001: 51ff., 71, 78).

In formal organizations 'din' –taking space literally and metaphorically, often noisily – is a privilege of men who routinely silence and diminish women (Harlow et al. 1995: 98ff.). Key actors in formal organizations also put much concerted effort into actively silencing their critics – as the burgeoning literature on whistleblowing testifies. In the case of sexual harassment the entire organization can become attuned to the task of silencing and denial, even if these organizations have formal programmes allegedly devoted to discouraging, discovering and combating sexual harassment.

Interview material reveals that many women do not speak out, not because they are ashamed, but because they have realistic expectations that their complaints will be ignored and that they will receive no help from their male superiors. Instead they try to focus on their tasks and avoid the harasser (cf. Hoerning 1985). They may even choose to quit a job rather than to confront the perpetrator and the organization (Clair 1998: 77; see also Gruber/Bjorn 1982: 293).

Clair (1998: 74, 79ff., 90f.) argues that the organization's and women's silencing, avoidance and denial strategies overlap to a great extent, resulting in the overall sequestration of stories about sexual harassment. The perpetrator, the organization and the victim collude in producing silence. Their strategies overlap in the cases of:

1. corporate denial and women's denotative hesitancy: 'such things do not happen in this firm', 'are you sure the man wasn't just flirting', 'it was so subtle, I'm not sure, perhaps it was just flirting';

2. trivializing: by ridicule, joke or playing down the incident becomes an instance of a simple misunderstanding;
3. privatizing: saying it is a private problem of x or y; bringing in a boyfriend to intimidate the harasser;
4. reifying: 'men are men, this is unavoidable', 'all firms have such problems'.

Clair (1998) does not say why it is that organizations and women invest so much energy into denying cases of sexual harassment. She takes it for granted that we know what is at stake. One can guess that complicity in complementary denials protects both these women's and their firms' reputations. However, given the paucity of research on this topic, more is needed on both the complicity and the strategies and forms of denial.

3.4 Sexual violations in the context of nationalist rape discourses

Let us now take the question of sexual violence and its hushing-up from the organizational to the structural level. In examining the case of covering up rape in work organizations, consideration of national discourses on (sexual) violence and rape helps to understand how extra-organizational discourses produce intra-organizational silence.

Although national discourses differ in their specific constructions of the nation and its gendered members, they do not differ so much in how they construct the male rapist and his female victim. Taken together with the phenomenon of rape in war, these national discourses reveal why silence about the actual rapes is both so common and so important.[2]

For many decades the prevalent discourses in the US and Europe have urged women to remain alert and avoid the threatening 'outside', and, the reverse, not to leave the safe, sheltering 'inside' (Marcus 1992: 387, 399). 'Safe', 'home' and 'inside' have been synonyms – violence always comes from outside (Wobbe 1995: 94). Similarly, in both the US and Germany the 'native' male has stood for shelter, security and a comforting, protective presence (Marcus 1992: 388, 392, 399; Wobbe 1995: 92, 94). This male became associated with safety and peace; other males became turned into strangers synonymous with threat, invasion, violence and rape. The strangers could be the attacking soldiers of the enemy army or the 'minority'/'migrant' males living among the 'natives'. While racist US discourses have since the time of slavery depicted male African-Americans as sex-crazed, dangerous, defiling rapists, the German and European nationalist/racist discourses today single out Turks, 'Arabs', Asians, Moslems and 'blacks' for this positioning. The discourses about these strangers – portrayed as disgusting, dangerous, dirty, oversexed and with a power to violate – suggest one single cognitive frame: 'These men are a threat' and one feeling rule: 'These men have to be feared, avoided and, if necessary, destroyed' (Wobbe 1995: 92ff.). The same discourses also underscore the status of the woman as a vulnerable potential rape victim.

As has already been well researched, female sexuality is defined as the property of a nation or a 'race'. It is only hers in trust (Marcus 1992: 392). It belongs to her nation/'race' and the designated man of this nation/'race'. Rape has historically been defined by men, as equal to invasion, to the violation of another's property (Marcus 1992: 392, 397ff.). As such, rape is seen by some as 'the fixed reality in women's life' that makes for 'pained', 'damaged' inner space – a reality that best remains unnameable, unrepresented, shameful, horrendous and equal to or worse than death (Marcus 1992: 398).

These discourses help to answer the question of why so many women keep silent about sexual harassment and rape, and also why keeping silent about sexual harassment and rape – whether domestic or intra-organizational – is of such a great importance. Nationalist and racist discourses remain for the most part silent about sexual harassment and rape among 'natives' and in this manner construct home and nation as pure, sex-free, pacified or peaceful territories. These discourses stress the native woman's vulnerability and desirability to strangers. What they deny is that 'native' women are equally vulnerable and desirable to the 'native' men, and that rapists most frequently are not strangers. In fact most (sexual) violence takes place at home or at work. To keep real-life cases of violence and rape unreported is essential to maintaining the illusion that home and nation state are pure, secure and non-violent territories and that the domestic man is protective, just and safe. At stake here are the very *loyalties* of women to these 'native' men, to their homes and to their nation states. To provide one example stemming from Erika Hoerning's (1985; 1988) research on rapes by Russian soldiers in Berlin in 1945: against the background of war propaganda and hearsay, German women actually expected to be raped by the enemy, did not expect 'their own' men to come to their rescue, forgave those men who led Russian soldiers looking for women to their hiding places, and, finally, forgot their own suffering in solidarity with their own 'poor' 'home-returning' men. This illustrates the enormous power of nationalist rape discourse.

3.5 In-group, intra-organizational loyalty

When some women define war or an oppressive racist regime as a 'reason' to stay loyal to or behind 'their' men, it is perhaps understandable in view of the powerful discourses and socio-political pressures that they face. But it remains puzzling why a hardworking woman thinks that it is better to quit her job, subject herself to the stress of avoidance strategy or live in denial of the sexual harassment to which she is exposed rather than to confront her harasser officially. The answer, as surprising at it may be, seems to be that these women – just like (sic!) men – feel strong *loyalty* to their firm and the (male) company world. Arguably, it is not only the shame, humiliation or anxiety about speaking out loud about sexual harassment that silences women. Powerful male discourses may be internalized by women as well as by men, along with the cognitive and communicative denial strategies that sustain loyalty and silence.

Consistent with the interpretation that silence about sexual violation done to women by 'their' men is essential to keeping women's solidarity with the 'native' men, and the unity of families and nations intact, is the silence surrounding the rapes of 'enemy women' by their 'own' men during and after the war. For the 'native' men also rape 'enemy women,' that is, co-nationals, brothers, fathers and friends also behave like only 'strangers' supposedly do. This silence creates and helps to sustain the seductive illusion of the peaceful, innocent, civilized, honourable native men, so different from the rest of the entire male species and for this reason preferable to every stranger – whether the stranger among 'us' or the one living across the border. This illusion is necessary to create and support nationalist emotions of solidarity, mutual belonging and heterosexual love that combine to grant to native men a privileged access – to 'native' women as much as to protected national labour markets.

4   Conclusion

This chapter has examined the issue of violations in and around organizations at three interconnected levels of analysis – the macro, meso and micro. It provides a framework for investigating organization violations, gender relations and emotions. Macro plural forms of inequality, oppression and violation often translate into meso supposedly 'neutral' organizational principles and cultures that are conducive to various forms of veiled and open violations, and that result in widespread micro taken-for-granted violating processes, such as more or less subtle verbal insults, as well as physical (gendered and sexualized) violence.

We have argued that the concept of violations is more useful than a narrower concept of violence, since it helps to see that unjustified hurt takes many forms and has multiple causes that have to be addressed simultaneously in research, politics and practice. This framework recognizes that day-to-day experience of racism, sexism or ageism can be emotionally, and sometimes even physically, more harmful and damaging than a single physically violent event. As research shows, harassment and bullying experienced, for example, by women in military, police and business settings leads to emotional and mental ill-health, exacerbated by the negative responses to any complaints. The negative health effects of objective oppression and discrimination, whether or not these are also subjectively recognized by their victims, are a cause for alarm not only in themselves (Krieger/Sidney 1996; Landrine/Klonoff 1997), but because '[a]ccumulations of microaggressions' can negatively affect self-confidence and self-respect of those who are targeted (Benokraitis 1998: 8ff.).

The latter sections took up sexual violence, sexual harassment and, more specifically, rape in organizations to show how macro nationalist and meso organizational discourses constitute sexual harassment and rape as 'shameful impossibilities' that have to be denied. These discourses pressure both organizations and victims to engage in what appear to be 'collusive' defensive strategies to generate silence about what has happened. Not only shame, but also several other disparate 'silencing emotions' caused by structures of inequality, organizational work logics, patriarchal-fraternal bonds and masculinized cultures push the victim, her family, friends and institutions meant to help her into sustaining this silence. The silence, in turn, reproduces the vicious circle that condones sexual violence and rape. This vicious circle takes its point of departure, but also its ends, in the organizational myths of 'rational organizational' and 'loving family men', ever ready to protect 'their' women against 'barbaric', 'violent' 'foreign' men.

Notes

1. These argument patterns can be found also in very recently published texts concerned with rape in very different settings and countries: Moe's (2007) article is about domestic violence in the US, Schäfer's (2005) about family violence, rape and incest in (post-)apartheid South Africa. Hearn's and Parkin's (2001) book is about violence and violations in organizations, and Clair's (1998) about sexual harassment in formal organizations. Finally, Hoerning's (1985; 1988) chapter is on rapes by Russian soldiers' in Berlin in 1945 and Scharlach's (2002) on the state-encouraged mass rapes by Pakistani, Serbian and Rwandan Hutu soldiers. One could conclude that this common line of argument is due to the authors' common background. As feminists, we may assume, they have a strong, shared view on (sexual) violence that to helps

structure their texts in a similar way, resulting in an almost tedious reading. But the alternative conclusion is that it is not the feminist discourse unifies these texts, but instead the patriarchal-fraternal relations that permeate modern, western families and institutions just as they do the non-western ones. It is the patriarchy and the fraternity that are at the root of both (sexual) violence and the silence about it.

2. For this purpose three papers were analysed: Marcus (1992) on rape prevention, Smith (1990) on interracial rape, both written in the US 'peace-time' national context, and Wobbe (1995), written in the peace time, but marked by the neo-fascist-mobilization in Germany.

References

Bennett, J.B. and Lehman, W.E.K. (1996) 'Alcohol, antagonism, and witnessing violence in the workplace: drinking climates and social alienation-integration', in VandenBos/Bulatao (1996), 105–52.

Benokraitis, N.J. (1998) *Subtle Sexism*, Thousand Oaks, CA: Sage.

Bessant, J. (1998) 'Women in academia and opaque violence', *Melbourne Studies in Education*, 39(2), 41–67.

Bishop V., Korczynski, M. and Cohen, L. (2005) 'The invisibility of violence: constructing violence out of the job centre workplace in the UK', *Work, Employment & Society*, 19(3), 584–602.

Bourne, J. (2004) *Fear: A Cultural History of the Twentieth Century*, London: Virago.

Cardy, C. (1992) *Training for Personal Safety at Work*, Aldershot: Gower.

Chamberlain L.J., Crowly, M., Tope, D. and Hodson, R. (2008) 'Sexual harassment in organizational context', *Work and Occupations*, 35(3), 262–95.

Clair, R.P. (1998) *Organizing Silence: A World of Possibilities*, Albany, NY: State University of New York Press.

Collinson, D.L. (1988) ' "Engineering humour": masculinity, joking and conflict in shopfloor relations', *Organization Studies*, 9(2), 181–99.

Collinson, D.L. and Hearn, J. (eds) (1996) *Men as Managers, Managers as Men. Critical Perspectives on Men, Masculinities and Managements*, London: Sage.

de Coster, S., Estes, S.B. and Mueller, Ch.W. (1999) 'Routine activities and sexual harassment in the workplace', *Work and Occupations*, 26(1), 21–49.

Dixon, N. (1976) *On the Psychology of Military Incompetence*, London: Jonathan Cape.

EEOC (The U.S. Equal Employment Opportunity Commission) (2009) *Sexual Harrassment*, http://archive.eeoc.gov/types/sexual_harassment.html (last modified 11 March 2009, accessed 1 December 2009).

Einarsen, S. and Raknes, B.I. (1997) 'Harassment in the workplace and the victimization of men', *Violence and Victims*, 12, 247–63.

Einarsen, S., Raknes, B.I. and Mathieson, S.B. (1994) 'Bullying and harassment at work and their relationships to work environment quality: an exploratory study', *European Work and Organizational Psychologist*, 4(4), 381–401.

Ferguson, H., Hearn, J., Holter, Ø.G., Jalmert, L., Kimmel, M., Lang, J., Morrell, R. and de Vylders, S. (2004) *Ending Gender-based Violence: A Call for Global Action to Involve Men*, Stockholm: SIDA.

Fineman, S. (ed.) (1993) *Emotion in Organizations*, London: Sage.

Fineman, S. (ed.) (2000) *Emotion in Organizations*, 2nd edn, London: Sage.
Fineman, S. (ed.) (2007) *The Emotional Organization: Passion and Power*, Oxford: Blackwell.
Flam, H. (1990) 'Emotional "man": Corporate actors as emotion-motivated emotion managers', *International Sociology*, 5(2), 225–34.
Flam, H. (1993) 'Fear, loyalty and greedy organizations', in Fineman (1993), 58–75.
Flam, H. (2000) *The Emotional Man and the Problem of Collective Action*, Frankfurt a.M.: Lang.
Flam, H. (2008) 'The emotions behind the unspeakable', paper presented in session II devoted to Emotions, Identities and Civic Society at the 38th World Congress of the International Institute of Sociology (IIS), held in Budapest, Hungary, in June 26–30.
Folgerø, R. and Baron, R.A. (1996) 'Violence and hostility at work: A model of reactions to perceived injustice', in VandenBos/Bulatao (1996), 51–81.
Folgerø, S.I. and Fjeldstad, I.H. (1995) 'On duty – off guard: Cultural norms and sexual harassment in service organizations', *Organization Studies*, 16(2), 299–313.
Gabriel, Y. (1993) 'Organizational nostalgia – reflections on "The Golden Age"', in Fineman (1993), 118–41.
Gabriel, Y. (1995) 'The unmanaged organization: Stories, fantasies and objectivity', *Organization Studies*, 16(3), 447–501.
Gabriel, Y. (1998) 'An introduction to the social psychology of insults in organizations', *Human Relations*, 9(3), 1329–54.
Gruber J.E. and Bjorn, L. (1982) 'Blue-collar blues: The sexual harassment of women autoworkers, *Work and Occupations*, 9(3), 271–98.
Guerrier Y. and Adib, A.S. (2000) ' "No, we don't provide that service": The harassment of hotel employees by customers', *Work, Employment & Society*, 14(4), 689–705.
Gutek, B.A. (1989) 'Sexuality in the workplace: Key issues in social research and organizational practice', in J. Hearn, D.L. Sheppard, P. Tancred-Sheriff and G. Burrell (eds) *The Sexuality of Organization*, London: Sage, 56–70.
Gwartney-Gibbs, P.A. and Lach, D.H. (1994) 'Gender and workplace dispute resolution: A conceptual and theoretical model', *Law and Society Review*, 23(1), 265–96.
Hearn, J. (1993) 'Emotive subjects: Organizational men, organizational masculinities and the (de)construction of "emotions"', in Fineman (1993), 148–66.
Hearn, J. (1998) *The Violences of Men: How Men Talk About and How Agencies Respond to Men's Violence to Women*, London: Sage.
Hearn, J. (2003) 'Organization violations in practice: A case study in a university setting', *Culture and Organization*, 9(4), 253–73.
Hearn, J. and Parkin, W. (1995) *'Sex' at 'Work'. The Power and Paradox of Organisation Sexuality*. Revised and Updated (1st edn 1987), London: Prentice Hall.
Hearn, J. and Parkin, W. (2001) *Gender, Sexuality and Violence in Organizations: The Unspoken Forces of Organization Violations*, London: Sage.
Hearn, J. and Parkin, W. (2007) 'The emotionality of organization violations. Gender relations in practice', in R. Simpson and P. Lewis (eds) *Gender and Emotions*, London: Palgrave, 161–82.

Heise, L., Ellsberg, M. and Gottmoeller, M. (2002) 'A global overview of gender-based violence', *International Journal of Gynecology and Obstretics*, 78, Supplement 1, 5–14.

Hodgkinson, P. and Stewart, M. (1991) *Coping with Catastrophe*, London: Routledge.

Hoerning, E.M. (1985) 'Frauen als Kriegsbeute', in L. Niethammer and A. von Plato (eds) *Wir kriegen jetzt andere Zeiten: Auf der Suche nach der Erfahrungen des Volkes in Nachfaschistischen Ländern*, Band 3, Berlin: J.H.W. Dietz Nachf.

Hoerning, E.M. (1988) 'The Myth of Female Loyalty', *The Journal of Psychohistory*, 16(1), 19–45.

Howell, D. and Willis, R. (eds) (1990) *Societies at Peace*, New York: Routledge.

Jermier, J.M., Knights, D. and Nord, W.R. (eds) (1994) *Resistance and Power in Organizations*, London: Routledge.

Johnson, R. (1986) 'Institutions and the promotion of violence', in A. Campbell and J.J. Gibbs (eds) *Violent Transactions*, Oxford: Blackwell, 181–205.

Kondo, D. (1990) *Crafting Selves: Power, Gender, and Discourses of Identity in a Japanese Workplace*, Chicago: University of Chicago Press.

Krieger, N. and Sidney, S. (1996) 'Racial discrimination and blood pressure: The CARDIA study of young Black and White adults', *American Journal of Public Health*, 86(10), 1370–78.

Landrine, H. and Klonoff, E.A. (1997) *Discrimination Against Women: Prevalence, Consequences, Remedies*, Thousand Oaks, CA: Sage.

Marcus, S. (1992) 'Fighting bodies, fighting words: A theory and politics of rape prevention', in J. Butler and J.W. Scott (eds) *Feminists Theorize the Political*, New York: Routledge, 385–403.

Martin, P.Y. (2001) 'Mobilizing masculinities: Women's experiences of men at work', *Organization*, 8(4), 587–618.

Martin, P.Y. (2005) *Rape Work: Victims, Gender, and Emotions in Organization and Community Context*, New York: Routledge.

Moe, A.M. (2007) 'Silenced voices and structured survival: Battered women's help seeking', *Violence Against Women*, 13(7), 676–95.

Mueller, Ch.W., De Coster, S. and Estes, S.B. (2001) 'Sexual harassment in the workplace: Unanticipated consequences of modern social control in organizations', *Work and Occupations*, 28(4), 411–46.

O'Toole, L.L. and Schiffman, J.R. (eds) (1997) *Gender Violence: Interdisciplinary Perspectives*, New York: New York University Press.

Rastetter, D. (1994) *Sexualität und Herrschaft in Organisationen. Eine geschlechtervergleichende Analyse*, Opladen: Westdeutscher Verlag.

Salin, D. (2003) *Workplace Bullying among Business Professionals: Prevalence, Organisational Antecedents and Gender Differences*, Doctoral dissertation. Research Reports, Serie A, no 117, Helsinki: Swedish School of Economics and Business Administration.

Schäfer, R. (2005) 'Geschlechtergleichheit versus Gewalt gegen Frauen in Südafrika – Verfassungsgrundlagen, Erbe der Apartheid und Rechtsrealität', *Streit*, 4/2005, 139–49.

Scott, S. (2001) *The Politics and Experience of Ritual Abuse. Beyond Disbelief*, Buckingham: Open University Press.

Sharlach, L. (2002) 'Sexual violence as genocide', in K. Worcester, S. Avery Bermanzohn and M. Ungar (eds) *Violence and Politics: Globalization's Paradox*, London: Routledge, 107–23.

Sluka, J.A. (ed.) (2000) *Death Squad: The Anthropology of State Terror*, Philadelphia: University of Pennsylvania Press.

Smith, V. (1990) 'Split Affinities: The Case of Interracial Rape', in M. Hirsch and E. Fox Keller (eds) *Conflicts in Feminism*, New York: Routledge, 271–87.

VandenBos, G.R. and Bulatao, E.Q. (eds) (1996) *Violence on the Job: Identifying risks and developing solutions*, Washington, DC: APA.

Vartia, M. (1996) 'The sources of bullying – psychological work environment and organizational climate', *European Journal of Work and Organizational Psychology*, 5(2), 203–14.

WHO (2002) *World Report on Violence and Health*, Geneva: World Health Organization.

Wobbe, T. (1995) 'The boundaries of community: Gender relations and racial violence', in H. Lutz, A. Phoenix and N. Yuval-Davis (eds) *Crossfires: Nationalism, Racism and Gender*, London: Pluto, 89–120.

Woods, M. and Whitehead, J. with Lamplugh, D. (1993) *Working Alone: Surviving and Thriving*, London: IPM/Pitman.

Wright, L. and Smye, M. (1997) *Corporate Abuse*, New York: Simon and Schuster.

Young, I.M. (1990) *Justice and the Politics of Difference*, Princeton: Princeton University Press.

Yuval-Davis, N. (1997) *Gender & Nation*, London: Sage.

8
Emotions of Queuing: A Mirror of Immigrants' Social Condition

Alberto Martín Pérez

1 Introduction

In many European cities, hundreds of immigrants queue up every day in front of government offices. This is not just a recurring image of immigration in the media, but an everyday reality. They stand in waiting lines in order to get access to scarce public services, especially to get their work and residence permits issued or extended. Immigrants' relationships to the bureaucracy of their host country tend to be moulded by this specific inconvenience, as this obligation usually reflects their social condition: in most cases 'legal' immigrants are allowed social and economic citizenship, but still seem to be treated differently because of the fact that they remain foreigners in their host society.

On the basis of an ethnographic study, in this chapter I analyse the emotions interwoven into this particular type of queuing – both the immigrants' emotions while waiting and the civil servants' emotions towards them, emerging from their daily interaction with their migrant clients. The aim is to show in which ways these 'emotions of queuing' reflect the immigrants' social condition: framed by current immigration policies they reveal how distinctions are drawn between immigrants and citizens. It results that immigration and immigration policy implementation are mainly seen as a problem, and become a political issue within the host country. Although a broad range of immigrants' emotions result from, and also reinforce, their feelings of subordination, some instances of resistance show up in my results; some emotional reactions reveal individual as well as collective struggles for some kind of citizenship recognition, for instance through immigrants' claims for better treatment.

In my study I focus on the social condition of immigrants in Spain, one of the 'new' immigration countries in Southern Europe. In the last two decades Spain has become one of the major destinations within the EU for migrant workers from Latin America (Ecuador, Colombia, Peru, Argentina and the Dominican Republic), Eastern Europe (Poland, Romania, Bulgaria and Ukraine) and Northern Africa (Morocco). Whereas in 1991 foreigners represented less than 1 per cent of the total population of Spain, in 2008 foreigners made up more than 12 per cent.

In 2004 and 2005 the Spanish authorities carried out a particularly broad regularization of immigrants' status: work and residence permits were issued for about 700,000 'illegal' immigrants already living in the country. At this same period, I conducted my study in the city of Madrid. As my analysis of the resulting waiting lines shows, the queues may be described as a set of actors and interactions that produce and reveal social norms and roles. At the same time, they reflect institutional mechanisms of power and sociability, and display a peculiar social organization, autonomous on many occasions, but basically in the context of the access of immigrants to public services. This is the framework in which immigrants' and civil servants' emotional expressions and reactions develop: their social experiences of bureaucracy and more specifically their emotional experiences of the waiting line provide evidence on the social construction of immigration and the immigrants' social status.

2   Conceptual approach: Sociological research on waiting lines, migrant bureaucracy and emotions

The study of waiting lines is a quite rare topic in sociological research. However, some empirical contributions have explored the functioning of queues as social organizations in different periods and contexts, by analysing them as social systems made by different actors, practices and interactions (Mann 1969; Schwartz 1975; Coenen-Huther 1992). These specific organizations have mostly been interpreted as cultural expressions. For instance, Mann (1969) examines a particular example of a western culture of waiting lines: the 'queue tradition' in selling tickets for major sporting events. Boudon (1979) observes queues in front of French theatres. The presence of queuers in these lines usually depends on their wish to attend the event for which they are waiting (Schwartz 1975; Meyer 2001). Other researchers focused on the distinctive traits of a clearly different 'queue tradition' in former east European communist regimes (Czwartosz 1988; Rukavishnikov 1990; Coenen-Huther 1992). These queues seem to be less voluntary and a bit more compulsory than the western ones, in so far as they used to give access to staple foods and hence were understood as part of everyday life, producing some kind of 'soviet way of living' (Czwartosz 1988; Rukavishnikov 1990). Further studies of 'queue cultures' refer for instance to south-east Asian waiting lines (Lee 1984) or north African ones (Sabry 2005). The last case provides a useful example for the present chapter as it refers to the 'other side' of the migration experience: Sabry (2005) analysed waiting lines in Morocco, particularly those formed in front of western embassies in the city of Casablanca by Moroccan candidates for emigration. He shows how queues formed by migrants seem to resemble 'soviet queues': the goods at stake in lining up are basically understood as staple foods, as these queuers wish to emigrate in search of a better life in which their basic needs are fulfilled. To do so they need a compulsory visa. Moreover, Sabry's study points to inequalities in access to public services. In this, it re-echoes further studies which prove the existence of privileged users who manage to be served without queuing (Schwartz 1975; Moessinger 1977; Lipsky 1980); an aspect I also realized during my research. Finally, Sabry (2005) demonstrates the importance of the emotional aspects of the organization of access to the embassies studied. In this, his results resemble a blueprint of what I call 'multiply linked emotions': the emotional landscape of queuing filled with feelings of anguish, humiliation and attitudes of resignation, but also with a particular social organization that allows queuers to cope with such negative feelings.

Despite the diversity of contexts, all these studies have one trait in common: the analysis of the way the actors who participate in the social organization of waiting lines deal with the time spent in queuing. Most researchers describe similar strategies to keep public order (especially by impeding queue jumping) and regulate the serving time through different types of sociability (Mann 1969; Coenen-Huther 1992). Therefore, waiting time in queues is neither empty time before being served (Larson 1987) nor a particular time to be managed by organizations, mainly by trying to reduce it (Katz et al. 1991). Instead, waiting time becomes the basis of the social organization of access and delay (Schwartz 1975), as happens in other dimensions of social life (Hochschild 1997; Sennett 1998).

Several approaches are especially apt for examining waiting lines as a particular type of social organization. Therefore, it is important to understand queues as a kind of gathering where, according to McPhail and Wohlstein (1983), individual and collective behaviours have to be explored. For the analysis of behaviour in public places, Goffman (1963) provides relevant tools, especially for the observation of interaction rituals (Goffman 1967), which seem to epitomize the social organization of waiting lines. Goffman shows that individual behaviour is in fact a social issue. As Hochschild (1979) argues, this also explains the way rules are felt by the individuals involved in a particular social structure – and the feeling rules to which they are bound. This points to the importance of analysing emotions when studying organizations. Moreover, emotions are a social phenomenon, as emotion sociologists have long demonstrated (Halbwachs 1947; Bericat 2000; Von Scheve et al. 2005). With respect to organizations, there is a considerable body of research treating emotions such as shame and humiliation, which also build the core of my analysis. For instance, Goffman (1956) studied the effects of embarrassment and shame in deploying unequal social structures, as Scheff did by linking shame, humiliation and conformity. Shame is, in Scheff's (1988: 397f.) terms, 'the most frequent and possibly the most important of emotions'. Thus, emotion theorists state that a 'humiliation process' (Smith 2001) has to be taken into account when dealing with the power relations that imbue every social relation.

The special case of immigrants' emotions within their host countries has rarely been treated. Exceptions are, for example, Graham's (2003) analysis of 'emotional bureaucracies' concerning immigrants in Sweden and Flam's (2007) contribution on the symbolic violence reflected in immigrants' emotions. Both contributions are relevant to my study, because they show the way immigrants' as well as natives' emotions reflect the inequality of treatment that usually inspires social relations within migrants' host societies and, as I show for the Spanish case, within their bureaucracies.

3 The empirical approach: An ethnography of the waiting line

As mentioned above, I conducted my study in 2004 and 2005 in Madrid, a period during which a particularly broad immigrant regularization campaign took place in Spain. This resulted in a remarkably huge number of up to then 'illegal' immigrants applying for work and residence permits.

My initial research purpose was to explore the daily practice of immigration policies – the bureaucratic procedures that direct the interaction between immigrants and civil servants. However, even during my first contacts with the immigration offices I realized how relevant the interactions taking place outside the office were: before getting access, immigrants waited patiently on the streets for their turn, usually for hours and sometimes for more than a day. My impression was that something important in political terms was happening there, so I decided to focus on that particular scene.

In my research design, I combined systematic participant observations with formal and informal interviews conducted with both immigrants and civil servants. The observation criteria and the interview guidelines were elaborated on the basis of the concepts outlined above.

The observations took place in front of four police stations deling with different kinds of residence permits and Madrid's only office where work permits were issued. Apart from the immigrants, my fieldwork included some specific civil servants who ensured that they formed well-organized waiting lines. In the police stations, these were both uniformed policemen and agents in civilian clothes; in the work permits' office, a porter and a security agent had this role. Moreover, some other actors gradually appeared on the scene: further civil servants, people living next to the offices, storekeepers, journalists, members of religious groups, sales agents, pollsters and not least myself, the participant observer. All of us were playing different roles in the social organization of immigrant access to the government offices.

As a whole, my research project lasted from March 2004 to December 2005. During the observation phases, I usually remained in the area alongside the immigrants for the whole day. After the first observations, I gradually started to participate in informal conversations and then made appointments for some more formal interviews, which also took place during the waiting time. In autumn 2005, I also conducted interviews with the executive officials in charge of the services and with the 'street-level bureaucrats' (Lipsky 1980) who were meeting immigrants directly. These took place inside the immigration offices and lasted approximately one hour each.

In this way, I was able to gather rich data for an ethnography of the waiting line, which allowed me to analyse the practice and the experience of the social condition of these specific foreigners: migrant residents and workers who are forced to wait in front of immigration offices in order to achieve 'legal' status. Altogether, this was a rich experience filled with different emotions, which have inspired the following analysis.

4   Emotions in the Spanish migration procedure

In this section I first present the emotional landscape of queuing. I start with immigrants' emotions, which make up their social experience of the waiting line. These emotions seem to emerge following an 'ideal chain' and may be grouped as emotions of subordination (section 4.1) and emotions of resistance and coping (section 4.2). Then I go into the emotions the civil servants experience in view of the waiting lines (section 4.3). Finally, I discuss my findings (section 4.4).

4.1 Immigrants' emotions of subordination

4.1.1 Anguish

Anguish characterizes almost all the steps immigrants have to follow before obtaining a residence permit. That is why it appears quite long before they get access to the offices. For some immigrants, this happens when the date of expiry of their previous permit approaches. For newly regularized immigrants in 2005, it appeared when the opening of the regularization process was announced, even unofficially.

Anguish is visibly expressed and felt for three reasons. The first concerns the bureaucratic obligations: both the administrative steps to be followed and the mere fact of having to go to the offices on a particular date. The second is coupled to the time to be spent in the queues and the expected waiting conditions. The third refers to a stable condition of immigrants' lives: the continuous social experience of a provisional status caused by the constant request to provide 'papers' results in almost permanent anguish. On this basis I discern three 'types' of anguish.

The first type called 'previous anguish' is usually expressed in the following way:

> When you see approaching the date of expiry of the permit ... well ... I don't know, you get excited ... You and the others around you. (Nicoleta,[1] Romania)

> Well, the stress ... for everything, just for the fact of coming here ... the date, whether I can go or not, how to do at work ...(Anita, Colombia)

> Think of all this, line up, spend your time here, this bothered me, all this stuff to be planned....(Mónica, Ecuador)

The second type I call 'anguish in the queue'. This is reinforced by the prospect of a very long waiting time: 'Yes, time, time ... because you see how long the queue is, you see it doesn't move, but you try to think: 'well, maybe this is going to be quick', you try to calculate, but not, it is not like that, I don't know ...' (Catalin, Romania).

While lining up, immigrants often consider themselves as victims of some injustice – especially when conflicts arise within the queue. Anguish is then identified with the permanent tension provoked by the mere fact of waiting under these conditions. Moreover, this reveals the weak social position of these immigrants:

> You see, here, it depends, but here you can't stay like that, calm, you queue and you wait. Here, every time, there are problems, fights, people shouting ... I am really anguished because of this, I assure you! (Mónica, Ecuador)

> Well, here, OK, there are people, you see, who stay calm, they stay calm, but most of us feel tension. When there is a problem, I don't know, everybody wants to know what happens ... We all feel tension, every time ... well ... going there or being here, knowing what's happening. (Alicia, Peru)

Finally, a feeling of 'permanent anguish' can be clearly identified. On the one hand, this anguish is related to the fact of periodically having to renew one's residence permit: 'I will be better with my papers, that's for sure, but I will have to be aware, because I won't have these papers forever!' (Anita, Colombia). On the other, 'permanent anguish' is strictly connected to the fact of not being a citizen of the host country: 'Of course, with these papers I am going to be calmer, but I don't know if I am going to calm down completely. There are plenty of concerns for us, for foreigners ... That's what I can say ...' (Hugo, Ecuador). Thus, anguish appears as a crucial feature of immigrants' social condition. It is continuously experienced by immigrants confronted with the obligation of remaining 'legal' within the host country. This periodical and compulsory requirement transforms anguish into a permanent emotion.

4.1.2   Humiliation

Various researchers have pointed out that the main basis of humiliation is the awareness of being subjected to injustice (Margalit 1996; Scheff 2000; Smith 2001). This also holds true for the queuers I studied. They felt humiliated due to the difficult waiting conditions, which in turn reflected the unequal treatment of foreigners and citizens in the host country. Moreover, the obligation to queue makes them remember similar unpleasant experiences in front of public services in their home countries. Some recall political corruption – and that of civil servants, others remember painful waiting experiences in the former communist countries of Eastern Europe.

Emotions of humiliation are for instance expressed as follows: 'The queue is just for foreigners ... That's clear, isn't it? So, it's like ... you are a foreigner, you must queue up, that's it ... It's like a label, like cattle, well, I exaggerate maybe, but for me, that's humiliation' (Belkasem, Morocco). In a similar vein, two Colombian women agreed after a long conversation on their lives and the obligation to wait so long for their immigrant identity cards: 'What a humiliation they make us suffer!' Special feelings of humiliation arise for eastern Europeans who negatively associate the queues in front of the Spanish immigration offices with the waiting lines in their former communist home countries. Here is an example:

> I think that for the permits it is the only place where there are queues... I ask myself this question... because, okay, in Romania, before, at the time of Ceaucescu, there were a lot of queues. We were used to them, we saw a queue and just sat down because... well, no matter if they were selling this or that, now or later, we needed it anyway... This was twelve years ago... And, I tell you this, here I hadn't seen the same queues as in Romania and I wonder if... no, no, if I look closer, no, the queues... the only place where there are queues it's at the migration offices... I don't know... not anywhere else, for sure. (Helena, Romania)

4.1.3 Resignation

Most immigrants wait without complaining. They almost never react to conflicts in queues between immigrants, police officers or other civil servants, and usually strictly respect the organization of access. Regularly, immigrants say that they do not want to complain for fear of negative consequences. For instance, they could run the risk of being denied the renewal of their residence permits. The result is a feeling of resignation: if immigrants detect a lack of fairness or a lack of justice, they take into account the costs and profits. Obtaining the desired permit represents an extraordinary profit, endangered by complaining. In contrast, the costs of complaints are high, because of the possibility of unpleasant and painful consequences. Consequently, immigrants tend to avoid complaints, no matter how rightful or lawful these may be, before their 'papers' are handed out. Thus they accept queuing, no matter how long it takes, with resignation.

Resignation is formulated as follows: 'And what else can we do?' (Milton, Ecuador). The underlying comparison of costs and profits may be seen in the following quote:

> We all need our papers... Well, without papers we don't go anywhere... That's why we have to wait here, you don't have to do

anything bad... Papers, the identity card, that's everything for us. If we don't have it, we can't go on, so... we have to wait as much as necessary, follow all the steps and that's all, without any problem... We talk about our papers, that's the most important thing. (Milton, Ecuador)

Most immigrants I interviewed made similar statements. They see almost no possibility of complaining, either about the rules of access to the immigration offices or to denounce the reasons for their anguish and feelings of humiliation. They seem to avoid causing additional uncertainty in their lives, as the only basis of their 'legal' presence in the host country is the required permit. Thus, waiting calmly is seen as the only way to gain access to the offices, and this is coupled to feelings of resignation:

But we can do nothing... You spend all your time in obtaining your papers and that is the most important thing. (Anna, Bulgaria)

No, no... you must just stay calm and not react... Our papers, that's the most important thing... You don't need to do any stupid thing, you know? (Evelyn, Ecuador)

It makes no sense to complain. You must just follow all the steps, have your identity card in hand and that's all... you have to avoid problems. (Alicia, Peru)

Here, it's about our future that we are talking about... You don't have to make noise like other people do. In the end, if they complain, that's worse for them. (Olga, Ukraine)

4.2 Immigrants' resistance and coping

4.2.1 *Complaining*

Even if immigrants tend to fear negative consequences of making a complaint, and the probability of it being successful in terms of changing the situation is marginal, sometimes they do opt to do so. I can identify two kinds of complaints. *First*, an active, visible and audible one, manifested through fighting, quarrelling, arguing or shouting, both against policemen or civil servants and against other immigrants. These are actions in response to a perceived injustice; usually they represent a desperate reaction to the anguish caused by particular waiting conditions. *Second*, there is verbal complaining, an option I found more often than the first type: while queuing and waiting calmly, immigrants verbalized their anguish or feelings of humiliation – mostly in conversations with other immigrants in the queue. Such conversations dealt with perceived injustices, concerns about waiting time and waiting conditions, decisions made by police officers and civil servants perceived as incongruous and unreasonable, decisions that immigrants collectively decided not to respect, unacceptable compulsory bureaucratic procedures and even racism or other disdainful attitudes towards immigrants. However, verbal complaining also appeared in interviews with journalists (who frequent the queues when immigration becomes breaking news) and in the interviews I conducted. The following examples stem from three of my interviews:

> This is unacceptable, this is unbearable... You are here, since I don't know when and you can do nothing, and they treat us very badly. There, when you get in, if at least they where nice, but not, inside it's the same... You see, you queue up, without sleeping and then they almost throw you your card without saying anything, even hello. (Eduardo, Bolivia)

> And what do you think? Do you think people are happy being here? That's disgusting, disgusting. These queues, what they do, this is not fair. (Belkasem, Morocco)

> Listen, all the things that happen here, it's a shame, it's a shame... Police officers who are... well... I don't want to swear, but everybody feel tension, we wait here, they just let in very few people each time, and then, they don't come back until half an our later... How do you want me to feel about this? (Hicham, Morocco)

By complaining, the immigrants are not just looking for evidence on painful waiting conditions. They also seek responses and accurate solutions to their problems such as the mere existence of waiting lines:

> How to change this? Well... I don't know. Maybe they should hire more civil servants and they should work harder as well because, you know, when you get in and you are in front of the officials and you see they stand up and leave when your turn arrive... That's annoying! And you stay there... as an idiot, because, I don't know, they're going to rest or something... when there are a lot of people in the queue! So, more civil servants, that's it. (Eduardo, Bolivia)

4.2.2 Coping

Immigrants state that there are also positive aspects to waiting. This goes along with a reinterpretation of emotions that are primarily understood as negative, such as anguish and humiliation. In this case, queuers look for additional explanations in order to cope with the circumstances and finally they detect positive aspects in queuing. As Schnapper (1981) indicates, it might first be necessary to accept the negative consequences of a situation before coming to value some of its aspects as positive: 'Finally, it is not so bad to be here ... there's always a saving grace, isn't it?' (Andrés, Ecuador). For the immigrants, this 'saving grace' often appears in comparisons with the public administration of their home countries. If someone says that 'there, this is worse' (Milton, Ecuador), this also means that 'here, this is better' (Félix, Ecuador). Such comparisons seemed to make my interviewees feel more confident. Here are more specific examples:

> I told you ... here, this is very slow, that's true ... But, there ... well ... in Bulgaria ... that's really worse ... I already told you. (Anna, Bulgaria)

> There, the problem is corruption. Officials are corrupted ... You can't do anything without money. Here at least, there is more control. (Hicham, Morocco)

> There, for public services, you prepare your money and you go there. If you don't do this, you've nothing to do. No matter if you do have the most important paper ... no, no, here ... here people ... everything is more correct, more honest ... It's true, it's much better here. (Gladys, Colombia)

Positive aspects are also drawn from comparisons with immigrants who are living illegally in Spain. Compared to the latter, the queuers perceive their social condition as less unfortunate. Then, they seem to interpret their waiting in front of the immigration office as a privilege: 'People complain but, in the end ... this is worse for those who don't have papers, isn't it? Here we are something like ... privileged if you compare us to those who don't have papers' (Hicham, Morocco).

Furthermore, immigrants appreciate the quality of sociability within queues. The social contacts transform their experience into a more acceptable one. As Dubet (2006) argues with respect to individual perceptions of inequalities at work, immigrants also reason in terms of symmetry between justice and injustice. In particular, positive feelings arise from being in touch with other immigrants, sharing information both on administrative matters and on daily life with them or meeting people from different countries and cultures:

> If there is something I like here, is the fact of giving information to other people ... and, of course, receiving this information for

yourself...Information about papers, about residence permits...
(Alicia, Peru)

That's the best, meeting people from everywhere...from every country, different cultures, all these things...people saying things...I
don't know, I think this diversity of nationalities, cultures, is extraordinary. (Hugo, Ecuador)

4.2.3   The aftermath: Liberation

Let me turn to the 'aftermath', the moment when immigrants leave
the office with the desired 'papers'. I observed a whole range of visible and audible reactions in front of the police station where residence
permits are issued. Some immigrants keep their identity cards inside
their bags and leave the place without expressing any discernible feeling. But most frequently I perceived joyful emotions reflecting a feeling
of liberation: finally, after many bureaucratic steps and a long period of
waiting, the residence permit represents the recognition of the immigrant's rights. This is an occasion of relief, and the time of an exceptional celebration.

Some express these joyful emotions by evident gestures: leaping up,
crying or inviting people around them to have a drink at the nearest
bar. Others show their relief by more intimate gestures; they kiss their
husbands, wives or friends. Some share a last moment of sociability
with a 'queue mate', for example, through looking at each other's cards
and laughing about each other's photos.

The feeling of liberation is due to the fact that the immigrants have
successfully regularized their residence in the country. However, immigrants usually realize that joy is ephemeral, because the residence permit will expire and will have to be renewed. Thus, I interpret liberation
as a provisional emotion. Moreover, 'provisional liberation' becomes
the positive counterpart of 'permanent anguish': it appears as the last
link of the chain of emotions and, at the same time, as the first one in
new multiply chained emotions. The following examples from my field
notes illustrate the feelings of liberation and joy:

A young man and a young woman from Ecuador, looking at each other's
card, decide to go have a drink: 'And now, let's have a whisky!'
Two Eastern European women, visibly excited, hug each other and
shout: 'I've my card and you've yours!'
A woman from Ecuador says broadly smiling to three men waiting
for her outside 'At last, I will go back to Ecuador!'

But liberation quickly becomes provisional, as the following examples show:

> Two Latin Americans, looking at their brand new identity cards focus on the date of expiry. One of them says: 'Look, the date of expiry is April ... In less than nine months we will have to restart all these procedure!' The other replies: 'You are right ... we should start thinking about this!'
>
> One of the men waiting for the Ecuadorian woman says: 'Before you travel back, you have to look at the date of expiry, because you will have to renew your permit in less than a year.' She listens carefully to this advice, but still smiles without stopping.

4.3   Immigration officers' emotions

Let me turn to the civil servants' emotions during the process. As I recognized from my interviews, civil servants describe their activity in the immigration offices in emotional terms. At the same time, this emotion-laden evaluation of their work reveals their attitude towards immigrants and immigration, which is imbued with a paternalistic tone. Rather than being perceived as 'normal' users of general public services, immigrants are depicted as uncommon users of an exceptional service. Immigration officers describe them for instance as 'poor people', 'people who are scared' or 'people who make one feel sorry'.

> Difficulties? To tell you the truth ... I think that it's people who come and don't understand the language. The way of understanding each other – it's the only thing, I think ... When there are some of them, poor guys, who come from countries ... so far away, who don't really understand what you mean ... they don't understand and, poor guys, leave without having understood anything. (Sonia)
>
> It's people who are scared ... because everything depends for them on papers, on renewing their permits, they accept everything, they are very grateful ... whatever you do for them, they thank you a thousand times. (Nuria)
>
> They are scared ... for instance, I work basically on permit renewing, and I think they are scared of not being renewed and they ask you: 'am I going to be renewed?' That's routine ... Sometimes there is someone who tells you his case ... a difficult case, and then they

make you feel sorry, you know, and you try to guide them better. (Nuria)

Moreover, civil servants insist on their own fragile position. They think that immigrants perceive them as being those who decide on work and residence permits, as they are the only visible face of the migration authorities. However, this is not the case, as the officers state. Thus, they consider themselves as just an insignificant wheel of the bureaucratic machinery of the Spanish government. They judge the immigrants' perception of them as unfair, as an ascription of a responsibility they are not supposed to assume. In this way they justify their own feelings of anguish.

They think you are somebody important, as if it was us who accept or reject their permits. (Sergio)

They think it depends on us... the future of their papers, that's what they think. (Sonia)

They think it's us who decide... we don't decide about anything! (Nuria)

We try to make them understand... to make them understand this... That is, it must be clear for them that we are just following orders and we are not able to decide, we can't do anything... but they try everything. (Sergio)

Feelings of anguish are also caused by doing a tiring job with very demanding users:

This job is stimulating, that's true, but it's tiring, tiring... It's not like: 'here is this paper to be filled in and signed and that's all'. No, no... sometimes... well, it takes a long time because they think you are a psychologist, you know? They tell you their life and so on... to analyse it and see what you can do, and you have to listen to very hard things! (Carmen)

Waiting lines, in civil servants' opinions, make them share this feeling of anguish with immigrants, more or less in the same terms, as they tend to state:

Queues are a problem. They are a problem, for them and for us. That is... In days like today, when it's cold or when it snows, so... for them it's a serious problem. But it's also for us because ... you know, it's ... some days you arrive, you sit down and you don't stop meeting people until lunch time ... Without stop, and that, as a civil servant, you feel that also ... you finish your day really tired. (Sergio)

The queue in the corridor ... the whole corridor was full ... That was anguishing, also when you are on this side of the window ... Wof! ... You look and you see forty people there, waiting, you say: 'Fuck! I'll never finish!' That's very anguishing ... 'Come on, come on, quick, quick!', Very bad, very bad ... (Sonia)

However, civil servants usually adopt an attitude of conformity or, in some way, a sense of resignation. Thus, they say they would appreciate being able to do more for these people who often make them feel sorry: 'If this depended upon me ... I would give papers to anybody! But we have to respect the law, that's the point!' (Sonia) Resignation also appears to be a useful strategy for protecting officers from the negative consequences of their work. In some sense, resignation works as a reaction against the emotional aspects of their relationship with immigrants, filled with anguish, distress and pity:

Well, in the end, you must be a bit objective and cold to say: 'that story is not my problem, I don't need to take this problem home with me and ...', because, maybe, humanly, you could do anything more but, well, as a civil servant you have to respect the law. If you can't do it that way, you can't do it. (Carmen)

There are stories that upset you because sometimes what happens is unfair and so on ... All this upsets you because you can't do it in another way. You can help them if you have the chance, but that's all ... That's why, in general, I try ... I try to switch off, that's what I do. If I have to go back home with all these problems, I become crazy. (Sergio)

As Graham (2003) pointed out in his study, these statements on civil servants' emotions also show their wish to seek some kind of 'emotional consensus' with immigrants, one which is nevertheless unbalanced by a stronger feeling of guilt, as they perceive the position of immigrants within the bureaucracy as being inferior. On the one hand, civil servants judge this inferior position as an injustice. On the other, this very position makes immigrants appear as the uncommon users of an exceptional service, as they are not full citizens of the host country. Finally, civil servants think they are compelled to accept with resignation the immigrants' social condition and its expression within the bureaucracy.

4.4 Discussion

As I have shown, immigrants' social experience of the waiting line is made up of various emotions, linked to feelings of subordination as well as resistance and coping. An individual may be restricted to one of these experiences, but as Pollak (1990) pointed out, social experiences are very frequently linked in many different ways. This observation is echoed in my findings: the immigrants usually experienced most of the emotions described above. For example, resignation, which defines the acceptance of anguish and humiliation, can be followed by complaining (by trying to refuse the stigma of 'the immigrants who queue') or by coping with the situation and looking for positive aspects of queuing.

These emotions are experienced from the very first moment when immigrants learn the steps to take until the moment they finally receive their work or residence permit. Even if each individual has a different view on what happens during that period, the emotions of queuing appear to form an 'ideal' chain. The first link in the chain is anguish, based both on the obligation to undergo the administrative procedures and the prospect of waiting a long time. Then, immigrants tend to experience humiliation, mainly caused by the fact of being compelled to queue. For some immigrants, this recalls similar unpleasant experiences in their home countries. This is especially the case for Romanians, Bulgarians, Ukrainians and other eastern Europeans who remember their life under the former communist regimes where 'there were queues everywhere.' Immigrants from other countries (Latin Americans, Moroccans or central Africans) usually remember the disastrous functioning of public services and public administration in their home countries, which also results in feelings of humiliation.

At the same time such a comparison of home and host countries explains the next linked emotion: often immigrants think that it was worse *there*, in the home country. As a result, feelings of humiliation are turned into a search for the positive aspects of waiting. There are further ways of coping with negative emotions and of finding reasons through which the waiting experience may be transformed into a positive practice, as Hachimi Alaoui (2007) also points out with respect to the whole migration experience. The immigrants in my study do so by emphasizing the importance of sociability: the positive experience is then based on a practical exchange (in terms of information and mutual aid) or an emotional exchange enacted in the queues.

At the same time, an attitude of complaining emerges. This is especially the case for immigrants who are not queuing for the first time.

They are usually quite sensitive to humiliating practices and cannot bear them any more. In contrast, 'newcomers' do not show this dissenting attitude as clearly. However, complaints rarely succeed. Therefore, most immigrants tolerate the waiting conditions with resignation – 'and what else can we do?'

Finally, after having waited for hours or longer, a new emotion appears, which I called liberation. It marks the end of the bureaucratic procedure, when the permit is issued: then pleasure is expressed in various forms. However, liberation is provisional: usually, the residence or work permit expires and the whole procedure starts again, causing anew anguish and humiliation. As such, my observations re-echo Paugam's (1991) argument on the way the experience of social disqualification develops: feelings of liberation like joy are only provisionally comforting; immigrants soon realize that these feelings are not the last link of the chain, but become a new one.

Reconsidering this 'ideal chain' of emotions, it becomes clear that all of them are closely linked to specific bureaucratic activities. Anguish is related to uncertainty concerning the governmental decision on the allocation of 'papers'. Humiliation is experienced during an unacceptable waiting period. Resignation seems to be a common attitude for immigrants who have no choice but to wait in front of the offices. Liberation and the search for positive aspects of lining up stand for a kind of dream: in some way, having their 'papers' in their hands gives immigrants' freedom of movement and access to limited citizenship, at least within the host country. In this sense, the queues studied symbolize the power of the government to decide on immigrants' 'legal' or 'illegal' future. At the same time the queues represent the sphere of immigrants' sociability, which reflects the collective search for a better life.

Turning to the civil servants, I have shown that their social experience of immigrants' queuing is basically made up of two emotional reactions. On the one hand, they experience anguish due to the disorganization of the immigration offices, especially the long waiting lines both outside and inside. On the other, they declare that they work with a sense of resignation, in so far as they feel just like a small wheel of bureaucracy, that is, of a process they cannot really control. At the same time, these emotional experiences reveal specific paternalistic – and sometimes explicitly negative – images of immigrants and immigration in Spain. Following Vaughan's (1999) approach to organizations, such negatively interpreted emotions are a common reaction among employees who picture the organization they work for as being characterized by misconduct and disaster.

As such, civil servants' emotions reveal important features of the social construction of immigration and the immigrants' social status. They reflect the dominant interpretation of immigration in the country: through a shared paternalistic attitude, immigration and immigrants appear as a social problem. The somehow chaotic organization of this particular public service appears as a logical effect of the second-degree citizenship allowed to its users, compared to those of other, more general public services.

5 Conclusion

As my ethnographic study of the emotions of queuing in front of the Spanish immigration offices has shown, such an exploration of emotions leads directly to a more general reflection on immigration and citizenship. For instance, immigrants' emotions such as anguish and humiliation, as well as their weary acceptance of their social condition, are strongly related to their daily confrontation with the political logics guiding immigration policies and policy-making. In other words, the multiply linked emotions I have analysed are strongly linked to attitudes towards immigrants and immigration in the host society. My analysis of civil servants' emotions confirms this idea: as their emotional reactions reveal, to them immigrants represent a 'problem', the atypical users of an exceptional service.

For 'normal' citizens, their relationship to the public administration is a fundamental element of their political condition. In their case, their entitlements do not depend on this relationship, but are the main basis of their citizenship. This has clear consequences: for example, citizens' claims against the authorities appear not just as a possibility, but as a duty. As to the government (at least in democratic countries), it ought to take into account these claims in some degree, because it is supposed to be responsible for citizens' welfare.

However for immigrants, access to public services has a completely different sense, as the analysis of their emotions has shown. In their case, access is a necessary condition of the recognition of rights. Thus, immigrants must apply for 'legal' status; an authority regulates compulsory administrative procedures and decides if recognition is granted. This leads to a deep sense of restriction in immigrants' relation to the public administration. Their continuous experience of a provisional status results from the compulsory and periodical requirement for proof of 'legality' imposed by the government. Obeying these regulations is the only way to be accepted as a 'legal' foreigner. It is also the only way of avoiding failure – a condition that would lead to even more disgraceful consequences than the painful waiting conditions as reflected in immigrants' feelings of anguish and humiliation. Moreover, the waiting lines I studied clearly reflect the immigrants' position within these power relations. To give an example: at the time when I conducted my study the queues in front of the immigration offices were broadly considered to be a social and political 'problem', for instance in the media. Nevertheless, no effort was made to change this situation, either to improve public services in charge of the immigrants' residence and work permits or to avoid having waiting lines outside the offices. In most cases, immigrants accept their resulting inferior position with resignation. However, they do demonstrate as well that they can change, at least, the negative experience of their waiting conditions, by valuing sociability within queues and by coping with anguish and humiliation through a struggle for better treatment. As a result, their resistance may be read as a struggle for social inclusion, the struggle to count as 'normal' users of general public services, which on their part should be interpreted as 'normal' and not as the exception.

The analysis of immigrants' emotions appears as a useful tool for the understanding of the integration of immigrants into their host societies. Thus, in the context of immigrants' struggle for entitlements, further research must be carried out in other general public services whose users are both immigrants and citizens. This is the case, for instance, of welfare services where immigrants 'compete' with natives for the same provisions. In this way, research will provide more evidence on the emotional proximity between citizens and immigrants and, as a result, on the access of the latter to citizenship.

Note

1. All the names of my interviewees are fictional in order to protect their privacy.

References

Bericat, E. (2000) 'La sociología de la emoción y la emoción en la sociología', *Papers*, 62, 145–76.

Boudon, R. (1979) *La logique du social. Introduction à l'analyse sociologique*, Paris: Hachette.

Coenen-Huther, J. (1992) 'Production informelle de normes: les files d'attente en Russie soviétique', *Revue française de sociologie*, 33(2), 213–32.

Czwartosz, Z. (1988) 'On queueing', *Archives européennes de sociologie*, 29(1), 3–11.

Dubet, F. (2006) *Injustices. L'expérience des inégalités au travail*, Paris: Seuil.

Flam, H. and Beauzamy, B. (2007) 'Symbolic violence', in G. Delanty, P. Jones and R. Wodak (eds) *Identity, Belonging and Migration*, Liverpool: Liverpool University Press, 221–40.

Graham, M. (2003) 'Emotional bureaucracies: Emotions, civil servants, and immigrants in the Swedish welfare state', *Ethos*, 30(3), 199–226.

Goffman, E. (1956) 'Embarrassment and social organization', *American Journal of Sociology*, 62(3), 264–71.

Goffman, E. (1963) *Behavior in Public Places*, New York: Free Press.

Goffman, E. (1967) *Interaction Ritual*, New York: Doubleday.

Hachimi-Alaoui, M. (2007) *Les chemins de l'exil*. *Les Algériens exilés en France et au Canada depuis les années 1990*, Paris: L'Harmattan.

Halbwachs, M. (1947) 'L'expression des émotions et la société', *Échanges sociologiques*, Paris: Centre de documentation universitaire, http://classiques.uqac. ca/classiques/Halbwachs_maurice/classes_morphologie/partie_2/texte_2_4/ expression_emotions.pdf (accessed 23 September 2009).

Hochschild, A. (1979) 'Emotion work, feeling rules, and social structure', *American Journal of Sociology*, 85(3), 551–75.

Hochschild, A. (1997) *The Time Bind. When Work Becomes Home and Home Becomes Work*, New York: Henry Holt.

Katz, K., Larson, B. and Larson, R. (1991) 'Prescription for the waiting-in-line blues: Entertain, enlighten, and engage', *Sloan Management Review*, 32(2), 44–53.

Larson, R. (1987) 'Perspectives on queues: Social justice and the psychology of queuing', *Operations Research*, 34(6), 895–905.

Lee, R. (1984) 'Malaysian queue culture: An ethnography of urban public behaviour', *South East Asian Journal of Social Science*, 12(2), 36–50.

Lipsky, M. (1980) *Street-level Bureaucracy. Dilemmas of the Individual in Public Services*, New York: Russell Sage.

Mann, L. (1969) 'Queue culture: The waiting line as a social system', *American Journal of Sociology*, 75(3), 340–54.

Margalit, A. (1996) *The Decent Society*, Cambridge: Harvard University Press.

McPhail, C. and Wohlstein, R. (1983), 'Individual and collective behaviors within gatherings, demonstrations, and riots', *Annual Review of Sociology*, 9, 579–600.

Meyer, T. (2001) 'Subjective importance of goal and reactions to waiting in line', *The Journal of Social Psychology*, 134(6), 819–27.

Moessinger, P. (1977) 'Developmental study of the idea of lining up', *The Journal of Psychology*, 95, 173–78.

Paugam, S. (1991) *La disqualification sociale*, Paris: Seuil.

Pollak, M. (1990) *L'expérience concentrationnaire. Essai sur le maintien de l'identité sociale*, Paris: Métailié.

Rukavishnikov, V. (1990) 'The queue', *Soviet Sociology*, 29(5), 20–36.

Sabry, T. (2005) 'Emigration as popular culture. The case of Morocco', *European Journal of Cultural Studies*, 8(1), 5–22.

Sennett, R. (1998) *The Corrosion of Character: The Personal Consequences of Work in the New Capitalism*, New York: Norton.

Scheff, T. (1988) 'Shame and conformity: The deference-emotion system', *American Sociological Review*, 53(3), 395–406.

Scheff, T. (2000) 'Shame and the social bond: A sociological theory', *Sociological Theory*, 18(1), 84–99.

Schnapper, D. (1981) *L'épreuve du chômage*, Paris: Gallimard.

Schwartz, B. (1975) *Queuing and Waiting: Studies in the Social Organization of Access and Delay*, Chicago: University of Chicago Press.

Smith, D. (2001) 'Organizations and humiliation: Looking beyond Elias', *Organization*, 8(3), 537–60.

Vaughan, D. (1999) 'The dark side of organizations: Mistake, misconduct, and disaster', *Annual Review of Sociology*, 25, 271–305.

Von Scheve, C. and Von Luede, R. (2005) 'Emotion and social structures: Towards an interdisciplinary approach', *Journal for the Theory of Social Behaviour*, 35(3), 303–28.

Part II
Organizing Emotions

9
Talking (and Silencing) Emotions: The Culture of Mobilization in the Italian Communist Party During the 1940s

Andrea Cossu

1 Introduction

The tale of most communist organizations is a tale of discipline and preparation that tends to see distinct emotional cultures as problematic and residual. We can commonly witness not only a lack of attention to political symbolism in their own reflection on culture (though in practice the development and communication of political culture played a great role), but also that emotions are even more problematic than this expressive dimension when it comes to defining the characteristics and meanings of 'being' and 'acting' like a communist. Political organizations that have a background in the Marxist and Leninist traditions usually conceive the role that emotions and symbolism play in mobilization with an unsurprising suspicion: they mainly stress the nature of politics as being inherently rational and goal-oriented (Barbalet 1998). However, an effective mobilization of emotions is crucial for the formation of communist and class identity (Barbalet 1992), especially in transitional and 'effervescent moments' (Durkheim 1995) which go 'against bureaucracy' but are nonetheless governed by bureaucratic principles of efficiency and commitment to the organization's values. In addition the everyday, ordinary and routinized party life features a constant reference to how emotions should be 'used', governed and repressed.

This chapter deals with the relation of emotions, power and organizational constraints in the Italian Communist Party (PCI) during the late 1940s. I will argue that emotions played a role beyond 'effervescence', and that they were also disciplined in such a way as to shape effectively the 'communist self' of the militant and the cadre, a part of what Halfin (2003: 7) has described as a communist way to pursue a 'hermeneutics of the soul'.

My question is aimed at the emergence of a somehow counterintuitive aspect: what role do emotions play in an organizational culture that systematically discards them? Moreover, given the pivotal ambiguity in the party's perception of emotions as a powerful (and unavoidable) element of both political socialization and mobilization, according to what principles are the processes of affiliation of the individual to the collective moulded?

These questions may best be answered by framing them in terms of both a cultural history and a cultural sociology of emotions. Placing the use of emotions in its historical context (the peculiar situation of 1940s Italy) allows a consideration of some extra-organizational reasons for the demise of emotions in communist politics. Among these reasons, the most important is the attempt of the PCI to distance itself from the permanent mobilization of feelings pursued by the fascist regime. In turn, a cultural sociology of emotions helps in tracing the vicissitudes of emotional politics with reference to two major aspects that governed the shaping of the communist self in that period: the management of the relationship between the public and the private, on the one hand, and the dialectic between the individual and the collective, on the other. Needless to say, the communist pedagogy of the self (including the discipline of emotions) placed itself on the *collective* and *public* sector that resulted from the intersection of these two analytic axes. But since it was also a 'total' pedagogy aimed at a simultaneous reconfiguration of the private and the individual, I contend that emotions served to attenuate these boundaries and were instrumental in the creation of the PCI as a community of feelings (Berezin 2002) and as a community of practice and beliefs.

2   Conceptualizing the study of emotion in political organizations

The traditional conceptualization of political culture, centred on the cognitive aspects and on the prominence of values and beliefs in the constitution of culture (Almond/Verba 1965), quite systematically treated emotions as a residual and 'extrinsic' aspect of political orientation *qua* cognitive (and only secondarily affective) orientation (Berezin 2002: 34; Goodwin/Jasper 2006). More recent approaches to political culture that have emerged since the 1980s, however, have reconceptualized the relationship between the cognitive and socio-psychological aspects of political symbolism and their concrete expression, a turn that has assigned a new centrality to practices and performances. This attention to symbolism in action has often referred to the category of ritual, with the assumption that political identity is shaped *in vivo*, through interaction among social actors (Kertzer 1987; Bell 1997).

The tradition of ritual theory as a whole has always kept emotions at the centre of any culture-based account of political identity. Emotions, in this perspective, are one of the significant outcomes of ritual action, which is itself a highly sophisticated social practice that simultaneously sparks emotions and controls them: '*Rituals* serve to *channel emotions*, guide new experiences and knowledge, and promote group formation' (Kertzer 1987: 9).

If it were not for this performative dimension, emotional life could hardly be possible at a level that transcends individual experience and social interaction in the limited context of face-to-face interaction.

Political rituals have been often perceived as expressions of an irrational cult (e.g. Mosse 1975) that disrupts the normal pursuit of political goals in accordance to principles of interest and rationality. They direct the view onto individuals' collective and public action and reshape or soften the fundamental boundaries of modern life: i.e. the one between the public and the private sphere, and the one between the individual and the collective. The ritual agent is neither private nor 'completely' individual, because ritual prescribes total commitment to a situation in which the backstage (to use the analogy of Goffman 1959) is required to be suppressed. However, the relegation of emotions to the domain of irrational politics and authoritarian regimes is not satisfactory from an empirical point of view. In an increasing body of research, it is indeed argued that emotions are inextricably connected to various instances of collective action and mobilization (e.g. Aminzade/McAdam 2001), including ritual, and that some emotional activity is not simply *refined* but entirely created by action and mobilization, whether these emotions are *reciprocal* or *shared* (Jasper 1997: 185).

Researchers of political ritual have usually focused on shared emotions, as a consequence of the enduring power of functional interpretations of what ritual does and how it achieves its functions (e.g. creation of identity, solidarity, group integration). Yet the rituals that always accompany and shape political life are more complex and ambivalent, especially if we do not restrain ourselves to the vision of ritual as a type of action, but also take into consideration the fact that ritual can be most of the time conceived of as an 'element of action' (Roth 1995). Randall Collins' (2005) sociology of emotions clearly fits this perspective, since 'interaction rituals' are the context in which emotions are created and reproduced, but also because the adoption of a clearly micro-sociological point of view helps in defining rituals as broad activities that inhabit our everyday life. Ritual is present on the whole continuum of social interaction, from face-to-face encounters to mass gatherings, with the important implication that human behaviour is rooted in emotions and – in turn – that emotions shape social order, in terms of the alignment of the individual to collective norms, and produce social solidarity.

However, ritual celebrations are also highly ordered and coordinated social practices. In order for rituals to be effective, ritual agents and participants have to recognize the ritual as such and not as a seemingly chaotic juxtaposition of sounds movements, words, colours and gestures. Like other forms of collective action, they have somehow to be coded, scripted, staged and performed (Benford/Hunt 1992; see also, from a more pragmatic perspective, Eyerman 2006).

Theoretically, the issue of the scripting of ritual is crucial because the relationship between the scripts that govern performance (ritual included) have to be assessed in their relationship to the scripts that govern the expression of emotions in the ritual context. While the concept of scripting has achieved wide popularity in performance and ritual studies (for an overview see Schechner 2002), and in the sociology of emotions alike, the mutual relationship between performative scripts and emotional patterns has not been sufficiently assessed. Are they analytically independent? Do they constitute different facets of dealing with deeper structures and rules of conduct? How, in any case, can they be rejoined in an effective way?

If we consider one of the most recent and powerful proposals for the analysis of ritual *qua* performance – Alexander's (2004) cultural pragmatics – this tension between the scripts and rules that govern performance and the rules that govern emotions is most manifest. Emotions operate in the relationship between the actor and the cultural text that she/he brings to life in the performance. As such, emotional activity is filed under the category of *cathexis,* the actor's affective projection towards the representations and the rules of performance that are required to be executed in order to transform and translate the representations into action.

Cultural pragmatics' understanding of scripting hints to a macro-oriented theory (Alexander 2003) that focuses on some degree of cultural *autonomy*.[1] Moreover, it has the great advantage of making a distinction between different structural levels, and we can conceive of the process of scripting (that is, adapting the general rules to the situation, or socially constructing the situation with reference to the general rules) as the *trait d'union* between basic codes and the concrete expression of cultural meanings and feelings in social situations.

This attention to social performance and to its structural elements can prove useful in staying clear of the cognitivist and instrumentalist assumptions that have characterized many scholarly visions of culture (Swidler 1986; Eyerman/Jamison 1991).

The seminal work of Hochschild (1979) on feeling rules provides a starting point for a successful incorporation of emotions into the broader framework of the discussion about ritual, and political ritual in particular. Hochschild's argument stresses the existence of feeling rules that guide emotion work and that are defined as 'guidelines for the assessment of fits and misfits between feeling and situation' (ibid.: 566). Coupled with these rules, display rules prescribe how emotions have to be made public, or silenced, in agreement with the norms and practices of specific cultures (or social settings). In other words, display rules are embedded in the procedures that govern the *mise-en-scène* of emotions in social situations. This focus on rules and parameters of acceptability hints to a vision of culture that is simultaneously enabling and constraining. Not only does culture define what emotions can or must be expressed and how, but there is also a normative dimension, which actors cannot avoid when they 'feel' and express how they are supposed or required to feel in public.

This is the more ideological side of the argument. With regards to the domain of politics, organization (and organizations which are highly bureaucratic in their general form) should not be understood simply as a residual aspect. Organizational culture and organizational best practices shape both how action has to be performed and how individuals should feel in the context of it. This is exactly what political theories that dismiss the relevance of cultural factors have neglected, along with the relevant findings of sociologists who have focused on the specific role that emotions play in shaping the life of organizations.

In the case of the PCI 'organization' tended to be perceived according to highly original principles; they defined a characteristic culture that was both opposed to the wider culture of society and shaped according to a cosmological vision that was supposed to guide individual life and collective action alike. The problem of the emotional identity of the communists is located in this quite narrow space, whose boundaries were drawn simultaneously by an utopian vision, a positive evaluation of highly structured organization, a counterintuitive attention to the symbolic and cultural aspects of politics and an ambiguity in the perception and use of emotions. I will now turn to the example of the PCI and a reconstruction of its context, its idea of bureaucracy and its use of ritual, through which I will demonstrate the ambivalence of both using and silencing emotions. The empirical material for the analysis comes from sources as diverse as reports from the party press, internal instructions and documents about the celebration of ritual that make the scripts more explicit than any other available source. I conducted research in the archives of the PCI, looking especially for minutes of the meetings of the Political Office and the Secretariat, where political matters and the organization of major political mobilizations were discussed. I also checked the files regarding the activities of the Commissions for Organization and Propaganda (*Il Propagandista* and *Il Quaderno dell'Attivista*). Since my focus is on the life and political culture of the PCI during the 1940s, I considered documents that regarded the period from 1943 to 1949. I also selected articles published in the daily newspaper *L'Unità* (several editions), and in the publications of the Commissions for Propaganda and Organization.

3   Making bureaucracy work in 1940s Italy: The rise and consolidation of the PCI

In the wake of the fall of fascism, in late July 1943, the PCI had about 5000 active members in the whole country (Secchia 1954), with many more serving sentences in prison. It was a typical Leninist organization of professional revolutionaries devoted to underground work and conspiracy. This picture changed with the onset of the Resistance and with the liberation of more and more areas following the Allied invasion.[2] By March 1944, the party's membership rose to 80,000 in the liberated regions of the south, and after the so called 'svolta di Salerno' the party expanded to an estimate of 700,000 members by the end of 1944 in the regions of central and southern Italy.[3] At the end of the war, in April 1945, there were more members, about 100,000 of them in the areas of northern Italy where the Resistance had been fiercer and lasted longer. The official report of the Political Office to the Party's 5th congress (December 1945 to January 1946) claims an even bigger organization, with an alleged 1,800,000 members by September 1945. A year later, the total number of members rose to 2,068,000, and by September 1947 it reached its highest point with an alleged 2,252,000 members (PCI 1947: 9).

These figures describe the huge development of the party in just two years, but they merely hint at the myriads of organizational and political problems that the rise in the membership brought to the communist elite that had been socialized to politics in a different context. This elite was, in some respect, unprepared to govern what Gundle (2000: 7) has described as the creation of the 'last great left-wing political culture in Europe'. The new generation of communists, which entered the party during the Resistance or after the Liberation, was alien to the rational and goal-oriented vision of politics that many of the older cadres and activists had. The leaders stigmatized an attachment to the party based only on 'feelings' and a non-rational desire for radical and immediate social change, and they felt that the main task of the PCI was to educate the masses to political action and to build a disciplined organization.

This internal view is, however, potentially misleading. It offers a vision of the optimal path that had to be followed in the creation of the disciplined organization that the party leaders had in mind, while at the same time silencing the much richer process of the creation of a distinct communist culture in the postwar years. The 'art of the organization', to quote a widely circulated article by deputy-secretary Pietro Secchia (1945), conceived organization first and foremost as a *techne*, with little room for improvization or an amateurish attitude: 'A party is made up of men, and we should take them as they are. But we must also try to improve and educate them, to give them the qualities they currently lack of, and in the meantime it is also necessary that we do our ordinary work'. Indeed, organization was 'neither a game nor a 'field for experimentation' (ibid.: 269).

At the same time the party feared the excesses of bureaucratization that could undermine its capacity to mobilize and make organization an end rather than a means to achieve political goals. Secchia (1946: 20) spoke explicitly and quite freely of the predominance of 'bureaucratic work' at the expense of activity among the masses. And it was again Secchia (1948), as the person in charge for organizational matters, who stigmatized the existence of a 'bureaucratic tendency that consists in expectations that everything [directives and orders; A.C.] comes from above' (ibid.: 16).

What kind of solutions did the PCI's leadership envisage? Not surprisingly, the Leninist (and Stalinist) beliefs of the leaders, and their old procedures rooted in decades of clandestine activity, had to be adapted to the polymorphous character of the 'new party'. The party sought a balance between autonomy, discipline and control, in which 'being a communist' was a major reference both normatively and in terms of everyday practice. Rituals specifically aimed at the construction of the communist self played a major role here, in a seemingly manifest contradiction with the rationalistic and 'scientific' discourse that was simultaneously the object and the means of political socialization.

4   Rituals, emotions and the moulding of the communist self

Political organizations of the mass-party type are always characterized by a high degree of ritual activity. This includes not only the large, recurrent mobilizations that take place periodically (rallies, congresses, feasts) but also a more nuanced, sophisticated series of rituals that punctuate the daily life of the militant. The top-down construction of the militant's identity is performed in a double way: first, by softening the boundaries between the private and public aspects of personality and individual identity, and second by subordinating the individual to the collective. Emotions (felt, discussed, and sanctioned) are at the centre of this double process. I argue that it was mainly thanks to feeling distinct emotions, which were perceived and evaluated differently in the organization, that the key tasks of making and becoming a communist were carried out. Thus being a communist was a totalizing experience and the militants were most of the time willing to subordinate themselves to the decisions of the organization, even in matters that were *prima facie* alien to political intervention (Bellassai 2000). Emotion work was employed both to incorporate the individual into the collective and to signal the distinction between the members of the party and the external others. Emotional tone signified differences, almost irreducible, between the in- and out-groups, and was particularly effective in both the construction of communist identity and the labelling of the enemy, especially in times of political confrontation.

4.1   Continuity and anti-fascism

The definition of 'the communist' regarded any aspect of the individual, and it was all the more important in the Italian context which had witnessed a parallel attempt, that had lasted 20 years, to mould a genuinely Italian 'fascist self' (Berezin 1997). There was an explicit concern, on the communist leaders' side, to distance themselves from the kind of politics of emotions that had characterized fascism's spectacular state (Falasca Zamponi 1997).

Accordingly, in the PCI's vision, politics had to be detached from emotions and the latter had to be strategically employed for more practical purposes such as the ones of agitation and propaganda. This can be seen in a party document that dates back to the political campaign for the local elections of 1946, which clearly stresses the separation between politics and emotions. The party leadership, at that point, feared a dismissal of the catchwords associated with anti-fascism as a central element of propaganda. Therefore, instructions to local organizations criticized the fact that the theme of anti-fascism had become used less and less in the party's political campaign. Reference to anti-fascism was useful in fulfilling two objectives; 'one which is mainly political, the other *affective-emotional*' (Sezione Propaganda 1946). Although external to the common interpretation of politics as a rational calculation, emotions were thus not completely disregarded in the vision the party had of political participation, mobilization and socialization.

But there was also another concern in trying to exploit the powerful symbolism of anti-fascism in the first years of the transition to democracy. The stress on anti-fascist, socialist and, particularly, communist symbols served to express the continuity between the underground party that had fought the battle for liberation during the Resistance and the mass party that was making a contribution to the Italian transition.

Since the Resistance, which especially for the communist partisans of central and northern Italy had been a violent and sometimes traumatic event, public celebrations often implied both a cult of the dead and a civic discourse on the survivors. In communities where communist hegemony was widespread, this also created a sense of continuity and provided the ground for a bonded political community that turned around a very organized and ritualized daily life. Even in the years when anti-communism was more dominant in Italy (from 1947 to 1956) the PCI built an alternative world and an alternative symbolic system.

4.2 Scripting the rituals

The PCI faced the problem of a double incorporation of subaltern masses in republican Italy: into the party and into the state, two tasks that potentially meant the recourse to contradictory frames, discourses and practices. It is surprising, in this context, how ritual was actually used to a great extent in the achievement of this double objective. As a consequence, organizational concerns informed both the way communist rituals were performed and the way they were talked about in public.

Like many organizations with a centralized propaganda commission, the PCI paid great attention to the uniformity of ritual and other forms of political communication. Local organizations had to conform to best practices established by the centre, and there was a general drive towards emulation and competition among local organizations in inventing and developing useful forms of propaganda.

The centre of the party exercised great formal control on celebrations and ceremonies, especially for what concerned the two main types of ritual activity by the party: commemorations (Cossu forthcoming) and political campaigns (including more radical forms of mobilization such as strikes). Guidelines were issued regularly in the communist press and in the publications that were meant mainly for internal use, like *Propaganda*, *Il Quaderno del Propagandista* and later *Il Quaderno dell'Attivista*. Here we find one of the most important and neglected sources for the analysis of the top-down process of the creation of political symbolism among the communists.

These short, one-page instructions for the celebration of communist rituals usually focused on what the communist propagandists perceived as the relevant elements of symbolic action. These elements were shaped by the propagandists' particular vision of politics as inherently rational, and of symbolic action as having an educational goal. The participants *had* to learn and educate themselves through ritual, and thus the dominant stress was placed on *words* and *discourse* as the central element of celebration. History and current affairs were merged in the unitary and teleological communist vision of progress and struggle for the advancement of the subaltern classes.

However, rituals had to be staged, and their *mise-en-scène* often revealed something more than was in the words or in the intentions of the organizers. Whereas explicit instructions focused mostly on the *scripts* that had to guide the performance of ritual and its alignment to the dominant verbal culture of the party, little was explicitly said about the way the outcome of ritual action (in terms of heightened emotion and sense of community) had to be handled by the organizer. This silence highlighted either a vision of symbolic action as something that did not generate problematic outcomes in terms of identity or one of the audience of ritual as an undifferentiated and mostly passive 'mass'.

But since the goal of the communists in promoting public gatherings and celebrations was also the awakening of 'consciousness' in the participants, it was clear to the organization that the communitarian dimension generated by aesthetic politics was a crucial element that had to be governed in the process of consolidating and strengthening the communist party. The incorporation of ritual into everyday communist practices owed much to that analysis of culture and action, and also to the practical lessons that the communist leadership drew from the development of Soviet ritual as a way to 'become Bolshevik' in Lenin's and Stalin's Soviet Union. Indeed, since many of the prominent leaders had lived in exile in the Soviet Union, they were exposed to Soviet rituals and learned much about their organization and efficacy (Lane 1981). Commemorations, in particular, were designed as occasions for the display of party symbols and the production of narratives about the party, the class and their role in the democratization of the republic (either within the context of national unity or within the framework of 'progressive' people's democracy). The celebrations of November 7, June 21 (the anniversary of the foundation of the party), April 25 (Liberation Day), May Day and April 27 (the anniversary of Gramsci's death) were usually performed according to centralized scripts. The rituals often featured a combination of political rallies and popular feasts that incorporated into the PCI's cultural system the element of local and national folklore (Gundle 2000). Not surprisingly, however, the central element was the celebratory speech by a local or national party leader.

If we consider that one of the main goals of these gatherings was to provide the masses with a basic level of political education, this focus on the dimension of discourse is understandable. But we also have to consider at least one important aspect that shaped communist ritual in the late 1940s; implicitly or not, the communist leadership held a cognitive vision of the function of ritual practices. Ritual, in other words, had to (and was effective only in so far as it was able to) generate shared beliefs that could guide a specific communist interpretation of the world, one of power and class relations.

This vision of symbolic action was consistent with the more general system of beliefs of the communists. Ritual was not just a specific action but part of the broader environment in which speeches and discourses could achieve their performative function, the transformation of identity. Since the process of transformation was conceived of as a transition between different levels of individual consciousness, involving a rational and reasoning actor, communist rituals were explicitly designed as word-centred, in sharp opposition to the type of political symbolism that had been exploited by fascism.

Yet a focus only on these limited written sources tells us less about the organization and functions of communist rituals than one could expect. If we take into consideration only the understanding of these ritualized occasions from the point of view of the communist leadership, many relevant characteristics can be missed and emotions are certainly among them.

4.3 The discourse of emotions

So far, indeed, one could argue that one of the central features of communist rituals was the implicit suppression of any emotion in favour of a completely rationalized vision of political action that was, of course, attuned to the bureaucratic principles that shaped the 'art of organization'. Were the feeling rules of the PCI something close to *suppression rules*, a set of implicit and explicit guidelines for the domestication of emotional life within the context of symbolic action? Or were there some more invisible features that a mere consideration of the top-down organization of ritual activities cannot reveal?

Indeed, the communist leaders and activists could not simply ignore that the rituals they staged also owed their pragmatic efficacy to the fact that they were able (in most cases) to generate feelings in their participants. So, while the suppression of emotions was often seen as an element for 'good' political action, communists (like any person or group facing the power of collective and symbolic action) could not escape the management of emotions. Their interpretations on the subject were constrained by their Marxist framework, but their accounts of ritual often reveal more than they intended.

First, one should consider carefully that discourse about emotions and feelings abounded in the PCI, even though it was often confined to some specific aspects of communist life and the education of activists and members as communists. Therefore, emotions were absent from the explicit discussion on culture and politics, but were present (and to a surprisingly large extent, in the press, in reports of the meetings and in the 'advices' for everyday life that were published in less serious magazines like *Vie Nuove* or *Noi Donne*). Indeed, in a party where the actions and the life of the individuals had to be lived in accordance with the normative standards of the organization, and in which the organization itself continuously assessed the alignment of the individual to its 'cosmology', the discourse about feelings and their presence in private and political life fulfilled, again, pedagogic objectives.

If emotions, as the communists understood them, belonged to the sphere of the individual, they had to be publicly assessed and politicized in the process of softening the boundaries between the individual and the collective, the private and the public, as discussed earlier. Accounts of the optimal life of the communist activist as a woman, male, father or worker, in his or her role, which transcended the political sphere, were often accompanied by an interpretation of emotions. As if by telling how a person should feel in performing that role, one could also tell what distinguished a good communist from a bad one – or from one who had only partially learnt the individual management of his or her own communist identity.

Quite notably, however, the reference to emotions was much more common when the press wrote about women, in accordance with a masculine vision of politics. However, these guidelines for the self focused more on the private/public boundary than on the one between the individual and the collective. The boundary between individual and collective, discussed endlessly both in the communist press and in the meetings of the central party organization, was challenged by the communist effort simultaneously to shape both the 'partito nuovo' and the communist self.

In fact, when it came to describing ritual and considering whether it was effective or not, the communist leadership quite counter-intuitively adopted some reference to emotions and displayed a clear idea about feelings as being in some cases a valuable outcome of ritual action. Yet, again, the assessment of emotions and their value was constrained by organizational factors as well as the specific communist worldview. The pattern of association between types and elements of ritual action was uneven, although some important regularities can be retrieved. These regularities highlight how rules of expression were associated to symbolic action and how the communists interpreted them, with particular reference to (a) the actors who felt emotions and (b) the specific aspect of ritual and the frame of execution of it that allowed or suppressed the expression of emotions.

Official rituals usually were described with hardly any reference to emotions. The crowd was seen in neutral terms, and described with reference to its size or, at best, its quiet behaviour (*L'Unità*, n.a. 1945a; 1945b; 1946 are just a few examples, regarding the celebrations of April 25 and May 1). Leisure activities that followed official celebrations, though, were portrayed in terms of the expression of joy, as if to point out that there was a time outside the performance of official ritual where emotions could be expressed and evaluated positively (*L'Unità*, A.R. 1946). Yet on all these occasions the subjects of emotions are not the communists, but rather the people as a whole – a vision that emotions can be talked about only with reference to external subjects (or to collective actors who are not entirely true believers) that also resurfaces when negative emotions are evoked, as I will illustrate later in the case of the attempted assassination of Togliatti.

I argue that accounts in the communist press about ritual speak of the communists as subjects of emotions and they hint at a dimension that has so far been neglected when it comes to the understanding of the general process of creating a communist identity. An analysis of the communist press and newspaper reports of rituals, mobilizations and celebrations supports the interpretation that some suppression of emotions in the ritual context was not only desired but also encouraged as a way to create the communist self.

One should note that the bulk of activity was systematically not correlated to emotions, ranging from political mobilizations such as strikes to some ritual celebrations that involved mostly party members and whose descriptions were standardized with the exclusion of any concrete or characteristic reference to any feeling, such as joy, rage or grief. Thus, the more an activity was understood as one that belonged to the domain of rational action or structured action organized by the party, the more it was portrayed in an 'objective' way that carried no mention of a vocabulary of feelings.

Political mobilizations, especially when they were perceived by the communists as goal-oriented and not permeated by ritual and symbolic elements, were indeed subject to this neutralization of emotions. One of the most important waves of strikes that shook fascist northern Italy in March 1944, for example, was described in completely 'objective' terms, meaning the strength and presence of the workers' movements, and featured accounts of the number of workers who decided to go on strike, the actions they took and an evaluation of the success of the strike in getting the support of the great majority of the workers in the industrial towns of the north (*L'Unità*, n.a. 1944).

After the liberation, when the PCI's membership rose and its activism was feared by conservative forces, the articles published in the communist press reported the 'orderliness' and 'quietness' of the rallies organized by the party, focusing only sporadically on the sentiments felt by the crowds of participants and usually only in positive terms. This was not just a strategy of representation. Since the press was at the time one of the most important elements that connected the party's central organization and its members, such portrayals of the communists implicitly suggested how they had to be, reproducing a normative discourse about communist identity that marginalized emotions into a periphery.

Both the explicit scripts for rituals and the post facto accounts in the communist press thus paid little attention to the affective dimension of mass politics and symbolic actions, especially when only party members or sympathizers were involved. However, when it came to the focus on the PCI as an actor pursuing the goal of 'nationalization' of the masses in the transition to democracy, the vocabulary of feelings reemerged. In many cases, this happened with reference to the occasions that the PCI saw as a legacy of the nation, where the party did not claim the rights to the symbolic property of an event or a celebration. May 1 and April 25 are probably the most important dates when this focus on emotions was present and different from the silence that characterized other descriptions of political rallies and mass gatherings. *L'Unità* described the celebration of May 1, 1945, held in Rome, as a 'May Day of joy and freedom' (it was the first celebration after the end of the War) (*L'Unità*, n.a. 1945a), and accounts of the people gathering in the main squares of Rome often made reference to this festive dimension.

Many communist rituals of the time were organized in such a way that festive elements (dances, sport competitions and even beauty pageants) were juxtaposed with the more 'serious' times and places of a political gathering that featured the dominant elements of communist propaganda and rituals: the discourses and the pedagogical connotations that the communists always attached to them. This doublesideedness of communist ritual thereby served simultaneously as a way to incorporate emotions in a ritual context and to keep them within the boundaries of its festive side.

Whereas positive emotions were deemed important in this context, as ancillary to political mobilization and its rational goals, the overall drive towards suppression that affected the expression and the description of positive emotions at the level of the central organization also functioned to dismiss and silence negative ones. Negative emotions were more commonly associated with political enemies and – if and when they were associated with members of the party – were always excluded from the description of both ritual action and mobilizations at large.

The most striking examples regard the popular and party reaction to the attempted murder of the party's secretary Palmiro Togliatti (who was almost shot dead on 14 July 1948), which offer particularly good evidence of the asymmetry in the management of feelings by the PCI.

The articles published by *L'Unità* in the days after the attempted assassination are striking for the portrayal of the actors involved in the event and the popular protests that followed. It was obviously a moment when feelings of rage and hatred towards the government and conservative forces flooded the hearts of the militants and guided their actions. Yet the communist press was silent about them; it only referred to the feelings of the communists once Togliatti was recovering and his life was no longer in danger. If the events of July 1948 were to be seen as a mobilization, and this certainly was almost an insurrectional mobilization at least in some areas, they had to be depicted as completely nonemotional, and *L'Unità* preferred to refer to the '48 hours of struggle' and to 'the red flags on the factories' (*L'Unità*, n.a. 1948a; 1948b). Emotional subjects in general and subjects of hatred, in particular, were positioned as adversaries of the party, and the accounts in the communist press used emotions and feelings to trace boundaries between social groups and to elevate the communists above their adversaries. Indeed, there was an uneven distribution of emotions between the communists and the government and police, with the latter being attacked for their 'hatred' and labelled as 'bandits', whereas there was no reference to resentment in the portrayal of the communist mobilizations (*L'Unità*, n.a. 1948c). It was only when the struggle was over and it was known that Togliatti would survive being shot, that positive emotions such as joy and relief erupted and were thus reported in the press, coupled with the quiet mourning for those who had died in the protests (*L'Unità*, n.a. 1948d).

This contradictary aspect of the discourse about emotions hints once more at the difficulty of representation within the communist political culture. The culture of the organization, and the procedures that were established right after the Liberation, influenced the accounts of emotions and pushed them *outside* what the communists perceived as the main element of their political actions. The socialization to politics and internalization of the emotions associated with the polity were mainly performed during these crucial years of the foundation of the 'new party'.

5 Conclusions

Ritual played a central role in the creation of a communist identity during the late 1940s; it was an important part of political education, both the socialization to the party's values and frames and the education to collective action. The common accounts in the communist press of rituals, descriptions of ritual activities and the prescriptions about the way rituals had to be scripted, staged and performed point to their role in shaping the communist self and in the creation of the communist party as a collectivity of action and beliefs.

Yet, within this context, the ambiguity of emotions in the organization was always on the surface. The asymmetry in evaluating emotions that emerges in the analysis of political mobilizations and ritual celebrations hints at the difficulty of thinking about emotions in a completely positive way. In turn, this was linked to the optimal vision of organization, a normative aspect that ultimately can be connected to the broader, 'cosmological' vision of the party and its struggle for socialism and political change.

Much of the ritual activity involved emotions to a greater or lesser degree. However, the way the communists talked and wrote about those practices was much more focused on their structural or 'rational' elements than on emotions per se. In political mobilizations, emotions (especially negative ones such as hatred) were stigmatized and linked to a perceived enemy that felt 'class' hatred. Positive emotions, such as relief or pride, associated to the communists, were often used to describe either the outcome of the mobilization or a 'cooling off' time that followed mobilization. But mobilization per se had to be (and had to be talked about) in completely nonemotional terms. There was room, indeed, for positive emotions, but they were almost always perceived as an ancillary aspect of politics, something that had to be almost eradicated if the communist self was to live up to the expectations of the leaders and the necessities of the organization.

On a more general level, the scripts that governed the expression of feelings, which paralleled the more detailed scripts for the performance of ritual, were much more problematic than the latter. One of the reasons for this is that communist rituals were specifically designed to highlight elements of political participation (reasoning and the understanding of the party's line), and this task was best accomplished by a focus on the formal elements of discourse. Therefore there was a marginalization of feelings and emotional politics. Organizational constraints played a role in giving the standards for the interpretation of best practices. The whole process of scripting and talking about emotions was affected by both the organizational culture and the established bureaucratic practices that constituted the 'art of the organization'. As a community (of practice, beliefs and feelings), the PCI was shaped as a major political actor *within* the constraints imposed by this contradiction. The goal of this chapter has been to illustrate how and to what extent broader representations about the cultural horizon of the organization, which are translated into ordinary practices of governing the party, create the legitimate framework for the expression or the suppression of feelings and the discourses about them.

Notes

1. It should be noted, however, that in its most complete formulation 'cultural pragmatics' is simultaneously a theory of action (hence the focus on *cathexis*), a theory of institutions and a theory of how culture works, and is not merely intentionalist or instrumentalist.
2. The Resistance started in the days following the armistice with the allied troops, in early September 1943. The communist party and the other anti-fascist forces organized military resistance and liberation committees in the zones occupied by the Germans. Although an accurate estimate of the number of partisans is impossible, it is commonly believed that about 80 per cent of the fighting partisans were communists or affiliated with the mainly communist 'Garibaldi' brigades. For a short introduction to the history of the Resistance, see Peli (2006).
3. The 'svolta di Salerno' is a major political change in the strategy of the party that started with the return of the secretary, Palmiro Togliatti, from the Soviet Union. In a series of speeches after his arrival in southern Italy, he called for collaboration by the major political forces with the monarchy, and for the temporary abandonment of the discussion about the form of the post-war political regime.

References

Almond, G. and Verba, S. (1965) *The Civic Culture*, Boston: Little Brown.
Alexander, J.C. (2003) *The Meanings of Social Life*, Oxford: Oxford University Press.
Alexander, J.C. (2004) 'Cultural pragmatics: Social performance between ritual and strategy', *Sociological Theory*, 22(4), 527–73.
Alexander, J.C., Giesen, B. and Mast, J.L. (eds) (2006) *Social Performance. Symbolic Action between Ritual and Strategy*, Cambridge: Cambridge University Press.
Aminzade, R.R. and McAdam, D. (2001) 'Emotions and contentious politics', in R.R. Aminzade, J.A. Goldstone, D. McAdam, E.J. Perry, W.H. Sewell jr., S. Tarrow and C. Tilly *Silence and Voice in the Study of Contentious Politics*, Cambridge: Cambridge University Press, 14–50.
Barbalet, J. (1992) 'A macro sociology of emotions: Class resentment', *Sociological Theory*, 2, 150–63.
Barbalet, J. (1998) *Emotions, Social Theory, Social Structure. A Macrosociological Approach*, Cambridge: Cambridge University Press.
Bell, C. (1997) *Ritual: Perspectives and Dimensions*, Oxford: Oxford University Press.
Bellassai, S. (2000) *La morale comunista*, Rome: Carocci.
Benford, R.D and Hunt, S.A. (1992) 'Dramaturgy and social movements: The social construction and communication of power', *Sociological Inquiry*, 62(1), 36–55.

Berezin, M. (1997) *Making the Fascist Self: The Political Culture of Interwar Italy*, New York: Cornell University Press.

Berezin, M. (2002) 'Secure states: Towards a political sociology of emotions', in J. Barbalet (ed.) (2002) *Emotions and Sociology*, London: Basil Blackwell, 33–52.

Collins, R. (2005) *Interaction Ritual Chains*, Princeton: Princeton University Press.

Cossu, A. (forthcoming) 'Making communist memory: The Italian Communist Party and the appropriation of the Italian Resistance, 1943–8', appears in *Memory Studies*.

Durkheim, E. (1995) *The Elementary Forms of Religious Life*, New York: Basic Books.

Eyerman, R. (2006) 'Performing opposition, or how social movements move', in Alexander et al. (2006), 193–217.

Eyerman, R. and Jamison, A. (1991) *Social Movements: A Cognitive Approach*, Oxford: Polity Press.

Falasca Zamponi, E. (1997) *Fascist Spectacle: The Aesthetics of Power in Mussolini's Italy*, Berkeley: University of California Press.

Goffman, E. (1959) *The Presentation of Self in Everyday Life*, New York: Doubleday.

Goodwin, J. and Jasper, J.M. (2006) 'Emotions and social movements', in J.E. Stets and J.H. Turner (eds) *Handbook of the Sociology of Emotions*, New York: Springer, 611–35.

Gundle, S. (2000) *Between Hollywood and Moscow: The Italian Communists and the Challenge of Mass Culture*, Durham: Duke University Press.

Halfin, I. (2003) *Terror in My Soul. Communist Autobiographies on Trial*, Cambridge: Harvard University Press.

Hochschild, A. (1979) 'Emotion work, feeling rules, and social structure', *American Journal of Sociology*, 85(3), 551–75.

Jasper, J.M. (1997) *The Art of Moral Protest. Culture, Biography and Creativity in Social Movements*, Chicago: University of Chicago Press.

Kertzer, D.I. (1987) *Ritual Politics and Power*, New Haven: Yale University Press.

Lane, C. (1981) *The Rites of Rulers. Ritual in Industrial Society: The Soviet Case*, Cambridge: Cambridge University Press.

L'Unità, A.R. (1946) '25 aprile. Il popolo balla nelle strade', *L'Unità*, Rome, 27 April 1946, 2.

L'Unità, (1944) 'Vittoriosi scioperi nel Nord', *L'Unità*, clandestine edition, March 1944.

L'Unità (1945a) 'Oltre centomila lavoratori salutano il Primo Maggio della libertà e della vittoria', *L'Unità*, 3 May 1945, 2.

L'Unità (1945b) 'Festa del popolo festa della repubblica', *L'Unità*, 27 April 1945, 1.

L'Unità (1946) 'Basta con la monarchia, hanno proclamato i lavoratori italiani', *L'Unità*, 3 May 1946, 1.

L'Unità (1948a) '48 ore di lotta di tutto il popolo italiano', *L'Unità*, 16 July 1948, 1.

L'Unità (1948b) 'Bandiere rosse sulle fabbriche', *L'Unità*, 16 July 1948, 1.

L'Unità (1948c) 'La lotta continua', *L'Unità*, 17 July 1948, 1.

L'Unità (1948d) 'Le bandiere rosse del lavoro saluteranno la salma di Glionna', *L'Unità*, Rome, 21 July 1948, 2.

Mosse, G. (1975) *The Nationalization of the Masses: Political Symbolism in Germany from the Napoleonic Wars through the Third Reich*, New York: Howard Fertig.

Peli, S. (2006) *Storia della Resistenza in Italia*, Turin: Einaudi.

PCI (Partito Comunista Italiano) (1947) *L'attività del partito in cifre*, Rome a cura della Commissione centrale d'organizzazione.

Roth, A. (1995) 'Men wearing masks: Issues of description in the analysis of ritual', *Sociological Theory*, 13(3), 301–27.

Schechner, R. (2002) *Performance Studies. An Introduction*, London: Routledge.

Secchia, P. (1945) 'L'arte dell'organizzazione', *Rinascita*, 2(12).

Secchia, P. (1946) *Migliorare il lavoro di partito. Rapporto di Organizzazione tenuto al V congresso nazionale del PCI*, Rome: Società Editrice de l'Unità.

Secchia, P. (1948) *Più forti i quadri, migliore l'organizzazione. Intervento al VI congresso del PCI*, January 1948, Rome: Casa Editrice de l'Unità.

Secchia, P. (1954) *I comunisti e l'insurrezione*, Rome: Editori Riuniti.

Sezione propaganda (1946) *Circolare n° 1, Propaganda per la campagna elettorale*, APC, Direzione, Sezioni di lavoro, Sezione propaganda 110/545, Rome, 2 February 1946.

Swidler, A. (1986) 'Culture in action: Symbols and strategies', *American Sociological Review*, 51(2), 273–86.

10
From Bureaucratic Agencies to Modern Service Providers: The Emotional Consequences of the Reformation of Labour Administration in Germany

Sylvia Terpe and Silvia Paierl

1 Introduction

In recent years, public employment services all over Europe have been restructured. The common intention of all these reforms was to overcome old administrative structures that were seen as ineffective and bureaucratic; new service-oriented administrations were to be established instead. Like other institutions in the public sector, the German Federal Employment Agency (FEA, *Bundesagentur für Arbeit*) was modernized along the lines of New Public Management. Our question is what emotional consequences ensued for FEA employees as a result of this reformation.

The chapter is organized as follows: in section 2, we present the reforms' central guidelines and principles. Against this background, we then turn our attention to the reforms' organizational core element: the jobcentres. Their employees are not just facing new processing tools like action programmes and client groups (3.1), they are expected to possess a variety of communication skills for their encounters with clients as well. In section 3.2, we analyse the FEA guidelines for these encounters and look for the feeling rules demanded of placement officers. Afterwards (3.3), we discuss whether these feeling rules request employees' voluntary emotion work or involuntary emotional labour, and then propose a classification of feeling rules according to their motivational force. In section 3.4, we finally present three groups of placement officers who feel obligated to adopt different feeling rules and can be characterized by typical emotional reactions with regard to their clients and the reforms' objectives. The empirical basis of these descriptions stems from a qualitative study with 65 placement officers conducted by Ludwig-Mayerhofer and colleagues. Although this study was not explicitly concerned with feeling rules and emotions, publications by this research group reveal manifold references to the affective dimensions of FEA employees' work.[1]

2 Reform of the German labour administration

In Germany, the reformation of the labour administration is closely connected to the report by the so-called Hartz Commission (*Hartz Kommission*), at whose suggestion an organizational restructuring was initiated in 2003. A new management-by-objectives approach was installed and a complex controlling and benchmarking system was set up, measuring a multitude of operating figures monthly to survey the degree to which the respective goals were attained. The process of service delivery (like counselling, training or placement) was reorganized according to cost-benefit logic (Bender et al. 2006: 58, 68; cf. Hielscher/ Ochs 2009: 19, 28;).

In addition to the desired strengthening of efficiency and effectiveness, the reforms were initiated with the ambition of transforming labour administration into a modern service provider based on the needs of clients, who from now on would be called 'customers'. The local employment offices were reorganized into jobcentres (*Kundenzentren*), which consist of specialized units responsible for different aspects of customer services in order to reduce waiting periods and long waiting lines. In scheduled appointments, a special placement service team takes care of customers in individual face-to-face interviews to advise and support them in finding a new job (cf. Bender et al. 2006: 61, 104, 115; Hielscher/Ochs 2009: 20f.).

At this point, it has to be emphasized that equating public service recipients with customers is quite problematic. The term 'customer' hides the fact that claimants are not enabled to choose between different services and products freely as customers in a market can do (cf. Hielscher/Ochs 2009: 32). Those who apply for or receive unemployment benefits usually have no other options– therefore we will use the term 'clients' in later sections to bear in mind their dependence on the labour administration services. Moreover, the FEA and its local branches are obliged to monitortheir clients' willingness to work and they have the right to impose sanctions in cases of abuse of benefits or misbehaviour (cf. Ludwig-Mayerhofer et al. 2009: 28). Since even an alleged lack of motivation or effort might give rise to sanctions, Jacobi and Mohr speak of a new 'distrusting welfare state' (2007: 226f.). Customer orientation on the one hand and authority rights on the other are inherently contradictory. This antagonism goes back to a shift in the idea of how the labour market functions. In contrast to the prior assumption of mainly structural unemployment, the new perspective lays its emphasis on the supply side of labour. It assumes unemployment to be the result of poorly qualified persons and/or people who are not motivated or flexible enough to find a new job (cf. Bieling 2006: 67). Based on this assumption, a new policy of activation has set in, which addresses the attitudes and motivations of the unemployed (van Berkel/Borghi 2008: 334; cf. Hielscher/Ochs 2009: 22;) and asks them to prove their efforts for labour market integration regularly.

Just like the new service orientation, this policy of activation emphasizes the communicative process between clients and staff; yet, while the term 'service' implies a rather equal relationship to a customer-like client, the term 'activation' points towards the clients' obligations and the staff's duties to monitor them, and therefore towards the unequal character of their relationship. This contradictory nature of the relation between the involved actors manifests in the proceedings and encounters in jobcentres.

3 Jobcentres as places of communication and emotion

3.1 Organizational standards of dealing with clients' and employees' emotional reactions

An essential element in the reform process was the introduction of new methods of customer management. The counselling and placement processes are structured by so called action programmes (*Handlungsprogramme*), which determine how to deal with clients. They prescribe different modes of support and define how often a client gets an 'invitation' for a personal interview. The selection of an action programme is decided upon according to the client's individual profile, which includes an in-depth assessment of the person's background, needs, aspirations, strengths and weaknesses (cf. Jacobi/Mohr 2007: 228; Arnkil et al. 2008: 9). For this profiling, the placement officer has to employ a standardized diagnostic tool which assigns the job seeker to one of four client groups (Behrend et al. 2006: 3; cf. Bender et al. 2006: 155ff.; Hielscher/Ochs 2009: 25;).

- 'Market clients' (*Marktkunden*) are considered ready for integration and have the best chance of finding employment. It is assumed that this type of client is able to find a new job without much support and counselling.
- 'Clients for counselling and activation' (*Beratungskunden Fordern*) are seen as being in need of activating measures to improve their search for a job. To increase their chances of reintegration, their attitudes towards motivation, effort, mobility and flexibility must be changed.
- 'Clients for counselling and qualification' (*Beratungskunden Fördern*) are judged as poorly or inadequately qualified. Most probably, they will be assigned to training programmes to improve their qualifications and skills.
- 'Intensive assistance clients' (*Betreuungskunden*) are considered to have the lowest chance of reintegration. It is assumed that even intensive counselling and support will not get them into a job. According to the cost-benefit logic of the service production, 'intensive assistance clients' receive no intensive support.[2]

After profiling and categorization – a process that is reviewed on a regular basis – the unemployed person has to sign a 'contract' with his or her local jobcentre which 'specifies obligations and the detailed steps that will be taken to seek work and to regain or enhance employability' (Jacobi/Mohr 2007: 228). The unequal nature of the relationship between clients and staff is revealed in the fact that the former cannot refuse to sign the contract without the threat of sanctions, e.g. a cut in their unemployment benefits.

How did placement team staff react emotionally to these new structures and tools?[3] This is a proper question since one can assume that processes of organizational restructuring generally interrupt formerly routine behaviour. In his experiments, Garfinkel (1967) has shown that every departure from normalcy gives rise to strong emotional reactions (cf. Terpe 2009: 69). How does this general observation translate to this case of a changing work context for placement officers? A standardized poll of about 2000 employees in jobcentres, carried out by Bender et al. (2006), shows inconsistent results: On the one hand, most employees feel great pressure and find the new working conditions exceptionally stressful. They complain about the high level of monitoring and state critically that they are working 'just for the figures' (ibid.: 199ff.). On the other hand, they perceive more scope for independent work. This contradiction between 'pressure and freedom' is a well-known effect of new management methods aimed at the empowerment of employees (cf. Glissman/Peters 2001; Moldaschl/ Voss 2002). Whereas it remains uncertain which aspects of placement officers' work are characterized by greater independence and freedom – we will make an educated guess about that in section 3.4.2 – their experiences of pressure and stress can be assumed to be a result of the internal benchmarking system. The application of explicit performance standards and measures of exposes them to greater supervision (Ludwig-Mayerhofer et al. 2009: 37). This tighter monitoring of work can promote feelings of anxiety at not keeping up with organizational expectations (cf. Brooks 2003).

These emotions of anxiety and fear might be complemented by anger and resentment at the standardized tools of the action programmes and client groups. Although it is difficult to quantify the number, a majority of employees object to these instruments and experience them as being too restrictive (Bender et al. 2006: 206, 209). They describe their work as 'not free' (Ludwig-Mayerhofer et al. 2007: 380); they complain about an 'increase in bureaucracy' and a reduction in their scope for discretion in judging clients. They feel their qualifications are devalued and consider themselves hampered in their decisions (ibid.: 372). An interviewee comments: 'This is like a castration of our work. One should have more trust in us [...] and our human judgement' (Ludwig-Mayerhofer et al. 2009: 135). If these restrictions are experienced as a loss of power within the organization, again, feelings of anxiety might arise, this time about diminished influence in comparison to the past. But not all placement officers are resigned to these emotions. Some of those who are angry, especially, seem to be motivated by their resentment to act against standardization – however, not in an open but in a rather clandestine way. We will come back to this type of officer in section 3.4.1.

3.2 Cooperation and coproduction: New directives to employees in the form of feelings rules and emotion management

While for internal proceedings the client group classification has to be transparent, placement officers are urged to conceal it from clients.[4] For the clients, the decisions of the placement team should appear to result from their individual cases' needs (Ludwig-Mayerhofer et al. 2007: 379). This corresponds to the service orientation described above, which pretends to allow for individual differences and needs. Alongside this declared customer orientation and the policy of activation with its focus on clients' attitudes and motivations, placement officers are expected to have considerable communication skills. Rather than being engaged in (technical) job placement services only, they have to fulfil pedagogic functions like counselling, caring and motivating (Behrend/Ludwig-Mayerhofer 2008: 38). They are asked to establish 'cooperative' relationships with their clients in order to work out 'common' solutions for labour market integration. It is expected that this customer-service-like communication will enhance clients' motivations and prevent opposition, resistance or passiveness (cf. Rübner 2006: 129; Hielscher/Ochs 2009: 36).

In order to equip placement officers with various conversational techniques, the FEA has provided a three-volume manual called RAT (FEA 2002).[5] The handbook consists of training materials that contain both theoretical and methodical reflections on 'how to counsel the right way'. An essential part of the manual pays attention to the role of emotions in encounters between employees and clients. Feelings are described as an inevitable constituent of every interaction – they cannot and should not be neglected or suppressed (RAT1: 121f.). Rather, their function as a 'signal' for motivations, opinions and the qualities of relationships is emphasized. Placement officers are encouraged to be aware of both their own and their clients' feelings; they are asked to verbalize emotions and to make use of them (ibid.: 122ff.). The reader is equipped with various suggestions about those feeling states regarded as necessary for a successful encounter between employee and client. These can be interpreted as *feeling rules*, since they prescribe 'the direction' of emotions, i.e. what should be felt in a given situation. Additionally, these rules suggest a certain 'extent' and 'duration' for the respective feelings, i.e. how much and for how long the emotion should be felt (Hochschild 1979: 565). Two feeling rules for employees can be differentiated:

1. *Don't be indifferent. Feel empathy for the client.*[6] Placement officers are urged to look from their clients' perspectives in order to comprehend their situations. Empathy is described as a kind of 'attentive care' for clients and a necessary ingredient for a positive 'atmosphere of interaction' (RAT1: 12f.). The latter is seen as a prerequisite for clients' 'active collaboration' (ibid.: 15), i.e. it should motivate their willingness to negotiate a common agreement. Nevertheless, too strong an empathy, in which an employee 'feels the situation' the same way as the client does and, by doing so, could embarrass him or her, is

warned against (ibid.: 12). At the same time, as stated in the guide-lines, real cooperation presupposes the genuine acceptance of clients as 'autonomous partners' (ibid.: 16). Hence, a second feeling rule has been formulated:

2. *Accept/respect the client – just as the person he is.*[7] This acceptance has to be unconditional, e.g. it should not depend on an initial feeling of sympathy for the client, on similar political orientations or on a similar social background. Furthermore, acceptance and respect have to be shown to clients openly: 'The attitude of acceptance succeeds only in so far as it is clearly visible in the consultant's behaviour' (ibid.: 9). The employee is to give distinct signals of his/her respect. She/he must not act in an irritable manner, and she/he should avoid irony, sarcasm or ridicule.

Both feeling rules ask for what Hochschild calls *emotion management* via deep acting: a real 'act of trying to change an emotion or feeling in degree or quality' (Hochschild 1979: 561). In contrast to surface acting, emotions in deep acting are not simply faked, but an attempt should be made actually to feel them. Accordingly, the advice manual suggests placement officers should be emotionally authentic and genuine persons. 'The aim [of showing respect to the client] will be reached only in so far, as the counsellor really tries to internalize the respective attitude and does not try to play-act' (RAT1: 8). The employee is encouraged to behave in an 'open and natural' way – she/he should be 'visible as a human being, as a real person' with honest feelings (ibid.: 10f.). The placement officers learn that their ability to solve conflicts is equal to their ability to manage their emotions, such as suppressing undesired feelings like fear or insecurity and evoking the desired emotions of empathy and respect (ibid: 19).

Emotion management does not only include managing one's own feelings; rather it is often directed at another person's emotions as well. In this case, it is aimed at the creation of a specific emotional state in the other (Hochschild 1983). The handbook's training material refers first to *clients' emotions*, which are seen as obstacles in the way of a common agreement that should be removed by placement officers. Such an obstacle may be a client's anxiety not to appear ridiculous or worthless in the eyes of the employee. The client should not feel that she/he can lose face in the encounter (cf. Goffman 1955, Sarangi/Slembrouck 1996: Ch. 5). 'The counsellor's respectful attitude should enable the consulter to speak in an open manner about himself and his problems, without fear of losing the counsellor's esteem towards him or of appearing ridiculous' (RAT1: 8). The dissipation of such fears of interaction, done by the employee showing respect and acceptance, is seen as a necessary condition to place clients in a feeling state (trust) in which they are willing to talk about other emotions as well. Clients might be angry about a dismissal, they might feel disappointed and ashamed about their unsuccessful attempts to get a job or they might be insecure and have doubts about their skills and competencies (RAT2: 143, 153). These troublesome feelings are seen as a starting point for the procedure the placement officer will choose: 'The counsellor's activities are oriented towards these feelings' (ibid.: 144). She/he is urged to observe the client attentively and to look for signs of these emotions.

On the basis of this diagnosis, placement officers can move on and try to evoke more positive emotions in the client. They are asked to make the clients feel confident, optimistic and trustful and should give the clients a sense of power to change the situation (ibid.: 148ff.). On the one hand, these positive emotions are seen as fuel to motivate and activate clients; on the other, they play a crucial role in dispelling mistrust, resistance and opposition to the FEA employees' decisions. The latter is grounded in the following assumption: a motivated client will propose his/her own solutions; therefore, it is up to the placement officer to shape these solutions as if they were made just by the client's own considerations. The manual explains:

> To prevent opposition, it is enough to let the client participate in the procedure as often as possible, even if some (usually most) of the suggestions are made by the counsellor. One can reach a state, in which the counsellor is focusing the problem in such a way that the counsellor's solution appears [...] like the logical consequence of the client's reflections. (RAT2: 257f.)

Hence, it is expected that clients tuned to being emotionally positive will not consider resistance, since they live with the manufactured illusion of solutions made by themselves – as (seemingly) autonomous persons.[8] For the placement officers this manual's advice reveals the contradictory nature of normative expectations: while they are encouraged to respect the client as an 'autonomous partner', and hence as a person who can and should take responsibility for their actions, they are nevertheless urged to dodge this guideline when problematic circumstances arise. In conflict situations, the placement officers should distance themselves from the idea that the client is an autonomous person and act only *as if* she/he was one. Whether these contradictory expectations result in a state of emotional ambivalence (cf. Flam/Terpe 2009) on the employee's side depends on the obligatory character of the feeling rules. This takes us to the question of if the required emotion management is a rather voluntary or involuntary one.

3.3 Empathy and respect as 'voluntary emotion work' or 'forced emotional labour'?

According to Hochschild, emotions generated in an economic context possess exchange value. Because they are sold for a wage, she speaks of a commodification of feelings and chooses the term 'emotional labour' if emotions are managed according to the feeling rules of an organization (Hochschild 1983). In contrast, the term 'emotion work' is confined to voluntary emotion management as people practise it in their private lives towards friends and family (cf. Bolton 2000: 156; Turner/Stets 2005: 38; Meanwell et al. 2008: 539). The interpretation of emotion management at work as a capitalistic commercialization of feelings was challenged by authors like Mastenbroek (1992; 1999) and Wouters (1989; 1992; 1998). Inspired by the works of Elias (1997), they contextualize emotions in a theoretical frame of figurational sociology and add a historical perspective lacking in Hochschild's analysis. For instance, in his treatise about the historical development of the 'art of negotiating' from the fifteenth century onwards, Mastenbroek portrays negotiating skills as techniques for dealing with emotions. The sophistication of negotiating styles indicates 'the changing ways in which people learn to deal with emotions' (1999: 49). Following Elias, Mastenbroek explains this civilizing of emotions as a result of ever tightening relationships of interdependence. The changing networks of power have required an emotional attitude of self-restraint, discretion and patience. In analysing the work of Francois de Callières, a civil servant of Louis XIV, Mastenbroek identifies feeling rules for diplomats, such as 'Do not behave arrogantly', 'Do not show contempt' and 'Do not immediately resort to threats' (ibid: 57). Although formulated in early eighteenth century, all of them could nowadays be applied to jobcentre employees as well. In a similar way, Wouters criticizes Hochschild for neglecting 'the general social track': 'Hochschild writes as if she deals with recent novelties, while in fact she is concerned with developments that have been going on for millennia.' (1989: 104). Negotiating skills and organizational feeling rules are far from being that unmistakable sign for a capitalistic commodification of emotions as stated by Hochschild. Instead, these rules have developed during a long-term historical process in networks of changing political and economic dependencies. What does that mean for this section's question? Referring to Callières' eighteenth-century feeling rules, Mastenbroek remarks: 'Today, most of these recommendations still apply, but they are far more matter-of-course and self-evident.' (1999: 58) Although not always fulfilled in its most sophisticated forms, the techniques of negotiating are held 'as a normal standard' (ibid.). Hence, one could conjecture that at least some of the respective feeling rules are realized in actual behaviour in a familiar and taken-for-granted manner. The normative character of these 'normal standards' fades away in routine interaction and comes into the focus of awareness only in unusual and potentially problematic situations. These considerations suggest a differentiation of feeling rules, which takes into account varying degrees of reflection and different motivational forces to be complied with.

Following Bolton and Boyd (2003), we differentiate three types of feeling rules: social, professional and commercial. On the basis of the study by Ludwig-Mayerhofer and colleagues, we will look at placement officers whose adherence to feeling rules corresponds to the categories of the typology depicted in Figure 10.1.[9]

- Actors become acquainted with *social feeling rules* during primary socialization. They are so familiar with them that they enact them routinely without special or conscious efforts (Bolton/Boyd 2003: 296). We assume that compliance with these social feeling rules is motivated by a genuine desire to do so, because they form an essential part of actors' identities and self-images. Actors meet the normative expectations of those rules because they *want* to comply with them. The study of Ludwig-Mayerhofer et al. contains a group of FEA placement officers who are bound to such a feeling rule: *Feel empathy for clients as human beings* (Type 1).

- *Professional feeling rules* are learnt in secondary socialization, for instance when an actor undergoes vocational training and acquires special codes of conduct typical for a profession (ibid.: 295f.). In early phases of training these professional feeling rules are probably still external to the actors. They follow them out of the reflection that they *should*, if they want to belong to an already established group of colleagues. The more the actors become familiar with those rules and internalize them as part of their professional identity, the more

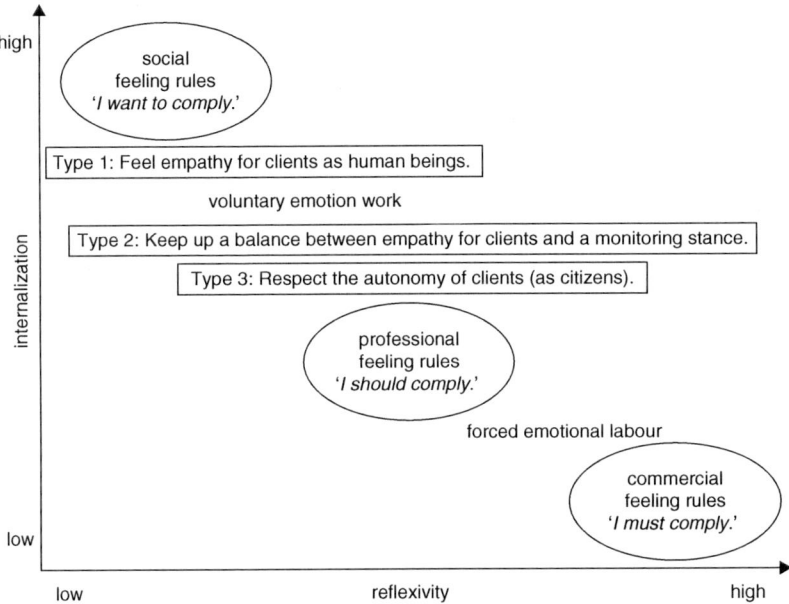

Figure 10.1 A typology of feeling rules and types of FEA placement officers

they *want* to comply with them. Among the FEA placement officers we detect two professional self-conceptions characterized by specific feeling rules: the first corresponds to the new ideal of employees as sympathetic yet monitoring counsellors, the second meets the image of a rather functional, however not unemotional personal adviser. Their feeling rules can be described as follows: *Keep up a balance between empathy for clients and a monitoring stance* (Type 2), *Respect the autonomy of clients* (Type 3).

- *Commercial feeling rules* are formulated by business companies and administrative corporations for regulating employees' behaviour towards customers and clients. Compliance with these commercial feeling rules is motivated 'instrumentally' and by 'pecuniary' means (ibid.: 296f.). Employees experience the demands of these rules as external forces they *must* comply with, if they want to get a promotion or, much more simply, if they do not want to lose their jobs. Only these commercial feeling rules demand what Hochschild calls 'emotional labour'. In the study of Ludwig-Mayerhofer and colleagues we could not identify cases that correspond to this category.

However, one should bear in mind that this research was not conducted with an explicit aim of examining placement officers' emotions and adherence to feeling rules. Nevertheless, the publications by Ludwig-Mayerhofer et al. convey an impression of employees acting according to feeling rules voluntarily most of the time, because these rules form a part of either their social (Type 1) or their professional (Types 2 and 3) identities.

In the next section, we give a detailed description of these types of placement officers. Additionally, we formulate suppositions about which emotions typically arise from adherence to the respective feeling rules. It has to be added that we understand the categories of this typology as ideal types in the sense of Weber (1976). As with every ideal type construction, the picture of the groups is somewhat overdrawn in order to clarify their special features. That is to say, they are not to be found in this straight form empirically (ibid: 13).

3.4 Placement officers' commitment to feeling rules and the resulting emotions

3.4.1 Feel empathy for clients as human beings (Type 1)

Placement officers who feel obliged to conform to this feeling rule criticize the instrument of client group classification most (Ludwig-Mayerhofer et al. 2009: 136). The basis of their criticism is formed by a deep-seated uneasiness about treating clients as a composition of those abstract figures contained in the standardized profiles. They do not feel able to reduce a 'whole person' of 'flesh and blood' (ibid.: 139) to a set of numbers for profiling, and complain about the wave of instructions (ibid.: 152). They recognize clients as human beings who should be judged as integral entities (2007: 374). Besides disapproving of the client groups classification, these employees also criticize the corresponding action plans as inappropriate. They feel troubled when it is up to them to refuse support to a client, because she/he belongs to a 'wrong' client group. They explain their uneasiness with reference to a 'humaneness' which obligates them to care for every client as a human being with specific needs (ibid.: 376). The feeling of obligation to 'humaneness' seems to be part of their identity beyond their professional self-image as placement officers. Against their employer's formal directives they rely on their own moral convictions, and these form the basis of their criticism. For instance, one interviewee comments with regard to the group of 'intensive assistance clients': 'What should I do then, should I shoot them?' (Ludwig-Mayerhofer et al. 2009: 149). She complains about the neglect of these clients in moral terms and calls it an 'antisocial' policy (ibid.: 154).

Additionally, employees of this type are characterized by a deeply felt empathy with the situations of the unemployed and a strong desire to help. What qualifies this empathy as being obliged to a social feeling rule is the fact that it seems to be a rather unreflective one. It is taken for granted and seen as an inherent feature of dealing with clients. In some cases, this deep-seated empathy is bound (again in an unreflective way) to a special group of clients, with whom the officer concerned feels connected because of their similar social background (ibid.: 130f.). It is important to note, however, that placement officers of this type expect a special kind of reciprocity in their encounters with clients. The latter must 'open up' in order to establish a personal and close relationship. Instead of formality and distance (ibid.: 137), an intimate bond should characterize the relationship; and to achieve that intimacy the employees expect a special attitude on the clients' side – they have to want, and must respond to, the placement officers' caring attention.

To sum up: placement officers in this category meet the official FEA feeling rule of empathy for clients out of their own moral convictions: they want to comply with this rule. But in contrast to the official rule they are not willing to limit this empathy, because for them there cannot be a 'too much' of it. Moreover, their expectation of an intimate bond contradicts the official rule of respect for clients' autonomy, if the latter contains an acceptance of the clients' right for privacy as well. But neither the demand for a balanced empathy nor the claim for client autonomy seems to bother placement officers of this type. Their reference to 'humaneness' justifies their behaviour and prevents them from doing 'forced' emotional labour.

What emotional reactions are typical for this group of employees? Above all, there seem to be compassion and pity for clients born out of deeply felt empathy on the one hand, as well as righteous anger and indignation about FEA's client group classification on the other. One could conjecture that they might feel guilty if they used this tool in a direct way – a demand that they do not follow completely. Instead, they take the liberty of manipulating figures to categorize clients into groups that they judge as adequate for their needs, e.g. to get them a training measure despite their being 'market clients' (Ludwig-Mayerhofer et al. 2007: 376). If they have the sense that they are doing the 'right' thing, this might promote their feeling of pride. Otherwise, a strict adherence to formal directives, just like the constant struggle against them, evokes frustration and discouragement (ibid.: 378). But these latter feelings might arise from a specific reaction on the clients' side as well: if clients do not cooperate, if they show resistance and do not allow for an intimate approach, these employees suffer from rejection (Ludwig-Mayerhofer et al. 2009: 153). Just as they experience successful encounters with clients as an acknowledgement of their private selves, they perceive a client's refusal as a personal defeat questioning their personality. They feel disappointed and helpless if their intimate attention and engagement is not honoured by their clients (Behrend et al. 2006: 4).

3.4.2   Keep up a balance between empathy for clients and a monitoring stance (Type 2)

Although placement officers who belong to this category might also criticize the new client group classification, they perceive enough room for individualized encounters with clients. Their perception of independence despite organizational directives seems to be a result of their manifold techniques in dealing with clients emotionally. Their self-conception as professional placement officers demands that they find a personal access to clients: They try to 'find each other' and strive towards 'mutual trust' (Behrend/Ludwig-Mayerhofer 2008: 42). These employees want clients to get the impression that they are really being attended to (ibid.: 43), and to convey this feeling, they take on an empathetic attitude. Placement officers of this type can be labelled as skilled emotion managers, because they are able to address clients' feelings in various ways. Take, for instance, one interviewee who explains: 'Whenever people get frustrated, I say "take yourself a time-out, bite into a pillow, yell into it; after that you'll make it in good spirits"' (Behrend et al. 2006: 3). She tries to cheer up her clients and wants to give them new hope. In a similar fashion, another officer says: 'A lot of them are afraid, they don't know what's going to happen, and I try to dispel these fears' (Ludwig-Mayerhofer et al. 2009: 138). Other strategies appeal to such negative emotions as a motivating force: one interviewee employs his clients' anxiety about social decline to push them into activity (ibid.: 133). In a more general way, another placement officer compares the encounters with a 'little play', in which one employs emotions in well-calculated doses (ibid.: 141).

At this point of illustration the dominant impression might be that encounters between such placement officers and their clients proceed smoothly in a sociable atmosphere characterized by the absence of direct threats. De Swaan calls this a shift 'from command principle to negotiation principle' (de Swaan 1981). For the second half of the twentieth century de Swaan and Wouters identify a trend designated as 'informalization', which is characterized by a 'growing negotiability and leniency in the ways people oppose to and co-operate with each other.' (Wouters 1989: 105f.). In the course of this process, 'the sensitivity for each other's emotional life has increased, allowing for a wider social acceptance of all kinds of emotions, with the exception of feelings of superiority and inferiority.' (Wouters 1992: 230f.). According to Wouters and de Swaan, this consideration of one's own and other persons' emotions is owing to diminished hierarchical differences between individuals and groups and the dissemination of 'ideals of equality' in western societies (Wouters 1992: 230; 1998).

Despite de Swaan's and Wouter's emphasis on an equalization of power differences, one should not neglect the imbalances of power inherent in the encounters between placement officers and clients. Although employees show 'sensitivity' for their own and for clients' emotions, the contact between them is far from being equal. For this reason, Mastenbroek's observation concerning such a flexible and informal style in emotion management is very important. He states: '[T]he flexible mixed style, while definitely not primarily focused on dominance and power, may become an instrument in gaining the upper hand.' (1999: 68). To put it in other words: a sophisticated management of emotion can be an efficient instrument for dominating others and is able to conceal power differences at the same time. Translated into the work of this category's placement officers, it means a skilled play with emotions in order to get clients to do voluntarily what could be forced otherwise.

This ever-present possibility of force in a relationship between nonequals is revealed only in those cases in which clients do not comply. These are the same cases in which placement officers' mechanisms of emotion management – which have the quality of voluntary emotion work – become visible. The aforementioned empathy and sympathy for clients are by no means unconditional, rather, they are limited to those clients who are perceived as motivated and who convey the impression 'to try really hard' (Ludwig-Mayerhofer et al. 2009: 132ff.). If they do not meet these expectations, employees resort to strategies of distancing themselves from them. These strategies take up the official interpretation of unemployment as an individual defect. This 'individualization of unemployment' (ibid.: 120ff.) not only allows for distancing, but also enables placement officers to impose or threaten sanctions. Because employees of this category have internalized the official perspective, they perceive these sanctions as justified and condemn (alleged) unmotivated clients in moral terms. Moreover, it is exactly this official perspective that prevents them from following the second feeling rule of respect for clients as autonomous persons who are allowed to make their own decisions. The FEA's own policy of activation annuls this feeling rule and hence, does not require emotion management to produce and guarantee respect for clients.

Two clusters of resulting emotions can be differentiated for employees of this type. If their strategy of balanced empathy is successful and clients can be persuaded to follow a specific course of action, they feel satisfied. Although they might perceive their relationship with clients as a cooperation between equals, this positive emotion is partially derived from a confirmation of their position of power. The officers' skilful playing with clients' emotions makes the latter act according to the former's will, even without the open threat of sanctions. Ludwig-Mayerhofer et al. (2009: 171) speak of a subtle enforcement of the institution's claims. A feeling like sympathetic care is used to direct the clients' behaviour in a desired direction and hence becomes an 'emotion of control' (Fineman/Sturdy 1999). In many cases, this supposedly non-authoritative approach seems to be successful indeed (Sondermann et al. 2007: 177). A different emotional landscape emerges in encounters with clients who are seen as uncooperative and unmotivated. Because placement officers of this type identify with the official policy of activation and believe in the necessity of an intrinsic and visible motivation on the clients' side (Ludwig-Mayerhofer et al. 2009: 112), they become distanced from supposedly unmotivated clients in a moral way. They feel righteous anger and indignation about clients being unreasonable, inflexible or lazy. These clients are seen as deserving sanctions in order to punish their 'wrong' behaviour and discipline them into a 'better' one.

3.4.3 Respect the autonomy of clients (Type 3)

Employees who feel obligated to adopt this feeling rule act on the basis of the assumption that most clients are already motivated to find a new job because their unemployment is causing them to suffer (Ludwig-Mayerhofer et al. 2009: 161). This is why they refuse to blame clients and, by doing so, refuse to 'torture' them even more (ibid.: 156). Placement officers in this category do not share a belief in the official FEA policy of individualizing unemployment; instead, they perceive this to be the result of unfavourable labour market conditions. They offer support to their clients in the form of suggestions, but leave it to their clients to decide whether to follow them or not – and therefore, they really judge clients as autonomous persons who can make decisions for themselves in a responsible way (ibid.: 157). In contrast to Type 2 officers, they share the conviction that one cannot change clients fundamentally. Although their relationship with their clients can be described as a rather functional one, it is not without feelings. According to Ludwig-Mayerhofer et al. only these placement officers develop an understanding for their clients' situations and feel sympathy for them (ibid.: 163). But this is not the exaggerated empathy of Type 1 officers; instead they try to stay objective in a sense that they do not get too close to their clients. At the same time, this distancing of themselves from their clients is not accompanied by an easy switch to threat and sanctions; they are quite aware and reflective of their position of power and employ only carefully measured sanctions (ibid.: 164). They assume their clients to be honest and trust their information.

Against this background, placement officers of this type are quite critical about the FEA's new policy; they are worried about the changing welfare state, which in focusing on individualization is losing its solidarity principles (ibid.: 162). The situation of these placement officers reveals clearly the contradiction between the FEA's proclaimed service orientation on the one hand and the logic of activation on the other. One can say that employees of this kind indeed consider their activities as a service, but one for citizens whose claims are seen as justified. In addition, this service orientation is far from being new for them; rather, their commitment to the feeling rule of respect for autonomous clients comes out of their pre-existing professional self-image. Even the feeling rule for a balanced empathy with clients applies to them, if one understands it to be a balance between empathy and distance – and not between empathy and control, as for Type 2 officers.

In comparison to employees of Types 1 and 2, placement officers of Type 3 might appear less emotional in regard to their clients: they experience neither exuberant joy and pride in helping them (Type 1), nor outrageous anger and indignation about clients who do not agree with their suggestions (Type 2). Likewise, they are not deeply disappointed or personally affected if clients act and decide differently. Nevertheless, one should not hastily judge them as indifferent or ignorant. We conjecture that their uppermost worry is aimed at general political developments, which are seen as dodging the principles of welfare state solidarity. Within this background, they do feel pity for clients who must accept bad employment contracts to escape further unemployment (ibid.: 162), and they might feel happy for those clients who find adequate employment.

4 Conclusion

The aim of our chapter was to examine the emotional landscapes of employees in the German labour administration after its reform. The new principle of 'customer orientation' manifests in organizational feeling rules that call for empathy and respect when encountering clients. The publications by Ludwig-Mayerhofer and colleagues suggest that employees do not follow these rules because they have to. Rather, the feeling rules seem to have become – or have already been – part of their professional and/or social identity: hence, placement officers wish to comply with them. However, the policy of 'activation' induces potentially conflicting demands, if it asks employees to monitor clients and process them in predefined ways that may undermine the latter's autonomy. We suppose that placement officers' emotional reactions towards the new policy and its instruments, as well as towards clients, depend on the motivational force of these feeling rules (see Figure 10.2). Our typology indicates different types of employees, whose dealings and interpretations of feeling rules vary.

Officers of Type 1 feel a deep-seated obligation to *help every client* as a 'human being', not respecting the clients' own wishes and decisions; their strong empathy seems to overcome the clients' right to autonomy.

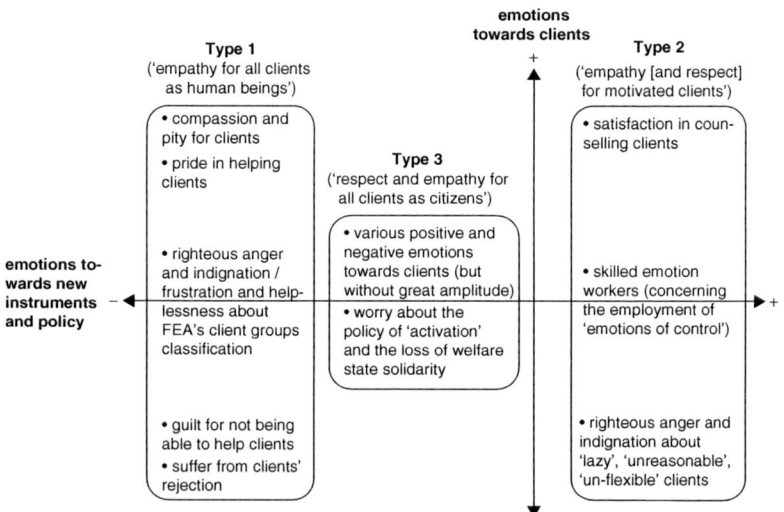

Figure 10.2 Types of FEA placement officers and their emotions

In contrast, Type 2 officers appear to 'use' empathy in a more reflective manner; they draw upon the official policy of 'activation' in confining their *empathy to 'motivated' clients*. These same clients seem to be granted respect and autonomy – but only as long as they behave as compliant 'customers'. As the exception, only employees of Type 3 are bound to the feeling rule of respect in an unconditional manner. At the same time, they feel sympathy for clients out of a mild sense of empathy for them. But although – or rather just because – these officers personify the *demand for both feeling rules* best, they are in conflict with their organization's policy. However, our typology and interpretation should not be understood as being final; they represent a first proposal in need of refinement by further research.

Notes

1. We used the following publications by this research group: Ludwig-Mayerhofer et al. (2007; 2009), Behrend et al. (2006), Behrend/Ludwig-Mayerhofer (2008), Sondermann et al. (2007). The English translation of the German material has been made by us.
2. The use of this typology reveals the still prevailing bureaucratic character of public labour administration. According to Sarangi and Slembrouck, 'bureaucracy is about processing people on the basis of information they provide' (1996: 36). An essential element of this processing is the application of classifications, i.e. the assignment of people to a predefined set of categories they must fit in order to get their requests processed (ibid.: 41f., 128).
3. Their feelings towards their clients will be the topic of section 3.4.
4. Sarangi and Slembrouck recognize in such a withholding of information a central feature of bureaucracies' endeavours to protect their power position. They are 'unwilling to make explicit the bases of their decisions' (1996: 178).
5. RAT means 1. *Richtig beraten* (counsel correctly), 2. *Anregungen* (suggestions), 3. *Techniken* (techniques). We refer to the different volumes of FEA (2002) as RAT1, RAT2 and RAT3. The English translation of the quotations has been made by us.
6. 'Counsellors have to be able to keep a balance between social closeness and detachment – but no indifferent neutrality' (RAT1: 7). 'Empathy means to understand another one's world as he does himself' (ibid.: 12).
7. 'Above all, respect means to take the other one seriously as the person he is' (RAT1: 7).
8. One could take that line of argumentation even further: if the 'clients' solution' does not work (i.e. if it does not result in a job), the clients can be blamed for it.
9. In contrast to Bolton and Boyd (2003), we do not distinguish the group of social feeling rules further. We tried to condense their considerations in Figure 10.1 (which is not part of their article) and combined their typology with various types of placement officers. We describe these types in detail in section 3.4.

References

Arnkil, R., di Domenico, G. and Konle-Seidl, R. (2008) 'Joblessness as a major challenge for Public Employment Services. Country reports from Finland, Italy and Germany', in R. Blanpain and M. Tiraboschi (eds) *The Global Labour Market: From Globalization to Flexicurity*, Alphen: Kluwer, 81–107.

Behrend, O. and Ludwig-Mayerhofer, W. (2008) 'Sisyphos motivieren, oder: Der Umgang von Arbeitsvermittlern mit Chancenlosigkeit', *Zeitschrift für Sozialreform*, 54, 37–56.

Behrend, O., Ludwig-Mayerhofer, W., Sondermann, A. and Hirseland, A. (2006) 'Im Schatten der Aufmerksamkeit – die Arbeitsvermittler', *IAB Kurzbericht*, Nr. 21/2006.

Bender, G., Bieber, D., Hielscher, V., Marschall, J., Ochs, P. and Vaut, S. (2006) *Organisatorischer Umbau der Bundesagentur für Arbeit. Evaluation der Maßnahmen zur Umsetzung der Vorschläge der Hartz-Kommission*, Saarbrücken: Peter Ochs/ISO, www.iso-institut.de/download/2007_01_16_iso-ochs-Bericht_BAEval_%20AP2.pdf (accessed 1 December 2009).

Bieling, H.J. (2006) 'Arbeitsmarkt- und Beschäftigungspolitik in der Europäischen Union – Problemlagen, Krisendiagnosen, Strategieelemente', in C. Stelzer-Orthofer (ed.) *Arbeitsmarktpolitik im Aufbruch. Herausforderungen und innovative Konzepte*, Wien: Mandelbaum, 39–72.

Bolton, S.C. (2000) 'Emotion here, emotion there, emotional organisations everywhere', *Critical Perspectives on Accounting*, 11, 155–71.

Bolton, S.C. and Boyd, C. (2003) 'Trolley dolly or skilled emotion manager? Moving on from Hochschild's Managed Heart', *Work, Employment & Society*, 17, 289–308.

Brooks, I. (2003) 'Systemic exchange: Responsibility for angst', *Organization Studies*, 24, 125–41.

de Swaan, A. (1981) 'The politics of agoraphobia: On changes in emotional and relational management', *Theory and Society*, 10, 359–85.

Elias, N. (1997) *Über den Prozess der Zivilisation*, vol. 1–2, Frankfurt a.M: Suhrkamp.

FEA (Federal employment Agency, Bundesanstalt für Arbeit) (2002) *RAT. Richtig beraten, Anregungen, Techniken: Grundwerk individueller Beratung*, Vol. 1–3, Nürnberg: BfA.

Fineman, S. and Sturdy, A. (1999) 'The emotions of control. A qualitative exploration of environmental regulation', *Human Relations*, 52, 631–61.

Flam, H. and Terpe, S. (2009) 'About emotional ambivalence', paper presented at the 9th ESA conference at Lisbon (Portugal), September 2–5, 2009.

Garfinkel, H. (1967) *Studies in Ethnomethodology*, Cambridge: Polity Press.

Glissman, W. and Peters, K. (2001) *Mehr Druck durch mehr Freiheit: Die neue Autonomie in der Arbeit und ihre paradoxen Folgen*, Hamburg: VSA.

Hielscher, V. and Ochs, P. (2009) *Arbeitslose als Kunden? Beratungsgespräche in der Arbeitsvermittlung zwischen Druck und Dialog*, Berlin: Edition Sigma.

Goffman, E. (1955) 'On face work: An analysis of ritual elements in social interaction', *Psychiatry*, 18, 213–31.

Hochschild, A.R. (1979) 'Emotion work, feeling rules, and social structure', *American Journal for Sociology*, 85, 551–75.

Hochschild, A.R. (1983) *The Managed Heart*, Berkeley: University of California Press.

Jacobi, D. and Mohr, K. (2007) 'Rushing towards employability-centred activation: The 'Hartz reforms' in Germany', in R. van Berkel and B. Valkenburg (eds) *Making it Personal. Individualising Activation Services in the EU*, Bristol: Policy, 217–41.

Ludwig-Mayerhofer, W., Sondermann, A. and Behrend, O. (2007) ' "… Jedes starre Konzept ist schlecht und passt net' in diese Welt" – Nutzen und Nachteil der Standardisierung der Beratungs- und Vermittlungstätigkeit in der Arbeitsvermittlung', Prokla, *Zeitschrift für kritische Sozialwissenschaft*, 37, 369–81.

Ludwig-Mayerhofer, W., Sondermann, A. and Behrend, O. (2009) *Auf der Suche nach der verlorenen Arbeit. Arbeitslose und Arbeitsvermittler im neuen Arbeitsmarktregime*, Konstanz: UVK.

Mastenbroek, W.F.G. (1992) *Verhandeln: Strategie, Taktik, Technik*, Frankfurt a.M.: FAZ and Wiesbaden: Gabler.

Mastenbroek, W.F.G. (1999) 'Negotiating as emotion management', *Theory, Culture & Society*, 16, 49–73.

Meanwell, E., Wolfe, J.D. and Hallett, T. (2008) 'Old paths and new directions: Studying emotions in the workplace', *Sociology Compass*, 2, 537–59.

Moldaschl, M. and Voss, G.G. (2002) *Subjektivierung von Arbeit*, München: Hampp.

Rübner, M. (2006) 'Leitbildwechsel in der aktiven Arbeitsmarktpolitik? Professionelle Kundenkommunikation und Beratung als Erfolgsfaktoren neuer Integrationsstrategien in den Agenturen für Arbeit', in H.-D. Braun and B.-J. Ertelt (eds) *Paradigmenwechsel in der Arbeitsmarkt- und Sozialpolitik?*, Brühl/Rheinland: Fachhochschule des Bundes für Öffentliche Verwaltung, 126–37.

Sarangi, S. and Slembrouck, S. (1996) *Language, Bureaucracy and Social Control*, London: Longman.

Sondermann, A., Ludwig-Mayerhofer, W. and Behrend, O. (2007) ' "Willst du deine Freunde, oder willst du Geld verdienen?" Räumliche Mobilität in den Deutungen von Arbeitsvermittlern und Arbeitslosen', *Sozialer Fortschritt*, 56, 173–80.

Terpe, S. (2009) *Ungerechtigkeit und Duldung. Die Deutung sozialer Ungleichheit und das Ausbleiben von Protest*, Konstanz: UVK.

Turner, J.H. and Stets, J.E. (2005) *The Sociology of Emotions*, Cambridge: Cambridge University Press.

van Berkel, R. and V. Borghi (2008) 'Introduction: The governance of activation', *Social Policy & Society*, 7, 331–40.

Weber, M. (1976) *Wirtschaft und Gesellschaft*, Tübingen: Mohr.

Wouters, C. (1989) 'The sociology of emotions and flight attendants: Hochschild's Managed Heart', *Theory, Culture & Society*, 6, 95–123.

Wouters, C. (1992) 'On status competition and emotion management: The study of emotions as a new field', *Theory, Culture & Society*, 9, 229–52.

Wouters, C. (1998) 'How strange to ourselves are our feelings of superiority and inferiority?', *Theory, Culture & Society*, 15, 131–50.

11
Learning by Listening: Emotional Reflexivity and Organizational Change in Childcare

Debra King

1 Introduction

Organizational change, particularly radical change, can trigger an array of emotional and cognitive responses from employees that will influence whether or not the implementation process will be successful (Ashford 1988; George/Jones 2001). In response, many organizations are taking an active role in managing the emotions associated with such change (e.g. Garrety et al. 2003). Where the kind of change proposed requires a fundamental shift from employees in the emotional culture and their emotion skills, organizational leadership needs to tread carefully through 'sensitive territory' (Fineman 2003: 130).

When the directors of three Australian childcare centres decided to implement change specifically focused on the emotional culture and emotion skills within their centres, they realized that one of their biggest challenges would be how to manage their employees' reactions. They were proactive, undertaking training in responsive leadership styles, consulting with employees about the change, role-modelling what was required and providing extensive professional development. They also implemented an initiative called 'shared listening', which provided employees with a forum within which to discuss the implementation process. This chapter focuses on the contribution of shared listening to achieving the desired changes.

The change that the childcare centres sought to implement took emotions seriously as a strategic element of change management and as a completely different approach to working with children. Called Listening to Children (LtC), this approach considers itself to be at the cutting edge of facilitating styles of emotional awareness and emotional management that produce resilient, emotionally healthy children who can interact with others in emotionally aware and constructive ways (Wipfler n.d.). In many ways shared listening mirrored the LtC approach by enabling employees to 'listen to themselves' and each other. The practice of attending to the emotional dimensions of organizational change is relatively new. Emotions have traditionally been sidelined as irrelevant to organizational change processes or, at best, relegated to the domain of the individual. In contrast, shared listening was an organization-level response to working with employee emotions and creating a new emotional culture within the childcare centres. There are risks associated with this response. The childcare centres risked being viewed as manipulative by employees and alienating them even further from the change process. Employees risked having their emotions (and perhaps even their subjectivity) exploited in the process of achieving organizational goals. In this chapter I use the example of shared listening to examine how attending to employee emotions influences their engagement with organizational change. In examining this issue, I query whether the benefits of attending to emotions extend beyond achieving successful change for organizations to also achieving positive outcomes for childcare workers.

2 Contextualizing listening to children

Listening to Children is derived from an approach to parenting developed in the USA by Patty Wipfler called 'Hand in Hand' (formerly the Parents Leadership Institute). Wipfler established the Parents Leadership Institute in 1989, producing a variety of developmental tools aimed at strengthening the emotional connection between caregivers and children through actively listening to children's voices and emotions (Wipfler n.d). Her initiative stimulated a growth in parenting approaches based on emotional connection and the importance of play (e.g. Cohen 2001), whereby secure attachment to significant adults is seen as fundamental to the development of alert, confident and resilient children.

Underlying LtC is the belief that when children experience difficult or unpleasant feelings – sadness, grief, anger, fear, frustration, shame or embarrassment – they can become disconnected from their sense of themselves and their world. Nonetheless, such feelings are viewed as part of a growing child's ordinary life experience, from which they have an ability to recover if allowed to express them in a safe and caring environment. Crying, for example, is seen as a healthy form of stress release that allows a child to heal their upsets and hurts. The caregiver's role in this situation is to stay close to the child, offering emotional warmth. This process aims to re-establish the close connection between the caregiver and child, and recover the child's sense of well-being; it also conveys the message that crying is acceptable. This type of release is viewed as essential for reconnecting to a sense of well-being and enthusiasm for life.

The approach to emotions being advocated by LtC is one of developing emotional self-awareness, encouraging emotional expression and valuing emotional sensitivity for both parents and children. It contrasts markedly from other approaches based on emotional control, management and manipulation that have emerged in the popular child development literature. These often use cognitive behaviour management strategies, for example those popularized by *Supernanny* (Ricochet 2009). In the LtC approach there is no time out, reward chart or distraction from emotional distress; nor is there a focus on children as 'disciplinary problems'. Instead, they advocate strategies called Stay Listening, Play Listening, Special Time and Setting Limits (see Appendix), which address different aspects of children's feelings and behaviour and how to stay connected with children when they are expressing them.

Transferring LtC into a childcare setting was seen as a logical progression by the directors and consultant, especially as time in childcare is now such a regular occurrence for Australian pre-school children (ABS 2005: 3). The aim of integrating the types of parenting skills associated with LtC into an institutional setting is indicative of what Hochschild calls the 'warm modern' solution (2003: 222) to the care deficit, whereby childcare is provided in both institutional and domestic settings (by both men and women) in environments where care is valued as important and can be fulfilled on a personal basis (ibid.: 222). Childcare, however, is not the same as parenting and childcare workers are not simply substitute parents for children in their care: it is not simply a matter of purchasing a 'commodified version of parenthood' (Hochschild 1997: 232). Childcare centres operate according to routines, they have administrative and reporting responsibilities and are increasingly professionalizing in the field of early childhood education. This is quite different to a home setting, where parents have a small number of children to care for, have continuity of care over time and where schedules can usually be adapted around the needs of individuals (including children) within the family.

The directors of the childcare centres were introduced to LtC by Ann, a consultant working in the area of leadership training in early childhood education and care. They had been working together for about two years on developing their leadership skills and improving practices within their centres. During this time they became increasingly committed to LtC, identifying three reasons why it should be implemented into their centres. *First*, they were aware that a care deficit was being created within the centres. Just as Hochschild (2003) argues, this was due to the time-bind that childcare workers were increasingly feeling in response to the bureaucratization and marketization of childcare. Thus, they did not have the time to provide 'good' care. LtC was seen as a way of enabling childcarers to refocus their priorities and provide opportunities to interact with children and participate in their development, which, as Rush (2006) argues, are key motivations for workers entering the field of childcare. *Second*, the directors felt that the process of giving children good attention, of providing care to a child who is experiencing emotional distress and facilitating the release of emotional tension, would create a much stronger basis for the social, cognitive *and* emotional development of children. Previously, children were taught the feeling rules and display rules (see Hochschild 1983) associated with being in childcare, and childcarers distracted children from feeling 'inappropriate' emotions. In contrast, LtC focuses on what Meyerson (2000) called 'honouring' emotions – allowing them to be spontaneous rather than governed by societal rules – and was perceived as being more respectful of children and more likely to achieve longer-term emotional development goals. *Third*, the directors thought that offering childcare that used LtC would appeal to existing and potential parents and provide the centres with a competitive edge.

Prior to taking LtC into the centres, the leadership team sought funding for training and professional development. Funding was gained for two aspects of the programme. The Commonwealth Department of Family and Community Services and Indigenous Affairs allocated funding under its 'Stronger Families and Communities Strategy' for Ann to provide training to parents associated with the childcare centres. At the same time the South Australian Department of Education and Children's Services provided funding to release the childcare workers for professional development and to cover Ann's costs as a trainer/consultant. Once funding was approved, the centres began the implementation process.[1]

The implementation had four elements. *First*, the leadership group role-modelled good practice in LtC skills, which meant employees could see it in action and even shadow Ann as a learning technique. *Second*, Ann held introductory skill development workshops where the principles and practices of LtC were explicitly discussed and experiences shared. *Third*, the shared listening strategy provided support for employees during the implementation process. The *fourth* element was the development of leadership skills (to continue role-modelling and training) among those childcarers who showed enthusiasm and skill in using the strategies. In this chapter, I focus primarily on the shared listening strategy. The empirical results presented stem from a broader action research project conducted over seven months in collaboration with the directors of the childcare centres and the consultant who led the training. The three childcare centres involved in the LtC project were all non-profit, with two of them being attached to tertiary colleges of further education (although a significant proportion of the children still came from the broader community). The Valley Childcare (VC) and Hill Childcare (HC) centres were both in the southern suburbs of Adelaide and were relatively large. These centres were divided into age-related 'rooms', for example, babies, toddlers and kindergarten. Mount Childcare (MC) centre was smaller, located in an inner regional centre approximately 40 km from the city and vertically integrated; that is, it had only one room, in which children of all ages played.

The empirical approach included semi-structured interviews about the LtC implementation process. In January 2007, 20 interviews with childcare workers (eleven from VC, five from HC and four from MC) were conducted. The interviews took place in a separate room in each centre and lasted for about 30 minutes. Questions focused on the employees' approach to childcare, their attitudes toward LtC, how they learned about the strategies, their use of LtC and whether it had made a difference to the way they worked with children and colleagues. This included asking about shared listening and their experience using it. In addition, each member of the leadership team (directors and the consultant) was interviewed twice: in June 2006 to establish the stage they were at and what they thought LtC would achieve, and again in January 2007 to reflect on the implementation process. Furthermore, field notes were collected on the basis of professional observation in each centre and the workshops which incorporated shared listening time were tape recorded.

3   Organizational change: Attending to emotions

Organizational change is often accompanied by various levels of employee resistance, stress and insecurity depending largely on whether the change is incremental or transformational to existing practices, with the latter being more likely to induce a stronger reaction (Callan 1993; Huy 2002). This is particularly so when employees perceive the change as threatening, unpredictable, uneven or disempowering. In these instances employees are likely to find it difficult to draw on their existing problem-solving strategies and may even need support in adapting to the change (Callan 1993: 72).

The process of organizational change can highlight the extent to which organizations are indeed 'emotional arenas' (Fineman 2000a). Emotions are important for long-term adjustment to change and for dealing with problems relating to change, such as interpersonal conflict, perceived loss and unfair treatment (Robinson/Griffiths 2005). As George and Jones point out, emotions are also integral to employees' sense-making during periods of change, especially during those phases when discrepancies between individual schemas and the required change create the circumstances in which individuals re-evaluate or reiterate their schema or, conversely, reject the change. Indeed, emotion can be a trigger for, influence upon, or by-product of the change process (2001: 422).

Understanding emotional attachments to schema and how they are constructed, deconstructed and reconstructed is therefore likely to be integral to the success of any organizational change strategy. Attachments to schemas are partly developed through the emotional socialization of employees into a professional field (Cahill 1999). In the case of childcare, employees learn the appropriate feeling and display rules associated with particular childcare practices, including the management of children's emotions and behaviour. Such schemas become normalized through practice and can be integrated into their identity as childcare workers. A shift in schema will require learning the new feeling and display rules (Hochschild 1983) associated with the new childcare practices. This is likely to create a period of emotional dissonance, during which employees are required to display the feeling rules attached to the new schema, but are still feeling according to the rules attached to the old schema. The strain of maintaining the separation between display and feeling, which Hochschild (1983: 90) describes, may lead to different responses to organizational change: those who cannot reconcile the differences either reject the new schemas or retreat to surface acting while those who accept the change and shift to the new schema are likely to have reconciled the dissonance between display and feeling rules. The speed with which change can be implemented will largely depend on how an organization manages this process of reconstructing emotional attachments to schema.

Organizations are now playing a more central role in supporting employees through change (Turnbull 2002), and consultants are routinely employed by organizations specifically to facilitate the emotional aspects of organizational change (ABC 2006). As such, organizations are recognized as having emotional capability, that is, in Huy's terms, the organization's 'ability to acknowledge, recognize, monitor, discriminate and attend to its members' emotions' (1999: 325), which enables them to meet the processural challenges associated with employee receptivity, mobilization and learning during radical change (ibid.: 328). Huy argues that there are two basic requirements: (1) having people who are emotionally committed and championing the change, and (2) attending to recipients' emotions through group-level processes involving emotion-related activities (2002: 31ff.).

It is the second point that is of interest for this analysis of the LtC implementation, as the idea of attending to employee emotions is a core feature of the shared listening strategy. There are, however, different ways in which organizations can 'attend' to emotions. At one end of the spectrum are the more control-oriented strategies aimed at minimizing emotional displays perceived to be inappropriate for achieving change. Such strategies might require employees to relearn organizationally appropriate emotions and provide the requisite amount of emotional labour to ensure they are displayed (Hochschild 1983). It might require training employees in skills associated with emotional intelligence (EI), like the capacity to monitor and control one's own and others emotions, and to use this information to inform decisions (Salovey/Mayer 1990). For this, EI measures and training that promise to provide employees with the tools to enhance individual performance and organizational success have been developed. However, with regard to EI, critics question its value-bias, its individualist focus and its predominantly psychological measures (e.g. Fineman 2004). If used as a strategy to 'attend' to emotions during a change process, it is perhaps even more problematic that the success associated with EI is contextual. If the context is the organization, the strategies risk being manipulative. Thus, employees striving for EI are rendered more governable and/or left experiencing the discomfort of emotional dissonance (see also Baumeler in this volume).

At the other end of the spectrum are the more expressive, relational strategies aimed at legitimizing employees' emotional responses to change and ensuring that their issues are taken seriously by the organization. Fineman, for example, argues that organizations play a role in promoting emotional sensitivity among employees 'through processes of feminization, emotionally responsive leadership styles, valuing intuition, and tolerance for a wide range of emotional expression and candour' (2003: 54). The celebration of, engagement with and sharing of emotions within an organizational framework have been found to improve the development and delivery of professional development and training (Short/Yorks 2002) because they stimulate motivation and establish a climate of collective purpose. Meyerson contends that the very act of developing norms of organizational caregiving that honour emotions by encouraging employees to access and respect emotional experience is likely to totally transform the nature of work and work relationships (2000: 172ff.). In relinquishing control, however, organizations would need to attend to both positive and negative reactions to organizational change (Kiefer 2002), and realize that intended and unintended consequences of the change process will be triggered by, and require, different emotional responses (Turnbull 2002).

Organizational strategies at the more expressive end of the spectrum appear more compassionate and validating of individuals while fostering learning and change. However, questions could be raised as to whether this is yet another example of 'managerial discourses infiltrat[ing] the very cores of employees' identities and emotional lives', as Garrety et al. (2003: 212) put it. These authors analysed the use of a personality typing tool (the Myer-Briggs Type Indicator) in a male-dominated industrial company. Use of the tool was promoted as a means of enabling employees to manage themselves and others in a more 'emotionally intelligent manner' (ibid.: 216). Part of the process of change was to establish workshops aimed at training employees in attending to emotions by 'penetrat[ing] defensive barriers and feeling rules that maintained old identities' (ibid.: 221). Thus, a process was facilitated through which employees would re-evaluate their old schema and develop new modes of performing their attachments to new schemas. Although perhaps not going as far as to honour emotions, the workshops did aim to validate emotional responses and provided a forum within which emotions were accepted and respected. The workshops were integral to achieving shifts in patterns of power within the organization, with 'these shifts occur[ing] through active engagements with Discourse, mediated through reflexivity and emotions that linked subjective experiences to broader patterns of control and resistance' (ibid.: 222). They argued that while these managerial discourses had indeed infiltrated employee identities, this was not straightforward, and that through the reflexive process engaged in during the workshops, employees were able to be active participants in how discourses were framed and implemented.

The LtC project offers a similar opportunity to examine how organizations attend to the emotions of their employees while implementing organizational change. The shared listening strategy was, as with LtC itself, framed as a process of emotional expression, awareness and sensitivity.

4 Shared listening

Shared listening was a forum within which childcare workers could listen to each other and discuss their feelings and concerns about issues that impinged on their capacity to implement LtC. Previously, emotional reactions were either managed at an individual level or were 'vented', but not necessarily in a constructive way or a supportive environment. Prior to LtC's implementation, childcarers who displayed inappropriate emotions were considered to be 'bitching or moaning' (Sally VC). Sometimes they were distracted from negative emotions through laughing or joking – 'we laugh to the point of actually holding your stomach and that's, it's a relief of tension' (Sandra HC) – or they just vented their emotions, for example, 'we would just usually go back and forwards and say this is annoying me and they go, yeah, this is annoying me' (Tamzin HC). Shared listening provided an alternative strategy for dealing with emotions and emotional dissonance. Before the leadership group could tackle issues relating to the implementation of LtC, however, they had to deal with the emotional reactions to participating in shared listening itself – particularly among employees who were sceptical of or resistant to the change.

There were two ways in which childcare workers could use shared listening: one was in team meetings when time was allocated to discuss issues both in a group and in pairs; the other was more informal, and involved asking a colleague (or the director) to 'swap' listening time during the normal working day. The principles of shared listening are based on recognized peer counselling techniques: reciprocity, focused attention and support. In describing a shared listening workshop Trish (VC) says:

> You're given something to reflect on, to talk about for two minutes and the other person completely gives you their attention in the fact that they don't interrupt, they don't give an opinion, they just listen. And that in itself is very different ... it's almost a way of acknowledging the other person and what they have to say in a very positive manner.

Reactions to shared listening varied: some embraced it as part of the shift to LtC (n=4), some rejected it as unprofessional and an unnecessary intrusion on personal feelings (n=3)[2] and the majority were sceptical about it but were willing to 'play along' (n=13). Childcarers who embraced shared listening fell into Huy's (2002) category of 'champions'. Emotionally committed to the principles and practices of LtC, they were eventually earmarked by the leadership group as potential leaders and trainers in the strategies. For this group, shared listening was used as part of the process of learning-through-experience and dealing with practical issues that arose from their use of LtC strategies. As their view of the shift to LtC was one of incremental change, it is likely that the dissonance between the old and new schema was lower for them than for other groups. As Tracy (HV) said, 'I thought this sounds really interesting and, the more I looked at it, the more I thought this makes so much sense.' All the employees in this group had (or were studying for) advanced levels of childcare qualifications and viewed LtC as an extension of their learning about child-focused care, which may have contributed to their openness to change.

The employees who were highly resistant to the change process were still required to attend shared listening sessions, but did not always participate or engage in them. One of them eventually went on to use shared listening in informal listening partnerships with a colleague in the centre, but continued to refuse to disclose in group sessions. Another worker who initially rejected LtC altogether attended a shared listening session in which several childcarers stated their admiration for the way she worked with children and reaffirmed her status as a valued colleague. The emotional tension in this session was high, but it was relieved through an extended period of crying by several childcare workers, including the resistant one. The validation of this person acted as a means of dissipating the level of anger and anxiety that she felt and enabled her to begin to engage in the change process. She began to see the value of sharing feelings and stories with colleagues and became more open to the way of thinking engendered by shared listening.

The majority of childcarers were initially unsure about engaging in shared listening. In the interviews they recounted the emotional dissonance involved in participation: they were embarrassed to talk about personal issues in front of colleagues, frustrated about not having the skills to 'do' shared listening, scared about voicing their disagreement with LtC in front of Ann (who was known to be in the leadership group with the directors) and did not want to be 'counselled' out of their feelings. The levels of emotional dissonance about shared listening were therefore quite high. As a result, shared listening initially operated on a relatively superficial level:

> The very first time I felt very frustrated, she's [Ann's] going to come around again and say 'what's something you want to talk about from work?' ... So I'm thinking, 'oh no, another two minutes, I've got to make something up.' And so the first time, its just so frustrating, but the next time I thought, 'I can't deal with that level of frustration, I've actually got to share deeper and I'm going to tell them what's on my mind and what's happening at home, you know, and all the deep things. (Julia, VC)

Not everyone had such a noticeable transformative moment. Nevertheless, everyone in this group eventually engaged in shared listening, coming to see it as a useful strategy for themselves, as well as for implementing LtC. Childcare workers identified three benefits of shared listening: it enhanced team building, it was a self-care strategy and it provided them with the practical skills to implement LtC.

Shared listening brought a whole new dimension to team building, one in which emotions were viewed as central, rather than a distraction. Although still engaged in emotional labour with the children, the relationships between childcare workers seemed to become more spontaneous and interactive. They showed more appreciation of each other as a 'whole' person who was a childcarer, but who also had a private life, fears, needs, strengths and weaknesses.

The fact that shared listening contributed to improving relationships between childcarers was particularly important in those centres where childcare was divided into age-related rooms and provided by teams of carers. This aspect of shared listening was mentioned by over two-thirds of employees:

> I think that's one reason why our room works so well is because we listen to each other, but we also, we're not only the listener we're also the one that will say stuff. But we all have our chance to say stuff, something and we all have our chance to listen. (Shelley, VC)

Shared listening allowed childcarers to understand how their colleagues 'ticked' – why they made certain decisions when working with children, how they felt about working in the particular environment, about personal issues that impinged on their work, about what people wanted their work to be like and so on.

[Shared listening] worked for discussing good and not so good aspects of your professional life, getting to know people on another level ... it helps just to build some bonds with people outside of the room where you're so busy. (Trish, VC)

Previously, the capacity for getting to know colleagues was viewed as limited and secondary to their work with children. Through participating in a formal framework such as shared listening, childcare workers gradually realized that their work with children improved when they enhanced their team work.

Shared listening was also valued for providing self-care for childcare workers:

We have time for ourselves. Listening time for the staff! ... [in] our listening time no one butts in, we just say what we want to say and then the people don't question us about it afterwards. They just go 'well, how do you feel about it?' and to make us know how we feel about it because usually you're always caring for other people but no one's caring for yourselves. (Kylie, HC)

Therefore childcare workers not only became more attuned to children's emotions through shared listening time, but also to their own emotions and those of their colleagues. The self-care aspect of shared listening was evident in the ways in which it provided stress relief – regardless of whether the stress resulted from work or from home. The forum in which they could share their frustrations was highly valued because it allowed them to work better with the children and return to their work with renewed energy:

People say you leave your work at work and your home at home but really who can ever do that because what's stressing you at home can sometimes roll over into your work and you try not to let it happen but getting out some personal things in those times and part of what happens here in the times that we've had with Ann has really helped as well. (Patricia, MC)

Once childcarers became aware of their own and each others' emotions, they were able to build in time for listening to one another throughout their daily routine, or became so attuned to each other that they could accommodate stress amongst the team members. In reflecting upon and attending to their own emotions and those of their colleagues (as distinct to those of the children), childcare workers found the emotional context within which they did their work improved:

> [It means] not getting really angry and frustrated to the point where you just want to give up and also that the children get quality time from you so that you're left with enough mental energy to deal with the rest of the day. (Annette, MC)

One of the key reasons the leadership team implemented shared listening, however, was to allow employees to practise the LtC strategies between themselves and to deal with the emotional responses to implementing LtC with children. Nearly all the childcare workers found that shared listening helped them to improve their own listening skills and become more sensitive to children's feelings and more focused on giving children good attention:

> You get a bit more insight as to Listening to Children because you pick up on the cues and how you actually listen; things like not fiddling, staring into the eyes but not getting too close, and when to step in and not to step in. (Sally, VC)

It also provided opportunities to learn from colleagues:

> We become more focussed and more confident with what we're doing. Listening to other people's experiences and how their, I wouldn't say failures, but listening to their challenges and the things that they have achieved has been really good as well because... it gives us a better idea of how to deal with it, 'I could put that into practice too' kind of thing. (Patricia, MC)

Undoubtedly, the aspect of shared listening most helpful for the implementation of LtC was to provide a forum for discussing emotional responses to the use of LtC strategies. The levels of emotional dissonance that LtC created differed between the childcare workers, but all (even the champions) experienced emotional reactions when using LtC strategies. Each of the LtC strategies raised new emotional dilemmas for childcarers. Engaging in Stay Listening created worry and frustration:

> It was a bit awkward because I thought well this child is misbehaving I shouldn't be just letting him... just rant and rave and carry on without a good reason or an explanation.... I was thinking why am

I doing it, this child is being naughty I should be putting him in the quiet room or something like that. That was frustrating at first. (Kaylene, VC)

No, it was really weird, and I think that's what we find confronting is letting a child cry and everything ... we'll do things to distract the child or whatever but [Ann] says well then it's not being resolved. (Christine, VC)

Some childcarers expressed fear and self-consciousness with Play Listening. For example Gillian (MC) said that she 'was a bit uncomfortable to start with, a bit stupid, being silly with the children'. Others were worried that someone would get hurt, either colleagues or children, during the 'rough and tumble' of Play Listening. Childcarers also discussed quite high levels of guilt associated with Special Time:

You've got so many one on one children and you've only got a limited number of staff, it's really hard to spend that individual time with them. And to be able to sit there and listen to a child for five, ten, 15, 20 minutes that they may need to be listened to when you're also scanning the room because you know that this person over here has just fallen over or this person needs a bottle or this person needs a nappy change. That, I see, is the difficulty. (Tracy, VC)

Setting Limits, in turn, provoked feelings of anger and frustration:

See personally I haven't put [Setting Limits] into place with biting. *I: Why not?* Because I can't, I get so angry and so upset with the child that's bitten that I can't handle that child, I say to another educator you need to take that child and one that's been bitten I'll comfort the biter. (Leigh, VC)

[In LtC you say] things like 'good girl', 'good boy' – language that isn't really childcare appropriate. ... And it takes a long time to train, retrain your mind when you've been doing it for 5 or 6 years. (Sally, HC)[3]

From the above excerpts it is evident that there were several aspects of LtC that created emotional dissonance: supporting children in expressing strong emotions associated with sadness, anger and frustration; using the language associated with LtC; the idea of spending time with individual children rather than groups and the shift from a behaviour management approach to one of 'positive guidance'. Within shared listening it was revealed that childcarers found these things particularly challenging because of the emotional dissonance that LtC stimulated in contradicting feeling rules and norms associated with professional socialization and the broader societal patterns of behaviour. In facilitating shared listening time, Ann sought to disrupt the internalization of these norms and the feelings attached to them. In one instance, for example, two childcare workers were upset by having to allow, and even support, a small boy to cry (for over 30 minutes) after his parents dropped him off. Their training and their experience indicated that the correct way to provide care for this child was to calm him down as quickly as possible, often by distracting him from the cause of crying. Ann asked them why it was so hard for them to let the child cry. Their responses were insightful: they were embarrassed that their colleagues might think they were not providing adequate care, they were sad for the child in that he might think he was not cared about or had been abandoned and they became anxious and even tearful about seeing the child cry for so long. These issues were then delved into further, until it became evident that they were never allowed to cry for prolonged periods when *they* were children (or even as adults), and the thought of allowing a child to do so was very scary. Ann encouraged them to feel the fear and express it physically which, for one person, stimulated tears. Ann supported this person through a period of prolonged crying in the session, allowing her to experience the sensations associated with it. After shared listening, these childcarers agreed to participate in Stay Listening strategies, but modified it slightly for use within the childcare centres.

Although not explicit in the training materials, the approach used during shared listening is psychodynamic, engaging childcare workers in raising their emotional self-awareness and developing their skills in emotional reflexivity. To do so they needed both to objectify the emotions and to reflect *upon* them in order to understand the existing attachment and to reflect subjectively *through* the emotions to discharge those emotions attached to old schema and recreate emotional attachments to new schema (King 2006). During shared listening, linkages were made between current feelings associated with the change to LtC and feelings associated with working in an environment that is gendered, relatively lowly paid and undervalued, with high stress levels, high turnover, low numbers of qualified workers, increased bureaucratization and unsatisfactory childcarer-child ratios. Each of these issues created challenges for the employees in the implementation of LtC. In dealing with the feelings about these challenges, shared listening facilitated a realignment of individual schemas.

Nevertheless, the LtC practices were not uncritically accepted. Childcarers actively engaged with the practices and adapted them to suit the institutional practices and processes of childcare and their own ways of working with children. Play Listening was modified to have less of a focus on 'rough and tumble' and more on giving children a sense of taking the lead in play, learning the limits of play and releasing tensions within a safe environment. Some aspects of Stay Listening also changed. For example, childcarers did not hold a distressed child against their will (as a parent might), but stayed in close contact with the child while listening to them release their distress. Moreover, childcare workers tended to integrate Special Time into their routines when they were able to connect with children on a one-to-one basis – such as sleep time, nappy changing and at the end or start of the day when fewer children were in the centre.

5 Conclusion

In implementing LtC, shared listening was an important strategy. Its psychodynamic approach enabled the childcare centres to penetrate defensive barriers and challenge existing feeling rules. This was integral to disrupting established schemas and promoting the emotional awareness and reflexivity (King 2006) required for organizational change. In addition, by engaging in shared listening, employees began to learn the skills associated with validating emotions and facilitating the expression of emotion within a supportive environment. This experience helped them to understand the principles behind LtC and transfer this mode of communication to their work with children. In so doing, shared listening created an environment within which emotions were honoured, emotional dissonance was addressed, new feeling and display rules were learned and new forms of EI were developed. These, however, were not neutral outcomes. They specifically enhanced the process of organizational change. The outcome for childcarers was more ambiguous.

Both shared listening and LtC are strategies that revolve around honouring emotions: appreciating one's own and other's emotions, speaking about these emotions and endeavouring to understand more about why they arise and how to prevent them from blocking thinking and behaviour. Such an approach endeavoured to view colleagues as whole persons with emotions and lives that traversed personal and professional arenas. Although this may be regarded as a better way of working (Meyerson 2000), implementing it as an organizational strategy meant that there was a *requirement* for employees to do this emotion work. The extent to which this mitigates the level of 'honouring' of emotions is difficult to judge. For example, should those employees who did not want to do shared listening have been allowed to withdraw because this would have honoured their feelings? There is evidence to suggest that employees were 'counselled' out of their negative feelings toward LtC and shared listening, but whether this was as advantageous to the employee as it was to the organization requires further investigation. What is clear, however, is that in honouring emotions, employees were more likely to be able to deal with the emotional dissonance associated with implementing LtC and therefore be viewed in a more positive light by the childcare directors.

Emotional dissonance arose because LtC involved new ways of working with emotions, both in doing emotional labour and in being emotionally intelligent. Except for the employees who championed LtC from the beginning, the approach was viewed as contradictory to their professional socialization, to their views of what providing 'care' involved and, often, to their experience as women or mothers. Shared listening created a forum in which the consultant and directors could guide employees to reassess emotional attachments to their old schemas and construct emotional attachments to LtC. Doing this meant that childcarers had to be convinced of the benefits of LtC to children and the comparative 'harm' that could result from old schemas.

As a new schema, LtC required a shift in the use and construction of organization-level feeling rules and display rules. Established rules were disrupted and replaced with a new language of emotions and new ways of managing emotions. The new rules not only upset professional norms of the cognitive behaviour management approach to working with children, but also social norms about the relative power between adults and children. Shared listening was a forum within which these new feeling and display rules were practised and learned. In addition to being shown what was appropriate, employees were encouraged to experience it by working on their own and each other's feelings in an effort to realign their identity as a childcare worker with the rules of the new schema.

The difference between LtC and previous schemas was that it was (or attempted to be) much less directive in relation to the kinds of emotional labour required for working with children. It operated on the assumption that if provided with the appropriate levels of emotional attention and allowed to express emotions freely and spontaneously, then there is little need to manage emotions in the ways often associated with emotional labour (like in the case of flight attendants in Hochschild's study, 1983). There is no room for surface acting. For LtC to work and produce the required results for children, it required deep acting *and* a resultant shift in subjectivity. In being both inter- and intra-subjective, shared listening enabled employees to construct an internal dialogue through which they could assess themselves against a range of possibilities and reposition themselves. This is not to say that the childcarers were passive in this process. As the earlier discussion demonstrates, LtC was not adopted uncritically. Even though most employees committed to the strategies, they modified them, they worked with those with which they were most comfortable and they sought to find ways of integrating old schemas with the new one. Overall, however, it is clear that it was not just organizational change that was being promoted through LtC, but individual change.

Whether or not such individual change is beneficial for employees will depend on the extent to which it helps them in their personal and/ or professional lives. On the personal front, the principles of LtC suggest that it contributes to improved emotional resilience and well-being. The extent to which this occurred for the childcarers was beyond the scope of this research. On the professional front, they certainly felt that shared listening improved teamwork and their own sense of self-care. If LtC were to become widely accepted, they might also have the emotional capital that would assist them to find alternative jobs. Certainly the implementation of LtC involved learning new emotional skills and developing or relearning skills associated with EI. In so doing, it highlighted the contextual nature of EI. Far from being a neutral, generic form of intelligence, there are particular kinds of EI that are highly specific to not only the childcare context, but also that of particular childcare practices. The findings suggest that the concept of EI as espoused by Salovey and Mayer (1990) downplays the levels of emotion work required to achieve EI, the potential for emotional dissonance in developing or relearning EI in particular contexts and the different types of EI that have value. In contributing to Fineman's (2000b; 2004) critique of EI, this research advocates a more contextualized conceptualization, one that takes account of gender, emotion cultures and organizational milieu.

For the childcare centres in this research, shared listening was a key mechanism through which organizational change was facilitated. It provided a forum for employees to deal with emotional dissonance, develop their emotional intelligence, learn the language and practices associated with new feeling and display rules and recreate the emotional culture of the centres. As an organization-level initiative aimed at providing employees with emotion-focused coping strategies to deal with the implementation of LtC, shared listening helped to alleviate the levels of resistance associated with organizational change. From the viewpoint of the childcare centres, it proved highly successful in mediating the transition to new organizational goals and strategies. From the viewpoint of the childcarers, they felt that their feelings had been 'honoured' during the change process. Nevertheless, the research demonstrated that achieving all of this required levels of emotion work and emotional reflexivity that changed the professional and, possibly, personal identities of the childcarers. These processes were largely invisible, hidden in the language of self-awareness, care and children's well-being. To truly understand the long-term effects of these processes and the link between personal and organizational change, a longitudinal study covering the personal and professional lives of childcare workers would be required.

Appendix: Listening to children strategies

1. **Stay Listening:** Appreciate children's feelings and the source of the feelings (if known) and stay connected with a distressed child without distracting it from the distress, for however long the emotions are expressed.
2. **Play Listening:** Play with children to address their emotional distress. Do not distract them by playing, but to use it to connect with the children in meaningful ways. For instance, empower children to initiate play with adults. This strategy requires having good skills in emotional literacy as well as relational skills in recognizing what may work for particular children.
3. **Special Time:** An adult sets aside a period of time when they can work exclusively with one child, doing whatever that child wants to do.
4. **Setting Limits:** Provide clear boundaries of behaviour and implement them in a light, supportive way, one that recognizes the feelings associated with doing something perceived as 'wrong' or something that a child does not want to do. This strategy dissociates discipline from the use of harsh tones or punitive measures. It requires performing high levels of emotional labour to manage adults' own and others' emotions.

Notes

1. Funding did not include costs associated with the research. This was funded through a small grant from Flinders University.

2. It is recognized that the most resistant employees were unlikely to volunteer to be interviewed.
3. In Australia, childcarers are taught to use language that focuses on behaviour rather than the person. For example, it would be acceptable to say 'you have good manners' but not 'good boy/girl'.

References

ABC (2006) 'All in the mind: emotions at work', *ABC Radio National*, aired 1 July 2006, www.abc.net.au/rn/allinthemind/stories/2006/1673425.htm (accessed 30 July 2006).

ABS (2005) *Survey of Child Care (4402.0)*, Canberra: Australian Bureau of Statistics.

Ashford, S.J. (1988) 'Individual strategies for coping with stress during organisational transitions', *Journal of Applied Behavioural Science*, 24, 19–36.

Cahill, S.E. (1999) 'Emotional capital and professional socialization: the case of mortuary science students (and me)', *Social Psychology Quarterly*, 62(2), 101–17.

Callan, V.J. (1993) 'Individual and organizational strategies for coping with organizational change', *Work & Stress*, 7(1), 63–75.

Cohen, L.J. (2001) *Playful Parenting*, New York: Ballantine Books.

Fineman, S. (2000a) 'Commodifying the emotionally intelligent', in Fineman (2000c), 101–15.

Fineman, S. (2000b) 'Emotional arenas revisited', in Fineman (2000c), 1–24.

Fineman, S. (ed.) (2000c) Emotion in Organizations, 2nd edn, London: Sage.

Fineman, S. (2003) *Understanding Emotion at Work*, London: Sage.

Fineman, S. (2004) 'Getting the measure of emotion – and the cautionary tale of emotional intelligence', *Human Relations*, 57(6), 719–40.

Garrety, K., Badham, R., Morrigan, V., Rifkin, W. and Zanko, M. (2003) 'The use of personality typing in organizational change: discourse, emotions and the reflexive subject', *Human Relations*, 56(2), 211–35.

George, J.M. and Jones, G.R. (2001) 'Towards a process model of individual change in organizations', *Human Relations*, 54(4), 419–44.

Hochschild, A.R. (1983) *The Managed Heart. Commercialisation of Human Feeling*, Berkeley: University of California Press.

Hochschild, A.R. (1997) *The Time Bind: When Work Becomes Home and Home Becomes Work*, New York: Holt.

Hochschild, A.R. (2003) *The Commercialization of Intimate Life: Notes for Home and Work*, Berkeley: University of California Press.

Huy, Q.N. (2002) 'Emotional balancing of organizational continuity and radical change: the contributions of middle managers', *Administrative Science Quarterly*, 47(1), 31–69.

Kiefer, T. (2002) 'Understanding the emotional experience of organizational change: Evidence from a merger', *Advances in Developing Human Resources*, 4(1), 39–61.

King, D. (2006) 'Activists and emotional reflexivity: towards Touraine's Subject as social movement', *Sociology*, 40(5), 873–91.

Meyerson, D. (2000) 'If emotions were honoured: A cultural analysis', in Fineman (2000c), 167–83.

Ricochet Ltd. (2009) *Official Supernanny Parenting Advice*, www.supernanny. co.uk (accessed 21 January 2009).

Robinson, O. and Griffiths, A. (2005) 'Coping with the stress of transformational change in a government department,' *The Journal of Applied Behavioural Science*, 41(2), 204–21.

Rush, E. (2006) 'Child care quality in Australia', Discussion Paper No. 84, Sydney: The Australia Institute.

Salovey, P. and Mayer, J.D. (1990) 'Emotional intelligence', *Imagination, Cognition, and Personality*, 9, 185–211

Short, D.C. and Yorks, L. (2002) 'Analyzing training from an emotions perspective', *Advances in Developing Human Resources*, 4(1), 80–96.

Turnbull, S. (2002) 'The planned and unintended emotions generated by a corporate change program', *Advances in Developing Human Resources*, 4(1), 22–38.

Wipfler, P. (n.d) *Listening to Children Brochures*, Palo Alto, California: Parents Leadership Institute.

12
Emotional Neutrality as an Interactional Achievement: A Conversation Analysis of Primary Care Telenursing

Vesa Leppänen

1 Introduction

In this chapter I will analyse how emotional neutrality is achieved in social interaction, using the example of how telephone advice nurses in Swedish primary care manage the emotions of clients who call for medical help. The analysis focuses on the concluding parts of the calls, when nurses advise callers about whether they need to see a general practitioner, a point at which it may be especially relevant to display concerns and worries. I will describe how nurses routinely sustain emotional neutrality in this part of calls, while at other times they may allow callers' concerns and worries to surface. Lastly, the reasons for routinely sustaining emotional neutrality are discussed, primarily in terms of the nurses being organizationally and professionally accountable for their actions.

2 Emotional neutrality and the social sciences

2.1 Emotional neutrality in modern times

One of the main concerns of classical sociology was to describe and analyse the dramatic structural changes that took place in western society from the second half of the eighteenth century to the first half of the twentieth; in other words the transformation of an agrarian economy to first an industrial and then a service-based economy. They observed that modern society entailed social relationships that were increasingly anonymous, specialized and formal: Marx (1867/1967) analysed the mechanisms of capitalism and how they resulted in alienation between the members of society, Durkheim (1893/1964) described how society had changed from mechanical solidarity (with little division of labour) to an organic society (with a greater division of labour) that brought with it a growing number of highly specialized and impersonal social interactions and Weber (1921/1968) portrayed the western world as becoming increasingly rationalized. According to Weber, social life was increasingly permeated by norms and values of intellectualism, explicitness, efficiency and calculability (see also Eisen 1978). The prime manifestation of rationalization was the rise of the modern bureaucracies that Weber described as hierarchical, designed to achieve specific goals and with a high degree of division of labour and detailed rules that govern the behaviour of staff. The consequence was a general demystification and dehumanization of social life. Elias (1939/2000) saw the history of the west since the end of the Middle Ages as a process of civilization that imposed greater self-restraint on the members of society and increased the distance between them. Parsons (1951) analysed social action by using five pattern variables, of which one was affectivity versus affective neutrality. For example, he described interactions between doctors and patients as often being affectively neutral.

Emotional neutrality soon became a taken-for-granted background for emotional experience, and today many of us view emotions as phenomena that occur intermittently against a background of emotional neutrality. Figuratively, emotions are thought of as the stars and planets in the emptiness of space. Emotions such as anger, anxiety, shame, happiness, joy, love and pride are often understood as arising and vanishing in the void that is emotional neutrality.

Some of us tend to view emotional neutrality as a state in which the 'rational mind' can operate and control ourselves and the situation. Being emotional is thought of as a state in which our organism or visceral self 'expresses itself' and 'takes control'. Thus we may say we are 'gripped' by emotions and therefore act 'uncontrollably' (Averill 1974; Goffman 1978). While obviously there are emotions that we experience as 'taking control of us' and which may be desirable (such as love and hope), being overly emotional is widely seen as undesirable because with it we may lose the ability to control ourselves, and this may lead us to act in ways we may regret later.

At much the same time as the general public started to view emotional neutrality as a taken-for-granted background for other emotions, sociology fell silent on this topic (Barbalet 1999; Starrin et al. 2008).

There were some exceptions. Both Simmel (1901/1983) and Cooley (1902/1922) were interested in emotions, and both were especially interested in the role of shame. Their research on shame was later followed up by Elias (1939/2000), Goffman (1959, 1963a; 1963b; 1967) and Scheff (2000). One reason for their interest in this particular emotion is that it is a fundamentally social emotion, arising when individuals view their actions from the perspective of others and see that they have failed to meet normative requirements. Yet there may also be a more specific reason for their interest: if modern life, as the classical sociologists said, results in an increased number of social interactions – of which many are anonymous, specialized and formal – there will be increased demands on individuals to manage these interactions – frequently by being emotionally neutral. When individuals fail to live up to these demands, the result is shame. The study of shame may thus be viewed as an interest in social situations in which the normative requirement of being emotionally neutral is not fulfilled.

Emotional neutrality has become a normative ideal. This remains true even when we look at the social revaluation of emotionality now underway in many parts of society. Fineman (2000) points out that in public life politicians now often display their emotions and journalists frequently ask interviewees about their emotional experience; at work, employees are trained to manage their own and clients' emotions and the concept of 'emotional intelligence' has become a part of public discourse (ibid.). While this trend emphasises emotionality, it insists on emotional control – the underlying normative ideal is to stay cool, not to be overwhelmed by emotion.

2.2 Research approaches to emotion in social interaction

Goffman conducted pioneering research on how members of society interact with one another in a variety of natural public settings, and included the role of emotion in these processes (1959; 1963a; 1963b; 1967). While it has been acknowledged that he set out the path for much future research by providing a general framework for the analysis of social interaction, he has repeatedly been criticized for his methodological approach (cf. e.g. Drew/Wootton 1988; Garot 2004). His studies may therefore be viewed as 'suggestive sketches of interactional processes rather than definite maps' (Drew/Wootton 1988: 6). Goffman described many of the ways in which people perform interactional work in order to appear reserved and indifferent. In one analysis he describes how individuals manage to achieve 'civil inattention' in public places (Goffman 1963a). In another he describes how individuals with discreditable properties manage to 'pass' and maintain the image of 'being normal' (Goffman 1963b). There are a number of ethnographic studies of emotion inspired by Goffman's work. Some of them focus on how social actors manage others' emotions in general (Clark 1990), while others analyse how different types of workers manage their clients' emotions, for instance airline stewardesses (Hochschild 1983), emergency call operators (Tracy/ Tracy 1998), police officers (Ehrlich Martin 1999), nurses (Bolton 2001), sex workers (Sanders 2004) and home carers (Leppänen 2008).

A different research tradition, of which several prominent figures were Goffman's students, is conversation analysis (Sacks 1992; Schegloff 2007). Although inspired by Goffman, this approach is different in at least two respects. First, empirical data are more detailed and are more rigorously collected and analysed: audio and video recordings are transcribed in detail and subjected to analyses of how interactional processes unfold sequentially. Second, conversation analysts focus on a different aspect of emotion. While Goffman was interested in both the experiencing subject and the performance of social interaction, conversation analysts tend to pay less attention to human experience per se. Instead they aim to provide detailed descriptions of the design of actions, to analyse utterances as embodying social actions, to specify how actions are oriented to previous actions as well as other relevant aspects of social context and to analyse how actions provide new context for subsequent actions. In other words, conversation analysis, in accordance with its ethnomethodological roots, describes the design of participants' actions in social contexts and analyses their mundane practical epistemologies (Heritage 1984). Conversation analytic studies of emotion primarily focus on how individuals display and manage emotions in interactions, not on their experiences as such (Heath 1989; Jefferson/Lee 1992; Whalen/Zimmerman 1998; Wilkinson/Kitzinger 2006).

There are conversation analytic studies that focus on how neutrality is achieved in organizational settings, for instance in courts of law (Atkinson 1992), community mediation (Heisterkamp 2006) and news interviews (Clayman 1992). However, they do not conceptualize neutrality as an emotional phenomenon but rather as 'impartiality', and focus on contexts in which impartiality is a central issue.

A number of previous studies deal with social interaction between callers and professionals on medical helplines (Leppänen 2002; Baker et al. 2005; Drew 2006; Shaw/Kitzinger 2007; Holmkvist 2008). However, few of these studies have considered how professionals try to manage callers' emotions so as to achieve emotional neutrality. An exception is a study of emergency calls in the USA by Whalen and Zimmerman (1998). They describe situations in which callers had serious and often life-threatening problems and were openly hysterical. Tracy and Tracy (1998) examine similar situations, although they base their analysis on participant observations and interviews. In the calls discussed here, although callers may have been worried, at no point did they become openly hysterical and therefore nurses did not need to manage those types of emotional expressions.

3   Telenursing in Swedish primary care

3.1   Context and method

When the general public in Sweden need medical help they can call a primary care centre or a primary emergency care centre (out of hours), and in an acute situation they can call the emergency services. This study focuses on telephone calls to primary care centres. There are more than 1000 primary care centres, district nurse offices and general practice surgeries administered by the local authorities and regions (SALAR 2009). In 2006, some 40 per cent of the Swedish population (which totals 9.2 million) called primary care centres or general practice surgeries (SALAR 2007). In most cases calls were answered by fully registered nurses (see Andersson Bäck 2008 and Holmkvist 2008 for the organization of telenursing in Swedish primary care).

In order to learn more about the ethnographic context and to explore nurses' general experience of telenursing, qualitative interviews were conducted with 18 nurses at 12 different primary care centres. Telephone calls from the general public to nurses were audio-recorded at six primary care centres in 1999. In total, 276 calls to 13 different nurses were recorded. The average call length was 2 minutes and 57 seconds. They were transcribed with conversation analytic conventions (Sacks et al. 1974; Jefferson 2004) and subsequently translated into English. The data set has previously been used for analyses of the overall organization of calls, callers' presentations of problems and nurses' questioning strategies (Leppänen 2002; 2005).

The average age of the callers was 36 years, and about 53 per cent were female. About 27 per cent of calls concerned children up to 12 years, and 17 per cent people 65 years and older. Most of the callers did not present their problems as being acute, unlike the calls analysed by Whalen and Zimmerman (1998) as well as by Tracy and Tracy (1998). This presumably reflects their choice to call a primary care centre instead of the emergency services. The typical medical problems were of the upper respiratory tract, skin, muscles, joints, stomach, bowels, urinary tract, eyes, ears, dizziness, headaches and tiredness (Leppänen 2002).

3.2   Working over the phone

The nurses' main task was to perform triage to assess if further medical attention was necessary, how soon and from whom. This is reflected in the basic structure of such calls, which consists of a request for help from the caller and a response from the nurse (Whalen et al. 1988; Whalen/Zimmerman 1998). The request for help may be expressed in the form of an explicit request, a narrative that describes the problem or a question (Leppänen 2005). Between the request and the response, the nurses enquire about the caller's problems, take their personal details and fill in various forms. Their most important task is thus to construct 'cases', some of which are then handed on to general practitioners at the primary care centres (Whalen et al. 1988; Whalen/Zimmerman 1998).

In the present study, once the callers had described their problems and answered the nurses' questions about their condition, one relevant thing to do for nurses was to *assess* the problems. When assessing medical problems, nurses have to take into account the professional division of labour between themselves and doctors, by which only the latter have the right to diagnose medical problems. The nurses in the study were well aware of this division of labour, which became evident when they named problems. When uttering diagnosis-like descriptions of problems, they did so cautiously, using formulations such as 'even though I can't say with any certainty, I think this could be X'.

Another relevant thing for nurses to do, when callers had described their problems and the former had inquired into them, was to *respond* by saying what needed to be done. The commonest response by nurses was about whether the caller needed – or did not need – an appointment to see a general practitioner at the centre. In 39 per cent of all calls, nurses scheduled a visit to a general practitioner at their primary care centre. In 4 per cent of cases, decisions were postponed, for instance by referring the caller to the general practitioners' telephone hours or by asking the caller to ring back later. More than 15 per cent of callers were referred to a district nurse and about 3 per cent to other caregivers. In other calls, nurses gave self-help advice, gave test results, rescheduled appointments, discussed prescriptions or told callers to wait and see how a problem developed.

One routine uncertainty in assessing and giving advice is that nurses may be uncertain about how callers understand their situation and what they think they ought to do about it. Although there are callers who start by announcing that they want to see a general practitioner, the nurses cannot know what view most callers take of their problems. The nurses cannot adjust their responses to 'fit' these actors, i.e. to 'recipient design' their responses in the terms of Sacks et al. (1974). Furthermore, there is the issue of caller *compliance*. Compliance is a central issue in any medical practice and may be especially important in this context, when the problems are new and a successful outcome depends on the willingness and appropriateness of the caller's actions after the call has finished. Therefore, following assessment and advice, nurses may be especially keen to *monitor callers' reactions* in order to gauge whether they need to be convinced.

4 Sustaining emotional neutrality

We will see that the nurses had two approaches to telling callers they needed to visit a general practitioner: either they sustained emotional neutrality by informing callers indirectly that an appointment would be scheduled or they alarmed them by explicitly assessing their medical problems and advising them to see a general practitioner.

4.1 Indirect information

In the majority of calls, nurses did not explicitly assess callers' medical problems or give advice. Instead, they indirectly informed callers that they needed to see a general practitioner. In the following example[1] a woman has called about her sore throat, a possible case of tonsillitis. The nurse has asked a number of questions about the problem, of which the last is 'you don't have fever' (line 1):

Extract 1
```
1  N   you don't have fever
2  C   no I don't
3  N   no
4  C   h no because my daughter has had inflammation of the
       ears
5      this week so that [huh
6  N              [yes
7      (1.8)
8      now let's see ((whispering))
```

Following the callers' response (lines 2–5), the nurse gives an acknowledgement token, showing she has heard what the caller has just said.

Here it would be relevant for her to continue either by asking further questions or by expressing her overall response to the medical problem. Instead she remains silent for 1.8 seconds and then mutters 'now let's see' (line 8). This conveys that she is involved in an activity that may somehow be related to her line of questioning, although it does not explicitly give any information about what this activity may be or how it is related. This places the caller 'on hold' and temporarily releases the nurse from continuing the call as a 'questioner' and 'responder' to the medical problem. It may also be understood by the caller as an indication that the nurse is now engaged in the preliminaries to making an appointment. The call continues:

```
 9  C  huh
10  N  give me your birth date
11  C  it is sixtythree nine twentyeight
12     (1.2)
13  N  mm
14  C  thirtytwo fourtyseven
15     (2.0)
```

The nurse's question about the caller's date of birth (line 10) is a request for the information she needs to fill in the case form. The caller may or may not know this, and may understand it as another indication that the nurse is scheduling an appointment with a general practitioner. The call continues:

```
16  N  are you in nasty pain
17  C  h no not that enormously in pain
18     (0.8)
19     just a little like that
20  N  mm=
21  C  =but I can see that it is red and then there was that
       [white hh
22  N  [mm hm
23     (0.4)
24  C  [huh
```

The nurse's question, 'are you in nasty pain' (line 16), is a request for the caller to grade her pain, which is a piece of information relevant to the form. The request to grade pain, followed by the non-response to the callers' replies (lines 17–23), may be interpreted by the caller as a further indication that the nurse is involved in some other activity, perhaps the scheduling of an appointment. Finally, the nurse says, 'I will take a look at how it looks here today'. This explicitly tells the caller that access to a general practitioner is called for. More specifically, the nurse gives conditional access: the scheduling of an appointment depends on availability.

```
25  N  [eeehm (0.6) I will take a look at how it looks here today
26     (1.0)
27  C  hhhh [hhhmm
28  N  [in our scheduling
29  C  yes h
30     (4.5)
```

Then the nurse gives access by saying there is a time available and offering it to the caller, who accepts it:

```
31  N  here's an appointment at two if you can take it
32  C  (2.2) yes that's I guess just huh
33     (4.2)
34  N  two fifteen
35     (2.5)
36  C  yes that's I guess better [case
37  N  [it is better
40  C  yes
```

This example illustrates the most common method of telling callers that an appointment will be booked for them. The nurse first indicates that she will begin to schedule an appointment by allowing a silence to ensue, by saying 'let's see', by asking for the caller's personal identity number and by asking the caller to specify how much pain she is in. Other nurses indicated the scheduling of appointments by audibly starting to type on their computers, asking questions about telephone numbers or which general practitioners the caller generally visited or by going over various aspects of their problems. Then the nurse gives conditional access to the caller and finally explicitly offers an appointment.

In this example, as in the majority of calls, the nurse did not explicitly assess the caller's medical problem or give advice. Instead she informed the caller that an appointment would be booked, and thus indirectly signalled that a visit to a general practitioner was necessary.

4.2   Callers' responses to indirect information

When nurses informed callers indirectly that an appointment would be scheduled with a general practitioner, callers did not display emotion; there were no displays of surprise (Wilkinson/Kitzinger 2006) or response cries (Goffman 1978), for example. Extract 1 is typical of the standard response, with the caller simply answering the nurse's questions and following the nurse in the process of booking an appointment before the call is concluded.

There may be a number of social psychological reasons why callers do not express emotion in this position. One hypothesis may be that callers are psychologically prepared for any one of a range of responses that nurses typically give during such calls (including booking an appointment to see a general practitioner) and therefore remain emotionally neutral. Another may be that, based on prior experience, callers have already guessed that their problems will need medical attention and are therefore unsurprised when this turns out to be the case. A third hypothesis may be that callers may be oriented to the professional division of labour between nurses and general practitioners, so they do not expect medical assessments from the nurse but from the general practitioner they will eventually meet and therefore remain emotionally neutral.

However, there may also be interactional reasons why the callers do not express emotion after being informed indirectly. When, as at the start of Extract 1 above, the nurses are silent, say 'let's see' or indicate in other ways that they have turned to another activity, it may be unclear to the callers what this other activity might be. Callers may or may not conclude that the nurses are scheduling an appointment. As the nurses have not yet explicitly informed or advised them, it is not relevant for the callers to display emotion.

When the interaction continues and the nurses start to ask for date of birth and telephone number, and in other ways indicate that an appointment will be booked, the ambiguity remains. Although the callers may become increasingly aware that they will have an appointment, they have not yet been told so explicitly.

Finally, when nurses explicitly offer appointments, the advice to visit a general practitioner has already been given indirectly. The advice stage has already been passed sequentially, so it is no longer relevant for callers to respond to the advice, but instead to respond to the offer of an appointment. In other words, by using indirect information, nurses do not give callers any interactional position in which they can display emotion about the advice to visit a general practitioner.

5 Alarming callers

5.1 Direct advice and assessment

In a minority of calls (17 of a total of 276), nurses assessed, and gave advice about, medical problems directly. These calls consist of three phases: in all 17 calls the nurses uttered direct advice to see a general practitioner, in 11 of them the nurses then accounted for their decision by giving a medical assessment and, finally, in three (and only in conjunction with the second phase) offered a tentative diagnosis. The following three extracts illustrate this pattern.

Extract 2
N now let's see here you need to come in	*direct advice*
so that someone can take a look at you	

Extract 3
N hh yes no we almost have to take a look at it	*direct advice*
because he has	
got such high fever so he's I guess pretty much	*assessment*
generally affected because he has not been	
able to keep anything either	

Extract 4
N but then I think a doctor should take a look	*direct advice*
at it today	
because of this like you said it's hot	*assessment*
perhaps there's some kind of infection or	*tentative diagnosis*
something like that	

The first phase consists of direct advice to callers that they need to come in to the primary care centre. The direct advice was more or less normatively strong. Normatively weak advice, as in Extract 3, can be expressed as 'hh yes no we almost have to take a look at it' or, as in another call, 'we may just as well take a look at him'. Observe that the actor in both examples is described using the institutional 'we' (Drew/ Heritage 1992a). It is the health care system, not the nurse or the general practitioner personally, that will examine the medical problem. Observe also that the nurses in both instances do not describe the precise measures to be taken when callers visit the centres, but use the casual 'look at' to describe what will happen. This may also portray both the medical problem and the visit to the centre as non-alarming, perhaps even 'just in case'. This is further underscored elsewhere in the design of their utterances, such as the 'we almost have to' that precedes the 'take a look at it' (Extract 3), or, in other calls, 'just as well' before 'look at him', 'almost so that' before 'one has to bring him here for a visit' or 'we almost have to' before 'schedule an appointment' and 'look at it'. In other words, the seriousness of callers' medical conditions is downgraded.

Normatively strong advice is designed differently. Advice is sometimes personalized using 'I think' instead of the institutional 'we' (as in Extract 4). The nurses also use verbal auxiliaries such as 'must' when describing what will take place at the primary care centres, as in 'we must look at that'.

The second phase, which sometimes follows the direct advice, consists of assessments where the nurses explicate the specific observations that led them to decide the callers should come in. These are about alarming symptoms (as when callers risk dehydration because of not being able to keep down fluids, as in Extract 3) and symptoms that are difficult to understand.

In a few calls, there is a third phase that consists of a tentative diagnosis (as in Extract 4) such as 'may be that there is some kind of infection or something like that'. Observe that the diagnosis is uttered cautiously (see Drew 1991), which may reflect her orientation to the professional division of labour between telenurses and general practitioners.

5.2 Callers' responses to direct advice and assessment

Callers responded to direct assessments and advice differently: either they explicitly supported it, and provided additional observations that supported nurses' assessments, or they displayed concerns and worries.

One study that is relevant in this context concerns British health visitors who gave advice to first-time mothers during their first home visit (Heritage/Sefi 1992). The mothers responded in three ways: first, by asserting knowledge or competence about the issue, in so doing resisting advice but not openly rejecting it. Second, some responded with 'unmarked acknowledgments' (see Schegloff 1982; Jefferson 1984) such as 'mm hm' or 'yeah' or 'that's right'. These 'unmarked' acknowledgement tokens neither acknowledged advice as 'news' nor did they constitute an undertaking to follow it. They merely conveyed the fact that they were listening. Third, some of the mothers responded with 'marked acknowledgements' such as 'oh right'. These conveyed that the advice was news for the mothers ('oh') and that it was accepted ('right'). Some mothers also repeated parts of the advice, further underscoring that they had heard and accepted it.

In this study, no caller resisted or rejected the advice to visit a general practitioner. When nurses gave direct assessments and advice, callers expressed rather strong support. Subsequent to the nurse's advice in Extract 2, the caller, overlapping the end of the nurse's utterance, said, 'yes exactly'; in Extract 3 the nurse says, 'hh yes no we almost have to take a look at it because he has got such high fever', which is overlapped by the callers' 'yes:' and 'a–', followed by the nurse saying, 'so he gets I guess pretty much generally affected because he has not been able to keep anything either', which is overlapped by the caller's 'no no'; and in Extract 4 the caller responds to the nurse's advice by saying, 'almost think so yes'.

In those calls where the nurses assessed medical problems (11 out of 17 calls), callers often provided additional observations in support. In one example, a nurse (Extract 4) gives advice followed by an assessment: 'but then I think a doctor should take a look at it today because of this as you say it is hot may be that there is some kind of infection or something like that', whereupon she gives instructions about whom the caller should ring and at what time. The nurse accounts for this advice with the assessment, 'so you may come in there yes because you should not wait until tomorrow either, but that somebody takes a look at it today'. The caller then gives explicit support to the advice by saying, 'I think it just as well', and utters supportive evidence, 'because she just slept a little now but is it (.) and it is warm'. In another instance where a mother calls about her son, the nurse says, 'hh hh we better look at him because ee it is you know a little bit uncertain because I can't say (1.2) what it may be you know and possibly it is f- sometimes you can have tonsillitis for instance and have stomach-ache'. The caller adds evidence to the nurse's tentative diagnosis by saying that you can suffer from tonsillitis without having a sore throat, 'yes without feeling it perhaps', and backs it up with a supplementary piece of evidence, 'because he doesn't usually complain exactly'.

Callers also expressed concerns following direct advice and assessment. In its mildest form this took the shape of *wondering* about their problems. In one call the nurse said, 'one has to take a look at your throat what it looks like', at which the caller wondered by describing a possible type of problem: 'could it have something to do with the thyroid gland as well perhaps?'. In another instance the nurse said, 'no we have to I guess do so that some doctor listens to you here tomorrow', and, after briefly discussing which general practitioner the caller usually visits, continues 'there is I guess not so much else to do' and 'because some doctor needs to you know listen to you when you are so heavy in your chest so'. The caller responds with, 'yes that's right', and, 'it is you know no vascular – yes I don't it is in any case any vascular spasm or anything like that'.

Callers also described *threatening aggravation*. In one instance (Extract 3), when the nurse had given direct advice ('hh yes no we almost have to take a look at it because he has got such high fever so he gets I guess pretty much generally affected because he has not been able to keep anything either'), the caller strongly agrees by saying 'no no', and then continues, 'yes I mean so he doesn't get dehydrated since he doesn't get'. The caller thus utters a possible continuation of what the nurse may have implied in her previous statement. The caller spells out a possible threatening aggravation that may be realized if the child does not see a general practitioner.

Callers also expressed their concerns *prosodically* (e.g. rhythm, stress and intonation). In one instance the nurse gives direct advice by saying, 'no but you must come – we must check a HB in any case that is completely clear and then we find out what we shall do'. Overlapping, the callers whispers 'yes' and 'yes of course' and, after the nurse has finished, continues in a shaky voice, 'I need awfully lots of blood' and then, with emphasis, 'that's what I need tell them that'.

Some callers explicitly *say they are frightened*. When one nurse says, 'now let's see here you need to come in here so that somebody can take a look at you' (Extract 2), the caller says, 'yes exactly as soon as possible I am afraid that if it is a slipped disc or p- something going on'.

However, callers also *distance themselves from worry*, as when the nurse says 'it is you know so many days so we may just as well take a look at him', the caller says, 'h h yes, I am not worried a- about him but I – I feel like is it (.) because he needs treatment then it feels like one should not wait too long either then'. This distancing from worry may indicate the caller perceives that worry is a relevant feeling in this position.

6   Discussion

Nurses used two methods to tell callers that they needed to visit general practitioners: indirect informing or direct advice and assessment. In order to understand why they use these methods, we need to explicate the aspects of the ethnographic context that are highly relevant to nurses.

The work of nurses takes place in two contexts and their actions are accountable in both. On the one hand, these interactions take place between members of the general public and a public service organization. These organizations are tax-funded and are expected to be efficient, use specific methods and achieve stated goals. They are subject to various forms of control and need to be able to account for their actions organizationally. Thus nurses need to be able to provide *organizational accounts* for their actions. On the other hand, these interactions take place between the general public and professionals (Mintzberg 1979; Abbott 1988). Professionals are typically university educated, base their practice on scientific and theoretical knowledge, are often members of professional associations and/or are authorized by governmental organizations, are bound by collective ethical codes and work in organizations that are sanctioned and financed by society. Often their organizations give them wide discretionary powers to analyse and assess clients' problems and give advice based on their professional knowledge. Consequently they may experience a need to structure these interactions, for example by asking specific sets of questions, performing specific tests and taking specific measures once they have identified clients' problems in given ways. As professional workers, nurses need to be able to provide *professional accounts* for their actions.

Thus, nurses are oriented to both the organizational and the professional contexts when working over the phone. These orientations have a number of consequences for the overall organization of the calls.

First, public service workers are often gatekeepers who decide if clients will be given access to services that the organizations can provide (Lipsky 1980). They tend to accept only the cases that are deemed relevant, which is also the case in the calls analysed here.

Second, the basic asymmetry between an individual who needs help and a public service organization that has the means to provide it results in the typically dyadic interactional structure described above: a request for help, some kind of response (Whalen/Zimmerman 1998) and the activities that take place as preliminaries to providing this, such as enquiring into the problem and administrative tasks such as filling in forms. These activities are introduced as rational steps towards a response, and they entail specific norms and expectations about which contributions to the interaction will be considered relevant. For instance, callers who do not introduce their problems are interrupted and specifically told to come to the point (Leppänen 2005). Similarly, when calling the emergency services callers are expected to answer questions so that the operators can fill in the computerized forms necessary to start responding as quickly as possible (Whalen/Zimmerman 1998; Whalen et al. 1988).

Third, there are often asymmetries of knowledge in these interactions. As professionals, public service workers may apply to problems a professional stock of knowledge that is not directly available to their clients. Public service workers do not necessarily explain the rationale behind their questions, which maintains their clients' ignorance of organizational and professional methods of inference and decision-making. The participants may be oriented to the public service worker as having the 'right' to knowledge about the problem. This may become visible when clients express themselves cautiously when using professional vocabulary, for example when patients meet general practitioners (Drew 1991), or when problems are 'translated' into professional vocabularies, as is the case in the interactions studied here when nurses interview callers and consider their symptoms (Leppänen 2002).

Fourth, interactions between members of the general public and professional public service workers are typically monotopical. Public service workers tend to discuss cases from their professional perspectives and may not be interested in listening to 'irrelevant' information, 'the wider story' or 'the client's perspective generally' (ten Have 1991).

Fifth, the emotions evoked by the problems discussed may be asymmetrical. While clients may feel strongly about the issues in question, public service workers may take an emotionally neutral view, finding them interesting as instances of problems open to analysis using their professional stock of knowledge. Moreover, professional public service workers are prone to withholding their own emotions. In a study of general practitioners and homeopaths in Finland, it was shown that once patients had explained what their trouble was, the professionals systematically withheld their own personal experience but responded in ways that focused on the patients' experiences (Ruusuvuori 2005). In another study it was shown that when members of the public told professionals about things they felt to be extraordinary and surprising, the latter (who may have experienced similar things in the past) did not always respond to them as being surprising (Wilkinson/Kitzinger 2006). A similar pattern can also be found in the calls studied here: the nurses refrain from expressing their own opinions on the problems in question, and account for their decisions in organizational and professional terms.

Public service workers may also expect clients to deliver information in an emotionally neutral tone. In a study of patient examinations during general practice consultations, it was shown that doctors withhold their gaze from patients until 'pain expressions' cease in order to not encourage further pain expressions and to preserve an 'analytical stance' towards their problems (Heath 1989). In a study of emergency calls in the USA, it was shown that callers, who not infrequently experience their situation as stressful, often view the questions asked by the operators as an obstacle to receiving help quickly (Whalen/Zimmerman 1998; Whalen et al. 1988). While some callers may contain their anger and frustration in order to present their case 'calmly', there are still some who explicitly state their frustration over the slowness of case processing. The emergency operators may explicitly state the organizational reasons for asking questions, and thus socialize callers into emotional neutrality. This pattern can also be found in the calls studied here: nurses socialize callers to stay on topic and present their problems clearly by repeating any questions they do not think have been answered clearly (Leppänen 2002).

Of course, nurses do talk with callers about the latter's experience of physical pain or worry, but they do so primarily when these experiences are relevant to assessing the caller's medical problems by using their medical stock of knowledge. For instance, a nurse may be interested in 'what the chest pain feels like' as part of assessing whether the caller is suffering a heart attack, but may not be interested in the caller's emotions per se. The nurses do not align themselves as 'troubles recipients' (Jefferson/Lee 1992), but adopt a stance towards callers based on their position as professionals and representatives of primary health care organizations.

7 Conclusions

The transformation of western societies from agrarian to industrial and service-based economies brought in its wake social relationships that were anonymous, specialized and formal, and thus often experienced as emotionally neutral. Emotional neutrality became an ideal in much of public life, especially in public service organizations and their interactions with the general public. The classical sociologists conceptualized emotional neutrality in various ways, but it soon became the taken-for-granted background of emotional experience, both for sociologists and others.

This chapter describes how telenurses in Swedish primary care manage the emotions of callers who seek medical help. It focuses on the final parts of the calls, when nurses give advice to callers about the need to visit general practitioners. Two patterns were identified: on the one hand nurses routinely sustain emotional neutrality by indirectly informing callers that they need to visit general practitioners, while on the other they may give advice and assess callers' problems directly, which results in explicit displays of alarm by callers.

These patterns are the result of nurses being organizationally and professionally accountable for their actions. Sustaining neutrality by the use of indirect information may result from a need to process large numbers of cases efficiently and in accordance with specific organizational standards. It may be more time efficient to inform a caller indirectly and move quickly on to booking an appointment than to manage the emotions displayed by the caller. The use of indirect information may also be the result of professional medical considerations, for in some cases nurses may consider it harmful to worry callers by giving direct advice and assessments over the phone, the obvious example being callers with suspected cardiovascular disease (see Gabriel in this volume who discusses the ethics of care perspectives and the justifications for not informing patients). Nurses are also sensible of the professional division of labour with general practitioners, which denies them the right to diagnose. As a result they may be intent on the basic task of performing triage and pass up the opportunity to assess medical problems.

The use of direct advice and assessment – thus giving rise to alarm – may instead result from a different consideration: it may be an attempt to increase compliance with the nurses' advice. This may be felt to be necessary when the medical problems are acute and in need of a quick response, when the described symptoms are unusual or puzzling or when the calls concern children who may not be able to put their experience of sickness into words and thus need to see a general practitioner for an examination.

Note

1. The transcript follows Swedish word order, which differs from English. In the transcript, the nurse is marked with N and the caller is marked C. The letter 'h' marks breathing sounds. Parentheses mark pauses and lengths of pauses in seconds. Square brackets come in pairs and mark where overlapping speech starts.

References

Abbott, A. (1988) *The System of Professions*, Chicago: University of Chicago Press.
Andersson Bäck, M. (2008) *Conceptions, Conflicts and Contradictions at the Introduction of a Swedish Call Centre*, doctoral dissertation, Gothenburg: Department of Work Sciences, University of Gothenburg.

Atkinson, J.M. (1992) 'Displaying neutrality: Formal aspects of informal court proceedings', in Drew/Heritage (1992b), 199–211.

Baker, C.D., Emmison, M. and Firth, A. (eds) (2005) *Calling for Help: Language and Social Interaction in Telephone Helplines*, Amsterdam: Benjamins.

Barbalet, J. (1999) *Emotion, Social Theory, and Social Structure: A Macrosociological Approach*, Cambridge: Cambridge University Press.

Bolton, S.C. (2001) 'Changing faces: nurses as emotional jugglers', *Sociology of Health and Illness*, 23, 85–100.

Clark, C. (1990) 'Emotions and micropolitics in everyday life: Some patterns and paradoxes of place', in T. Kemper (ed.) *Research Agendas in the Sociology of Emotions*, Albany: State University of New York Press, 305–33.

Clayman, S. (1992) 'Footing in the achievement of neutrality: The case of news interviews discourse', in Drew/Heritage (1992b), 163–98.

Cooley, C.H. (1902/1922) *Human Nature and the Social Order*, New York: Scribner's.

Drew, P. (1991) 'Asymmetries of knowledge in conversational interactions', in I. Marková and K. Foppa (eds) *Asymmetries in Dialogue*, New York: Harvester Wheatsheaf, 21–48.

Drew, P. (2006) 'Mis-alignments in "After Hours" calls to a British GP's practice: A study in telephone medicine', in J. Heritage and D. Maynard (eds) *Communication in Medical Care: Interaction between Primary Care Physicians and Patients*, Cambridge University Press, 416–44.

Drew, P. and Heritage, J. (1992a) 'Analyzing talk at work: An introduction', in Drew/Heritage (1992b), 3–65.

Drew, P. and Heritage, J. (1992b) (eds) *Talk at Work: Interaction in Institutional Settings*, Cambridge: Cambridge University Press.

Drew, P. and Wootton, A. (1988) 'Introduction', in P. Drew and A. Wootton (eds) *Erving Goffman: Exploring the Interaction Order*, Boston: Northeastern University Press, 1–13.

Durkheim, E. (1893/1964) *The Division of Labour in Society*, New York: Free Press.

Ehrlich Martin, S. (1999) 'Police force or police service? Gender and emotional labour', *Annals of the American Academy*, 561, 111–26.

Eisen, A. (1978) 'The meanings and confusions of Weberian "rationality"', *British Journal of Sociology*, 29, 57–70.

Elias, N. (1939/2000) *The Civilizing Process*, Oxford: Blackwell.

Fineman, S. (2000) 'Commodifying the emotional intelligent', in S. Fineman (ed.) *Emotion in Organizations*, 2nd edn, London: Sage, 101–14.

Garot, R. (2004) '"You're not a stone". Emotional sensitivity in a bureaucratic setting', *Journal of Contemporary Ethnography*, 33, 735–66.

Goffman, E. (1959) *The Presentation of Self in Everyday Life*, New York: Doubleday Anchor.

Goffman, E. (1963a) *Behavior in Public Places*, New York: Free Press.

Goffman, E. (1963b) *Stigma*, Englewood Cliffs, New Jersey: Prentice-Hall.

Goffman, E. (1967) *Interaction Ritual*, New York: Anchor.

Goffman, E. (1978) 'Response cries', *Language*, 54, 787–815.

Heath, C. (1989) 'Pain talk: The expression of suffering in medical consultations', *Social Psychology Quarterly*, 52, 113–25.

Heisterkamp, B.L. (2006) 'Conversational displays of mediator neutrality in a court-based program', *Journal of Pragmatics*, 38, 2051–64.

Heritage, J. (1984) *Garfinkel and Ethnomethodology*, Cambridge: Polity Press.
Heritage, J. and Sefi, S. (1992) 'Dilemmas of advice: Aspects of the delivery and reception of advice in interactions between health visitors and first-time mothers', in Drew/Heritage (1992b), 359–417.
Hochschild, A.R. (1983) *The Managed Heart: Commercialization of Human Feeling*, Berkeley: University of California Press.
Holmkvist, I. (ed.) (2008) *Telefonrådgivning inom hälso- och sjukvård*, Lund: Studentlitteratur.
Jefferson, G. (1984) 'Notes on the systematic deployment of the acknowledgment tokens "yeah" and "mm hm"', *Papers in linguistics*, 17, 197–206.
Jefferson, G. (2004) 'Glossary of transcript symbols with an introduction', in G.H. Lerner (ed.) *Conversation Analysis: Studies from the First Generation*, Amsterdam: Benjamins, 13–31.
Jefferson, G. and Lee, J.R.E. (1992) 'The rejection of advice: Managing the problematic convergence of a "troubles-telling" and a "service-encounter"', in Drew/Heritage (1992b), 521–48.
Leppänen, V. (2002) *Telefonsamtal till primärvården: Problem, utforskning, åtgärd*, Lund: Studentlitteratur.
Leppänen, V. (2005) '"Callers" presentations of problems in telephone calls to Swedish primary care', in Baker et al. (2005), 175–205.
Leppänen, V. (2008) 'Coping with troublesome clients in home care', *Qualitative Health Research*, 18, 1195–205.
Lipsky, M. (1980) *Street-Level Bureaucracy*, New York: Sage.
Marx, K. (1867/1967) *Capital: A Critique of Political Economy*, vol. 1, New York: International Publishers.
Mintzberg, H. (1979) *The Structuring of Organizations – A Synthesis of the Research*, Englewood Cliffs: Prentice Hall.
Parsons, T. (1951) *The Social System*, Glencoe, Ill: Free Press.
Ruusuvuori, J. (2005) '"Empathy" and "Sympathy" in action: Attending to patients' troubles in Finnish homeopathic and general practice consultations', *Social Psychology Quarterly*, 9, 597–622.
Sacks, H. (1992) *Lectures on Conversation*, 2 vols, Blackwell: Oxford.
Sacks, H., Schegloff, E.A. and Jefferson, G. (1974) 'A simplest systematics for the organisation of turn-taking for conversation', *Language*, 50, 696–735.
SALAR (2007) *Vårdbarometern: befolkningens syn på vården 2006*, Stockholm: Sveriges Kommuner och Landsting.
SALAR (2009) Primärvård – vårdcentraler, Sveriges Kommuner och Landsting, www.skl.se/artikel.asp?A=232&C=451> (accessed 1 February 2009).
Sanders, T. (2004) 'Controllable laughter: Managing sex work through humour', *Sociology*, 38, 273–91.
Scheff, T.J. (2000) 'Shame and the social bond: A sociological theory', *Sociological Theory*, 18, 84–99.
Schegloff, E.A. (1982) 'Discourse as an interactional achievement: Some uses of "uh huh" and other things that come in between sentences', in D. Tannen (ed.) *Analyzing Discourse: Text and Talk*, Washington, D.C: Georgetown University Press, 71–93.
Schegloff, E.A. (2007) *Sequence Organization in Interaction: A Primer in Conversation Analysis*, Cambridge: Cambridge University Press.

Shaw, R. and Kitzinger, C. (2007) 'Problem presentation and advice-giving on a home birth helpline: A feminist conversation analytic study', *Feminism & Social Psychology*, 17, 203–13.

Simmel, G. (1901/1983) 'Zur Psychologie der Scham', in G. Simmel *Schriften zur Soziologie*, Frankfurt a.M.: Suhrkamp, 140–50.

Starrin, B., Wettergren, Å. and Lindgren, G. (eds) (2008) *Det sociala livets emotionella grunder*, Malmö: Liber.

ten Have, P. (1991) 'Talk and institution: A reconsideration of the "asymmetry" of doctor-patient interaction', in D. Boden and D. Zimmerman (eds) *Talk & Social Structure*, Cambridge: Polity Press, 138–63.

Tracy, S.J. and Tracy, K. (1998) 'Emotion labor at 911: A case study and theoretical critique', *Journal of Applied Communication Research*, 26, 390–411.

Weber, M. (1921/1968) *Economy and society*, 3 vols, New York: Bedminster.

Whalen, J. and Zimmerman, D.H. (1998) 'Observations on the display and management of emotion in naturally occurring activities: The case of "Hysteria" in calls to 9-1-1', *Social Psychological Quarterly*, 61, 141–59.

Whalen, J., Zimmerman, D. and Whalen, M.R. (1988) 'When words fail: A single case analysis', *Social Problems*, 35, 335–61.

Wilkinson, S. and Kitzinger, C. (2006) 'Surprise as an interactional achievement: Reaction tokens in conversation', *Social Psychology Quarterly*, 69, 150–82.

13
Organizational Regimes of Emotional Conduct

Carmen Baumeler

1 Introduction

History shows that management ideas about the ideal organization of work deal not only with technical specialties but also with the psychological properties of employees. A dominant discursive stream reads that in the age of flexible capitalism, companies are in need of the enterprising capacities of their employees (Miller/Rose 1990; 1995). Consequently, the contemporary conception of the worker is as the enterprising subject, i.e. a person who solves bureaucratic inefficiency with his/her own creativity and innovation. One of today's widely popularized psychological approaches is called emotional intelligence and it deals explicitly with the enterprising subject's emotion management. In the following, I will show that emotional intelligence is a contemporary organizational regime of emotional conduct.

The chapter is structured as follows: first, I present theoretical perspectives that deal with the disciplining of the self and the management of emotions and are, therefore, relevant for the interpretation of organizational regimes of emotional conduct. In his seminal publication *The Civilizing Process*, Norbert Elias (1982a; 1982b/1939) described disciplinary action directed at the human body as a change of personality structure from medieval times under the condition of pacification through the nation state. Increasing control of spontaneous emotions and action led to the retention of impulses and to deliberate forms of action. Michel Foucault (1977; 1988) took a different perspective and dealt with the notion of disciplinary domination. He postulated a connection between (economic) power and the manipulation of the human body. In his view, the main goal of disciplinary power was the production of docile, productive bodies, which were related to the rise of capitalism. Nowadays, people discipline themselves freely with the help of technologies of the self. Whereas neither Elias nor Foucault deal explicitly with the disciplining of emotions, William Reddy (2001) and Arlie Hochschild (1979; 1983; 1998) fill this gap and propose theoretical concepts of emotional regime and emotional work in order to depict precisely the emotional management of the self in political and economic terms.

Second, I will show that the current economic order of flexible capitalism constructs an idealized productive subject that fits with it and requires a certain kind of emotion management. As a case in point, I present the psychological agenda of emotional intelligence. Finally, I will discuss the contemporary discourse of emotional intelligence as an organizational regime of emotional conduct on the basis of a reinterpretation of the theoretical perspectives presented. Thereby I show that this programme of self-transformation constitutes a guide to successful behaviour in the workplace, reflecting the contemporary conception of the enterprising subject and, therefore, the next step of the productive discipline of the body.

2 Theoretical background: Organizational regimes of conduct

2.1 Disciplining of the self

Dealing with emotional conduct, the question of the individual's disciplining needs closer examination. Discipline is a central concept that has been applied to explain the development of western subjectivity (van Krieken 1990), especially if one considers the crucial role Weber (1974 /1920) assigned to the disciplining character of ascetic Protestantism in the development of capitalist society. Elias' and Foucault's analyses of European history dealt with the impact of social changes on the human psyche and the rise of the increasingly self-disciplined individual. In the following, both approaches will be presented and the differences outlined.

Elias (1982a; 1982b/1939; 2000) postulated a connection between the long-term structural development of societies and the changes in people's social character.[1] He viewed European social history as a gradual imposition of sophisticated self-constraints – as a transformation in which the regulation of individual violent impulses, passions, sexual desires, table manners, bodily functions and forms of speech underwent a civilizing process. Whereas, in his view, the medieval personality was highly volatile, unpredictable and violent, the subsequent civilized individual was increasingly self-controlled. The transformation of interpersonal constraints into internal self-control, often described as internalization, resulted in a declining spontaneity regarding affect expression.

On the empirical basis of manners books, Elias showed that, gradually, from the Middle Ages, codes of behaviour became more differentiated and thresholds of shame and embarrassment became higher, spreading from court etiquette to all social classes. In the development of civilized bodies, individuals learned to control their emotions, drives and instincts. Elias (1978: 239) attributed this change to the increasing monopolization of violence during the process of state formation. Due to pacification by the nation state, people did not have to fear for their lives every minute or live permanently in a state of self-defence but could concentrate on the acquisition of money or prestige. As a result, the fluctuations in behaviour and affects were moderated (Elias 1982b/1939: 238).

However, not only pacification but also rising functional specialization, the market economy with its intensified competition between and within social groups and the denser webs of social interdependency[2] between people were important social changes that affected psychological make-up. These changes in the nature of social relationships – figuration as Elias (ibid.: 231) calls it – asked for different forms of behaviour and personality structure and resulted in a more civilized conduct and sentiment.

Integrated into an increasingly complex nexus of social interdependency and competition, individuals became subject to more social constraints and had to pay more attention to other people (ibid.: 232). According to Elias this has led to a specific vulnerability of spontaneous emotional expressions:

> The closer the web of interdependence becomes in which the individual is enmeshed [...] – the more threatened is the social existence of the individual who gives way to spontaneous impulses and emotions, the greater is the social advantage of those able to moderate their affects, and the more strongly is each individual constrained from an early age to take account of the effects of his own or other people's actions on a whole series of links in the social chain. (ibid.: 236)

Although not focused on the evolution of emotional regimes,[3] Elias' analysis of the increasing control of affect reveals important mechanisms. According to him, self-control was not only intensified but also became more automatic. Consequently, the emotional state was less volatile than in former times, and self-constraint became more all-embracing, applying to the public sphere as well as the private and to all people irrespective of social status (cf. Mennell 1992: 80). Elias emphasized the difference between constraint and spontaneity, assuming that children possessed a 'natural' aggressiveness, lack of affect and body control (van Krieken 1990: 356). Therefore, the socialization of children towards adulthood became more elaborated over time and required more self-control. Thus, more and more, socialization processes induced a change from a violent spontaneity to a 'steadier, more evenly disposed, subdued, moderated, and calculating pattern of affect' (Aya 1978: 222).

In summary, Elias interpreted the rise of the civilized persons and their emotional conduct in an evolutionary manner (resulting in greater social advantage and strategic gain). He emphasized the extension of socialization processes owing to structural changes of society and, as a consequence, viewed this process as the connection between declining external and rising internal constraints (in the form of a gradually strengthened superego, according to Freud).

Foucault, on the other hand, examined disciplinary techniques from the perspective of power, which he located in a broad range of everyday relationships.[4] In contrast to Elias, Foucault did not see a direct relationship between structural change and the change of the human being, but pointed to an intermediate interpretative process whereby social institutions (i.e. the military, prisons, schools, the Church, asylums, etc.) imposed discipline coercively and defined the constitution of the soul's proper organization (van Krieken 1990: 361). From Foucault's point of view, disciplinary power was directed towards the body and converted into something useful and docile.

In *Discipline and Punish*, Foucault (1977) documented the change of criminal punishment from pre-modern society (traditional domination), which used public execution and torture, to modernity, which employed new forms of punishment (disciplinary domination), for example the close surveillance of the deviant human body by Jeremy Bentham's Panopticon. Then, within less than a century, punishment became increasingly directed towards the individual's internal life, and, increasingly, subtle and hidden forms of disciplinary techniques have since been applied to the human body. From the eighteenth century onwards, the human body has been considered as an object for manipulation and training. Increasingly, codes of normality have been established and individuals seen as objects that can be measured, described, evaluated, examined and compared. Certain professional groups such as teachers, doctors, psychologists and social workers established norms of (emotional) conduct and, in the case of deviancy, suitable therapy to normalize the human body and soul (Foucault 1977: 304).

Furthermore, Foucault asked how individuals create their own selves through self-discipline. He identified various technologies of power that interact in monitoring and fabricating useful, productive bodies. Regarding self-discipline, the type of the 'technologies of the self', derived from practices of confession, is decisive. These technologies permit:

> individuals to effect by their own means or with the help of others a certain number of operations on their own bodies and souls, thoughts, conduct, and way of being, so as to transform themselves in order to attain a certain state of happiness, purity, wisdom, perfection, or immortality. (Foucault 1988: 18)

Especially in liberal democracies, the government of the subjects was increasingly realized via education or psychological expertise (Rose 1997), which aimed to produce subjects with a psyche with particular desires and aspirations that fitted into the political and economic environment. As a consequence, publications promoting recipes for self-help became highly successful. In contrast with Elias's understanding of affect control, Foucault postulated that the new disciplinary powers 'owed their success precisely to their ability to "free" psychic and libidinal energy in the very process of tying it to the productive concerns of a rationalizing capitalist economy' (van Krieken 1990: 356). External control made the interior of the individual psyche the object of the disciplinary action. Confessions and thinking/self-analysis became an important technique for self-discipline. As Hahn (1982: 426) states, knowing oneself provides the basis for controlling oneself, knowing others (their emotions, their true nature) allows for better control of them.

2.2   Disciplining of emotions

Whereas neither Elias nor Foucault dealt exclusively with the disciplining of emotions, Reddy (2001) introduced the theoretical concept of an emotional regime in discussing the political dimension of emotions. On the basis of his historical studies, Reddy postulates that every political order has to establish a certain normative emotional regime and to define and separate highly valued emotions from deviant ones. From his perspective, emotional regimes underpin stable political regimes and are a 'set of normative emotions and the official rituals, practices, and emotives that express and inculcate them' (ibid.: 129). These politically shaped emotional regimes can be placed on a spectrum. At one end, in strict regimes individuals are required to express certain emotions, for example loyalty to an army, love for a certain god or the pride of a nation. If a person refuses to show these emotions, severe sanctions such as torture can be imposed. Regimes at the other end of the spectrum allow for more interpersonal variation and demand emotional discipline only in certain institutions, such as school or the priesthood.

Reddy (2001: 127f.) also applies his general concept to contemporary capitalist democracies. He argues that, at first sight, this political order appears to offer space for emotional navigation but, in fact, individual emotional display is limited by contractual relationships, mainly by access to money and property. Within capitalist democracies, there exists a variety of emotional regimes that are defined by different strata and workplace hierarchies. Furthermore, whereas majorities mostly conform to emotional regimes, marginalized minorities stand opposed.

Unlike Reddy, Hochschild (1979; 1983) has a more micro-oriented perspective on emotion management in everyday life, based on a Goffmanian tradition. In her view, acting out one's feelings is regulated by social contexts which define specific 'feeling rules'. Feeling rules are widely accepted guidelines that are culturally constructed, socially shared and often latent, because they are successfully internalized (Hochschild 1979: 563). Feeling rules define what a person should feel in a certain situation, for example at a funeral, at a wedding, giving birth, while divorcing, etc. Not complying with a feeling rule often leaves the subject ashamed (for example if a mother is not happy about the birth of her child and, therefore, offends the culturally constructed feeling rule of happiness that is attributed to this situation).

We may comply with feeling rules by surface acting, i.e. in the sense of Goffman's (1959) conception of impression management, to present ourselves as if complying with a respective social norm. Surface acting refers to a strategy of pretending to feel what one does not feel, and is a mere display act. It often goes hand-in-hand with a rational benefit calculation, for example when a person who applies for a job remains overtly polite even if he or she is asked inappropriate questions. In addition, Hochschild (1979) introduces with the concept of emotion work the notion of 'deep acting', which focuses on how people actually try to feel 'deep down' (ibid.: 560). By emotion work individuals try to comply with situational feeling rules in truly altering their inner state. This implies acts of evocation, where the person tries to elicit an initially absent desired feeling, or acts of suppression, where the person focuses on an undesired feeling in order to abandon it. Emotion work, furthermore, is not only applied by the self but can be done by the self upon others and by others upon the self. Thus, in contrast to 'surface acting', deep acting describes the actual work on a person's emotional state and, therefore, is the same as managing an emotion.

On the basis of her empirical studies, Hochschild (1979: 562) describes three techniques of everyday emotion work. First, a cognitive one, which attempts to change images, ideas or thoughts in order to alter the associated feelings. Second, a change of somatic or physical emotional symptoms such as trying to breathe slower, trying not to shake, etc. Finally, she also refers to expressive emotion work where the individual tries to change her/his expressive gestures, such as trying to smile or to cry so as to modify her/his inner feelings.

Hochschild (1983) applied her emotion theory to the commoditization of human feelings in late capitalist society and coined the term 'emotional labour', which describes a certain kind of emotion management where workers are expected to display appropriate emotions as part of their job. She identified feeling rules that are inherent in certain job profiles in order to reach organizational goals. Thus, for example, a police officer is not allowed to show fear in dangerous situations, a nurse disguises her revulsion for certain patients, and so on. Many job profiles in the service industry are regulated by occupational feeling rules and require the capacity for deep acting – such as flight attendants who are supposed to radiate cheeriness so as to promote profit for their airline.

3   Discourses on the ideal employee

So far, different conceptions of disciplining the self and emotion management have been presented. In order to apply these conceptions to the discourse about an idealized emotional conduct in organizations, it is important first to depict current discourses on the idealized organizational subject who fits into the new flexible workplace. I start with some general insights into the 'New Capitalism', as analysed by Boltanski and Chiapello (2007), and ensuing feeling rules and go on with the discourse on emotional intelligence as a point in case.

3.1 The feeling rules of flexible capitalism

The last decades have been described as a progressive erosion of bureaucratic structures, the transition to a hyper-working society and the emergence of a New Capitalism (Sennett 1998; Boltanski/Chiapello 2007). Companies try to increase their capability for flexible and innovative reaction to turbulent business environments by enhancing their employees' own responsibility through strategies of increased flexibility and 'self-organization' in the workplace. New organizational forms (company networks and virtual organizations) go along with new workplaces characterized by flexitime, teamwork, delayering and virtual networking. The rules of economy have changed, one main reason being the widespread use of information technologies (Sennett 1998). The prevalence of virtual work, which collapses conventional boundaries of space, may be supposed to have great impact on feeling and emotional rules (Fineman et al. 2007; Sieben 2007b).

According to Boltanski's and Chiapello's (2007) content analysis of popular French management literature, the network pattern is the key element of the new ideological configuration of the capitalist spirit. It has superseded former capitalist modes as Taylorism, Fordism, mass production and bureaucratization that were at the centre of the capitalist production process until the middle of the twentieth century. With its key ideas of lean firms and network structures, the capitalist spirit postulates adaptation, change, communication and creativity on the part of managers as well as employees, and it is said to reject bureaucratic hierarchies and authoritarian order.

Rational bureaucratic authority was characterized by Weber (1978/1922) as relying on intellectually analysable rules and as eliminating personal, irrational and emotional elements. In the ideal passionless bureaucracy, there is a dominance of a spirit of formalism. Modern rational organizations, therefore, demanded the separation of the enterprise and the private realm. As organizations had to be the place of pure rationality in order to promote efficiency, emotionality was assigned to the family and therefore banned from the workplace.[5] The fear was that if processes in enterprises were increasingly to be rationalized, the 'iron cage' of an over-bureaucratized social order would result in limits on individual human freedom, potential and spirituality.

In the current economic order, the normative discourse on the relationship between the organization and the individual has changed. Analyses of flexible capitalism understand subjectification as a process intended to integrate individual characteristics and needs into the workplace. Whereas in former times emotions were regarded as an obstacle to rational decision-making, nowadays, the display and management of emotions is a sign of a new rationality in the workplace (Hughes 2005). From this perspective, emotionality and efficiency require each other. Not all emotions, however, are welcomed: certain emotions have been regarded as necessary for organizational success but others have been deemed unimportant or even harmful.[6] As a consequence, emotions still have to be controlled in the service of organizational needs.

The emerging spirit of flexible capitalism required a new kind of employee, which was invented in the discourses of the preferred organizational self. The organizational discourse of entrepreneurialism has created an idealized productive subject who reflects the interest of the organization. The current idea is that enterprises should release the individual's autonomy and creativity and direct them towards organizational excellence and success (Miller/Rose 1990; 1995). Thus, employees are supposed to be transformed into entrepreneurial selves who are personally responsible for innovation, economic growth and the safeguarding of their own employability (Pongratz/Voß 2003). To achieve these aims, the entrepreneurial subject is engaged in self-motivation and 'auto-dressage' (Tracy/Tretheway 2005).

Taylorist work organization has been considered as inappropriate because it treated human beings as machines and, therefore, could not employ their emotions, moral sense, honour and inventive capacity in order to increase productivity. Against this background, the management ideas of flexible capitalism have been considered as more human. However, in effect, they entail other and further-reaching possibilities of (self-) exploitation. As Boltanski and Chiapello state:

> Conversely, the new mechanisms, which rely on more sophisticated ergonomics, integrating the contributions of post-behaviourist psychology and the cognitive sciences, precisely because they are more human in a way, also penetrate more deeply into people's inner selves – people are expected to 'give' themselves to their work – and facilitate an instrumentalization of human beings in their most specifically human dimensions. (2007: 98)

In contrast to Weber's ideal passionless bureaucracy (1978), these demands for personal commitment and identification postulate an abandonment of the separation between work and private life. The demand for a project-oriented work organization without direct bureaucratic control implies that employees shall organize themselves, and identify themselves with the project. Moreover, the demand to connect with others in the project-oriented work, which is central to the depicted network world, shows once again the ongoing process of rising social interdependency identified by Elias.

If direct bureaucratic supervision is omitted, a new problem of control is identified: how to control self-organized teams working in networks that are not in a single place. One functional equivalent of direct hierarchical control is an increased self-control; another is the leader's vision, a shared meaning, which is said to guarantee the motivation and commitment of the employees. This conceptualizes managers from a different point of view, because they can no longer rely on hierarchical legitimacy, formal power and traditional in-house careers but of personal qualities, such as their charisma.

From Boltanski's and Chiapello's analysis of management literature it is possible to derive feeling rules for the idealized employee that fit into flexible organizations. Personal characteristics are demanded that are closely tied to emotions such as commitment, identification, engagement (giving oneself to work), enthusiasm and the ability to trust others. Feelings of timidity, rigidity and distrust are inappropriate. For managers, it is also important to have the ability actively to elicit enthusiasm, commitment and identification in employees, whereas employees should be open and willing to produce the required emotions.

In conclusion, flexible capitalism can be interpreted as a political order that establishes a certain normative emotional regime in the sense of Reddy and defines feeling rules in the sense of Hochschild that include highly valued as well as deviant emotions.

3.2 Constructions of the emotional intelligent employee

One of the contemporary discursive constructions that add to the preferred organizational self is emotional intelligence. Originally introduced into the psychological scientific debate by Salovey and Mayer (1990), the concept of emotional intelligence was popularized by Goleman (1995). This psychologist and author of several popular science bestsellers was highly influential in establishing a discursive field of emotional intelligence that attracts both lay people and scientists, especially in the realm of management (Fineman 2000; 2004; Sieben 2007a). As Matthews et al. (2002: 76) remark, measures based on emotional intelligence have become common practice in career selection in many organizations. According to Neckel (2005), emotional intelligence is currently the most influential concept of emotional self-management.

Generally, emotional intelligence is defined as a competence that allows the identification, expression and understanding of emotions, the assimilation of them in thought and the regulation of them in the self and in others. This includes the regulation of pleasant emotions and the deactivation of unpleasant ones (Matthews et al. 2002). As a psychological programme, emotional intelligence adopts an evolutionary perspective and draws scientific credibility from research results in the neurosciences and in cognitive psychology, especially from the research on brain functioning by LeDoux (1986; 1992). 'Correct brain practice' is said to prevent the hijacking by negative emotions. Goleman (1998) claims that if the brain is trained appropriately, people will be able to choose the emotions that are most useful and appropriate to specific situations. Emotional intelligence is therefore conceived as a capacity that can be learned when one is intentionally changing behaviour and habits with mindfulness training, which will result in a brain change. The promises of emotional intelligence are manifold: whereas individuals are said to lead happier lives if they are more aware of their own emotions and those of others, societal problems such as violent crime and drug abuse will also decline because of better emotion management skills (Goleman 1995). Furthermore, there is said to be increased productivity, better teamwork and a higher organizational commitment thanks to emotionally intelligent employees (Goleman 1998).[7]

As Goleman (1998) argues, nowadays, skill and expertise are not the only yardsticks by which individuals are judged. Increasingly important is 'how we handle ourselves and each other' (ibid.: 3). As his statement indicates, the successful management of emotions promises professional success. Whereas the intellectual ability or technical expertise to do the job is taken for granted, the new rules of work focus on personal qualities, for example initiative, empathy, adaptability and persuasiveness. Goleman calls them 'portable skills' that define the individual's employability in times of declining job security. Moreover, Cherniss and Goleman (2001) declare emotional intelligence to be predictive of superior performance at the workplace, and Goleman et al. (2002) as the key factor for effective leadership.

Goleman regards the self as a project that can be improved by mental training. He declares that emotionally intelligent subjects have abilities in the fields of knowing their emotions, managing their emotions, motivating themselves, recognizing emotions in others and handling relationships. Some authors in the field of emotional intelligence even speak of the necessity of repairing harmful emotions (Matthews et al. 2002: 286).

Furthermore, emotional intelligence is proposed as a topic for management training. According to the training model of Cherniss and Goleman (2001), it is above all important to *promote self-awareness*, i.e. people should use certain techniques to know their internal state better. Suggested methods are psychological tests; visits to assessment centres, where experimental behaviour is observed and evaluated; 360-degree assessment; ratings by family members and friends; self-monitoring (for example observing one's feelings and actions while writing a diary); in-depth interviews and meditation. If self-awareness is reached, *self-regulation* is the next step. Here, employees are assumed to manage their internal state, for example with programmes that resemble anger management or counter-conditioning (i.e. managing anxiety by confronting certain situations). Third, there is the *promotion of self-motivation* (so-called emotional tendencies facilitating success). A widespread technique in this field is achievement motivation training where participants develop self-motivation stories. In *promoting empathy*, learners are made aware of others' feelings through sensitivity training. The last domain, called *promoting social skills*, is reached via behaviour modelling, for example with role play.

There are two fields of emotion management that are important features of the enterprising subject: enthusiasm and stress. In terms of desired emotions, there is a demand for *enthusiasm*, which Goleman (1998) relates to the strength of leadership. According to him leaders should 'articulate and arouse enthusiasm for a shared vision and mission, step forward to lead as needed, regardless of position, guide the performance of others while holding them accountable, lead by example' (ibid.: 183). The committed employee, therefore, is enthusiastic, a person in whom passion for the enterprise runs deep.[8]

The construction of a leader who elicits enthusiasm strongly recalls the charismatic authority of Weber as one type of authority that is opposed to rational bureaucracy (see also Krell/Weiskopf 2006). Charisma, in Weber's notion, refers to 'a certain quality of an individual personality by virtue of which he is considered extraordinary and treated as endowed of supernatural, superhuman, or at least specifically exceptional powers or qualities' (Weber 1978: 241). Those who are subject to authority devote themselves to charismatic leadership, be it out of enthusiasm, despair or hope. Weber called an organized group that is subjected to charismatic authority a charismatic community, which contains disciples, has no hierarchical structure and is based on an emotional form of communal relationship (*Vergemeinschaftung*). Whereas Weber regarded charismatic authority as receding because of the rise of passionless bureaucracy, emotional intelligence's emphasis on enthusiasm seems to reinvent charismatic leadership.

Occupational *stress* is an emotional conglomerate that should be avoided or managed in the flexible workplace. More emotionally intelligent individuals are said to cope more successfully (Salovey et al. 1999; Bar-On 1997). According to Goleman et al. (2002), emotionally intelligent managers raise their self-control under stress and keep calm when confronted with challenges of working life such as rising uncertainties or constant change:

> Leaders with emotional self-control find ways to manage their disturbance and impulses, even to channel them in useful ways. A hallmark of self-control is a leader who stays calm and clear-headed under high stress or during a crisis – or who remains unflappable even when confronted by a trying situation. (ibid.: 254)

Occupational stress is owed to demands at work that include excessive workloads, short deadlines or lay-off threats (Rafaeli/Worline 2001: 104). Stress is regarded as representing a misalignment between demands from the external environment and personal motivations and abilities. Today, because of the widespread pressure of rising performance expectations, occupational uncertainty because of organizational restructuring and concerns for job security, occupational stress is even labelled as the Black Plague of the post-industrial era (Matthews et al. 2002: 489). Emotional intelligence is presented as a cure for this plague.

4   Emotional intelligence as a case in point of a contemporary organizational regime of emotional conduct

As has been shown, society constructs the ideal productive subject, be it the (ahistorical and naturalistic) *homo oeconomicus*, the passionless bureaucrat or – as discussed in this chapter – the *homo emotionalis* who fits into the political economy of flexible capitalism. Emotional intelligence is a case in point of a (sometimes merely discursive, sometimes actually practised) contemporary organizational regime of emotion conduct that recommends self-regulatory exercises which reflect propositions for self-management according to the feeling rules of flexible capitalism. With the help of the appropriate training, the productive subject is said to be able to manage his/her emotions more strategically and successfully.

If we interpret this organizational regime of emotional conduct from the point of view of Elias, the discourse of emotional intelligence and its potential realization is just a further evolutionary step in the long-term structural development of societies and the changes in people's social character. The increasing social interdependency that is based on de-bureaucratization, project orientation, social networking and rising dependencies on other people in order to get permanent employability results in increasing affect control and demand for emotion management. As Elias observed, within an expanding social nexus, spontaneous emotional expression renders the individual vulnerable and threatens his/her social existence, whereas increasing affect control results in social advantage and strategic gain. The organizational discourse of emotional intelligence can therefore be understood as a suggestion for a further step in the civilizing process, as a further transformation of personality structures regulated by a certain kind of emotion management. However, and in contrary to Elias's conclusion, the imposition of sophisticated self-constraints results not only in the intensified regulation of violent impulses and passions but also in the strategic and deliberate elicitation of passionate feelings such as, for example, enthusiasm. As Neckel (2005) observes, emotional intelligence represents a programme of 'emotion by design', which postulates generating emotions and also utilizing them strategically for organizational aims. This is one of the ways in which emotions become commodified (Fineman 2000).

From a Foucaultian point of view, the discourse of emotional intelligence has far-reaching power effects. Through measures of emotional intelligence for selection and training purposes, professional groups in the fields of education or psychological expertise establish norms of normality and suitable therapy in order to normalize deviant behaviour. This turns individuals into documentable and curable cases (Krell/Weiskopf 2006; Sieben 2007a), through a mechanism that represents one form of disciplinary power. Moreover, emotional intelligence may be read as a technology of the self. In creating their own selves through self-discipline, subjects transform themselves freely in order to fit into the contemporary political economy of flexible capitalism. The training model for emotional intelligence suggested by Cherniss and Goleman (2001) is a case in point: it includes techniques for knowing one's emotions, which can also be regarded as the basis for better regulation and control of them. Self-motivation and the promotion of empathy and social skills are further applications of the technologies of the self. Furthermore, knowing the emotions of others allows also for better control of them – and here, one also finds suggestions within emotional intelligence. The technologies of the self are applied by the individuals themselves in order to attain certain states such as happiness, and this is actually what emotional intelligence promises: a happier life, becoming a star performer, coping better with stress etc. (cf. also Krell/Weiskopf 2006; Sieben 2007a). Freedom, however, is not only a choice but an obligation: individuals have to cope with the risks that are socially produced. They are responsible for their own well-being in repairing harmful feelings of stress or eliciting enthusiasm in order to get promoted. As Bauman (2000) and Lemke (2001) point out, the duty to cope with economic risks that are socially produced is individualized. The deep acting of emotional intelligence regarding occupational stress is an example for this (Baumeler 2008).

Referring to the current political economy, Reddy showed that certain normative emotional regimes define the values of emotions – from highly valued to unimportant or even harmful ones. Within flexible capitalism, the normative emotional regime is constructed on the basis of the enterprising subject, who is seen as the solution to bureaucratic idleness. Organizational regimes of emotional conduct are defined by contractual relationships and construct a certain emotional atmosphere. Reddy postulates that in capitalist democracies there is a variety of emotional regimes, which are defined by different strata or workplace hierarchies. Emotional intelligence, on the contrary, formulates an overall emotional regime for each organizational self, independent from its social attributes such as class, gender or ethnicity. This individualization of employees does not take into account their different integration into society. As Illouz (2008) for example showed, emotional intelligence can be interpreted as a concept that reaffirms the social privileges of the middle classes, who, in contrast to members of the working class, have learned to talk about their feelings. Hochschild (1979), too, refers to the point that in contrast to working-class families, middle-class families prepare their children more for emotion management. In conclusion, the individualized approach of emotional intelligence blurs the social inequalities due to social attributes that still exist in the workplace.

Analysing emotional intelligence from the point of view of Hochschild, it is possible to say that it represents a universalized concept of feeling rules for the flexible workplace in the project-oriented network world – an ideology of how employees should feel in their work sphere and how they should do their emotional labour irrespective of their profession. Actually, the proponents of emotional intelligence postulate that people consciously change themselves in order to comply with these feeling rules. To this purpose, they develop educational programmes and give advice on how to realize the highly valued feeling rules with the help of mental training. The envisaged result is a 'deep acting', i.e. changing inappropriate emotions (such as stress) and eliciting appropriate ones (such as enthusiasm) – to be achieved by the same techniques that Hochschild points out, for example, the attempts to change images, ideas or thoughts in order to alter the associated feelings.

As Hochschild (1979: 568) elaborates, feeling rules can work as ideological tools used by elites in order to gain access to the emotive life of subordinates. How these normative ideas are actually applied in organizational everyday life, however, is another question. What are the possible consequences of complying with the organizational regime of emotional intelligence? As Hochschild (1979) states, feeling rules – the same as other rules – may be half-heartedly obeyed or even broken. In her perspective, what is actually done in the field of emotion management has to be analysed on the basis of situational interactions and this is currently lacking in the field of emotional intelligence.

5 Conclusion

The aim of this chapter was to show that emotional intelligence represents a contemporary organizational regime of emotional conduct – imposed by the flexible new capitalism, which requires an enterprising subject equipped with autonomy, creativity and a capacity for self-motivation. Different conceptions of disciplining of the self and the management of emotions have been used for this purpose.

Based on Elias' historical perspective on affect control, it has been argued that emotional intelligence may be interpreted as a further step in the civilizing process and, what is more, as a quest for the strategic and deliberate elicitation of passionate feelings. From a Foucauldian point of view, the discourse of emotional intelligence has far-reaching power effects: measurement and training are a form of disciplinary power, commodifying emotion and emotion management. Moreover, emotional intelligence produces techniques of the self – which result in compliance with constructed emotional ideals like eliciting empathy or coping with stress. Based on Reddy's analysis of emotion regimes, it was argued that emotional intelligence creates an overall emotional regime for each organizational self that disregards existing inequalities in the workplace. Lastly, from the point of view of Hochschild's conception of emotion work it was shown that emotional intelligence represents an educational programme for achieving the entrepreneurial self who complies with the norms of new capitalism by deep acting.

However, suggestions for mental training and future applications of new technologies (of the self) and refashioned subjects are by no means self-fulfilling prophecies. As Latour (2005) shows, ideas of technologies spread out in networks and are translated according to the interests of allies, so that they are willing to participate and maintain the network. During this journey, ideas and technologies may change their content as well as the usage that is made of them. The ways in which we use technologies have an influence on the potentialities that will be realized. Ideas of technologies are fluid, and their realization and application are highly insecure. Therefore, they rely on adaptation to and integration into everyday life, where individual resistance (Fleming/Sewell 2002; Hughes 2005) against the commodification of emotions is also always possible.

Notes

1. Like Elias, Wouters (1992) accentuates the relations between society and emotions. In his view, personal relationships influence the development of emotional impulses and counter-impulses of the individual, which are attuned to the contingent standards of behaviour and attitude of their society.
2. The argument that since medieval times rising social interdependencies have given way to increasing self-discipline has been contested by Duerr (1988), who argues that all societies regulate emotions, especially the traditional ones where the control imposed on individuals is thought to be even greater that in modern times.
3. See e.g. van Krieken (1990: 359), who criticizes Elias's concept of affect control: while it applies well to bodily functions, physical violence and table manners, it does not do so as easily to emotional states such as love, caring, honesty and steadfastness. For those emotions, a confessional and therapeutic culture has arisen that, rather, demands their exposure and revelation to public view.
4. That is also to say that Foucault does not conceptualize disciplinary power as residing in hierarchical relations in organizations, so e.g. managers are as much subjugated to it as their subordinates (Burrell 1998: 20).
5. Needless to say that this separation of spheres is intimately linked with their gendering. For a historical analysis of these changes see Hausen (1976). Against this background, Krell (2003) analyses the gendered (re)production of human resources from a Foulcauldian perspective and Krell and Weiskopf (2006) direct the view even more explicitly on the interwovenness with the ascription of emotionality.

6. Whereas Rafaeli and Worline (2001) depict emotions such as aggression, forcefulness, assertiveness, confidence or competition as necessary for the workplace, weakness, submission, modesty and caring are regarded as unimportant.
7. The concept of emotional intelligence has attracted a considerable amount of criticism. One line of this is that the scientific investigation of a clearly identifiable construct of emotional intelligence is lacking (Matthews et al. 2002). A further critique from the field of intelligence research is that the concept of intelligence is blurred with the one of personality and, furthermore, the situational context is not taken into account (for further comments on this topics see Bechtoldt 2008). Moreover, the neuroscientific argumentation is debated, especially its transfer to management recommendations for training and selection (Sieben 2007a).
8. In general, enthusiasm is defined by a great excitement and above-average interest and engagement in a topic. Its Greek source *'enthousiasmos'* originally meant to be inspired or even possessed by a god (*The American Heritage Dictionary of the English Language* 2000).

References

Aya, R. (1978) 'Norbert Elias and "the civilizing process"', *Theory and Society*, 5, 219–28.

Bar-On, R. (1997) *The Emotional Intelligence Inventory (EQ-i): Technical Manual*, Toronto: Multi-Health Systems.

Bauman, Z. (2000) *Liquid Modernity*, Cambridge: Polity.

Baumeler, C. (2008) 'Technologies of the emotional self: Affective computing and the "enhanced second skin" for flexible employees', in Karafyllis/Ulshöfer (2008), 179–90.

Bechtoldt, M.N. (2008) 'Emotional intelligence, professional qualifications, and psychologists' need for gender research', in Karafyllis/Ulshöfer (2008), 117–30.

Boltanski, L. and Chiapello, E. (2007) *The New Spirit of Capitalism*, London: Verso.

Burrell, G. (1998) 'Modernism, postmodernism and organizational analysis: The contribution of Michel Foucault', in A. Mckinlay and K. Starkey (eds) *Foucault, Management and Organization Theory. From Panopticon to Technologies of Self*, London: Sage, 14–28.

Cherniss, C. and Goleman, D. (2001) 'Training for emotional intelligence. A Model', in C. Cherniss and D. Goleman (eds) *The Emotionally Intelligent Workplace. How to Select For, Measure, and Improve Emotional Intelligence in Individuals, Groups, and Organizations*, San Francisco: Jossey-Bass, 209–33.

Duerr, H.P. (1988) *Nacktheit und Scham. Der Mythos vom Zivilisationsprozess*, Frankfurt a.M.: Suhrkamp.

Elias, N. (1978) 'On transformations of aggressiveness', *Theory and Society*, 5, 229–42.

Elias, N. (1982a) *The Civilizing Process. The History of Manners*, Oxford: Blackwell.

Elias, N. (1982b) *The Civilizing Process. State Formation and Civilization*, Oxford: Blackwell.

Elias, N. (2000) *The Civilizing Process: Sociogenetic and Psychogenetic Investigations*, Oxford: Blackwell.

Fineman, S. (2000) 'Commodifying the emotionally intelligent', in S. Fineman (ed.) *Emotion in Organizations*, London: Sage, 101–14.

Fineman, S. (2004) 'Getting the measure of emotion – and the cautionary tale of emotional intelligence', *Human Relations*, 57, 719–40.

Fineman, S., Maitlis, S. and Panteli, P. (2007) 'Themed articles: Virtuality and emotion: Introduction', *Human Relations*, 60, 555–60.

Fleming, P. and Sewell, G. (2002) 'Looking for the good soldier, Svejk: Alternative modalities of resistance in the contemporary workplace', *Sociology*, 36, 857–73.

Foucault, M. (1977) *Discipline and Punish: the Birth of the Prison*, Harmondsworth: Penguin.

Foucault, M. (1988) 'Technologies of the self', in L.H. Martin, H. Gutman and P.H. Hutton (eds) *Technologies of the Self. A Seminar with Michel Foucault*, Amherst: University of Massachusetts Press, 16–49.

Goffman, E. (1959) *The Presentation of Self in Every Day Life*, New York: Doubleday.

Goleman, D. (1995) *Emotional Intelligence. Why It Can Matter More Than IQ*, New York: Bantam Books.

Goleman, D. (1998) *Working with Emotional Intelligence*, New York: Bantam Books.

Goleman, D., Boyatzis R. and McKee, A. (2002) *Primal Leadership: Learning to Lead with Emotional Intelligence*, Boston: Harvard Business School Press.

Hahn, A. (1982) 'Zur Soziologie der Beichte und anderer Formen institution-alisierter Bekenntnisse: Selbstthematisierung und Zivilisationsprozess', *Kölner Zeitschrift für Soziologie und Sozialpsychologie*, 34, 408–34.

Hausen, K. (1976) 'Die Polarisierung der "Geschlechtscharaktere" – Eine Spiegelung der Dissoziation von Erwerbs- und Familienleben', in W. Conze (ed.) *Sozialgeschichte der Familie in der Neuzeit Europas*, Stuttgart: Klett, 363–93.

Hochschild, A. (1979) 'Emotion work, feeling rules, and social structure', *American Journal of Sociology*, 85, 551–75.

Hochschild, A. (1983) *The Managed Heart: The Commercialization of Human Feeling*, California: University of California Press.

Hochschild, A. (1998) 'Sociology of emotion as a way of seeing', in G. Bendelow and S.J. Williams (eds) *Emotions in Social Life. Critical Themes and Contemporary Issues*, London: Routledge, 3–15.

Hughes, J. (2005) 'Bringing emotion to work: Emotional intelligence, employee resistance and the reinvention of character', *Work, Employment & Society*, 19, 603–25.

Illouz, E. (2008) 'Emotional capital, therapeutic language and the habitus of the "New Man" ', in Karafyllis/Ulshöfer (2008), 151–77.

Karafyllis, N.C. and Ulshöfer, G. (eds) (2008) *Sexualized Brains. Scientific Modeling of Emotional Intelligence from a Cultural Perspective*, Cambridge: MIT Press.

Krell, G. (2003) 'Die Ordnung der "Humanressourcen" als Ordnung der Geschlechter', in R. Weiskopf (ed.) *Menschenregierungskünste. Anwendungen poststrukturalistischer Analyse auf Management und Organisation*, Opladen: Westdeutscher Verlag, 65–90.

Krell, G. and Weiskopf, R. (2006) *Die Anordnung der Leidenschaften*, Wien: Passagen.

Latour, B. (2005) Reassembling the Social: *An Introduction to Actor-Network-Theory*, Oxford: Oxford University Press.

LeDoux, J. (1986) 'Sensory systems and emotion: a model of affective processing', *Integrative Psychiatry*, 4: 237–248.

LeDoux, J. (1992) 'Emotion and the limbic system concept', *Concepts in Neuroscience*, 2, 169–99.

Lemke, T. (2001) ' "The birth of bio-politics" – Michel Foucault's lecture at the Collège de France on neo-liberal governmentality', *Economy & Society*, 30, 190–207.

Matthews, G., Zeidner, M. and Roberts, R.D. (2002) *Emotional Intelligence, Science and Myth*, Cambridge: MIT Press.

Mennell, S. (1992) 'Norbert Elias', in P. Beilhartz (ed.) *Social Theory. A Guide to Central Thinkers*, Sydney: Allen and Unwin, 76–83.

Miller, P. and Rose, N. (1990) 'Governing economic life', *Economy and Society*, 19, 1–31.

Miller, P. and Rose, N. (1995) 'Production, identity, and democracy', *Theory and Society*, 24, 427–67.

Neckel, S. (2005) 'Emotion by Design. Das Selbstmanagement der Gefühle als kulturelles Programm', *Berliner Journal für Soziologie*, 3, 419–30.

Pongratz, H.J. and Voß, G.G. (2003) 'From employee to "entreployee". Towards a "self-entrepreneurial" work force?', *Concepts and Transformation*, 8, 239–54.

Rafaeli, A. and Worline, M. (2001) 'Individual emotion in work organizations', *Social Science Information*, 40, 95–123.

Reddy, W. (2001) *The Navigation of Feeling. A Framework for the History of Emotions*, Cambridge: Cambridge University Press.

Rose, N. (1997) *Inventing Ourselves: Psychology, Power and Personhood*, Cambridge: Cambridge University Press.

Salovey, P. and Mayer, J.D. (1990) 'Emotional intelligence', *Imagination, Cognition & Personality*, 9, 185–211.

Salovey, P., Bedell, B.T., Detweiler, J.B. and Mayer, J.D. (1999) 'Coping intelligently: Emotional intelligence and the coping process', in C.R. Snyder (ed.) *Coping: The Psychology of What Works*, New York: Oxford University Press, 141–64.

Sennett, R. (1998) *Corrosion of Character: The Personal Consequences of Work in the New Capitalism*, New York: Norton.

Sieben, B. (2007a) *Management und Emotionen. Analyse einer ambivalenten Verbindung*, Frankfurt a.M.: Campus.

Sieben, B. (2007b) 'Doing research on emotion and virtual work: a compass to assist orientation', *Human Relations*, 60, 561–80.

The American Heritage Dictionary of the English Language (2000) 'Enthusiasm', www.thefreedictionary.com/enthusiasm (accessed 20 April 2009).

Tracy, S.J. and Trethewey, A. (2005) 'Fracturing the real-self – fake-self dichotomy: moving toward "crystallized" organizational discourses and identities', *Communication Theory*, 15, 168–95.

van Krieken, R. (1990) 'The organisation of the soul: Elias and Foucault on discipline and the self', *Archives Europeénes de Sociologie*, 31, 353–71.

Weber, M. (1974) *The Protestant Ethic and the Spirit of Capitalism*, London: Allen & Unwin.

Weber, M. (1978) *Economy and Society: An Outline of Interpretive Sociology*, California: University of California Press.

Wouters, C. (1992) 'On status competition and emotion management: The study of emotions as a new field', *Theory, Culture and Society*, 9, 229–52.

Index